Always Different, Always the Same

POPULAR MUSICS MATTER:
SOCIAL, POLITICAL AND CULTURAL INTERVENTIONS

Series Editors:
Eoin Devereux, Aileen Dillane and Martin J. Power

The Popular Musics Matter: Social, Political and Cultural Interventions series will publish internationally informed edited collections, monographs, and textbooks that engage in the critical study of popular music performance (live and recorded), historical and contemporary popular music practitioners and artists, and participants and audiences for whom such musics embody aesthetic, cultural, and, particularly, socio-political values. The series sees music not only as a manifestation of global popular culture but also as a form that profoundly shapes and continually seeks to redefine our understandings of how society operates in a given location and era.

Titles in the Series

Soundtracking Germany: Popular Music and National Identity,
   Melanie Schiller
Heart and Soul: Critical Essays on Joy Division, edited by Martin J. Power,
   Eoin Devereux and Aileen Dillane
*Deindustrialisation and Popular Music: Punk and 'Post-Punk' in
   Manchester*, Düsseldorf, Torino and Tampere, Giacomo Bottà
Always Different, Always the Same: Critical Essays on The Fall,
   edited by Eoin Devereux and Martin J. Power

Always Different, Always the Same

Critical Essays on The Fall

Edited by
Eoin Devereux and Martin J. Power

ROWMAN & LITTLEFIELD
Lanham • Boulder • New York • London

Published by Rowman & Littlefield
An imprint of The Rowman & Littlefield Publishing Group, Inc.
4501 Forbes Boulevard, Suite 200, Lanham, Maryland 20706
www.rowman.com

86-90 Paul Street, London EC2A 4NE

Copyright © 2023 by The Rowman & Littlefield Publishing Group, Inc.

Selection and editorial matter © Rowman & Littlefield, 2021

Copyright in individual chapters is held by the respective chapter authors.

All rights reserved. No part of this book may be reproduced in any form or by any electronic or mechanical means, including information storage and retrieval systems, without written permission from the publisher, except by a reviewer who may quote passages in a review.

British Library Cataloguing in Publication Information Available

Library of Congress Cataloging-in-Publication Data

Names: Devereux, Eoin, editor. | Power, Martin J., editor.
Title: Always different, always the same : critical essays on The Fall / edited by Eoin Devereux and Martin J. Power.
Description: Lanham : Rowman & Littlefield, 2023. | Series: Popular musics matter: social, political and cultural interventions | Includes bibliographical references and index. | Summary: "The Fall were one of the most influential bands to emerge in the British post-punk scene. Drawing upon a wide range of academic disciplines, including ethnomusicology, sociology, literary theory, linguistics, journalism, cultural studies, and film and media studies, this book investigates The Fall's significant contribution to music"— Provided by publisher.
Identifiers: LCCN 2022042802 (print) | LCCN 2022042803 (ebook) | ISBN 9781538165355 (cloth) | ISBN 9781538199220 (paper) | ISBN 9781538165362 (ebook)
Subjects: LCSH: Fall (Musical group) | Post-punk music—England—History and criticism.
Classification: LCC ML421.F327 A58 2022 (print) | LCC ML421.F327 (ebook) | DDC 782.42166092/2—dc23/eng/20220906
LC record available at https://lccn.loc.gov/2022042802
LC ebook record available at https://lccn.loc.gov/2022042803

Contents

Foreword ... vii
    Gavin Friday

Introduction: Mr Sociological Memory Man 1
    Martin J. Power and Eoin Devereux

1. Spoiling all the Paintwork: Mark E. Smith, Art Renegade ... 9
    K. A. Laity

2. Suzanne Smith in Conversation with Eoin Devereux ... 25

3. 'A letter so simple, yet disgusting in a stroke': Writing-out the (Typo)Graphic Strangeness of The Fall ... 41
    Paul Wilson

4. Psykick Dancehall: The Paranormal Strategies of Mark E. Smith and The Fall ... 61
    Ben Lawley

5. 'You can leave me on the shelf': The Death of The Fall and Mark E. Smith ... 83
    Martin Myers

6. Dead Beat Descendant: Mark E. Smith's Life, Death, and Mourning as a Cult Hero ... 101
    John Fleming

7. "What's a computer?" Intuition Meets the Science Law in a Complete Fall Lyrics Corpus ... 119
    Matt Davies

8	Searching for the Right Word or Phrase that Would Put a Chill Up the Spine: A Corpus-based Discourse Analysis of Mark E. Smith's Lyrics *Elaine Vaughan, Brian Clancy, and Eoin Devereux*	149
9	I Am Damo Suzuki Lost in Music (Dub) *Mike Glennon*	171
10	Remembrancer/Rememorator/Amorator!: The *Remainderer* EP and the Roots of The Fall's Late Obscurity *Samuel Flannagan*	185
11	Linguistic Perversion: Ezra Pound and The Fall *Kieran Cashell*	203
12	The Fall and Ireland: What a Manchester Band Can Tell Us about Ireland and Its Music Scene *Michael Mary Murphy*	231
13	The Madness in My Area: Montagu Lomax and the Psychodrama of The Fall: An Examination of the Use of Psychiatric Imagery in 'Early Fall '77–'79' *David Meagher and John McFarland*	245

Index	257
About the Editors and Contributors	267

Foreword
The Fall's Friendly Visitor
Gavin Friday

'Two swans in front of his eyes . . . a glass of lager in his hand / silver mitcrophone in his hand / wasting time in numbers and rhymes . . . .' 'Bingo Masters Breakout' a song about a suicidal Bingo caller and the very first thing I heard by The Fall, courtesy of John Peel on BBC Radio 1. It was impossible to find early indie punk music in Ireland back then. My good friend 'Tommy the Bottle of Milk' had already started to go over to Probe Records in Liverpool to buy rare and indie vinyl on a once-a-month post-punk vinyl shopping spree. I'd give him a list of records I wanted, along with the latest fanzines. 'Bingo Masters Breakout' was closely followed by the purchase of the album *Live at The Witchtrials* and thus my adoration/admiration of all things The Fall and Mark E. Smith began.

The abrasiveness of those early Fall records struck me hard. Especially the words. Surreal, suburban tales from the pen of the budding genius that was Mark E. Smith. What was beautiful about the early DIY, indie world of post-punk, was that on the back cover of singles, there were usually addresses to contact bands. That was a real breakthrough; before that, in the pre-punk era, if you were a fan of Bowie or Roxy Music, for example, and wanted to contact them, they were untouchable. Certainly, you could join their fan clubs, but they were generic in nature. You didn't feel you were getting the personal touch. In the case of The Fall, however, there was an address to write to Mark E. Smith, and I did. He replied and he gave me his actual home address in Prestwich. And with that commenced a long and constant conversation through writing postcards to each other. It started in late 1978 and went on until, I'd say, the mid-1980s.

Fuckin' Pen Pals with Mark E. Smith. I still have the postcards somewhere in the attic. In writing his postcards and notes, Mark showed not only his surreal creativity, but more than anything his dark and wry sense of humour . . . he was a truly funny geezer . . . they were usually banal British holiday postcards, but more often old cut-up Christmas cards; he'd rip off the printed greeting and write on the back of the picture. He was very anti-U2—even in the early days. I remember one card, an old Christmas yuletide thing with a Dickens-like preacher guy on the front of it with his hands up, where you'd also see his scrawl via an arrow, with the message: "Yet another bone of another Bono type, teaching, converting . . . ." He'd always put some jab in it! He had a keen sense of Irish history and literature. I remember discussing the Black and Tans with him and clearly recall him saying, "Most of those Bastards came from Manchester ya know." He genuinely seemed quite fond of the Irish.

For me, in early days of The Fall, it was Mark E. Smith's lyrics more so than the music. I found the lyrics/words/rants so curiously attractive, challenging and mind bending, small and manic vignettes of ordinary/extraordinary laymen, then his persona and his stance—there was no one like him even visually; he was anti, anti-visual, dressed in what looked like M+S secondhand hand-me-downs. Then his voice. He didn't sing; he had his own unique-Ah. Phrasing-Ah, he used his voice and words like an abrasive weapon, more like a musical instrument. His words and the physicality of his vocals were the most challenging and magnetic thing in the group's overall sound—especially in the early Fall. I must admit that the presence of the Hammond organ or keyboard in the early years used to drive me mad. It was way too hippy for the potent poison Mark was spitting out, or was that the point? Musically, I preferred when their sound became more alternative and experimental in later years. Many of the chapters in this collection attest to his clever wordplay. His use of language was almost Joycean. It immediately struck a chord with me, as my band, The Virgin Prunes, were attempting something similar by making up our own words—admittedly, in a far more naïve way. I found Mark's use of language and imagery extraordinary. It was so otherworldly but in a Joe Soapish, everyday Brit Lingo way, like his own revenge on the Queen's language. I suppose that's where I get his Joycean vibe from . . . and there were so many words it was like he was writing his own *War and Peace* set in Prestwich. Mark's words were the real force, because the music wasn't yet on that innovative curve like Joy Division was in 1978–1979 but then, the music got more and more complex and more interesting as the various phases of The Fall developed over time. It was like the group was always musically trying to catch up with him and he was always miles ahead and moving faster and faster. They were a musical frenzy, and there was no one like them.

Our friendship grew in the early days of The Virgin Prunes. We signed to Rough Trade in 1980, the same record label as The Fall. It was in early 1980 or so, and my friend 'Tommy the Bottle of Milk' asked Mark if we could come to one of The Fall's Manchester gigs. Mark invited us to stay in his flat. We got the boat over to Liverpool, travelled by train to Manchester, and then went straight to the gig. After the show, we went to Mark's flat. When I say flat, it was more like an overgrown bedsit full of books, empty beer cans, and wine bottles . . . the place was chaotic! He played us a mixture of records by some of his favourite German groups as well as playing new recordings and demos that The Fall had made, and crazy snippets from interviews, rehearsals, television, and films. It was extraordinary. Here was Mark giving us a live demonstration of how he writes—very much of Burrough's 'Cut Up' technique into practice—him and that old Dansette or Dictaphone he forever brought with him everywhere. It was like he was a sound archivist, curating his own life, something he did with great effect, for many years, by using, most possibly, that same old Dansette or Dictaphone onstage. As well as playing us all these recordings, he was ranting out new words. To be honest, we were a little awestruck and exhausted from the verbal and musical onslaught. It was a lot to take in. Away from all that, I have such a fond memory of how sweet he was. He was kind and charming, and I think quite chuffed that two Irish kids came all the way to see The Fall, and was so interested in us telling him about our ideas for The Virgin Prunes.

Over the years, The Virgin Prunes played with The Fall—I'd say maybe five times. There was a good camaraderie between us all. When The Virgin Prunes signed to Rough Trade, he was great at giving advice—especially warning us about who might rip us off and to keep an eye on the quality of the artwork and not to overspend in studios. He was almost parental. The Fall's manager, Kay Carroll, was very taken with The Virgin Prunes. I sensed she had Irish blood and loved hanging out and looking after us. She and the group's members were also very good to us. Once, when we were playing with The Fall in Manchester, we had no money to pay for a hotel, and Steve and Paul Hanly asked their mother if we could stay at their house. Mrs Hanly put the six Virgin Prunes up—again it was us being Irish. She gave us breakfast the next day. I remember how taken aback she was when we went out and bought her flowers and chocolates to say thank you.

Years later, after he and Kay Carroll parted, he met and married Brix. Brix loved The Virgin Prunes and loved the way I looked—especially my wearing of dresses. She encouraged Mark for me to perform with the band even more. I distinctly remember in summer of 1984 being onstage with The Fall in the infamous Hacienda venue in Manchester and the audience hating me being onstage with them, which made Mark like it even more. I have to say the energy that Brix brought to the ensemble was so powerful they seemed to suddenly become a lot more musically articulate and focused. After this,

Mark rang me and asked if I would do a recording session. The Virgin Prunes were effectively falling apart at this stage, so it was a welcome call. I contributed to three songs on the group's 1984 album *The Wonderful and Frightening World of The Fall*. We worked at Olympic Studios in London with the renowned producer John Leckie. Leckie was decked out head to toe in a papal purple, something to do with his spiritual beliefs at the time, and Mark had great fun slagging him and giving him grief over that. When I arrived for the recording sessions, I had no idea of what he wanted me to do. All I remember was the group constantly putting down some very loud music nonstop. I had no sense as to what the lyrics might be. So, we went to a nearby pub and Mark pulled out some pieces of paper from a plastic carrier bag—envelopes, cigarette boxes, etc.—with bits of lyrics written on them. Laying them out on the table, jigsaw-like, these lyrics were the basis of 'Clear Off.' Mark revealed, "It's about a Civil Servant a lost and lonely sad old fucker. . . ." His only other advice to me was to be intimate. "Do your sad thing", he said. For 'Copped It', which is a big noisy, niggling, relentless monster of a song, he cackled at me, jokingly but serious, to do 'your Johnny Rotten trying to be David Bowie' vocal . . . 'they've Copped It. . . .' He hated both of them at the time! It was a live take, had no words, and was just improvising, but the noise was so loud I couldn't hear myself, so out desperation, with tongue in cheek, I ranted à la Lydon a line from an old Carpenters' song as my starting point. 'Sing . . . Sing a Song'. Mark loved that and pushed me no end. This recording process involved having a full PA set up in the studio as a monitor system. It was something that had to be seen and heard to be believed. So loud was the sound that my ears were deaf for days afterwards. Mark asked me how I might like to be credited on the album, so I suggested the phrase 'Friendly Visitor'. "Who do ya think you are, fucking E.T. or something?" he replied, laughing, but that's what I was credited as.

I've always considered Craig Scanlon to be a bit of a musical genius. He was one of the greatest members of the group. The guitars are something incredible. I also loved Paul and Steven Hanly's contribution as a rhythm section. Brix pushed The Fall in a very interesting and musically brilliant direction, adding, as she did, lots of glam and glitz. There were so many 'classic' Fall albums with her on board. She most definitely pushed Michael Clark at Mark, not to mention the group embracing the Top Twenty.

Mark E. Smith and The Fall have left an enduring legacy that will keep growing as the world catches up with the force and vision of his writings. I think he would have been amused by the very idea of a group of academics/fans writing about his work in such an attentive and considered way. Ultimately, I think Mark's contribution was his words, his vision. He was a master of lyric writing. He invented his own genre. He knew his vision.

Mark's poetry, or his rant, was the big vision; it was his beating heart in that mad skinny body of his. He never succumbed to anything other than his own obsessive vision. I don't think that he wanted the music to ever distract from his words, even though he'd almost purposely mix couplets and rhymes way, way low in the music—I always assumed to piss off the Trainspotter fans. He ruled the group and its music with an iron fist, like a post-punk dictator with Tradesman-like finesse. In the end, as this collection evidences, he is best seen as an extraordinary writer who made an immense contribution to post punk. He was a total one-off. Rest in peace, old friend, and here's to The Fall lasting forever. . . .

Gavin Friday, Dublin, August 2022

Introduction
Mr Sociological Memory Man . . .
Martin J. Power and Eoin Devereux

THE FALL

Within the music press, music industry, and in the growing number of publications by former group members and music critics, the broad and often idiosyncratic history of The Fall (1976–2018) is generally well known. Across multiple incarnations, The Fall led by the late Mark E. Smith (1957–2018) were one of the most influential, important, and prolific *avant-garde* music groups to emerge on the British post-punk scene. Taking their name from Albert Camus's novel *La Chute* (*The Fall*) (1956), over four decades, the group (involving upwards of 66 members) released thirty-one studio albums and numerous live albums and bootlegs. Distinctly northern English and working class, but also drawing on wider European cultural influences including Can and Neu!, The Fall's unique abrasive sound attracted—and continues to attract—a dedicated fan-base (see, for example, https://thefall.org).

Perhaps more than any other artist of his generation, Mark E. Smith encapsulated the DIY ethic of punk and post-punk in terms of his song-writing, recording techniques, and distinctive live performances. In addition to his love of an expansive range of musical genres and art forms, Smith's life-long interest in literature, cult literature, cinema, and most importantly *wordplay* all heavily influenced his song-writing craft and The Fall's overall aesthetic and sound. As well as his boundless creative output with The Fall, Smith was also a solo-artiste, a playwright and writer, who was regularly in demand for collaboration with other groups and artists (see, for example, Smith and Duff 2021, as evidence of Smith's abilities as a scriptwriter). Mark E. Smith recorded and performed with, amongst others, Gorillaz, Coldcut, Edwin

Figure I.1. Poster for Fall Symposium 2019
Eoin Devereux © Reproduced by kind permission.

Collins, Mouse on Mars, and Inspiral Carpets, and is reputed to have been a significant influence on groups such as LCD Soundsytem, Sonic Youth, Pavement, Fontaines D.C., and The Murder Capital.

While there are clearly identifiable phases in The Fall's career in terms of output, 'chart success,' accessibility and musical styles, the uniqueness and *unpredictability* of Smith's delivery remained constant to the very end. In many respects, Smith's subversive capacity to disrupt and destabilize owes more to Dadaism and Surrealism than it does to practices associated with punk and post-punk. Indeed, Smith's songcraft and his delivery of those songs forces us to call into question any received notions we might have as to what constitutes a 'song'—or indeed a gig—in the first place and how we might expect them to be delivered. Eschewing the usual practice of playing 'hits' or songs from their latest release, Fall gigs were, more often than not, a full-on assault on the aural and visual senses. From our experience of watching the group play live, Fall gigs are best summarised as being chaotic, mesmerising, hypnotic gatherings of predominantly male fans, in communion with the shaman-like Smith.

ALWAYS DIFFERENT, ALWAYS THE SAME: THE SYMPOSIUM

Organised by the (then) *Popular Music and Popular Culture Research Cluster* at the University of Limerick, the eponymous symposium on which this

Figure I.2. Fall Symposium laminates
Eoin Devereux © Reproduced by kind permission.

edited collection is based, took place in Limerick City, Ireland, on November 7, 2019. A post-industrial city, its parallels with Manchester in terms of economic decline have not gone unnoticed by many commentators.

Smith's untimely passing in January 2018 and his salutary perseverance as a performer, in spite of his debilitating illness, had convinced us that it was time to convene an event that would underline the significance of his important contribution to contemporary music and culture. To the best of our knowledge, only one other academic conference on The Fall—'Messing Up the Paintwork' (2008)—has taken place, to date (see Goddard and Halligan 2010). The Limerick symposium's artwork featured the cover of the group's 2016 release *Wise Ol' Man*, reproduced by kind permission of Mark's sister Suzanne. Our chosen venue was the renowned Dolan's Warehouse. Set in the docklands of Limerick, we would like to think that Mark E. Smith would have been mildly amused, given his own early history as a shipping clerk and the fact that a symposium dedicated to respectfully dissecting his work was taking place in a pub.

"Hey Student!"

The symposium audience comprised fans, academics, students, and academics who were Fall fans. All aspects of the day were 'Fallified' to coin a new phrase. Coffee breaks referenced Smith's lyrics "I drank a jar of coffee . . ." and the lunch and dinner were styled "Eat Y'Self Fitter . . .". Given our commitment to practice as much as to theory, in addition to twelve academic papers from a diverse range of academic disciplines, the symposium featured an interview with ex–Fall drummer Simon Wolstencroft. Interviewed by Martin Power, Wolstencroft recalled his days working with Mark E. Smith

Figure I.3. Fall 'Friendly Visitor' Gavin Friday video contribution with The Frigid Stars
Eoin Devereux © Reproduced by kind permission.

and The Fall in the period 1986–1997. His drumming was first featured on the group's 1986 album *Bend Sinister*. Wolstencroft told the audience about recording and touring with The Fall as well as his experiences co-writing the group's hit single 'Free Range' (see Wolstencroft 2018). Unable to attend on the day owing to touring commitments, the former Virgin Prunes' singer Gavin Friday (together with two of the contributors to this volume—Eoin Devereux, synths, and David Meagher, guitars) performed as Frigid Stars and contributed to the symposium in the form of a new recording of the 1981 Fall song 'Slates, Slags etc.' complete with a video presentation of images and words. Friday of course was a one-time guest member of The Fall (Mark E. Smith described him as a 'Friendly Visitor' when he provided vocals on the songs 'Copped It', 'Stephen Song', and 'Clear Off' on 1984's *The Wonderful and Frightening World of The Fall*).

Through a very happy set of circumstances The Fall symposium took place on the same date as the appearance in the venue of Imperial Wax. Three members of Imperial Wax (Pete Greenway, Dave Spurr, and Kieron Melling) were part of the final lineup of The Fall, taking their name from the very first Fall album, *Imperial Wax Solvent* (2008), they had played on together. The symposium concluded with a group interview entitled 'Life in The Fall'. Interviewed by Eoin Devereux, Greenway, Spurr, and Melling, all fondly recalled working with Mark E. Smith. Smith's intelligence and, most of all, his wry sense of humour as the group leader was emphasised. Mark's former group members paid homage to their leader and friend by including some songs from The Fall's albums *New Facts Emerge* (2017) and *Re-Mit* (2013) in their set.

"NOTEBOOK'S OUT PLAGIARISTS..."

The essays contained in this book had their first outing at our Fall symposium. From the outset we wanted the subsequent collection of essays to be deliberately ambitious. Rather than repeating the received 'wisdom' in circulation about The Fall, we asked the contributors to further disassemble The Fall and Smith's significant contribution to contemporary culture. This resulted in up-to-date original research by academics and writers from a diverse range of backgrounds. Given The Fall's complexities (their wide range of influences and styles, multiple lineups, and sometimes 'anti-music' stance), the collection consciously draws upon a wide range of academic disciplines and approaches in order to unpack the group's influence and legacy. As editors, we would argue that the very multi-modality of The Fall demands a set of interdisciplinary lenses through which we can begin to unpack the group's cultural significance. While a growing number of publications ranging from essays and memorabilia (see Norton and Stanley 2021), memoirs, books focused on the individual experiences of group members, and band discography have been published, with the exception of Goddard and Halligan's (2010) edited collection, there is a surprising dearth of academic scholarship published on The Fall and Mark E. Smith.

As this collection evidences, we cast a very broad net in terms of subject matter and focus. Smith's passing is assessed in terms of both his lasting legacy and the resultant demise of The Fall (see chapters 5 and 6 by Martin Myers and John Fleming, in particular). The disruptive 'strangeness' of The Fall is a recurring theme across several chapters, most notably in the group's use of particular forms of typography (see chapter 3 by Paul Wilson). Smith's role as a curator, not only of odd typographical styles and sampled sounds, but also of images and words for possible use in the design of record covers is carefully explored. This edited collection includes a firsthand insight into Smith's curatorial role by means of an interview with his sister, the artist Suzanne Smith (see chapter 2). While Smith might have been understandably hostile to the use of a neat label such as the *Avant Garde*, The Fall are shown to have had much in common with this movement. To use K. A. Laity's term (see chapter 1), as an 'Art Renegade', Mark E. Smith and The Fall typify a form of Modernism that is distinctly working class. Although many of the formative influences on Mark E. Smith have been previously documented,

David Meagher and John McFarland focus on how the early Fall were shaped by the near presence in Prestwich of the largest psychiatric institution in Europe (see chapter 13). They evidence how Mark E. Smith's early lyrics are replete with references to psychiatric institutions, psychiatrists, and pharmacology. The Fall's *atypicality* is repeatedly referred to across this collection. Mike Glennon explores such tendencies within the work of The Fall, CAN, in dub reggae and within some of Mark E. Smith and The Fall's dance-related creative activities (see chapter 9). Smith's well-documented experiences of 'Pre-Cognition' and ESP are the subject of Ben Lawley's chapter. He offers an insightful and considered account of how 'Pre-Cognition' and 'ESP' were an integral part of Mark E. Smith's creative strategies in The Fall (see chapter 4). Smith's dexterity in terms of language surfaces time and time again in this collection. Two contributions in particular (see chapters 8 and 9) subject the particularities of Smith's lyrics to a fine-grained linguistic analysis. Elaine Vaughan, Brian Clancy, and Eoin Devereux experiment with the applicability of a corpus-based thematic and discourse analysis of Smith's lyrics from the group's first and last five studio albums, while Matt Davies's contribution is even more ambitious in examining as it does the entire Fall lyrical corpus (see chapter 7). Extensive touring by The Fall resulted in the group developing an international following. Building his narrative from his experiences of being an Irish Fall fan, Michael Mary Murphy's chapter discusses The Fall's presence in Ireland and discusses how the group contributed to an ever-burgeoning post-punk music scene (see chapter 12). An over-arching theme in this volume is the degree to which Mark E. Smith and The Fall drew upon literary influences to create the group's distinctive art (see chapter 1). Blake, Burroughs, and Lovecraft are common touchstones in terms of those who have attempted to unlock Smith's engagement with and use of literature. Kieran Cashell's exhaustive analysis (chapter 11) of the centrality of language in the world of The Fall sees Smith's writings as a form of neo-Vorticism, which have a structural affinity to the idiomatic poetic practices practiced by Ezra Pound. Smith's conscious perversion of language in terms of both semantics and delivery are the key to understanding the group's substantial contribution to a working-class (literary) modernism (see Chapter 10).

In an early interview with the NME (*New Musical Express* magazine) in 1980, Mark E. Smith proclaimed that "The Fall defies logic. Our past defies logic. A threat: The Fall is a threat" (cited in Penman 1980). In hindsight, Smith's pronouncement (or was it a prediction?) certainly has merit. His obstinate and learned perseverance meant that The Fall never deviated from their stated mission of "talking back" on their own terms and leaving an indelible mark on contemporary music and culture.

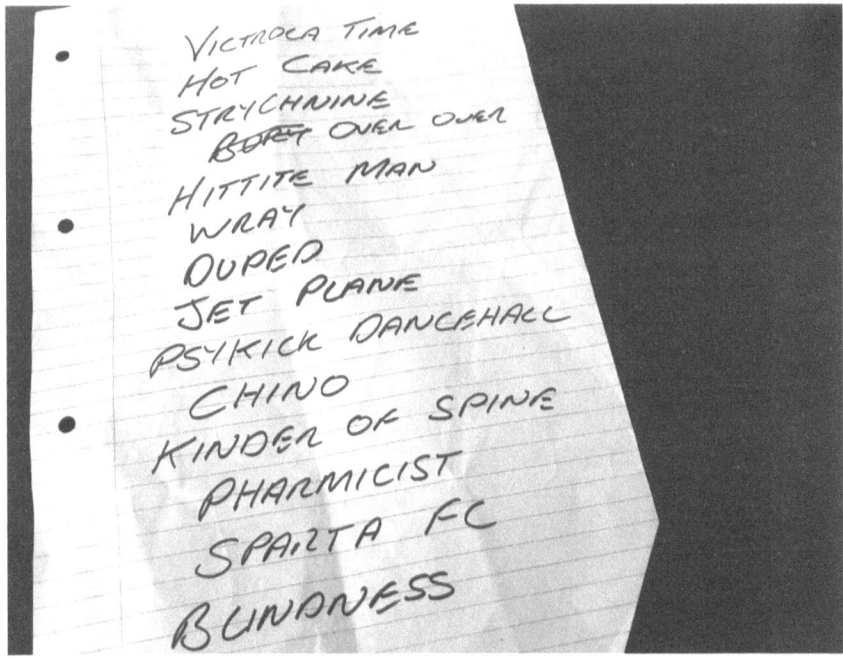

Figure I.4. The Fall Set List from The Set Theatre, Kilkenny, Ireland
Eoin Devereux © Reproduced by kind permission.

REFERENCES

Camus, Albert. (1956). *La Chute*. Paris: Gallimard.
Goddard, Michael, and Benjamin Halligan. (2010). *Mark E. Smith and The Fall: Art, Music and Politics*. Farnham: Ashgate.
Norton, Tessa, and Bob Stanley (eds.). (2021). *Excavate: The Wonderful and Frightening World of The Fall*. London: Faber & Faber.
Penman, Ian. (1980). "All Fall Down," *New Musical Express*, January 5, pp. 6–7.
Smith, Mark E, and Graham Duff. (2021). *The Otherwise*. London: Strange Attractor Press.
Wolstencroft, Simon. (2018). *You Can Drum, But You Can't Hide*. 2nd edition, London: Route Books.

Chapter One

Spoiling all the Paintwork
Mark E. Smith, Art Renegade
K. A. Laity

> *Course I'm an artist; I've been an artist for about twelve years . . . no one's called me an artist . . . the strength is being undercover.*
>
> —Mark E. Smith in interview with Michael Bracewell, ICA (1994)

The line between art and popular culture is a porous line, but one heavily policed by market forces and self-appointed guardians of taste, as well as by some of the practitioners themselves. People who swerve out of their lane often face great and lasting resistance—even ridicule. As Yoko Ono once said,

> That's the difference between entertainment and art. People just love to be entertained, and in order to entertain them, you have to do things in a way that they understand. So automatically, you have to go to a certain place, and I wasn't doing that. But then, also, I really think that any invention or discovery cannot be done unless you are totally free—free of those people. (Mitchell 2013)

This hostility has loosened up somewhat, but the truth is, human brains tend to like stable categories. According to MIT scientists, our striatum picks up the exemplars and our pre-frontal cortex builds categories from them (Trafton 2011). John Peel's famous edict aside, one would be hard pressed to come up with another band that lasted so long and sounded so different from its own past.

The Fall, of course, resists categories. 'We are the Fall / Northern white crap that talks back,' as Mark E. Smith snarls in 'Crap Rap2/Like to Blow'. The Fall's long career of cantankerous iconoclasm includes actual punch-ups onstage, and a rotating list of ex-members long enough to fill several books—as highlighted in Dave Simpson's *The Fallen* (2008)—fueling the burgeoning cottage industry of memoirs by former Fall members: a rich vein to mine, indeed. But it's good to remember that the group was always a collaboration, though it's always tempting (and at times impossible not) to focus on Smith: as ex-Fall member Paul Hanley writes in his volume specifically in the case of the iconic *Hex Induction Hour*, 'he wasn't the author of *Hex Induction Hour*, he was the co-author. There were six people involved in the writing, and seven in the performance . . . I know this because I was there' (2020, p.18).[1] Smith and the group may be inextricable in fans' minds, but for Smith—and for the ex-group members—it was a collaboration, one of many.

Always at the center of the maelstrom was leader and primary lyricist Smith, often mythologised by fans who give new meaning to 'fanaticism'[2] as members of the FallNet and The Mighty Fall Facebook group and their competing organisations can attest: or in the words of the first of these, 'a coterie of ketamine-coated cockroaches crawling across a keyboard' (FallNet 2006). Smith was as likely to dispute that mystique as to court it, coming out with surprising pronouncements of precognitive messages and improbable revelations like Fall fans inventing the internet in 1982 (see chapter 4 on Mark E. Smith and Pre-Cognition in this volume).

Yet his defiant working-class status always remained central. As David Wilkinson wrote in one of the many eulogies, 'Smith was no mystery. So much of his seemingly otherworldly vision was born of the Northern working-class culture that produced him', the autodidact who always believed that 'The Fall had to appeal to someone who was into cheap soul as much as someone who liked [the] avant-garde' (2018). The identity of the group as 'Northern white crap that talks back' became a throughline in its decades of existence.

Nonetheless, there's sometimes a resistance to acknowledge just how much the band planted its flags in the traditional art world. Perhaps more than any of the art school bands that rivaled The Fall for Manchester's crown, The Fall and Smith himself plunged into the *avant-garde* with a fearless zeal for experimentation matched only by a boundless enthusiasm for the popular and the reviled: with unflinching clarity, Manchester City supporter Smith saw no issue veering from presenting the football scores on BBC Sport, to namechecking comics, or weird writer Arthur Machen in his lyrics, or penning a musical about the short-lived Pope John Paul I. The Fall appeared on stage with the Michael Clark Dance Group in a production on royal succession. Smith himself appeared as Jesus in the BBC 3 series *Ideal* (2005-11), created by modern art lover, Graham Duff. Perhaps one of the least-well-explored areas of Smith's *avant-garde* appearances was in video installations including *Diary of a Madman* (1997), and Mark Aerial Waller's *Glow Boys* (1998) and *Midwatch* (1999–2001), the latter which appeared as an installation in the LUX gallery: literally in the fine art world.

Although an icon of post-punk music, Smith clearly had ambitions—which he sometimes denied—to step beyond the pop world into the *avant-garde* and achieved them with the same slouching aplomb that accompanied his ever-present carrier bags. He seemed to instinctively embody Oscar Wilde's assertion that while '[a]rt is the only serious thing in the world . . . the artist is the only person who is never serious' (1894). In a video for the Tate Modern, Smith says that 'art is good if you are very pure about it' and 'there's a difference between art and arty . . . art is a skill' (2010). Early on the band were making connections to iconoclastic artists like William Blake and Wyndham Lewis. The latter and his work amongst the Vorticists offered a particularly potent touchstone that shaped much of The Fall's approach to its work, at least from Smith's perspective. Lewis's idea of the artist as his own first creation seems to fit not only Smith but the first iterations of the band as it found its feet.

LITERARY

Let's begin with the name: according to Martin Bramah, Smith's initial suggestions included the toe-curlingly bad Master Race, Death's Heads, and the more rockabilly-esque the Shades—perhaps a little too close to the Shadows (quoted in Ford 2003, p.18). They finally settled on The Outsiders until discovering another band was using the name, so Tony Friel suggested they switch to Camus's other major work for their name and became The Fall (Ford 2003, p.18). While their initial choice aligned with the existentialist notion that defined their general attitude—being apart, being contrarian, being different from the rest of the burgeoning Manchester music scene—the final choice fits better than might have been initially supposed. Smith's monologues, which permeate the group's recordings, mirror the long confessions of narrator Jean-Baptiste Clamence. Fearing the judgment of others, he is quick to mock first. Everyone is guilty, God is dead, power and subjugation are the only possible relations—consequently, he is alone because all relationships are too confining. His words sound surprisingly familiar both in the lyrics and interviews given: 'I have always mocked the greed which, in our society, takes the place of ambition' (Camus 2006, p.14).

For Simon Ford, an important aspect of this choice puts the band in 'a different league' from the bands popping up in the wake of the punk explosion. 'The high-brow literary connections instantly set the group apart from the many bands with joke and ephemeral "punk" names', but he adds to that, 'The Fall was at pains to escape classification as a self-consciously artistic and experimental band' (Ford 2003, p.18), the ones who were generally seen as middle-class art-school types. While our culture reminds of the gulf between 'art' and the working class over and over again, and in the career of the group this relationship has proceeded without much fuss. Chucking out art with art-school types does a disservice to the band.

Nonetheless, there are tensions which caused Smith and other members of the band to bridle at suggestions of artiness and play up the working-class image. The class tensions around the contested area of 'art' and its practice run deep. Consider, for example, the Manchester Art Gallery, begun as the Royal Manchester Institution for the Promotion of Literature, Science and the Arts in 1882. Like similar nineteenth-century institutions, it was among 'the efforts by representatives of the upper and middle classes to organize the leisure of the working-class by offering educational, cultural and sporting opportunities. Frequently such activities were provided by "settlements" or "missions", close in inspiration and style to colonial enterprises' (Waterfield and Smith 1994, p.56). Not surprisingly, accusations of any connections to the arts could chafe.

Even when exploring the literary influences on the band's creative work—apart from Camus as the source of their name—the bulk of attention has tended to focus on the comfortably 'low brow' or genre authors, H. P. Lovecraft and Arthur Machen, immortalized together in *Dragnet*'s 'Spectre vs. Rector'; however, they appear along with M. R. James. With the latter, there's an extra whiff of intellect. The medieval scholar and ghost story hobbyist comes with all the trappings of the elite from his Eton school days to his career at Kings College, Cambridge—even if he does pen gruesome tales of rectors and spectres. Quite a heady mix for the Prole Art Threat. But the scholar's love for Latin chants, runic curses, and hidden secrets in medieval buildings and ancient places clearly fired the imagination of the group's primary lyricist. One need only glance at the complicated and much-contested commentary on the lyrics of that particular track at The Annotated Fall website to realise that Smith mixes high- and low-brow elements with pop culture artifacts without missing a beat. As the legendarily disastrous NY-MOMA exhibit 'High and Low: Modern Art and Popular Culture' demonstrated all too well, stealing from popular culture (as Picasso would say) could make great art, while merely copying it could not (Smith 2015). The difference between the dazzling spectacle of 'Spectre vs. Rector' and the mere assemblage of quirks like the average mundane Lovecraft pastiche is immense (see for contrast, the groundbreaking *Lovecraft Country* television series which takes every effort to undo all Lovecraft's worst impulses). The difficulty of parsing the final lyrics bears out Ken Price's encomium, 'A craftsman knows what he's going to make and an artist doesn't know what he's going to make, or what the finished product is going to look like' (Nasher Sculpture Centre

2013). While horror may strike most readers as decidedly low-brow, it continues to grip the power of literary minds: even Joyce Carol Oates has written Lovecraft pastiche.

Other bookish influences definitely throw the weight toward the more literary establishment but also exhibit an iconoclastic whimsy that refuses to be pigeonholed. Mark Goodall has written about the influence of Malcolm Lowry in songs such as 'Lunar Caustic' and 'Arms Control Poseur'; though less celebrated today, Lowry certainly has a solid reputation. It's striking that Smith referred to him as 'one of the *best* bloody writers, he wrote the *best* books' (Goodall 2010, p.45). In cut-up style (another art tradition dating to the early twentieth-century Dadaists, though probably best known for being employed by William S. Burroughs and adopted most famously by David Bowie), Smith appropriates lines from Lowry's diaries to blend seamlessly with his own inventions, a suggestion that the literary milieu is nothing alien to Smith's lyrics. It's easy to see why the tragic tale of the Consul, alienated, drunk, adrift in an 'alien' country, appealed to Smith's sensibilities. Lowry stumbled in the opposite direction from the Modernists he loved like Joyce and Eliot, creating what Stephen Spender has called 'not a statement about civilisation so much as an account of one man's soul within the circumstances of an historic phase' (Lowry 1966, p.xii). The Consul's fiery end seems all of a piece with many of the doomed heroes found in Fall songs:

> Yet no, it wasn't the volcano, the world itself was bursting into black spouts of villages catapulted into space, with himself fall through it all, through the inconceivable pandemonium of a million tanks, through the blazing of ten million burning bodies, falling into a forest, falling—Suddenly he screamed and it was as though this scream were being tossed from one tree to another, as its echoes returned, then, as though the trees themselves were crowding nearer, huddled together, closing over him pitying. (Lowry 1966, p.406)

As a final touch to have a dead dog thrown over him, it was a fate that would have made the cat-loving Smith shudder with horror.

Literary influences also include Camus's fellow countrymen, Jean-Paul Sartre, Vladimir Nabokov, and even Alfred Jarry, all of whom add intellectual cachet to the cauldron of inspiration. Before we get too rarified though, Smith calls on the Dice Man, Luke Rhinehart, for cult appeal. For the bouncing Bo Diddley–style homage to the novel, Smith sings 'throw the bones and the poison dice / no time for small moralists' and the preparatory notes for the LP warn, '(From the book, don't read it, the song's much safer)' and further that it is 'dedicated to all ex-members of The Fall & their petty materialism' (Norton and Stanley 2021, p.67). The lyrics present Smith's astute encapsulation of the novel in which Rhinehart's fictional alter-ego explores the perils of living every choice by the throw of the dice. 'With determination and dice, I am God,' the fictional Luke claims (1971, p.107), though he has already begun to complicate the matter by allowing himself to disobey the dice decisions. One can easily see the appeal for Smith of the complicated and porous divide between truth/fiction as well as playing a role just to see what reaction it gets. As Rhinehart puts it in the preface to the novel, 'A well-told lie is a gift of the gods' (1971, p.ix). Rigid adherence to a system is deadly, Rhinehart's character realises: 'Slowly and steadily, my friends, I was beginning to go insane . . . I discovered that I liked absurd comments, anecdotes, actions,' even beginning to shout 'I'm Batman' at his therapist (1971, p.97). For Smith, this was further ammunition for his desire to approach The Fall not as a band but as a project to resist the commodification of both music and daily life.

And that's not even getting to Jack Cole, Jack Kirby, and the world of comics, an often derided medium. As Wyndham Lewis has written, 'An artist should be impartial like a God' (2010, p.205), affirming the whimsy of this perspective a few sentences later: 'The artist who takes his job seriously gets his sensibilities blunted' (2010, p.205). All existence is the artist's palette: mix and match. 'High' and 'low' are meaningless, and this omnivorous sensibility has served The Fall well. While there will be more discussion of Lewis below, it is worth pointing out that while the visual influence of the Vorticist may be most apparent in the career of the group, Lewis has a similar influence on the writing, too. Lewis himself 'consciously tried to keep his writing and art apart' Richard Humphreys argues, though 'neither activity can be understood without reference to the other' (2004, p.7).

So it is, too, with Smith who never really sought to separate the two. While fans tend to ring-fence the music from the rest of his work, for Smith it seemed to be all of a piece. As Paul Hanley writes in *Have a Bleedin Guess*, the parallels between the two artists were plain, from Smith's envy of the *Blast* manifestos ('Nobody comes out with anything like that now, do they?') to their similar approach to publicity, and the desire to always 'contradict yourself. In order to live, you must remain broken up' (2020, p.154). He cites scholar Michael Nath, who writes that, 'both the words in the Blast manifestos and in Mark Smith's lyrics are very similar in their magic—they take the reader/listener by surprise, because they're not attached in normal ways' (2020, p.155). Eleni Poulou speaks to this broad-ranging imagination in the foreword to *The Otherwise*: 'I believe Mark could have directed and written films, written books. But he chose the medium of song' (2021, p.13). Duff agrees that 'in a different life Mark E. Smith would have made a superb short story writer. This assertion is easily borne out by even a cursory perusal of his lyrics' (p.211). In the most recent tome assessing the influence of The Fall and its front man,

Excavate! (2021), Michael Bracewell and Jon Wilde argue along similar lines that 'he assembles his lyrics in such a manner that found language, narrative, slang, double-talk, trigger phrases and rapid juxtapositions are combined to create a discourse which describes as it commemorates. The style is not artless, as it may look, but the product of careful design' (p.219).

Perhaps the best way to demonstrate the literary richness of Smith's lyrics is to point to a resource well known to most fans: the Annotated Fall site. Here the dedicated fans—not all 'look back bores'—minutely annotate lyrics, possible lyrics, and potential connections to everything from the aforementioned authors, to comedy legend Peter Cook, the OED, obscure BBC broadcasts, American and German slang—even Pythagorean numerology and Plutarch's lives. This rich body of critical, fan-fueled work speaks to the literary richness of The Fall's output over the years.

Of course, Smith has been examined a narrative writer, too. For example by Taylor Parkes in the *Quietus*, who argues that 'Mark doesn't write short stories any more—and besides, it's the one part of his "old" writing that's never been properly addressed' but also that there is another kind of narrative specific to the group: 'Fall-narrative is like this: free of the formal demands of literature, the words spin loose (and occasionally cop out), but always impose themselves through that assertive, insubordinate authorial voice rather than anything else' (Parkes 2018). In the foreword to *The Otherwise*, the horror movie script Smith wrote with *Ideal*'s Graham Duff, his widow Eleni Poulou writes, 'Mark . . . wanted to create something new all the time. I still think of him as a writer. Not a songwriter' (2021, p.13). Parkes thinks the particular style that appears in composition like 'Prole Art Threat' offers a story 'free of the formal demands of literature' resulting in 'salty word-storms' (2018). While The Fall's story songs never reach for the level of narrative coherence as say, Bobby Gentry's 'Ode to Billy Joe', it's primarily because that is not the mark they're aiming for—the surrealism which Parkes calls, 'the careful juxtaposition of disparate ideas which, when placed together, become explosive' (2018). But it's also the fun of it: as Eleni remarks, 'Mark was so effervescent and creative, a true writer and inventor. In his always curious and unjaded state he would play with the most banal of storylines and embellish them' (2021, p.13). The way she describes it makes watching television into a kind of exquisite corpse, the favourite Surrealist game.

But this playfulness and sureality are a choice. The release of the script of *The Otherwise* makes clear, Smith was quite capable of narrative coherence when he wished to employ it. As Duff has said in interviews, the project proceeded much differently than he had expected, and he echoes the view that Smith was a writer who turned to lyrics and not the reverse:

"I don't think he ever saw himself particularly as a lyricist," Duff says. "He saw himself as a writer who worked in the world of rock. Sometimes he'd send me bits of script, or we'd talk about stuff on the phone, and I'd think 'that's just perfect as it is, I don't need to do anything to that'. I mean, I don't want to give the impression that he spouted a load of ideas and I turned them into scenes, because he would literally send me fully written scenes that ended up in the script. It wasn't a case of him humming a couple of bars and me making a song out of it, if you know what I mean." (Murray 2021)

Similarly, when it came to constructing the project over a lengthy period of time, the collaboration took on a very different nature than Duff had anticipated, with Smith showing a particular interest in creating vivid dialogue: 'Initially I did think it would probably be more me, that we'd brainstorm and then I'd go and turn it into something. But actually, I was surprised. Not by Mark's ability to come up with fascinating ideas and weird ideas and great juxtapositions, but by his ear for natural dialogue' (Murray 2021). Smith's habit of inserting overheard dialogue into lyrics shows the careful attention he paid to the rhythms of natural speech, a key building block of popular fiction.

One of the other measures to show the literary influence of The Fall and Smith can be found in books inspired by the group and its songs. These range from the upmarket, established writers included in *Perverted by Language* (2008) which bears the imprimatur of Smith himself who wrote the introduction to the fan-fueled oddity *Dr. Buck's Letters: An Unauthorised Extrapolation of the Fall by Fall Net* (2005). The former effects to produce the gravitas of the literary including known names like Jeff Vandermeer and the ever-present Stewart Lee. The latter offers a raucous embodiment of the Mark E. Smith School of Writing School, stories of paranoia and marginal lives, interspliced with art and photography seemingly forming random snapshots of a cluttered past or future and mixing fonts aggressively enough to make any graphic designer cry. It's completely in the spirit of The Fall. In years to come there will doubtless be many more writers inspired by Smith and The Fall, but it's time to move along to the next category.

THEATRICAL

Of course, the primary connection to the theatrical world for the group comes via the Scottish dancer Michael Clark, but it's useful to remember too, as Martin Myers reminds us, that transgender artist Lanah P[illay] regularly opened for The Fall in the 1980s in an act paying tribute to Shirley Bassey, Eartha Kitt, and so on (2010, p.141). Lanah explains how it happened as a part of the rich cauldron of the Manchester art scene at the time:

> Through Maureen and Alan, I met up with somebody called Joe Quinn who had an antiques shop on Stockport Road, and through him I met Mark E. Smith of The Fall and Kay Carroll, his girlfriend and manager at the time. I ended up supporting The Fall at a few gigs at the Russell Club on Moss Side and even appeared in some of their videos as well. It was by becoming friends with Mark and Kay that I met someone called Adrian Sherwood who managed On-U Sound Records and a band called The London Underground. They were coming to play the Hebden Bridge Festival, and then they persuaded me to come down to London, like Judy Garland, with all my belongings in a trunk. (i-D staff 2017)

The theatricality of the performances set them apart from the more typical rock bands of the time. As Kay Carroll said at the time, 'The audience and the media didn't know what to make of it . . . but that was the intention, we wanted to push their "posingness" into their faces, and [Lanah] certainly did achieve that for us, I think' (Ford 2003, p.100). The dramatic effect came from orchestrating not just their own music but the whole experience of the evening.

Michael Clark's collaboration of course was a much more far reaching one. Recalling later how they first met, Smith said of Clark's appearance on a local news programme, 'He was dancing through a Manchester supermarket in a dress. Everyone was going, "he looks a right idiot," but I thought, "he looks pretty cool to me." That was my first impression—and first impressions are usually the best' (Cooper quoted in Ford 2003, p.134). Though surprised by Clark's desire to use The Fall's music for his *New Puritans* show, Smith readily agreed. Clark mentions being particularly attracted by the lyrical complexity as much as by the rhythmic power of the music. He appreciated the band taking a punt on the project. Clark said of Smith, 'I don't think he was very familiar with anything that I'd done, I think it was just one of those things that he basically took a chance on and hoped that something interesting would come out of it' (Nugent quoted in Ford 2003, p.134).

Smith, being 'pleasantly surprised' by the interpretation of his music sought out more opportunities to embrace the theatricality of the ballet company. Their joint performance of 'Lay of the Land' on *The Old Grey Whistle Test* brought the live audience an unprecedented experience that included the notorious cheek-revealing tights and a pantomime cow. The bright costumes of the dancers kept the cameras' focus; there's only one line of the song where a camera seeks out the singer, never mind the rest of the band. While commentators later disparaged 'the bare bottoms and The Fall's "accompanying noise"' (Push quoted in Ford 2003, p.136), the group thought well enough of the performance to brainstorm further collaboration.

In the meantime, Smith had written *Hey! Luciani*, 'according to Fall mythology' as Tommy Mackay puts it, 'on beer mats and delivered to its director in a shoebox' (2018, p.83). The two-week long production starred Leigh

Bowery, was described by its author as 'a cross between Shakespeare and *The Prisoner*' (2018, p.83). Typically, Smith links together the high and if not the low, the somewhat lower than the high. Patrick McGoohan's cult series exudes an air of paranoia that fits well the conspiracy-laden script about the short-lived pope 'incorporating Israeli commandos, demonic possession, Italian fascists, ex-Nazis and a Scottish communist' (Mackay 2018, p.83).[3]

The play is less interesting for these purposes than for how it inspired further ambition for stagework, which came to fruition with Michael Clark's invitation to the Holland Festival, he and Smith decided 'the "Glorious Revolution" of 1688 would make an appropriate starting point' (Ford 2010, p.180) for their collaborative performance. *I am Curious, Orange* was 'succinctly summarised by Mark E. Smith as: "The English get pissed off with their king, kick him out and get some Dutch bloke in."' (Stansfield 2020). Touching on religious controversy like the pope play, this triumphal Protestant narrative cemented the religion of Britain by inviting the Dutch prince and his Anglican wife to take the throne, ousting the Catholic James II and sealing the power of Parliament over the Crown.

Clark and Smith, however, were not much interested in the history as much as the spectacle, which included Leigh Bowery as a can of Heinz Beans, Brix on a giant hamburger, and Clark dancing with crutches. He considered it a success: 'It had that feeling of finally getting to a point that we'd been aiming towards for some time' (Ford 2003, p.181). While it puzzled some fans on both sides of the art/music divide—or as Smith would have it, 'We've got a lot in the art crowd, a lot in the football crowd' (Turner 2018)—the last effect of the performance has stood the test of time. In the recent *Michael Clark: Cosmic Dancer* exhibit at the Barbican, the performance warranted an entire room. Curator Florence Ostende commented, 'For me, I Am Curious, Orange goes much further than a radical deconstruction of Clark's ballet vocabulary. . . . It is a key artwork of 1980s British art' (Stansfield 2020).

Yet Smith refused to admit there was anything even art-adjacent about it. Quizzed by Radio One's Liz Kershaw about it being 'a bit poncey and arty farty' Smith countered, 'Not particularly, no' (FallNet 2000). For him it was all of a piece with the work of the group. Because it seemed so natural, Smith didn't see it as any different than the other experiments within the group. Looking back years later, Smith was able to see how it had been revolutionary, but still downplayed both the innovativeness and his astuteness in pursuing it. In conversation with Luke Turner in 2018, Smith remarked, 'That sort of collaboration's not so new nowadays, but we weren't aware of how it hadn't been done before. It was just a good project. We used to swap tunes and lyrics by post while he was doing the troupe' (Turner 2018). The essential curiosity of the artist is to pursue an idea without respect to the shape it takes—whether it's a post-punk LP or a ballet. As he expressed it in *Renegade*, 'I was on a roll at the time. I'm rarely short of ideas, and I'm not into preserving them too much, either. If it's in your head and you've got the right people around you, then there's no better time to tell the story. . . . I think too many writers hold too much back for another time and lose that spark' (2018, p.159).

But clearly these forays into the world of theatre and ballet inspired Smith to dip further into the realm of performance beyond The Fall, including spoken word recordings *The Post Nearly Man* and *Pander, Panda! Panzer!* as well as readings like his BBC Story for Xmas. In a sense these hearken back to the origins of The Fall as an arts collective, poetry read over music. At the BBC Collective Smith mentions writing his own book *Renegade*, which is more often dismissed as just transcriptions of pub chat. The posthumous release of *Molocular Meditation*, a collaboration between Smith and Mouse on Mars member Jan St Werner, features 're-editing a set of songs that were originally recorded in 2014 at the Cornerhouse, Manchester, in the guise of a multi-channel installation (as well as unreleased new material partly written around that same time)' and 'the music is cryptic, otherworldly, and uncanny' as befits the inadvertent haunting of the late Fall leader (Lehrer 2020). While traditional written narrative may not really be his medium, his embrace of performative texts shows that restless desire to keep innovating that is key to art. In some sense, too, these performances overlap with next section.

FILM

For many pop artists, music videos are an obvious entrée into filmmaking, but as usual Smith seems to have taken the long way around to film. Established early on, his knack for memorable sound bites and off-the-cuff diatribes made for good footage. As the BBC began to move operations north, more opportunities materialised, such as his memorable reading of the football scores, and of course, who could forget his turn as Jesus in modern art scholar Graham Duff's *Ideal*? The publication of the script for *The Otherwise* (2021) offers a tantalising dream of what might have been.

Duff offers insight into Smith's process as they work on the *The Otherwise* initially as a television project inspired by Rod Serling's *The Twilight Zone*, which both cite as influential on their creative work including several Fall songs (Smith and Duff 2021, p.36). The evolution and brainstorming on the project reveal the extent of both Smith's influences and free-ranging imagination. As Duff explains, 'Mark has the idea of developing it into a musical where the characters lip-synch to songs. Like [Dennis Potter's iconic 1986 television series]*The Singing Detective*, but with Fall songs. I immediately realise this is exactly the project that western culture has been lacking: a supernatural Fall musical for TV' (p.41). The book also reveals another film project Smith had been working on with Poulou, 'World Age 4 . . . about animals taking over society' (p.47). His ambitions in this area had been expanding even as he received the final cancer diagnosis. As she noted, 'He'd always be creating something out of the everydayness of life' (p.11).

But perhaps the most interesting thread of his film appearances began with BBC short *Diary of a Madman* (1997). Directed by John Humphries and starring Steve Evets, for once Smith plays not himself or a version of himself, but an actual character, a social worker. Evets next worked with video artist Mark Aerial Waller on *Glow Boys* (1999), which is perhaps how Smith came onboard to play The Caterer. 'It's all right. I like doing videos,' One-Take Willy Smith told *Melody Maker*. Despite his light tone, the film offers a grim picture of shift work in a nuclear plant. The vocal performance of 'The Caterer' which appears on the collection *A World Bewitched* conveys that tone succinctly.

Waller's follow-up on the same theme, *Midwatch*, appeared as an installation at the LUX gallery. Filmed entirely on infrared film, the film is Evets and Smith facing off in total darkness as a mutineer and the time-traveling caterer from the previous film. Waller name-checks Sartre's *In Camera* (AKA *Huis Clos* or *No Exit*) as well as *Das Boot* to describe the atmosphere which he hoped remained true to the experiences of the British nuclear test veterans he interviewed for *Glow Boys*. Like Smith, he sought to bring art gallery sensibilities to the experiences of the working class. Another tantalising titbit from *The Otherwise* is Eleni's offhand mention of 'an unreleased film of [Waller's] where Mark is playing Agamemnon' and that 'he understood Mark's essence like no other' (2021, p.12). Perhaps as the world begins to open up again after the plague, these films will again be shared in exhibition.

FINE ART

I return to Blake and Lewis again. Blake because he embodies the eternal iconoclast so well and I think in riffing on the sacred cow of 'Jerusalem' Smith knew this. In his essay *William Blake Now: Why He Matters More than Ever,* John Higgs writes about the 'metamodern' nature of the artist in 'His willingness to explore what is useful in seemingly opposite extremes' (2019, p.59). Luke Turner in his *Metamodern Manifesto* calls it 'the mercurial condition between and beyond irony and sincerity, naivety and knowingness, relativism and truth, optimism and doubt, in pursuit of a plurality of disparate and elusive horizons' (2015), which seems very Smith-like. Higgs notes how the memorial stone to Blake is not raised up but lowered into the ground to become 'the ground on which we walk' (2019, p.60). Smith takes this space, too, as psychogeographers of Manchester and Prestwich will tell you.

The metamodern explains Smith's lifelong connection to the work of Wyndham Lewis and his edict to 'contradict yourself'. Paul Hanley's *Have a Bleedin Guess* details the connection between Lewis's publications including of course *Blast!* and the construction of *Hex Induction Hour*: 'If Mark E. Smith modeled the worldview he saw fit to share with others on Wyndham Lewis, then it's entirely appropriate, if surprisingly on-the-nose, for him to mode the sleeve of arguably [very much an argument] his most important work on *Blast*' (2020, p.155). The Vorticist approach to manifestos colours also The Fall lyrics books, in the layout, the typefaces, the switch to handwritten typography and the insertion of drawings and photos—as well as the overall graphic aesthetic of the group through its LP artwork. As Paul Wilson argues, 'Mark E. Smith's handwriting has played a central role in establishing The Fall's visual identity and in cementing both his characteristic approach to music and The Fall's position as cultural "artifact" . . . signif[ying] spontaneity, informality, and non-standardised or informal production' (2010, p.120).

But is it art? Yes. If you want a simple answer: yes. If you want a longer answer, try BLAST!'s assertion that 'the art for these climates . . . must be a northern flower' then certainly Smith and The Fall fit the bill. The artist's job, as Grayson Perry (another Smith fan) says, 'is to notice things that other people don't notice' (2014, p.116). In late-stage capitalism, in the metamodern world, art remains an elusive endeavour but while he lived, Smith certainly gave it a good try.

NOTES

1. Although as numerous guests on Hanley's *Oh Brother!* podcast have noted, memories of those times vary greatly between those who were there.

2. For a detailed discussion of the roots of the word 'fan', see de Kloet and van Zoonen (2007), 'Fan culture', pp. 322–41. They highlight the often negative impression of the 'fan' who 'is more regularly accused of having silly pleasures, of leading vicarious lives and losing their mind over their idols or favourite programmes' (p. 323).

3. You can find the transcription of the performance—a partial, disputed, and needfully imperfect record—at TheFall.org thanks to 'harmless drudge' Pete Conkerton.

REFERENCES

Annotated Fall. N.d. http://annotatedfall.doomby.com/
Bracewell, Michael. 1994. 'Interview with Mark E. Smith at the ICA, 1994.' YouTube, https://www.youtube.com/watch?v=N6YuHaWQTBo

Camus, Albert, and Robin Buss. 2006. *The Fall*. London: Penguin.
de Kloet, J., and L. van Zoonen. 2007. Fan culture: Performing difference. In Devereux, E. (ed.), *Media Studies: Key Issues and Debates*. London: SAGE Publications, pp.322–41.
FallNet. 2000. 'Fall News—14 March 2000.' https://thefall.org/news/000314.html
———. 2006. *Dr Buck's Letters: The Unauthorised Extrapolation of the Fall*. Los Angeles: KeroseneBomb Publishing.
Ford, Simon. 2003. *Hip Priest: The Story of Mark E. Smith and the Fall*. London: Quartet.
Goodall, Mark. 2010. 'Salford Drift: A Psychogeography of The Fall.' In *Mark E. Smith and The Fall: Art, Music and Politics*, edited by Michael Goddard and Benjamin Halligan. Farnham, UK: Ashgate.
Hanley, Paul. 2020. *Have a Bleedin Guess: The Story of Hex Enduction Hour*. Pontefract, UK: Route.
Hanley, Paul, and Steve Hanley. *Oh! Brother podcast*. 2021–. https://twitter.com/OhBrotherShow
Higgs, John. 2019. *William Blake Now: Why He Matters More Than Ever*. London: Weidenfeld and Nicolson, Orion Publishing Group.
Humphreys, Richard, and Wyndham Lewis. 2004. *Tate British Artists: Wyndham Lewis (British Artists)*. London: Harry N. Abrams.
i-D staff. 2017. 'The untold story of lgbt pioneer lanah p.' i-D: 7 July 2017. https://i-d.vice.com/en_uk/article/nenbxb/the-untold-story-of-lgbt-pioneer-lanah-p
Lehrer, Adam. 2020. 'I Think That's The Lot: Mark E. Smith Signs Off on Jan St Werner's New Album.' *The Quietus*: 5 March 2020.
Lewis, Wyndham, and Scott W. Klein. 2010. *Tarr*. Oxford: Oxford University Press.
Lowry, Malcolm. 1966 (1947). *Under the Volcano*. Introduction by Stephen Spender. New York: Signet Books.
Mackay, Tommy. 2018. *40 Odd Years of The Fall*. Glasgow: Greg Moodie.
Mitchell, Elvis. 2013. 'Yoko Ono.' *Interview Magazine*, 26 November 2013. https://www.interviewmagazine.com/culture/yoko-ono-1
Murray, Andy. 2021. "It was an absolute buzz." Graham Duff talks about collaborating with Mark E. Smith on the horror script *The Otherwise*.' *Northern Soul*, 8 June 2021. https://www.northernsoul.me.uk/graham-duff-mark-e-smith-the-otherwise
Myers, Martin. 2010. 'The Fall, Mark E. Smith and "The Stranger": Ambiguity, Objectivity and the Transformative Power of a Band from Elsewhere.' In *Mark E. Smith and The Fall: Art, Music and Politics*, edited by Michael Goddard and Benjamin Halligan. Farnham, UK: Ashgate.
Nasher Sculpture Center. 2013. 'Ken Price: A Retrospective: Exhibition Information.' 9 February 2013. https://www.nashersculpturecenter.org/art/exhibitions/exhibition/id/45?ken-price-a-retrospective
Norton, Tessa, and Bob Stanley. 2021. *Excavate! The Wonderful and Frightening World of The Fall*. London: Faber & Faber.
Parkes, Taylor. 2018. 'The Fall and Mark E. Smith as a Narrative Writer.' *The Quietus*: 24 January 2018. https://thequietus.com/articles/03925-the-fall-and-mark-e-smith-as-a-narrative-lyric-writer

Perry, Grayson. 2014. *Playing to the Gallery*. London: Penguin.
Rhinehart, Luke. 1971. *The Dice Man*. Woodstock, NY: Overlook Press.
Smith, Mark E., and Austin Collings. 2009 (2008). *Renegade: The Lives and Tales of Mark E. Smith*. London: Penguin.
Smith, Mark E., and Graham Duff. 2021. *The Otherwise*. Foreword by Eleni Poulou. London: Strange Attractor Press.
Smith, William S. 2015. 'Overview: Between the High and the Low.' *Art News*: 19 August 2015. https://www.artnews.com/art-in-america/aia-reviews/overview-between-the-high-and-the-low-61976/
Stansfield, Ted. 2020. *The Story of Michael Clark's Game-Changing I Am Curious, Orange Performance*. AnOther: 9 December 2020. https://www.anothermag.com/design-living/13000/michael-clark-s-i-am-curious-orange-performance-the-fall-mark-e-smith
Tate Museum Collective. 2010. 'Mark E. Smith | Sound & Vision | Tate Shots.' 10 March 2010. https://www.youtube.com/watch?v=7KcqpBXl90Y
Trafton, Anne. 2011. 'How the brain assigns objects to categories.' *MIT News*: 27 July 2011. https://news.mit.edu/2011/category-learning-0727
Turner, Luke. 2015. 'Metamodernism: A Brief Introduction.' *Berfrois*: 10 January 2015. https://www.berfrois.com/2015/01/everything-always-wanted-know-metamodernism/
Turner, Luke. 2018. 'Mark E. Smith of The Fall on Art & The Artist.' *The Quietus*: 24 January 2018. https://thequietus.com/articles/04568-mark-e-smith-of-the-fall-on-art-the-artist
Waterfield, Giles, and Nicola Smith. 1994. 'Art for the People.' *History Today*, vol. 44, no. 5, June 1994, p. 55. EBSCOhost, search.ebscohost.com/login.aspx?direct=true&AuthType=sso&db=edb&AN=9406277628&site=eds-live
Wilde, Oscar. 1894. 'A Few Maxims for the Instruction of the Over-Educated.' *The Saturday Review*: 17 November 1894. Available via WikiSource https://en.wikisource.org/wiki/A_Few_Maxims_For_The_Instruction_Of_The_Over-Educated
Wilkinson, David. 2018. '"Northern white crap that talks back": The Fall's Mark E. Smith spoke for weird Manchester.' *The Conversation*: 25 January 2018. https://theconversation.com/northern-white-crap-that-talks-back-the-falls-mark-e-smith-spoke-for-weird-manchester-90710
Wilson, Paul. 2010. 'Language Scraps: Mark E. Smith's Handwriting and the Typography of The Fall.' In *Mark E. Smith and The Fall: Art, Music and Politics*, edited by Michael Goddard and Benjamin Halligan. Farnham, UK: Ashgate.

Chapter Two

Suzanne Smith in Conversation with Eoin Devereux

Suzanne Smith designed artwork for singles, EPs, and LPs by The Fall. She currently lives in Manchester, UK. She has exhibited her work in London, Berlin, and Copenhagen. Suzanne's works include the paintings *Remit 2*, *Joan Praying*, *Andrew 2*, and *Douglas* as well as a series called *Nothing to Fear*. She has just completed illustrations for two books on poetry (*Ordinary Others* [2020] and *Vulgar Variants* [2021]) in collaboration with poet Jonathan Wonham. In this conversation, Suzanne speaks with Eoin Devereux about working with her brother Mark on designing artwork for The Fall.

INTERVIEW

ED: Can you tell me about your own training as an artist? Were you formally trained?

SS: No, I'm not trained at all. It was just when I was in secondary school and the art teacher really liked my work and stuff [. . .] I did go to University about seven years ago and studied visual arts but I found that they take away a lot of your uniqueness. I found it took me a while to get it back again. But you do learn some things, so it wasn't all bad.

ED: Did you study art for GCSE's, O-Levels, A Levels or anything like that?

SS: I got an O-Level in art, because obviously, you take it at secondary school, don't you?

ED: When you started to draw and paint, when you were a teenager what were your influences? Who or what did you look to?

SS: Well, everybody likes Salvador Dali, don't they, but you see my favourite work really is illustration, so it's George Grosz[1] that I like now.

ED: How would you describe your work?

SS: I don't know [. . .] I think it's quite unique [. . .] Because I have a lot of people who are not quite able to copy it [. . .] what they used to describe it is Outsider Art [. . .] where people consider you not skilled enough. I can't remember what the name for it is for. You know there was a fellah in Cornwall wasn't there [Alfred Wallis[2]] [. . .] he used to paint the boats [. . .] and people went mad on it, but it is not classed as skilled artistry, do you know what I mean?

ED: You mentioned Salvador Dali [. . .] are there any other influences on your work? Are there influences, for example, from Pop Art or other album covers? Are there other things brought to bear on your work?

SS: My favourite album cover was Alex Harvey[3] *The Impossible Dream*, I don't know if you have ever seen it, it's like a comic [. . .] it's like a comic book. I'm trying to think of my favourite artist as well. [. . .] It's Ernst Kirchner[4] the German Expressionist, I love him.

ED: When you came to work on design with The Fall, what was the first piece of work that you did?

SS: It was *Fiery Jack*, wasn't it? I think I was aged seventeen when I did that. Mark was just starting out so I think he just asked me because he knew I was quite good at drawing [. . .] and then the second one was *Grotesque* and he asked me specifically what he wanted in them people on that cover. I was eighteen when I did that and I did it in me bedroom with poster paints. I remember taking it around to his flat and he opened it and he just stepped back and went "Wow". I think it's because it was so brightly coloured. I also drew City Hobgoblin—a figure of a goblin that was superimposed onto a building—for the single cover around that early time also.

ED: I am just looking at that cover. [. . .] I was curious about the cover for *Grotesque*. 'Fiery Jack' is one thing, but *Grotesque* obviously has the figures in it, there's a cassette, there's an image of a truck [. . .] were these suggested by Mark, or did he give you ideas?

Figure 2.1. 'Gerry'
By Suzanne Smith © Reproduced by kind permission.

SS: Yes. Do you see the lady with the blonde hair and a black hat on and she's got [. . .] I don't know if it is visible on that [. . .] it's a 'Kiss Me Quick' hat. Do you remember those from Blackpool? You used to go to Blackpool and get them.

ED: He wanted that included?

SS: Yes, and he wanted [. . .] in the Seventies and stuff and early Eighties there used to be a lot of White Rastas [. . .] and then there was the Skinhead. People dress like that nowadays. [. . .] He wanted a train or a motorbike receding into the distance and I couldn't do the motorbike so I did the truck and if you notice it's next to 'After the Gramme.' I don't know if that is a reference to when you are coming down off drugs. [. . .] I don't know if that is relevant.

ED: I am curious about Mark's role. [. . .] He obviously designed and co-designed. [. . .] He clearly had a very strong input on some album covers. He is credited in terms of designing and co-designing album covers later on. [. . .] Mark was clearly clued in to art and to what the cover might look like. Did he have very clear ideas?

SS: He gave me pretty much artistic licence, but I must state that he always gave me about three days to do it. It was always last minute. "Can you just do this? because somebody has let me down". [. . .] It wasn't a big [. . .] People probably think you are in a big discussion for ten days or two months about something, it was nothing like that—if you know what Mark was like.

ED: So even in the heat of creation then, when you were working on an EP cover or an album cover in that short period of time [. . .] did you ever listen to the record [. . .] was there a relationship between what the cover looked like and what the album or the EP sounded like or was it purely in terms of what let's say Mark suggested or if he said can you paint a cover? Did you listen to the record before you painted?

SS: I never listened to the records. He did give me the master copy for *Wise Ol' Man* and I don't think it was the same as the single that they brought out but it was mainly conversations with him, more so as to the design outlay of it. I've got interesting things to say about the cover of 'Hey Luciani'. [. . .] I did the two covers. I always do an alternative for every one that I have ever done and he decided to put both of them on that. This was before Google and I had to go to the library to find out what that pope[5] looked like.

Figure 2.2. 'Irene'
By Suzanne Smith © Reproduced by kind permission.

ED: That was the pope who was allegedly bumped off? There were financial scandals in the Vatican [. . .] so tell me about painting that cover then.

SS: I think I painted that in Mark's house, because sometimes when he would go on tour I'd look after the house for him, and I painted it *on* the table. I think I did that one and I did 'Ghost in My House' there while he was away.

ED: What medium did you use? You have obviously used a range of mediums when you have painted.

SS: All those there ('Luciani', 'Ghost') all those are poster paints and now you can't get those nice quality ones of them so later on, I would use acrylic paint but a lot of the early ones are just poster paints.

ED: Did Mark ever say: 'I don't like that cover, or I want it different or I want to change it or revised?'

SS: He did on *Re-Mit*. I don't think he liked *Re-Mit* because it was black and white.

ED: OK. I like that cover actually, I like it very much.

SS: He got the graphic designer to do different tonals. So, you know it's blue, but if you see the original, it's black and white. And then, I came across the Forum[6] once and everyone was discussing how I was ripping off Picasso for his 'Blue Period' and that had nothing to do with me! [Laughs]

ED: For *Re-Mit* there's a reference to Anthony Frost and Becky Stuart. . . .

SS: Becky Stuart was the graphic designer. She would have changed the colour. I'm not comfortable in doing lettering. I did on *Grotesque* and stuff, but you know it's not me strong point. And Anthony Frost did the eyes around *Re-Mit* . . . can you see that? and I think that was used as a backdrop onstage as well.

ED: I saw The Fall perform with that . . . and in the inner sleeve there's handwriting which talks about "Recycle Photo" and he's sketching out, you know, where various members of the group should be. Am I correct in assuming that's Mark's sketching?

SS: I just remembered about that. He gave me . . . what he did with that was . . . he always had scraps of paper with scribblings on and he'd actually give me like an envelope, and he went, you know, "Use things like this" and he wanted me to use this decorative frame around it that he had given me and it wasn't like them eyes, but in the end he used them because he liked them so much of Anthony Frost. He did want like a Roman theme so that's why that is like that.

ED: [Laughs] All he is short is a bunch of grapes on the cover, you know, the way he is sitting there. It struck me that it was quite Romanesque. I really like the blue. So, you did it in black and white first?

SS: Yeah, and that's the members of the band and I said I'll have to come and take photographs. He wouldn't let me draw him live or anything. [Laughs] I had to do it from memory!

ED: And did you photograph the rest of the group?

SS: It was a backstage gig. And they weren't very clear because me camera was rubbish. So, it's a matter of just . . . because it's cartoon and it's not realistic you can sort of get away with it a lot of the time. *Re-Mit* won best album cover of the week in the NME. It was for the joke aspect of it really . . . everybody kneeling at Mark's feet. . .[laughs].

ED: Go back to 'Fiery Jack' then . . . you were obviously very young when you drew that . . . where did that figure (of Fiery Jack) on the cover come from?

SS: It's funny that . . . I was telling me daughter . . . we're from Manchester . . . I don't know if you know Manchester?

ED: I know it well.

SS: So, you know Strangeways Prison? and there was like a lot of pubs around there and obviously when people were released from prison the first place they'd go were them pubs. But there was also a men's hostel on the corner (at Francis Street, a Salvation Army hostel) where in them days, they weren't homeless, there was . . . it was just tramp men and they always looked like that, you know, like *Aqualung*[7] out of Jethro Tull? You never see that anymore. You never saw any women. It was always men and it was, I don't know why I actually picked him as 'Fiery Jack' but obviously I done his reflection as the Devil 'adn't I, which if you notice I also took that theme back on 'Hey Luciani'?

ED: Yes, absolutely, it comes up again. Because the goat on the 'flip-side' we'll call it . . . because the goat is symbolic of the Devil.

SS: Because we all liked our horror, you see. We all used to watch *Appointment with Fear*[8]. We've all been brought up with that in our family. I remember, as it was a school night but our dad let us stay up late to watch it and we waited for him to come home from the pub with nuts for us to watch the feature.

[Laughs]

ED: Would you say that across time from 'Fiery Jack' to the last pieces of design work you did for The Fall and Mark that there are commonalities? Are there themes that recur over that stretch of time?

SS: I don't know . . . you see for *Wise Ol' Man*, I did two alternative pictures again and he wasn't happy with that and it was his idea to cut them in half and put them together.

ED: I had wondered about where that idea had come from.

SS: He was getting a bit angry; he was getting a bit annoyed about that. Because I don't think . . . it wasn't what he wanted. And then, a lot of people think, that's Mark and it isn't. So, you know, sometimes when you draw people, sometimes you draw them slightly like you, don't you?

ED: It is interesting that you say that because I would have just taken it that it was Mark and at the time, I thought it might be references to his illness. . . . I knew he wasn't well and so on and I thought it was just referring to that, but it's not him at all?

SS: No, it isn't, and I didn't know he was ill at that time.

ED: OK. Isn't it interesting how we look at things in retrospect, after you know something then, it changes the way you look at something? Was that a sketch in pencil or charcoal or how was it drawn originally?

SS: I tell you what. One of them was . . . (I like to draw in Biro) watercolour, and the other was Pro Marker pen, felt-tip.

ED: OK, so that's obviously what I am calling the black-and-white side of it, that's marker and the other is watercolour.

Figure 2.3. 'Melanie'
By Suzanne Smith © Reproduced by kind permission.

SS: Yeah. I actually sold both of those pictures as well to a fan.

ED: So, what had you in mind then when you were coming up with the idea for *Wise Ol' Man*? What was to the forefront of your mind when you were picturing what the cover might look like?

SS: You know, it's funny, because I was thinking how can I possibly say anything to you because I've got nothing to talk about but when you are asking me these questions, it's actually coming to me. It just reminds me . . . do you know about the Holts' pubs in Manchester? And Mark obviously lived in Prestwich and there's the Woodthorpe[9] and the Foresters[10] and in those pubs there's always a vault and there's always old withered-like type men. They are there at eleven o'clock in the morning and they are always on the Holts' Bitter. It was just that . . . the Wise Old Man . . . they always have nuggets of information I suppose.

ED: Was there ever any resistance from record labels about design or the way you designed covers?

Figure 2.4. 'Remit'
By Suzanne Smith © Reproduced by kind permission.

SS: No, I don't think so. No. I think the only problem was with that *Re-Mit* cover, because the original is quite big. I done it on cardboard, and I don't think it had squared properly and I think that's why in the end they had to put the border around it as well even though he wanted to incorporate Anthony Frost's eye thing, I think it was more oblong and they slightly stretched it. That's the only problem I can think of really.

ED: Is there anything else you'd like to add about working with Mark in terms of the design of album or EP covers?

SS: Well, he was always very supportive of me. For a lot of my birthdays, he'd buy me like artists stuff and everything. But I must confess, it was always like usually "Can you meet me in the pub, five days before, do you think you could just get this done because it just needs to be . . ." and then there was a lot of toing and froing between him and his wife because he didn't like using computers and you had to scan it over and send it to him . . . you know what I mean . . . I remember *Wise Ol' Man* it was just that conversation in the pub and then he'd go on to other subjects and then you'd sort of just go home and just get started on them, you know what I mean, and I always did, I never just did one, I always did a few alternatives, so it was never "Oh, this is it", you know what I mean, so he'd always have a choice.

ED: I have this picture of Mark being really well read, in terms of reading lots of books and being familiar with film. He was clearly clued in to so many things. Would art and artists have been part of his interests? He seems quite well versed in art and design.

SS: I know that he raved about Tintoretti[11] if that helps and we are all into film.

ED: 'Hit the North' is a really interesting cover. How was that designed?

SS: Mark said can you do a map of the world? We discussed doing a map of England. He said on Hull, I want you to put a 'No Entry' sign! There's a dart and Manchester's got the sunshine, hasn't it?

ED: The first time I saw the 'Hit the North' cover it reminded me of *Dad's Army*.[12] For some reason, the Union Jack down in London reminded me of *Dad's Army*. There's a lot going on. You have what look like bagpipes. You have a frog. You have, obviously, Loch Ness. You have a shamrock out in the

Figure 2.5. *Remit 2*
By Suzanne Smith © Reproduced by kind permission.

Irish Sea. There's a lot going on in that painting. It's really, interesting. He specified where you should put where Hull is, where there is a 'No Go' sign, the red marker . . . did he give you any other instruction in terms of what it might look like?

ED: I wanted to ask you also about 'A Ghost in My House' because that reminds me of that painting *The Scream*.[13]

SS: I don't think I was aware of that then. I wasn't so much into artists until I went to Uni in me early fifties. That's what it is . . . when I did *Grotesque* I was in the pub, and somebody came up to me and went 'Did you do that cover for *Grotesque*?' I went yeah and he said: 'I thought to myself, it was either a child that done it or a genius'. I took it as a compliment.

Figure 2.6. *Remit*
By Suzanne Smith © Reproduced by kind permission.

Figure 2.7. 'Wise Ol' Man 1'
by Suzanne Smith © Reproduced by kind permission.

Figure 2.8. 'Wise Ol' Man 2'
by Suzanne Smith © Reproduced by kind permission.

NOTES

1. George Grosz (1893–1959), member of the Berlin Dadaist movement.
2. Alfred Wallis (1855–1942), a Cornish fisherman and self-taught artist. His paintings are sometimes referred to as being examples of "Naive Art".
3. Glasgow born Alex Harvey (1935–1982), leader of The Sensational Alex Harvey Band.
4. Ernst Kirchner (1880–1938), member of the Die Bruke (the Bridge) art movement.
5. Pope John Paul I (1912–1978) who died just thirty-three days after assuming the role of Pontiff.
6. Presumably in reference to The Fall Fan Forum.
7. Released in 1973 on Island Records, *Aqualung*'s cover art features a derelict homeless man from a watercolour by Burton Silverman, which in turn was based on a photograph taken by Jenny Anderson from a series of pictures of homeless men on the Thames Embankment in London, UK.
8. *Appointment with Fear* was shown on Yorkshire television. The Smith family watched it on Granada (local region) on Monday nights at 11.00 pm.
9. The Woodthorpe Hotel and Pub, Bury New Road, Prestwich, Manchester.
10. The Foresters Arms, Prestwich High Street, Prestwich, Manchester.
11. Renaissance artist from the Venetian School who lived and worked in the sixteenth century. By coincidence, he painted a series about Saint Mark.
12. BBC Television Series which ran from 1961 to 1977.
13. Edvard Munch's painting *The Scream* (1893).

Chapter Three

'A letter so simple, yet disgusting in a stroke'

Writing-out the (Typo)Graphic Strangeness of The Fall

Paul Wilson

STRANGE WORDS

This essay considers the typographical aspects of The Fall's visual communication and those words that work to shape and create the group's graphic appearance. It looks to explore an application of design and designed words onto the collateral and associated ephemera of music industry communications as something inherently *strange*. Such an idea of strangeness can be located within Mark E. Smith's intended or deliberate desire for a music and visual identity which in some way expressed an idea of the fantastic or weird, and also in an impulse which resisted any formal preconceptions, perceptions, or expectations that an audience or organisation or community might have of these designed experiences.

From their appearance and methods of visual presentation to the affects they sought to conjure, it can be observed that ways The Fall *used* typography—considered as some kind of meaningful arrangement of visible language, the manipulation of letters, words and sentences, or phrases—within a graphic design context reflect Smith's shifting and slippery subjectivities, and his continual testing of any fixed preconceptions within the conservative contexts of music, musicianship, and the music industry's own habitual routines.

While there has been recognition and some discussion of Smith's forays into graphic and typographic design and, in particular, in his selection of cover artists, this essay aims to locate the ways in which his use of strategies for visualising language perform a role which questions and connects to some of design's broader social and cultural functions and purposes: a coalition of approaches in which things and experiences are commodified and the attribution of a culturally pre-determined meaning. Such a role (designer as aesthetician, taste-maker, hidden persuader, etc.) perhaps mirrors Smith's vision of himself as a writer within a tradition of speculative, odd or unsettling, or grotesque fictions where the material conditions and experiences of everyday life would be forcibly unfixed from their now untrustworthy moorings, and where the horror or shock of such reality-warping events causes deeply felt and long-lasting impact. His interest in such authors as M. R. James and Philip K. Dick (and Smith's own work in the publication of *The Otherwise* with Graham Duff) clearly demonstrates a fascination with the potential for everyday oddness which was such a strong theme in The Fall's lyrics and music and is, as I hope to show, also reflected in the techniques which Smith applied to their typographic, visual, and material experience.

This sense of being strange, of strangeness, or of something becoming or being made strange runs through both Smith's life and the time during which The Fall were in existence and was a theme in popular cultural history he showed clear knowledge of. Lyrics and interviews would make frequent references to horror literature, to the eerie and otherworldliness of everyday life, and, at times, to Smith's own experiences of mediumship such as the services of tarot readership he once provided. There would also be a mention of the occasional psychic or clairvoyant awareness and of an ability to divine an unsettling sense impression such as future fairground horrors in Disneyland, echoes of atrocities in Germany, or a glimpse of near-future conflict in the former Yugoslavia.

Graphic and typographic design—as aesthetic resource and cultural practice—are often unappreciated in terms of the extent to which they impact upon how we experience everyday life and the role they play in the production of meaning through a manipulation and mediation of meaningful words and images on the surfaces of the world.

How, then, have the approaches to graphic design and, in particular, Smith's deliberate manipulation or deformation of visible words and uses of typographic design methods sought to reflect or suggest a particular idea or experience of strangeness, and an attendant defamiliarization, when encountered on The Fall's music packaging? Mark E. Smith's use of design mirrors his use of sound and language, and the techniques he makes use of in the creation of typographic and graphic design, I contend, extend such an aesthetic towards the visual.

MAKING STRANGE AND THE ABNORMAL NORMAL

'Designers, as creators and shapers of our social reality, are deeply involved in the operations and processes of habitualisation in contemporary life. It follows that designers must also therefore take some responsibility for the consequences of these effects . . .' (Buwert 2016, p.26).

Highlighting design's role in the formation and absorption of routines within everyday experience, Buwert draws attention to how it functions as co-creator (of the habitualised) and as a key method through it also becomes normalized. And while there is some suggestion of benefit, their insinuation of undesirable consequences seems to reflect Mark E. Smith's own, oft-stated antipathy to any idea or experience of such habitualisation, such as his claim that 'routine is the enemy of music', and which he saw as a source of oppression and a negative tension to be resisted at every turn. For Smith, however, habit and routine were not the same as and should not be compared with *repetition*, which when employed deliberately and creatively would be positioned as central to The Fall's approach. He would defend a desire for repetition as a means to avoid anything that suggested a sheen of slick, polished professionalism in The Fall's musicianship—which he regarded as the byproduct of too much practice, or from too much time spent seeking an idealised perfection in playing. He was equally resistant to the visual equivalent: an overly produced, artificial, glossy sheen of design 'style' which strives for aesthetic refinement and desires perfection. Such a tendency is particularly evident in graphic design's willingness to be guided by digital technology's capacities for smoothing, correcting, polishing, and the tidy over-refinement which helps determine the monophonic, cool, and visually repetitive tropes which encase the majority of our contemporary experiences of digitally derived design.

> Habitualisation is a functional necessity for us, managed by our conditioned responses to past experience and replayed when necessary to avoid an anxiety of constant response to the unknown or the just-known. (Shklovksy 1917)

Viktor Shklovksy's definition of habitualisation further suggests the idea of a deliberate or strategic ideal of familiarity which is beyond our immediate perception or recognition. The benefits of familiarity as a positive outcome from adopting certain habits can also be located in typography's Modernist history, and they were made very clear by Beatrice Warde's lecture 'The Crystal Goblet' to the British Typographer's Guild in 1930. The form of printed texts, Warde argued, should be as clear and as unobtrusive as possible and should pass as unnoticed as the glass which holds a drinker's wine. To aim for any effect which interferes, impedes, or spoils the enjoyment of a text (or a drink) is to fall prey to the temptations of the ego-driven artist or designer. Visible language, therefore, should always respect that which it serves, and the preservation of meaning and ensuring clarity of communication of any text is a typographic designer's primary purpose. To achieve this aim, it was necessary to formalise, habitualise, and systematise everything—to transform the craft of printing into a typographic science through an adoption of strict rules which would go on to govern the practice of typography and graphic design for the next fifty years.

As Shklovsky acknowledges, having or keeping habits is often a *functional necessity*, meaning that we and others and the systems within which we work and live are sustained and benefit from our dependency upon them and the processes which they underpin. That we might have to renegotiate the fundamental practices of human life each time we experienced them does suggest such habitual behaviours are useful, and our contemporary lived experience is often generally founded upon principles which depend upon rational, objective, and rules-based systems or processes and this is certainly true in how, where, and why we encounter design in its many forms.

However, Buwert (2016, p.26) continues that

> (certain) things . . . should be known not as normal but as wonderful, or terrible. If we degrade things which are truly extraordinary by accepting them as merely ordinary, we are either denying ourselves the pleasure of appreciating the abnormally good, or wilfully subjecting ourselves to the horrors of the abnormally bad.

Given Mark E. Smith's comments on what he termed the 'middle mass', such a threat of ordinariness (as a barrier to certain experience) and it being a consequence of uncritical habitualisation is something to be resisted and confronted where necessary as it threatens to limit human experience in certain ways, preventing us from grasping certain things which exist outside or beyond the ordinary. For author Colin Wilson, so-called ordinary consciousness was something to be shocked awake and disrupted so that an evolutionary breakthrough might take place. Like Smith, Wilson would often make use of familiar forms in order to subvert—styles of fiction and storytelling (science fiction tropes or thriller narratives, for example) as a covert means for the introduction of philosophical ideas or themes to the often unsuspecting reader.

While Smith continually resisted those limitations that are acknowledged as being present in a habitualised ordinary, he was not strictly in opposition to it ('he's neither left nor right . . . he's basically critical of everything'—Alan Wise, BBC documentary) and so would also seek to identify and glorify the abnormally normal, certainly in a recognition of the value in aspects of normality in terms of how one lived, where one lived, and the cultures of such places.

A TACTIC OF DEFAMILIARISATION

The deliberate development of methods for making things *strange*, and with the purpose of creating some kind of unsettling or shocking experience which results in an audience seeing something as if new, has a notable history. Viktor Shklovksy (1917, p.17) defined these intentional acts of estrangement as *ostranenie* and regarded this as the fundamental purpose of art: 'to make one feel things . . . to make objects unfamiliar, to make forms difficult'. He argued that such an experience should be prolonged to encourage audience recognition of the creative act as a process and forcing *an acknowledgment of the form of a thing* so that such a perceptual act would, in fact, become a conscious realisation of creativity itself. With such an awareness, the audience therefore is able to arrive at an understanding of the artistic object that has been revitalised and would be, in some way, more *authentic* rather than one which is automated by any over-familiarity.

For Buwert (2016, pp.27–28), the transformative potential of such a tactic also raises the troubling opportunity to disturb human experience itself:

> Defamiliarisation . . . is the deeply unsettling moment of psychological disorientation experienced when something which has always appeared familiar suddenly becomes unfamiliar: the moment when something is comprehended in a new way . . . because the item in question had been considered so ordinary and acceptable, and is now . . . found to be truly extraordinary.

Echoing Smith's own descriptions of his intentions for linguistic and visual defamiliarisation (and pointing out the consistent value in taking such an approach) Shklovsky (2017 [1917]) would make much of Aristotle's claim that *all poetry should possess qualities of strangeness and wonder*. Further inspired by these ideas, playwright Berthold Brecht believed that a productive defamiliarisation of the theatre experiences could be achieved by way of creative strategies which force an audience's active and critical participation in the production. His development of strategically employed methods for intentional unfamiliarity would be applied via very concrete activities which sought to subvert audience expectations of theatrical form—methods for interrupting and the disruption of a production's linear narrative, by looking to create conditions of tension between audience and performer with *deliberately* bad acting and unsympathetic characterisation, and through moments which revealed the inner workings of a performance itself.

MAKING STRANGE, MAKING FAMILIAR

Practices of design play a fundamental role in defining aspects of both ourselves and those things that surround us, and are a key influence in determining our experiences and interactions within and through how we carry out much of our analogue and digital lives. Design's significance, via the value we continue to assign to such experience, is based largely upon a carefully negotiated mediation of innovation and familiarity and, in some cases, we can see how design thrives on the reproduction of familiar form. In the contexts of *graphic* or *fashion* design, for example, we recognise a need to supply something which is already recognised as having value by an audience primed to either consume a message or wear a garment which reflects an existing familiarity. As Buwert acknowledges, design's role in such habitualisation and how it works to deliver such pre-determined experiences in response to pre-determined expectations is a functional requirement for the management of how we work and live. As Shklovsky (1917) reassures, such habitualisation, is a necessity so that we can go about our lives, and we mostly manage to carry on due to our pre-conditioned responses formed by our past experience. Without this bulwark of familiarity, we'd most likely find it necessary to approach everything as if it were new and whatever we didn't know or were just-knowing would prove a constant source of anxiety. So, those routine experiences which form and support our habitualised expectations offer us a reassurance and provide some sense of understanding that helps prevent any overwhelm by sensory experiences if everything were constantly uncommon and unexpected.

Conditions for habitualisation by design, therefore, are nurtured through a consistency of form, a reassurance that's reinforced by its tendency towards risk-aversion together with a commitment to the routine, and for following a proven and successful formula. Such behaviours, however, can embed a reactionary disposition and a conservatism which results in the predominance of ordinariness. Dominant modes of graphic design practice, for instance, seem rightly concerned with a reproduction of existing form and for a usefulness that's determined by an ability to *visualise*, *connect*, and *create links* between people and the materials that wrap the surfaces of the world. Its value to such readers or users could not be located in the production of objects or experiences which worked to push people away or by making them feel uncomfortable if they can't or don't understand a thing, or how they might use it or what it might mean. Such pursuit of familiarity in and of things, and the skills necessary for the generation of persuasive facsimiles of these things, are often highly valued within the professional practices of design since they carry very useful resources of cultural capital.

The rise and *success* of the *International Typographic Style* in the second half of the twentieth century was largely a byproduct of theoretical and conceptual groundwork established in the 1930s and 1940s: a distillation and expansion of rules that were initially popularised by typographic scholar Beatrice Warde's vision for the discipline which would themselves be systematised by designer Jan Tschichold, and which would also be reflected in the overtly scientific tendencies of an emergent Swiss Modernism. Such activities would work to establish the grammar for a globalised visual and typographic language (of what we now know as branding and advertising) whose primary function was to be *universal, ahistorical,* and deliberately *deterritorialised.* The aesthetic hallmarks of the International Typographic Style (often known as the *Swiss Style*) were fashioned to be *rigorous, rational,* and *objective,* and would lack any notable visual characteristics or any defining sense of *personality.* The resultant publications, posters, typefaces, etc. sought out a position of *neutrality* as they went to participate in the complex systems and processes of communication that were being shaped and concretised during the post-war period. Such a heroic ideal and desire to be *beyond stylistic frippery* (a position often argued with dogmatic zeal) would, ironically, become the main means to define it *as* a style—one highly dependent upon a limited and restrictive system of rules and where only that most hegemonic of sanserif typefaces, Helvetica, was allowed. As design critic Jeffrey Keedy (2013, 191) observed, the International Typographic Style was to be adopted as *the default visual language* for the emerging corporate capitalist culture of the 1950s and 1960s and, to a certain extent, it remains—continuing to circulate, too, as a vision for design and typography which drives most brands and their globalised activities of marketing, advertising, and communication.

Keedy goes on to describe an upgraded, re-tooled *Global Style* (a Swiss Style *redux*) whose impact seems to further demonstrate a desire for design to reassure or guarantee some sense of familiarity within the contemporary experiences of graphic and typographic design, now supplying an inescapable *anonymity* and *homogeneity*. It's likely that any approach or contemporary strategy for design which seriously considered an intentional unfamiliarity would be the least desirable and most unnecessary strategic direction to take in the circumstances which have given rise to the International Typographic Style and its digitally derived simulacra as a Global Style—each responds to a popular need for reassurance and for the comfort that comes when encountering the *already-known* (a familiar brand in an unfamiliar city, for example). One notable visual characteristic of the now-dominant Global Style highlighted by Keedy, is a drive for simplification in the face of complexity, and where the challenges of *aesthetics, intentions,* and *decision-making* are replaced by a relatively short list of *default* design options which guarantee the designer an array of very familiar typefaces and styles, commonplace compositional arrangements, along with an assortment of routine non-linguistic graphical elements and comfortable choices in colour. For Keedy, this is most likely a consequence of the de-skilling that's taken place in the graphic design industry since the introduction of digital tools which have given rise to the global visual language he's scrutinising. The upswing in consumer demand for popular communications technology experienced over the last ten to fifteen years further democratises an access to the means of production of graphic and typographic design which, via an in-app functionality that's similar in how such stylistic limitations are baked-in to the user experience, encourages a participation in the creation and dissemination of Global Style, lessening the need for a professional designer in many contexts.

THE *UNSTRANGE* STRANGE, REFORMATION AS *DEFORMATION*

Discussing Shklovsky, Victor Erlich (1965, p.179) argued that, 'as opposed to a pure art for art's sake doctrine, [Shklovsky] came to define poetry not in terms of what it is but in terms of what it is for'; and that, instead, he showed a 'rather unexpected preoccupation with the uses of poetry and therapeutic value of creative deformation on our routine-dulled perception of the world'. Here Erlich describes an ideal (seemingly one pursued by Shklovsky) which repurposes creativity with the express intention of disrupting the habitual, and which desires for something so unfamiliar as to be unrecognisable. A potential for such reinvention and for the instrumentalisation of any creative activity (such as poetry, or rock music, or even graphic design) allows, therefore, for an abandonment of passivity, neutrality, or a pursuit of familiarity. Instead, such *creative deformation* would look not for difference for its own sake, but one driven by a purpose or rationale that's *purposeful*, *helpful*, and, perhaps, *therapeutic*.

In particular, Mark E. Smith's ideals for creative transformation often seemed to proceed from an innate predisposition towards distortion as an ameliorative, both in terms of an aesthetic experience (for others) and as a practice (for himself and the group). Whether as music or via graphic and typographic design, Smith's unforced aim to grasp or manifest some kind of notional primitive would often be utterly reliant on an approach that venerated being *deliberately unlearned*. Such strategies were purposefully crude or offensive (towards ideas of a learned and practiced professionalism) and, in particular, embraced those non-professional (or un-professional) modes and methods for making, playing, creating, or communicating. In the spirit of an image of the maverick (or, more likely in his case, an idea of the *renegade*), Smith's attitude reflects and celebrates the non-expert creativity found in the low-brow or everyday, where any pursuit of perfection misses many opportunities for real affect and there is much to be loved in moments of genuine error. Demonstrations of his being consciously in opposition to performed virtuosity can found across Smith's efforts to design The Fall, and are, of course, most visible in his ideas of and for their music packaging (alongside their other graphic ephemera such as promotional posters, press releases, etc.). As he described to journalist Sandy Robinson in 1980, there was little difference in his approach, whether for The Fall's public image or in their published product: "I like the cover to reflect what's inside . . . my attitude to the sleeve is the same as my attitude to music." Robinson would further situate The Fall's aesthetic as being located in the *fantastical* everyday, highlighting Smith's eye for error-strewn instances of found (or ignored) commonplace typographic design:

> "The Fall are true alchemists in their recognition that shit masks gold, the apparently worthless can be the source of the thrill of it all. Mark loves 'Those cheap printed cash 'n' carry signs with inverted commas where you don't need them. Things like that. . . .' (U)nlike all those grey groups [Smith] still sees the potential for ecstasy, magic. The Fall's album graphics seem to reflect all this with a meticulous shoddiness that refuses to offer a focus unlike most covers with their repetition of empty impact." (Robinson, 'Hex Education', SOUNDS, 8 May 1980)

Robinson's observation that The Fall's cover graphics don't volunteer or submit to a preconceived demand to require a *focus* (a sense of the spectacular, something to grab the attention) suggests that Smith's strategies for creative deformation were intended to make audiences work to fully understand or, as is more likely, come to appreciate a message or idea that he would attempt to communicate. The cover of the 2001 single 'Rude All the Time' lacks any visual element as its focus (other than the group's name) and is remarkable for the absence or lack of what might be formally acknowledged or recognised *as* graphic design. The sleeve offers *no big idea*, no further information on what we're looking at with Smith, makes no use of any common visual or graphic devices to meet a viewer's expectations of what the function and purpose of a record cover might actually be: *there is no attempt to correspond or persuade, to intrigue, or even to surprise*. The words THE FALL seem crudely attached to whatever surface this is, as if they have been copied and cut from another source as the grey background behind the letters works to aggravate the eye against the plain white background colour of the rest of the sleeve—no doubt, a deliberate effect.

From the same year, and in contrast, the cover of *Are You Are Missing Winner* has clearly been through *a process of design*, although one marked by the intention to be ambiguous, deliberately unpleasant, not wholly coherent. Seemingly, Smith had little or no mind for it to appear *pleasant* or that it should give ground to any established ideas of aesthetic beauty or ideals of whatever *good* design might mean. The cover image is rendered largely illegible by being inverted so that whatever content it contains is rendered out of the viewer's reach as only abstract shapes result from its colour values being reversed, resulting in its visual negative. Further, the image is playfully cropped and tightly focused upon two faces and the typographic content (for both the album title and group's name) is warped and manipulated, either stretched vertically or defined by some faraway vanishing point. Brought together, these three elements result in a composition or arrangement which has no clear logic or purpose (and results in Smith's right eye being most dominant) and laughs-off any notion of a designer being interested in satisfying audience tastes or needs for a meaning or message communicated by the cover's design.

EVERYDAY WEIRDNESS: NEITHER PLEASURABLE NOR UNPLEASANT

In his definition and discussion of weirdness in the everyday and how it's present in the music and design of The Fall, writer and theorist Mark Fisher draws attention to the idea that Mark E. Smith's intentions and approaches for developing a visual language were very deliberate in how they sought to force or affect an estrangement in the minds of his audience. Certainly, when seen alongside other music packaging (either from the history of The Fall or in contemporary design), Smith's belligerent vision stands out for its dissonance and in being notably *unlovely*. As Fisher (2016, p.33) speculates, Smith's intention was for 'a popular Modernist weird', characterised by 'its unfamiliarity, its combination of elements previously held to be incommensurable, its compression, its challenges to standard models of legibility . . . the conflict between the claustrophobic mundaneness of England and the grotesque-weird'.

The identification of these principles brings many features of Smith's strategies for producing typographic design into focus: taking a deliberately *strange* approach which challenges expectations, projecting the sensation that combinations or collections of elements included within the design shouldn't belong together, and that their being together isn't easily understood in terms of whether form *or* content. In his juxtaposition of visual material whose presentation communicates an impression or experience of *both the ordinary and the extraordinary*, Smith demonstrates an understanding of both collage and concision (both fundamental design skills): the potential for meaningful or persuasive *collision* and of a communicative *compression* which mirrors the Modernist tenet of *less is more*.

Fisher details how we are clearly able to identify these principles as applied on the cover for the 1980 single 'How I Wrote "Elastic Man"' in its portrayal of an urban scene invaded by '"emigres from old green glades"; a leering, malevolent kobold [which] looms over a dilapidated tenement. But rather than being smoothly integrated into the photographed scene, the crudely rendered hobgoblin has been etched onto the background. This is a war of worlds, an ontological struggle, a struggle over the means of representation' (Fisher 2016, p.33). Looking further into the image, the hard edge of an upended collaged patch of brickwork is forced firmly against the figure and runs to the physical boundary of the sleeve. This pressure seemingly causes the hobgoblin's body to warp, forcing it into a hump-backed posture which exaggerates a sense of discomfort and oddness being conjured from the collection of elements being presented. The cold blue tone used as the cover's sole colour acts to merge or weave these elements together, casting a pale, cool pallor over the scene and suggesting the end (or beginning) of a day—or that we might be viewing the scene through some kind of eerie haze or smog. For the single's back cover, the typographic execution of the hand-written track titles echoes the uncertain linework employed to define the hobgoblin figure pictured on the front. These words are placed alongside a set of cryptic, pseudo-symbolic illustrations which appear to represent scenes of distress or discomfort where figures suffer in ways that can barely be perceived.

The covers of *Grotesque (After the Gramme)* and *Room to Live* (from 1980 and 1982, respectively) each explores further Smith's interest in how images of the ordinary can be imbued with qualities of the eerie and the *everyday strange*, where design decisions for placement and alignment and how such collections work together suggest meanings and connections via their visual relations and proximity. The back cover of *Grotesque* echoes Smith's earlier interests in the ambiguous potential of everyday architectural photography by placing a typically opaque or uncertain image at the centre of a series of photographs which seemingly show Fall members *at leisure*, indoors (somewhere) with drinks in their hands. The arrangement of these images, and their placement next to each another, is managed by Smith with a series of hard edits and crops which work to force the group's bodies together, although it is notable that he is shown as physically separate from this scene while also seemingly part of it. In contrast to such images of domesticity, another photograph, again deliberately apart from the others and this time featuring group member Marc Riley, is more affected with the side of his face emerging from the monochrome, ghostly darkness of a venue's stage. Among this collage another face, seemingly asleep and cropped very tightly so little else is visible, emerges from Smith's midriff and the group's name (again, *hand-drawn* and placed over another image) appearing to the right of his tightly closed eyes.

The front cover image of *Grotesque*, illustrated by Smith's sister Suzanne, again shows a collection of figures although this time they are pictured outdoors and, perhaps, part of a crowd. Echoing the back cover's photograph of Marc Riley, these characters emerge from a murky, darkened landscape which seems to consist of either heads, hats, or gravestones with their faces contorted into sneers or smiles (in contrast with the group members' flat, non-expressive poses in their photographs). A startled sprite appears from the hands of one figure whose hair moves as if channeling Medusa. Dressed gaudily, the bodies of each of the members of this troupe are misshapen, their heads and faces swollen, and shoulders and backs bulging. The sky's planetary body is, in fact, a microscopic patch of someone's pock-marked face ('a spotty exterior hides a spotty interior') and this shift in perspective draws attention to another scene featuring another familiar figure (seemingly Smith, holding a microphone) who sneers or grimaces with eyes closed, unaware or perhaps shielding his gaze from what's taking place in his own field of vision.

Room to Live continues Smith's use of found or non-expert photography in an extraordinarily ordinary portrayal of group life in The Fall although, in this case, we join them outdoors. The exterior brickwork glimpsed in their background is reused as a border which marks the sleeve's physical and visual boundaries, where the monospaced regular pattern of brick and mortar echoes the fixed-width typewritten typographic design that takes up much of the space on both back and front covers. Here, the repetitive spacing of an individual letterform is dictated by the need for the typewriter's carriage to move the same distance whichever key has been pressed and so results in the removal of an unevenness often seen in other machine-made lettering (whether analogue or digital) where such spaces are most often individually considered by a designer to make type more easily readable.

A MASS OF FRAGMENTS

Mark E. Smith's cover for the 1982 album *Hex Enduction Hour* is notorious for establishing the typographic approach that's most commonly associated with a *design genre* unique to The Fall: a deliberately confused collection of fragmentary words, garbled viewpoints (seemingly marked by communication from sources unknown), and the abandonment of the aesthetic norms for form and content that might most commonly be expected, and considered essential, for music packaging. Here Smith makes deliberate choices of low-fi, low-technology, and non-appropriate methods for a *shocking* design which pointedly foregrounds its own ugliness and crudity, and asks the reader to steady themselves in the face of such confusion. As discussed earlier, Mark Fisher (2016, p.34) notes Smith's deployment of Modernist techniques of collage and compression in terms of lyric writing and approaches to typography and graphic design which are joined here by an improvisational tactic which marshals immediacy or urgency in order to dictate the final outcome:

> My idea was just to get people's heads going, because they don't fucking read. But also with computer graphics coming in, it became quite impossible to do that. If you're on a major label you can't do this [he arranges the contents of our table—notebooks, scraps of paper, fag packets, beer mats—into a hasty collage], you can't do that and say: that's the back cover. The computer graphics and the art department can't handle it, because it doesn't fit on the bloody computer does it? (*The Wire*, September 2006, p.29)

This description of a design process with no clear curatorial or compositional strategy other than what's to hand, is one that is dependent on the effects of an abrupt collision of objects and surfaces in response to the dominance of digital technologies for production which were firmly entrenched in the business of graphic design by the end of the 1990s. Perhaps unsurprisingly, such changes in design practice shifted the discipline further towards a sense of perfection, introducing the desire for a *visual smoothness* and a sheen of *enhanced artificiality* which clearly ran counter to Smith's inclination towards the grainy and gritty, and a desire to capture the surface noise of everyday life. As can be seen across his *career* in designing the Fall's music packaging, Smith sought to create designs which were at best uninterested in any preconceived notion of how the objects containing recorded music should be presented.

Both *The 27 Points* (1995) and *Interim* (2004) appear to have been designed as a prime exemplars (and reminders, given their dates) of a typographic design genre that's both confounding and absorbing. From the improvised collagist approach (described in Smith's *Wire* interview above) to the proof that the computers of the record company art departments could, in fact, be *forced* to *handle it*, these covers operationalise his belief that any creative act should also be considered an improvisational one, and that any inclination towards over-thinking or an attempt at theorisation should be deliberately avoided and, if necessary, eradicated. For *The 27 Points*, collection, assemblage, and collision are employed as techniques to document a momentary gathering of ephemeral items, and this recording of their relationships is to be completed by whatever meaning or attachment a viewer would wish to create. Such fluidity and slipperiness in terms of intent for any communication and whether there actually was any particular desire to make a meaningful message by virtue of any new visual relationships is never explained, or even inferred. *The 27 Points* perhaps acts as a travel journal since it shows glimpses into various places through a use of objects such as a labelled cassette tape, and a pocketful of loose change which is presumably the remnants of one or more countries on the groups' tour itinerary. Further reinforcing sensations of disconnection, the words *The Fall* are scratched out with little attention to whether the shape of each letter appears complete or *clean*, and where they only appear to partially consider whether any glyph in this series should strive for meaning.

The cover concept for *Interim* embraces a *Brechtian ideal of transparency*, pulling back the curtain on itself so that the design works explicitly to reveal an approach to graphic production which is *aggressively non-expert*. By foregrounding its visceral and creased or scuffed form, Smith celebrates the *unprocessed, unfinished materiality* that is determined by the *fax machine*: a communications technology now held to be defunct or obsolete. He shows wilful disregard for meaning, function, or legibility ('*Comments will be ignored—MAELSTROM*') and also, perhaps intentionally, demonstrates a virtue in persistence and a value in the fax as a secure and decentralised form of communication that shows no sign of being superseded by newer forms of digital messaging—his communications are sent % *Saunders & Co. Prestwich*.

STRANGE WRITING: A BLACK ART

In his opening lines to 'Junger Cloth', the fifth track on 2015's *Sub-Lingual Tablet*, Smith relates the narrator's terrifying experience of a slow act of reading. While decoding or attempting a translation, Smith describes the interpretation of a written text whose typographic form possessing characteristics which, as individual letters are read, induces both physical and psychical response, and generates a sense of revulsion which apparently connects to or channels an unknowable, perhaps extra-dimensional force.

Smith's lyric for 'Junger Cloth' is perhaps most notable for two reasons. First, it's uncommon that he would refer to writing, written language, or typographic form as directly as he does in here. Second, as the narrative makes clear, he is telling the story of an estrangement *from* words and of his narrator's growing disgust and distress in response to *the shapes of the letterforms themselves*. Perhaps this is as a result of their being obscured in some way, or that he is cursed to suffer this almost Lovecraftian repulsion as their true form is gradually revealed upon close reading. It is clear, however, that some kind of magical or occultist force is working *through* the written word, a magic which is itself further described, expressed and materialised through the medium of the song itself.

A connection between the occult and visible language is, perhaps, no surprise when considered in the context of Smith's keen history for horror literature, and his enduring enthusiasm for creating narratives often populated by unknown or disgusting terror and his occasional tales of inter-dimensional transgression. The potential for dangerous emotional, magical, or spiritual consequences of acts of speaking, writing, reading, and spelling, together with the deep-rooted connections between language and the body, have long haunted how we perceive and believe, in particular within a context of technologies for writing and print. The plot of Ben Marcus's 2012 novel *The Flame Alphabet* centres on a mysterious affliction (a pathogen or virus) that affects adults *when subjected to the vocalisation of the young*, as the words of children work to poison and kill their parents. In order to somehow re-establish language as something safe, cured, or non-toxic, the book's narrator is employed within a mysterious facility to redesign the form of the alphabet—to invent new glyphs which might somehow be freed from their deadly infection. And so, time must be spent designing and testing these experiments in non-alphabetic typography, often with resulting in the *execution* of human readers whose role is as in-vivo laboratory subject. The narrator's own safety means that they are unable to look directly at the letters being shaped and so they must look via an arrangement of interconnected mirrors, or only through a glimpse out of the corner of their eye otherwise, as with Smith's narration of 'Junger Cloth', they would be revealed to him in their true, deadly form.

Similarly, Tony Burgess's 1995 novel *Pontypool Changes Everything* reports on a world where language is the carrier of a plague which, apparently, is contained only within certain English words and which results in its sufferers being transformed into cannibalistic zombies condemned to utter a poetic nonsense of words or phrases, locked-in and heading towards their terminal phase while repeating the same gibberish. In the story, the authorities' only solution is to declare communication itself illegal and, as hilariously demonstrated in the final scenes of Bruce McDonald's filmed adaptation (2008), upon infection the only cure is for individuals to *unlearn the contaminated word*, replacing its meaning with another through a repetition of old and new words until the symptoms cease.

> Sound ... exists only when it is going out of existence ... [t]he alphabet implies that matters are otherwise, that a word is a thing, not an event, that it is present all at once, and that it can be cut up into little pieces ... [the alphabet] ... has lost all connection with things as things. It represents sound itself as a thing, transforming the evanescent world of sound to the quiescent, quasi-permanent world of space. (Walter J. Ong, *Orality and Literacy*, Routledge 1982, p.91)

Here, scholar Walter J. Ong outlines the idea that, as a consequence of language navigating through its many technologies of mediation, there is an increasingly greater distance created between words and their originator.

Whether via vocalised sound and their cultures of orality, or the array of 'secondary modelling systems' which are defined by the adoption of pre-determined systems of phonetic symbols written onto the surfaces of physical objects via a range of inscriptive tools, each *technological shift* has brought with it the threat (or promise) to *displace*, *replace*, and *remake* existing attitudes, behaviours, and hierarchies which have been determined by the role that language found for itself in human culture and society.

In Western Europe this has often resulted in a threat or challenge to how established power is performed, and the encroachment or disruption of new technologies into pre-established systems of a production and reproduction of knowledge. The practice of writing, for example, was initially regarded as something *inhuman* and *unnatural* which would weaken the human mind by way of its *encouragement to forget* and in nurturing the need to rely upon text instead of our own memories. Plato's Phaedrus, itself re-told as the firsthand account of a spoken conversation, contains a warning of the perils of one invention of writing. The Egyptian god Thoth (or Theuth) so desired to improve human wisdom that he sought to encourage humanity to make use of writing in order to better their capacity for learning via memory. Presenting this to the other gods, however, he was challenged—the opposite would be the most likely outcome for a lazy human race, and this invention would result not in knowledge but only in the appearance of knowledge, and, consequently, a weakening of the mind as a further separation of words from their original source is carried out.

While writing would go on to be employed largely within administrative contexts, it would continue to carry with it the whiff of the dangerous, of the unknown or mysterious and often regarded as 'an instrument of secret and magic power' (Goody 1968, p.236). Written texts would be used to form or cast spells, and the figure of the *reader* (as intermediary, as *medium*) establishes that sense of otherworldliness or esoteric which may require caution and suspicion, or perhaps, obedience and deference.

> At the beginning of the sixteenth century, if you were used to seeing handwriting . . . it must have been unsettling, eerie and almost inconceivable to see writing mechanically reproduced. Each copy was identical, like a kind of perfectly multiplied individual. (Reinfurt 2019, p.23)

The inbuilt and inescapable repetition of Johannes Gutenberg's invention of movable type in the fifteenth century transformed how readers would relate to the written word, with print-embedded alphabet more firmly onto the surface of the page and fixed into the visual space of *typographic* text. With that came new concerns, in particular an anxiety regarding its potential for reorienting a reader's relationship with their world and, most worryingly for some, an erosion of the authority then held by organised religion. *John Fust* (Johannes Gutenberg's partner and financier) was accused of practising witchcraft because of the non-natural qualities of the letters being produced by the new technology of printing and its impossibly high speed of production. Fust is thought, by some, to be the source of the Dr. Faustus myth, as the boom in printing and book production which erupted in the sixteenth century coincided with a witch craze across Europe—many of the new opportunities for publication would be used to carry images and reports of witch trials which related both the witches' blasphemous behaviours and their resulting persecution, often reported with a sensationalism and a salacious focus.

The places where writing and printing were practiced were not immune to such dark or *spectral presences*, and some would learn of the dangers of textual manipulation which could damn both author and reader to eternal punishment. Titivillus, the patron demon of scribes, was said to haunt *both* the monastic spaces of the scriptorium and among the type cases of the print workshop. Since monks were required to complete the laborious and tiring job of hand-copying religious texts, unintended mistakes were likely to be made which might suggest a lack of attention or failure to maintain the required degree of dedication. It was Titivillus, therefore, who would be held responsible for any unintentional errors that might appear in the manuscript's production. Similarly, mistakes could also be found in copies of a printed text and it was the so-called *printers devil* who would be blamed, a term often used to refer to the printer's assistant who'd likely be held accountable for any error.

As The Fall's career progressed, there seemed a marked change in Mark E. Smith's belief in, and attitude towards, the number of words which should be included in his lyrics. His concern seemed to shift towards believing in a value of achieving a high level of concision and brevity as opposed to the abundance of words constructed in his longer-form or improvised lyrics in The Fall's earlier releases. This shift *away* from words is also evident in terms of Smith's use of typography on The Fall's record sleeves where, following *Room to Live*, there is an increasing tendency towards the dominant cover image usually in the form of commissioned painting or photography. His role becomes more curatorial or editorial and so, in the occupational terminology and management structures of creative industries, he moved upwards to assume a position as The Fall's nominal *art director*. It seems clear that he did remain deeply involved in guiding the form that The Fall's visual communication would take, and his communications to record companies collected in the recent *Excavate* publication show ample evidence of this. When he did return to the task, with the occasional cameo as cover *designer*, Smith would confirm his ongoing commitment to *compression* as a tactic in the typographic and visual language used to differentiate and distinguish The Fall.

CONCLUSION: THE MELTING SURFACE

During interviews, Mark E. Smith would often refer to his own mediumship and to a psychic ability which allowed him to scry past and future scenarios. Occasionally, these scenes might manifest themselves within a Fall lyric and then be further expanded upon in subsequent interviews. Historian of occult cultures Helen Sword (2002, p.161) frames a typical Spiritualist séance as a richly dynamic and polyvocal experience and, perhaps, this becomes a useful lens through which The Fall's typographic approaches might be considered:

> On the middle of one subject another will be interpolated; solemn sentences, in the midst of matter of fact statement, sometimes a meaningless sentence ... the mood shifts, the surface seems to melt away and then another surface and another—a perpetual change of consciousness.

In particular, Sword's description seemingly describes those examples where the surfaces of a Fall cover (packaging for vinyl or CD, posters, or other advertising media) were packed with a chaotic or overwhelming collection of words or phrases whose connection isn't immediately clear, or where an idea of innumerable voices being channeled via automatic writing into or upon the page via an unseen hand is conjured.

Sword also discusses W. B. Yeats's unpublished *Preliminary Examination of the Script of ER*, the spirit medium (**E**lizabeth **R**adcliffe), and reflects on her use of *fragmented scraps of language* in the production of automatic writing. Such a 'mass of fragments, of interrupted sentences, of unfinished thoughts' (Sword 2002, p.161) work to produce or communicate something more truthful than humans might otherwise be capable of, and these more marginal thoughts are, in fact, *more valuable* and more powerful than so-called ordinary language. If there is one idea that encapsulates Smith's attitude and his values, and which was often used to describe The Fall and Smith's work ethic and rate of production, it is this sense of celebrating *incompleteness* and of abruptly leaving things (often unfinished) so that newer, equally interesting or valuable work might be made. By virtue of their seeming or appearing incomplete or unfinished, Smith's work to create a particularly challenging vision for The Fall invites particular types of response and confronts any expectations audiences might have.

The use of a range of methods which explore the opportunities for being *partial* or seemingly deficient, sketchy, and imperfect seems evident when considering the visual and typographic output of Mark E. Smith, and certainly when reflecting on the career of The Fall. Such an approach is, of course, *strange* in the context of an industry that might prioritise ideals of perfection, but it almost also guarantees a strangeness in *whatever mate-*

rialises as a consequence of doing things in this way. For Smith, those illegible, or ugly, or odd combinations of words—positioned alongside other words, and around images and more words—which make up so many of the group's output was *necessary work* in order to shape the surfaces upon which The Fall appeared in the world.

REFERENCES

Buwert, Peter. 2016. "Defamiliarisation, Brecht and Criticality in Graphic Design". In *Modes of Criticism 2*, edited by Francisco Laranjo, 25–38. Porto, Portugal: Modes of Criticism.

Drucker, Johanna. 1998. *Figuring the Word: Essays on Books, Writing and Visual Poetics*. New York: Granary Books.

Erlich, Victor. 1965 [1955]. *Russian Formalism: History-Doctrine*. London: Mouton.

Fisher, Mark. 2016. *The Weird and the Eerie*. London: Repeater Books.

Goody, Jack. 1968. "Restricted Literacy in Northern Ghana". In *Literacy in Traditional Societies*, edited by Jack Goody, 198–264. Cambridge, England: Cambridge University Press.

Keedy, Jeffrey. 2013. "The Global Style". In Slanted 22 - Art Type, edited by Slanted Publishers, 190–195. Karlsruhe, Germany: Slanted Publishers.

Laranjo, Francisco, ed. 2016. *Modes of Criticism 2: Critique of Method.* Porto, Portugal: Modes of Criticism.

Nelson, Harold, and Erik Stolterman. 2003. *The Design Way: Intentional Change in an Unpredictable World*. Englewood Cliffs, NJ: Educational Technology Publications.

Reinfurt, David. 2019. *A New Program for Graphic Design*. Los Angeles: Inventory Press.

Shklovsky, Viktor. 2017 [1917]. "Art as Device". In *Viktor Shklovsky: A Reader*, edited and translated by Alexandra Berlina, 73–96. London: Bloomsbury Publishing.

Sword, Helen. 2002. *Ghostwriting Modernism*. Ithaca, NY: Cornell University Press.

van Toorn, Jan. 2006. *Design's Delight.* Rotterdam: 010 Publishers.

van Toorn, Jan. 2016. "Operationalising the Means: Communication Design as Critical Practice". In *Modes of Criticism 2*, edited by Francisco Laranjo, 25–38. Porto, Portugal: Modes of Criticism.

Chapter Four

Psykick Dancehall

The Paranormal Strategies of Mark E. Smith and The Fall

Ben Lawley

During forty years of lyric writing for The Fall, Mark E. Smith's words were often considered to have predicted newsworthy events yet to occur when songs were written. This led some (including Smith) to suggest supernatural precognition had occurred. Certainly, many would agree with comedian and Fall fan Frank Skinner: "It's a bit spooky, isn't it?" (BBC 2007). For the rational sceptic, this is easy to dismiss, but Smith often claimed to possess psychic powers, particularly precognition of future events. His claims remain important to understanding the construction and strategies of The Fall.

It is tempting to indulge in imaginative historicism, casting Smith as a working-class prophet, each performance a seance swirling with spectres of Salfordian industrial history, but Crosthwaite rightly dismisses such romanticism (Crosthwaite 2016). For a more analytical approach, one might consider precognition in the light of psychological theories. Mainstream psychology offers a wealth of empirical study evidence to debunk and pathologise delusional precognition alongside some patient-centred therapeutic approaches more tolerant of subjective beliefs. Denying Smith's psychic self-narratives as invalid claims to truth is insufficient, because regardless of evidence, precognition was undoubtedly significant to Mark E. Smith's writing and outlook. Precognition was a recurrent lyrical theme, becoming embedded in the Fall mythology Mark constructed and communicated through lyrics and interviews, substantiated by group members' statements and recollections. Music magazines and newspapers ran stories without verification and even the most oblique lyrical allusions could be dissected by listeners seeking portentous elements. The internet's rise amplified fan narratives and accelerated journalistic recycling of apocryphal tales of clairvoyance.

"UNSEEN KNOWLEDGE, UNSEEN FACTS"— ON PRECOGNITION

Within the field of psychology, research literature identifies three classifications of paranormal belief: experience involving life after death; psychokinesis; and extra sensory perception (Thalbourne & Delin 1994, p.3). The term *extra sensory perception* (E.S.P.) was coined by J. B. Rhine early in the scientific study of these phenomena. On observing fake seances in the 1920s, this American botanist launched parapsychology as a rational sub-discipline in the youthful science of psychology, and founded the first parapsychology laboratory (Mock 2009). *Precognition* is a sub-type of E.S.P. whereby individuals gain advance knowledge of future events by some unknown mechanism of transmission, unrecognised by mainstream science.

One frequently cited example of Smithian precognition was 'Terry Waite Sez' (1986), a concise garage blast conveying a barbed lyrical tirade against the perceived hubris of Terry Waite, who was serving as the Archbishop of Canterbury's special envoy to the Middle East. The lyrics sneer at a "50 plus" reverend who is "out to heal provincial pus". The track is not audibly impaired by mastering from compact cassette at Smith's insistence, paranoid that producer John Leckie had been "secretly mixing the tracks without his permission and fucking it up," as Leckie recalled, decades later (Easlea 2019, p.15).

Mr Waite, or "Mr Big" as Smith drawls disparagingly—had negotiated several hostage releases in the Middle East. After flying to Tehran on Christmas Day 1980 to negotiate a release, he gained media prominence through successive hostage crises (*Newcastle Journal*, 27.12.80). Frequent TV talk show appearances made him a household name in the early 1980s (*Belfast Telegraph*, 7.8.82). By 1985, he maintained a high profile across the media, publicly intervening in defence of a yachtsman facing drug charges and launching fund-raising campaigns for Bangladesh cyclone recovery and water in Sudan (*Reading Evening Post*, 2.4.85; *Newcastle Journal*, 30.5.85; *Liverpool Echo*, 22.2.85).

In Lebanon, 1985 saw at least a dozen Western hostages taken by Islamic Jihad/Hezbollah militia (*Guardian* 15.11.85). 'Terry Waite Sez' was recorded in June 1986 for *Bend Sinister* (released September 1986). Four months later, Terry Waite was kidnapped by militia in Lebanon. This was confirmed on 20 January 1987, a week after disappearing while visiting West Beirut to negotiate with Islamic Jihad for four hostages, including British journalist John McCarthy (Kaj 1987). Claiming he failed to honour promises from a previous hostage negotiation, the faction suggested Waite was working for the C.I.A., so negotiator became hostage. After arduous imprisonment and terrible treatment, Terry Waite was finally released in 1991 (Waite 1993).

People jumped to the conclusion this record "predicted" the kidnapping. So widespread was this idea, that it often arose in interviews. Typically, Mark chose deflection as a strategy playing down the connection, even suggesting Terry Waite was a drinker he met in a Stockport pub with no relation to the more famous namesake (Lowe 1987, p.25; reformationposttpm, accessed 2021).

Listeners and journalists cultivated the paranormal explanation, but how did the song come about? The publishing credits are attributed to Smith M.E./Smith B. (then wife and lead guitarist Brix Smith-Start), but Fall writing credits were often casual and inaccurate (Smith-Start 2016, p.207; Ford 2003, p.221). In recent years, Brix says she wrote the music, possibly extending to the title and even lyrics (Smith-Start 2016, p.207; Easlea 2019, p.14). Brix has also claimed psychic powers and believes in communication of energies (Smith-Start 2016, p.350). Could Brix's own second sight have contributed? In this instance, authorship may be unclear, so a collaborative endeavour may be suggested, a perspective which somewhat undermines the proposition of Mark E. Smith as singular psychic visionary. However, Brix's recollections from the 2000s (before so much time had elapsed) did contradict her later claims. She recalled having written the driving riff but suggested the lyrics were an instance of Mark's powers of precognition (Ford 2003, p.159; Simpson 2009, p.151).

Rationally, Terry Waite's kidnap and mention in song is a remarkable but explainable coincidence. Terry Waite featured heavily in UK media and the song doesn't specifically predict kidnap. Smith's references were often topical, cutting up daytime TV, pop culture, local newspapers. Perhaps the suggestion of psychic powers in relation to 'Terry Waite Sez' is just the cultivation of a myth of Mark's occult powers or psychic abilities, which was already well established as a journalistic framing. In this instance, Brix's recollections and journalists' questions elevated the myth, as did Terry Waite's relatives, who contacted Beggars Banquet Records to request lyric transcription, desperate to glean clues. Brix suggested this was for "remote viewing" so a medium could "look back and try and trace the path of where a person went" (Easlea 2019, p.14).

Fans and keen listeners, such as those at *The Fall Online* forum, have detected dozens more cases of potential lyrical precognition, said to have foretold events featured in news media, including terrorist attacks, wars, and politicians' downfalls where the events happened after the songs had been recorded (The Fall Online 2003–2021). Many listeners enjoy Smith's E.S.P. but often without giving it credence. However, belief trumps scepticism in society at large: Gallup opinion polls have consistently found a majority of Americans, sometimes 75 percent, believe in paranormal phenomena, with 41 percent believing specifically in psychics/E.S.P. (Gecewicz 2018; Gallup 2005). Older studies from Scandinavia and Britain returned similar results with one British survey finding 70 percent believed in E.S.P. specifically, but between 1985 and 2005 paranormal belief declined considerably, with a corresponding increase in respondents who accepted conspiracy theories (Haraldsson 1985).

"DICE MAN"—MISATTRIBUTION AND PROBABILITY MISJUDGMENT

Why do people jump to pre-cognitive connections between lyrics and newsworthy events? Cognitive psychology offers the *misattribution hypothesis* which suggests some individuals' psychological characteristics render them more likely to ascribe paranormal causes to uncommon events despite rational explanations (Wiseman & Watt 2006).

The *probability misjudgement model* proposes how this misattribution occurs in the mind. It suggests believers are simply miscalculating the frequency of coincidence (Wiseman & Watt 2006, p.328). These individuals suffer a weak or erroneous ability to estimate probability. In tests they frequently underestimate the probability of such events happening by chance. A succession of psychological research projects has constructed experiments in which subjects were triaged using survey scores reflecting their level of belief in psychic phenomena, comparing performance of strong believers versus strong sceptics—*sheep versus goats* to use the terminology coined by Gertrude Schmeidler (1945). Those with strong faith tended to perform poorly at probability judgment tasks such as predicting dice throws, coin flip outcomes, or generating random number sequences. This suggests they simply miscalculate the likelihood of events occurring randomly (Blackmore & Trościanko 1985; Houtkooper & Haraldsson 1997).

Several of Mark's lyrical predictions seem to exemplify the probability misjudgment model. Smith found inspiration in random daytime TV (Poulou 2021, p.11) and appropriated current affairs and societal trends as lyrical material. His assemblage of so many zeitgeist snippets made it likely some references would coincide with later news stories. Notable coincidences (like the Terry Waite kidnap) happen frequently yet many people perceive them as rare and exceptional occurrences thus ascribing disproportionate significance and meaning to events.

"MR HUGHES WAS RIGHT IN RETROSPECT"— RETROSPECTIVE CONFIRMATION BIAS

Retrospective confirmation bias is another class of cognitive error driving belief in precognition. In retrospect we seize on seemingly exceptionally rare coincidences between selected memories and new events. Rapid rule of thumb thinking (heuristic reasoning) accentuates bias allowing the mind to misattribute special significance, viewing coincidence as "too good to just be chance" (Blackmore 1992, p.368).

This problem of bias in reasoning was noted by Francis Bacon in the seventeenth century: "The human understanding when it has once adopted an opinion . . . draws all things else to support and agree with it" (rejecting contrary evidence), "in order that by this great and pernicious predetermination the authority of its former conclusions may remain inviolate" (Bacon 1620, p.50). We pay disproportionate attention to data confirming pre-existing knowledge and present or ingrained past beliefs, while discounting dissonant information which contradicts pre-existing beliefs. For example, people note when aspects of a fortune-teller's dialogue are confirmed by later events, while forgetting numerous unfulfilled predictions (Gray & Gallo 2016, p.242).

This bias towards selective recall made it easy to perceive a link between the news headline: "Diana Dead"—which announced the fatal Mercedez-Benz limousine crash of Diana Spencer in Paris (*News of the World* 31.8.97; *Sunday Mirror* 31.8.97)—and the memory of the song title 'Spencer Must Die'. First recorded over a year earlier for the John Peel BBC radio show as 'Spencer' (June 1996) and re-recorded a couple of months prior to the crash for *Levitate* (released September 1997). Sceptics (and listeners who didn't like the album) can point out the other thirteen tracks may be forgotten here as only 'Spencer Must Die' benefits from retrospective confirmation bias. Yet notably, zinc was used by Mercedes-Benz to reduce steel corrosion (Meyer 1986, p.826), a fact which becomes pertinent in light of the lyrics which include the words "bend zinc" and pained moaning. These factors seem uncanny in retrospect and support suggestions of precognition.

It is more likely the song name-checked Simon Spencer, the producer with whom Smith fell out while recording *Levitate*. This explains the progression from 'Spencer' to 'Spencer Must Die', a year later. It is also consistent with a succession of Fall song titles naming musicians: 'The Quartet of Doc Shanley', 'Stephensong'—Stephen Hanley; 'Craigness'—Craig Scanlon; '(Jung Nev's) Antidotes'—Neville Wilding; '(Birtwistle's) Girl in a Shop'—Spencer Birtwistle; 'Xmas with Simon'—Simon Wolstencroft. Rationally, Simon makes a more likely titular Spencer. However, consideration of whether the song predicts an untimely death is less readily dispelled, given the tragic death of Simon Spencer after being taken ill at the end of the 2003 Glastonbury Festival (BBC 2003).

Any suggestion the song predicts Diana's death relies on selective use of supporting data, while screening out coincidental explanations like frequent use of musicians' names in song titles. This type of retrospective confirmation bias would have annoyed Francis Bacon, but demonstrates the human love of narrative patterns as well as selective bias.

"I SAY E.S.P. MEDIUM DISCORD"—CLAIMS OF E.S.P.

Alongside the occult, psychic phenomena were a recurrent source of lyrical inspiration for Smith. Perhaps most clearly demonstrated in early Fall by 'Psykick Dancehall' (1979). In this "formative classic" (Thompson 2003, p.39), Smith invites us to 'Step aboard, for E.S.P. medium discord,' explaining: "When I'm dead and gone, my vibrations will live on." Kay Carroll (partner, manager, and backing vocalist) pointed to a psychic centre her mother opened in Prestwich (Ford 2003, 72), whereas Martin Bramah (guitarist and friend) suggested an under-eighteen's club "above a spiritualist church in Prestwich, Questors Psychic Disco" (Bramah 2016). Whether one or both are the place where "They know your questions about no words," *Dragnet*'s opener was re-versioned as 'Psyckick Dancehall #2' for the 'Fiery Jack' single (1980). Smith added an account of clairvoyant medium Helen Duncan, "Scotland's last witch", whose 1944 prosecution was the last under the 1735 Witchcraft Act. Her "gift" led to her downfall when she claimed contact with spirits of dead sailors had revealed the location of the sunken HMS *Barham* (torpedoed by a German U-boat in 1941 with loss of 861 lives). The location was not public knowledge, which made authorities suspicious, fearing she had access to naval intelligence and might divulge the forthcoming Normandy landings (Johnson 2018). It clearly made her a person of interest to Smith who wove her psychic mediumship alongside other recurrent Fall themes—the hounding of a persecuted performer, military history, and Prestwich psycho-geography.

Smith's own visionary geographical clairvoyance crops up in a live 'Cash 'N' Carry' (New Orleans, 23.6.81): "I can see, I have dreams. I was in three places at once. I was in Hof, I was in Trenton." Similar disruptions occur in 'Dissolute Singer' (1998), a spoken-word collage where a disoriented Smith attempts to navigate to the calamitous appearance at Brownies (Manhattan, 7.4.98). The night would culminate in three musicians quitting and Mark's arrest for assault (Kaufman 1998). A rainy night in New York is half blotted out by his fugue state, experiencing an awake dream, remote viewing directions through Manchester. Two topographies intersect around the common axis of Canal Street (which exists in both cities). In the midst of this dissociative trance, some arcane process of ancestral mediumship provides clairvoyant audience with Smith's deceased father and grandfather: "their respective faces appear gigantic, left and right, above the city skyline like Hawkman or

Lex Luthor. In embarrassment they see dissolute singer." Philip K. Dick–style E.S.P. also occurs in 1992's 'Arid Al's Dream': "And he gets pre-psi-cognition, everywhere he goes. It screams psi-cog from doorways, and upper shut off windows". As often, it's unclear whether pre-psi-cognition is experienced by the eponymous *Arid Al* or by Smith, but it relates Mark's sense that second sight is as much a negative experience as a gift. E.S.P. continues in later Fall, with songs like 'Coach and Horses' (2007) offering another dissociative dream of the 1860s. These narratives disrupt geography and chronology to grant Smith access to a subjective realm of remote viewings and visitations.

Lyrical references to para-scientific phenomena abound, as do allusions to Mark's own psychic sensitivity and precognition, but lyrics offer little explanation. Mick Middles interviewed Smith extensively for the book they co-wrote and said Smith "doesn't like talking about his psychic edge" (Middles & Smith 2003, p.264), but did manage to glean that Smith felt surrounded by strange powers from his childhood days. "There used to be this thing where watches would explode on me. . . . It was all extremely disturbing to be honest. . . . But I realised it was a bit pointless being a psychic." Mark explained his reasoning: the psychics he encountered while employed as a shipping clerk at Salford docks in the 1970s could foretell death, yet couldn't predict a winning racehorse (Middles & Smith 2003, p.264). Smith used a similarly humorous slant on the lack of practical benefit gained from E.S.P. on his second spoken word disc, the freeform tape splice of *Pander! Panda! Panzer!* (2002): "Being psychic has never done me any good whatsoever, as I always knew it would not." Sometimes he discussed this openly, sometimes he remained stubbornly, defensively guarded. Earlier in The Fall's development, Mark was asked about the psychic question: "Yeah, I believe in all those things. . . I don't think about them much. I'm not an "enthusiast" for that sort of thing." (Marvin 1981). He told the same interviewer he still read tarot cards but was more interested in "the way writings can prophesize things. Like I've found a lot of my writing is actual prophecy. It's really strange" (Marvin 1981). By the 1990s, this early candidness had been replaced by a more guarded phase with a new tone evident in interview answers on many subjects. Perhaps a mistrust of the press set in after too many "northern man in the pub" caricatures, or a fatigue with unresearched journalistic laziness (Smith & Collings 2009, p.217). Evidently the psychic question had entered the press-clipping libraries and become a stock in trade interview cliché. Frequently Mark would shut down this line of enquiry: "I used to be psychic but I drunk my way out of it" (Herrington 1996, p.26).

In later years Smith did offer one definitive and surprisingly frank statement during a more amiable television interview where Frank Skinner asked directly whether Mark had psychic powers. Speaking softly and with some hesitation,

Mark replied, "Oh, I have." . . . "All my life." . . . "It's summat you've got to keep under control really. . . . It's no use being psychic. It's a gift, but well, it's not a gift. It's no good." Echoing his equestrian remarks to Mick Middles, Smith affirmed he still couldn't pick a Grand National winner (BBC 2007).

Clearly Mark believed in his powers and also considered his mother Irene Smith possessed the gift. He discussed his disturbing early life psychic experiences when visiting her with Mick Middles (Middles & Smith 2003, pp.23 and 30). Kay Carrol and Brix Smith-Start have also suggested they had psychic gifts, and believed that Mark did (Ford 2003, p.72; Smith-Start 2016, pp.191 and 260). Family belief in E.S.P. may have been particularly significant. Developmental psychologists have mapped the familial influence of these beliefs. Research demonstrates correlation: if parents believe in supernatural occurrences, their children are more likely to develop similar beliefs (Braswell, Rosengren & Berenbaum 2012, p.104). Having grown up in surroundings where these beliefs were commonplace would have predisposed Smith to believe in his own psychic powers.

Brix still believes—and with considerable certainty—that Mark possessed psychic powers. Journalist Dave Simpson was aware of the psychic question, confirming: "Brix thinks he is." She went on to cite 'Terry Waite Sez' (1986), 'Free Range' (1992), though she might have meant 'Zagreb' (1990), and 'Powder Keg' (1996) to evidence the consistency of precognition (Simpson 2009, 151). Supposedly, these predicted Waite's kidnapping (1987), the breakup of Yugoslavia (1992), and a Manchester city centre bomb (1996).

A more personal example for Brix came with events surrounding 'Disney's Dream Debased' (1984). In January 1984, Mark, Brix, and her uncle vacationed at Disneyland, Anaheim, California. She wanted to share her deep appreciation of Disneyland, which was significant in her West Coast childhood. They rode The Matterhorn, a high-speed Bavarian alpine-themed roller coaster with bobsleds. Brix recalled, "As we were waiting in line he said 'This ride is evil.'" Brix remembered when Mark got off the roller coaster he was deathly pale, shaking with tears of fear in his eyes. "That ride is fucking evil, Brix. It's evil." Fire engines and security mobilised and later they learned a woman had been thrown from her bobsled and killed (Easlea 2010, p.6). Brix was clear, "Mark is psychic and he knows it. He's a precognitive psychic, able to pick up on snatches of future incidents before they happen" (Smith-Start 2016, p.192). The tragic incident was evidently deeply distressing and informed both 'Disney's Dream Debased' (1984) and later an introductory dreamlike preface to Brix's autobiography (Smith-Start 2016). The time frame of this case of precognition is different from some other examples; the events having happened so soon after the E.S.P. transmission, with the song digesting traumatic events in retrospect.

"MUST WE RETREAT INTO MYSTICISM?"—
DEVELOPING BELIEF IN THE ESOTERIC AND OCCULT

In addition to family members' influence, the psychology literature suggests the credence given by others in his social environment could have increased Smith's certainty regarding these beliefs. Tony Friel recalls Smith introducing him to the writing of both Philip K. Dick and H. P. Lovecraft in 1975 (Simpson 2009, p.72). Shadows of Lovecraft, M. R. James, and Arthur Machen are evident on *Dragnet* (1979), where tracks like 'Spectre vs. Rector' demonstrate an early fascination with the occult, gothic literature, and arcane knowledge. Mark Fisher used these links to construct a view of The Fall as literary high modernism (K-Punk 2006). Predictably, Smith rarely engaged directly or positively with these academic discussions of his work, despite presentation at a University of Salford symposium (Goddard & Halligan 2010).

Clearly Mark's social group enjoyed literature concerning cosmic and supernatural themes and sometimes this was accompanied by belief in E.S.P. and para-scientific phenomena. Martin Bramah had an interest in the teachings of G. I. Gurdjieff, the early twentieth-century Greco-Armenian mystic and spiritual teacher who became a high society guru and money magnet in New York and Paris (Lachman 2014, p.194). His teachings were disseminated in England by Russian follower and former theosophist, P. D. Ouspensky (Josephson-Storm 2017, p.123). There were still Gurdjieff Fourth Way groups running in Manchester in the 1980s which Martin recalls attending while Mark had less interest (Smith 2009). In common with Smith who told fortunes for money, Bramah also gave tarot readings, but as Smith recalled, with psychoactive drugs being introduced to the equation, things became "really insane" (Middles & Smith 2003, p.67; Marvin 1981).

Experiments showed how people's belief in supernatural claims increases when endorsed by others in their social environment. Experiments show social factors strongly influenced credence, acceptance being more likely where belief was evident "in networks of significant others—family, friends, work colleagues and so forth" (Markovsky & Thye 2001, p.37). Smith's milieu clearly had a large number of believers, not only relatives but also dock office colleagues, early Fall members, and partners who shared his belief.

Another aspect acknowledged as influencing the formation of belief is transmission from powerful or highly esteemed individuals. Smith's belief could have been influenced by consideration of pseudo-rational theories regarding time slips, prophecy, and E.S.P. described in Philip K. Dick novels like *Time Out of Joint* (1959). Smith had great respect for Dick, whose influence he acknowledged (Smith 1986), perhaps feeling an affinity towards a fellow paranoic and accelerant user who reported his own pre-cog experiences. Though Smith and Dick never met, Claude Bessy, who edited West Coast punk magazine *Slash* was introduced to Dick, visiting him in L.A. during 1978 where he gave him a Fall record which was positively received (Smith 1986, p.33). Psychological research experiments have shown paranormal claims to truth made by respected individuals (i.e., a college professor, maybe a respected author) have a strong influence on an individual's beliefs, which extends to written testimony from absent respected individuals (Markovsky & Thye 2001, p.35). Furthermore, the same experimenters hypothesised a synergistic increased impact on the level of credence given to paranormal claims where the various factors combined: friends, family, colleagues, trusted individuals, authority figures (Markovsky & Thye 2001, p.37).

Smith's early autodidact occult reading was no mere literary exploration, this spilled over into practical mediumship through the tarot. Smith recounted making money reading tarot cards for rich housewives when The Fall formed in the 1970s: "I had a natural talent for it. I've always been able to read people" (Smith & Collings 2009, p.67). In 1981 Smith said he still read tarot cards although countered this by confirming he had become more interested in the power of writing to predict events (Marvin 1981). A few years later Smith shunned fantasy as a genre, and had less interest in the occult, telling *New Musical Express*, "It was a funny time in my life but it was good to have. . . . I think the occult is a morbid fascination. That's what got me out of it" (Martin 1986). Much later Smith (perhaps jokingly) said he contemplated a return to tarot readings when he hit the financial doldrums in 2000 but didn't take this up (Smith & Collings 2009, p.68). In retrospect it appears back catalogue licencing deals and rejuvenating The Fall provided a more fruitful financial lifeline at the turn of the century.

"MILLENNIUM CONSPIRACY, FOREVER"— TIME TRAVEL AND CONSPIRACY THEORY

Back in 1981, Smith described a shift in focus from an adolescent interest in the occult, to concern with the power of words to predict the future and perhaps even interfere with the physics of time. The weird of H. P. Lovecraft gives way to Dick like musings regarding time, reality, E.S.P., and prophesy. Dick remained highly valued by Smith who acknowledged 1977's paranoic semi-autobiographical drug novel *A Scanner Darkly* as informing 'The Aphid' on 1995's *Cerebral Caustic*. The album contains a duet with Brix, 'Feeling Numb' where "I'll stick with Kindred," is likely a nod to Philip Kindred Dick, just as 'Leave the Capitol' (1981) mentions 'Monty,' another of his literary heroes, Montague Rhodes James (Sinker 2001). Smith did 'stick with Kindred', still praising the psychic novelist to his last days, despite loathing all film versions bar one, *Total Recall* (1990): "It's faithful to the book. Arnie gets it" (Wray 2018).

Other more conspiracy-focused lyrical snippets seem drawn from *Morning of the Magicians* (Pauwels & Bergier 1971) such as "The nine unknown men knew this" ('Putta Block' 1980), and "This is the Thule Group" ('Gut of the Quantifier' 1985). Originally published in France (1960), the English translation was popular in the 1970s, perhaps sitting alongside paperbacks by Colin Wilson and J. G. Ballard in Smith's carrier bag. The authors enjoyed concocting a pulp brew of portentous claims using an array of esoteric mystery mixed with conspiracy theory and pseudo-history. It's difficult to imagine Smith took it any more seriously than the authors, but the significance lies in bridging Smith's youthful occult interest and his later focus on conspiracy, perhaps accounting for its continued interest as a source of lyrical content.

As the occult references waned, other more contemporary political conspiracies became apparent during the 1980s. Bantam best seller *In God's Name* (Yallop 1984) inspired Smith's 1986 stage play *Hey! Luciani: The Life and Codex of John Paul I*, featuring Leigh Bowery, Lanah Pellay, and The Fall among its cast. The script used Yallop's material concerning the 1978 alleged murder of the short-lived pope. Smith's concerns extended to other machinations Yallop covered: freemasonry, banking corruption, smuggling Nazis to South America, links to the CIA and international mafia. Smith told Jools Holland the connections involved were what interested him, highlighting Paul Marcinkus as one of the characters he found fascinating (Channel 4 1986). Marcinkus, the American archbishop who controlled the Vatican Bank, was thought to be a CIA operative. When he died in America (2006), the cause of death was never revealed by the church (*New York Times* 2006). One can't rule out old age, but Yallop describes the subtle poisoning techniques of the P2 masonic lodge. The title and chorus of 'Mark'll Sink Us' (1987) seem to riff on the name Marcinkus, perhaps offering a Smithian precog of another murder.

The cover of banned espionage autobiography *Spycatcher* (Wright 1987) appeared on the *Seminal Live* (1989) album cover, emblazoned on Craig Scanlon's T-shirt. Mark wrote the paranoid E.S.P. phone-tapping song 'Telephone Thing' (1990) after reading the book, according to Martin Bramah (Bramah 2019, p. 94). Peter Wright, a retired senior MI5 officer published a candid memoir which revealed numerous illegal secret service conspiracies including MI6 plans to assassinate Egyptian premier Abdel Nasser and a joint MI5/CIA plot against Prime Minister Harold Wilson. His book was published in Australia, having been banned in London, but copies found their way around the world. It's a very Fall-like conspiracy: Wright even revealed frequencies used by radio bugs he had helped develop. Perhaps Peter Wright had become the real-life subject of 'New Face in Hell' (1980), the radio operator who "uncovers secrets and scandals of deceitful type proportions," which could be another Smithian precognition. "What a turn up for the books" as Smith's lyric goes on to say.

Regardless of whether the conspiracy material features pre-cognitive predictions, or whether this is just retrospective confirmation bias, pre-cog still crops up elsewhere. Old themes were never completely abandoned, with mediumship, haunting, and prophecy continuing to feature. For example, references to elves persist through the Beggars Banquet years from 'Elves' (1984) to 'Elf Prefix' (1989).

"I BECAME A SEMI ARTISTIC PERSON"—CREATIVITY, PSYCHOPATHOLOGY, AND PATTERN RECOGNITION

A rich seam of psychological conjecture and research has focused on commonalities and interactions between the mental processes and personality traits which give rise to creativity, mysticism, and psychopathology. Freud first posited a theory of "flexibility of repression" in which the creative artist is more readily able to shift mental mode, allowing subconscious impulses to manifest and combine in conscious thought (Freud 1917, in Thalbourne & Delin 1994, p.32).

Psychology studies suggest believers in psychic and paranormal phenomena operate with distinctly different cognitive mechanisms, compared to non-believers. Their mental processes predispose them to believe in precognition through detecting patterns, attributing psychic causation to unrelated phenomena. These individuals have a "propensity to find correspondences in distantly related material" (Wiseman & Watt 2006, p.329). In experiments these subjects are more likely to conceive of interactions between unconnected events. Their minds have a stronger sensitivity towards coincidence, thus forming unsupported connections (Bressan 2002).

"Everyone likes a good story" is a truism many psychologists and evolutionary biologists endorse, viewing humans as having evolved to construct meaning through discerning patterns: narrative, numerical, and visual. Evolutionary biologists hypothesise that humans developed pattern recognition to build cognitive environment maps (food sources, danger zones, etc.), later evolving further to facilitate recognition of emotion and gesture in social groups, eventually leading to verbal language (Mattson 2014). The human mind is predisposed to make sense of the world by picking out patterns used to navigate life's physical and social terrain. At times, this system of cognitive functioning may over-attenuate, yielding false patterns. Experimental subjects were more likely to believe in psychic phenomena if they perceived numerical patterns in random coin toss sequences, or discerned visual patterns where none existed, such as in unstructured abstract paintings (Van Prooijen et al. 2018, p.320).

Much psychology refutes the psychic singer narrative as attributable to failures of cognition and critical reasoning: probability misjudgement; misattribution; retrospective confirmation bias; and erroneous pattern recognition. Despite this scepticism, psychic experiences such as hearing voices (historically considered psychopathological) are regarded differently by some contemporary psychologists who take a more discursive approach, valuing the meaning and significance these beliefs hold for individual experience (Wooffitt & Allistone 2005). They offer a more benign view of E.S.P. as providing potential therapeutic benefit for some individuals (Powers, Kelley & Corlett 2017; Evrard 2014). From this perspective, while cognitive shortcomings may readily explain and refute the pre-cog trope, they cannot deny its personal significance to Smith, nor do they account for his successful employment of precognition as method and theme.

"MY GOSSAMER THIN GATE WILL KEEP OUT THE TRASH IN WHICH MY PSYCHIC STREET'S EMERSHED"— ON TRANSLIMINALITY

A psychology experiment demonstrated that although manic-depressives and schizophrenics were more likely to believe in psychokinesis than a control group, there was no significant difference between cohorts regarding levels of E.S.P. belief. Rather, researchers identified some support for a hypothesised single factor, correlating strongly with both creative personality type and paranormal belief (as well as mania and depression): *transliminality*. Defined as the experience of "novel ideas or solutions to problems; connections between elements—that appear not to be the result of direct reasoning, though pieces of the puzzle may have been allowed to lie dormant to incubate" (Thalbourne & Delin 1994, p.22). It can be said creative people have a more permeable threshold (*limen*), allowing subconscious subliminal thought to permeate the conscious mind. This transliminal threshold resembles the zone where Smith's E.S.P. manifests. He seems to speak of this subconscious threshold or psychic gate most directly with 'In These Times' (1988) slipping in a revealing personal line: "I often hope in days ahead my gossamer thin gate, will keep out the trash in which my psychic street's emershed." Emershed is a neologism published with the *Victoria* 7" box (1988), but in live recordings it could variously be enmeshed, immersed or immured, retaining a similar sense. The same lyric refers to Mark's "spectral filter", echoing mediums' accounts of the need to screen out some voices whose unwanted intrusions may penetrate the liminal veil.

'Bremen Nacht' (1998) recounted Smith's experiences of supposed spiritual possession, "The child's four-fingered bruises on my hip, meant I had been one day possessed." Presumably the spirits were from Bremen's WWII history, heavily bombed by allied forces, while upriver was the Bremen-Farge concentration camp (The Annotated Fall, accessed 2021; Wilkinson 1988). These songs deal with E.S.P. of previous rather than future events, old spirits breaking through the liminal veil from Smith's troubled subconscious, rather than prophetic visions of as yet unarrived futures. Again Smith sounds besieged and seeks to filter out the messages and visions, perhaps fearing the popular idea that psychic powers come at terrible cost to the individual, like the tragic predetermined fates awaiting the Faustian characters who frequent the screen in his beloved *Twilight Zone* episodes. At times he clearly considered E.S.P. a danger, wanting to close the gossamer thin gates of his transliminal threshold.

Through the lens of transliminality, the precognitive aspect of Smith's thinking parallels other favourite techniques like forging unexpected links between disparate elements, whether employing a Walkers crisps advertising campaign as Brexit analogy at the 2015 Green Man Festival (Wright 2019), or weaving together Nietzsche, Arthur C. Clarke, and the spectre of war in Eastern Europe in the lyrics of 'Free Range' (1992). We witness subliminal ruminations filtering over Smith's mental threshold into conscious articulation. Juxtaposed tangential data coalesces into an apparently prophetic vision of conflict in Eastern Europe. Direct mention is made of Zagreb and Moldavia (now Romania, Moldova, and Ukraine).

"I'M FEELING NUMB NOW, FROM REMEDIES AND PROZAC"—DEPRESSION AND MENTAL HEALTH

Depression is sometimes viewed as "a result of excessive transliminality" whereby subliminal material including negative memories and morbid delusions permeate the threshold and force their way, uninvited, into the conscious mind. Antidepressant drugs have been described as anti-transliminals, their target being to strengthen the liminal threshold, suppressing excess transliminal intrusions to a manageable level (Thalbourne & Delin 1994, pp.23–24). Depression is mentioned in several Fall songs, "The black dog on your back" in 'Backdrop' (1982), "Friend depression comes now and again" in 'Mark'll Sink Us' (1987), "I got down, I was depressed" in 'Dr Buck's Letter' (2000). Smith talks about prescription SSRI's in 'Feeling Numb' (1995): "I'm feeling numb now, from remedies and Prozac".

Undoubtedly, sustaining the Fall was extremely stressful at times and caused Smith considerable mental anguish (Ford 2003, p.235). Psychologists have noted how belief systems, particularly irrational ones, can become more important during stressful life events, helping create meaning out of uncontrollable circumstances (Park 2010, 292). The psychology literature suggests a lack of control over life circumstances statistically increases predisposition towards identifying illusory patterns, including conspiracy theories and superstitions (Whitson & Galinsky 2008, p.115). It's possible Smith's belief in his own psychic abilities became more pertinent during tough times in the face of uncontrollable events like tax demands and tour cancellations.

"WE'RE STILL ONE STEP AHEAD OF YOU"— PRECOGNITION AS CONSCIOUS STRATEGY

In 1977, before the Fall were well established, *New Musical Express* (N.M.E.) journalists Julie Burchill and Tony Parsons had a role in mind for The Fall, inviting them to the N.M.E.'s offices and offering them front page exposure if they would agree to be branded as the new working-class, anti-racist, communist band, "The Band Who Stand Against The N.F." (Middles 1987, p.22). Smith and partner/manager Kay Carroll instinctively refused the bait. The Fall were inherently anti-fascist, playing Rock Against Racism events *pro bono* and ridiculing National Front boss John Tyndall before launching into *Hey! Fascist* (Stretford Civic Centre 23.12.77). Yet Smith and Carroll feared The Fall project could fall victim to journalistic pigeonholing where short-term exposure as a single-issue band would come with a short shelf life, likely consigning The Fall to "the '77 shit pile" ('In My Area', 1979).

In the early days this approach expressed the "no sell out" punk philosophy of Kay's robust management style, but negating the expectations of journalists, record companies, fans, and retailers became something more; it evolved into a strategy to renew the multifaceted identity of The Fall, a project which might become almost anything, constrained only by the workings of Smith's arcane internal mechanisms. Repeatedly refusing to buckle under media definitions and showbusiness diktats was a constant assertion of independence as Smith resisted stagnation and typecasting. When it came to The Fall, there were to be "No boxes for us" ('Crap Rap 2', 1979). The Fall's shifting difference and continual becoming refused to be defined by ever narrower compartmental identity categories, echoing Deleuze and Guattari. There is no record of Smith encountering their schizo-analysis in the 1970s, with *Anti-Oedipus* untranslated until 1977, but counter-culture proponents of anti-psychiatry like R. D. Laing were already influential and accessible via Penguin paperbacks. One imagines these ideas permeating Smith's circle, which included mental health workers linked to Prestwich Hospital, built as a vast Victorian lunatic asylum. Kay Carroll and Una Baines (partner/keyboards) worked and trained there as psychiatric nurses, and Don Montgomery (neighbour/friend) was boilerman (Collings 2021, p.12). Early Fall lyrics take a subversive view of psychiatry in 'Repetition' (1978), 'Psycho Mafia' (1978), and 'Rowche Rumble' (1979). Anti-psychiatry may have validated Smith's lyrical foregrounding of his own inner realities and E.S.P. experiences.

Just as he shunned musical categories (punk, Madchester, Britpop), and negated journalistic framings, so Smith's use of supernatural and psychic themes acted to support his consistent guiding strategy—to maintain creative freedom through flux, rejecting external constraints. Predictably, Smith sometimes denied the term *prophecy* and said "It's just precog. . . . You write things down and you don't know what they mean but you know they're true and they come true later" (Bracewell & Wilde 1992). Despite the typical offhand deflection, in practice Smith would invoke the existence of extrasensory back channels quite often, both to bolster the authority of his particular subjective method of assemblage and to harden his personal resolve. An openness to the possibility of E.S.P. offered opportune narrative links to both futures and pasts, whereby temporal distortions granted a "step sideways" in perspectives, maintaining distance from received contemporary political and cultural viewpoints: "Just step outside this future world today, don't let it beat yer," 'Just Step Sideways' (1982).

"AND WAS JERUSALEM IN THE DARK SATANIC MILLS?" (WILLIAM BLAKE/M. E. SMITH)

Perhaps this psychic aperture on futures and pasts was at play in references to William Blake. Smith quoted *Milton a Poem's* preface (1804) in the ironic, anthemic reimagined 'Jerusalem' (1988) resulting in the wonderful publishing credit (William Blake/M. E. Smith). Edwardian composer Hubert Parry goes uncredited, in typical Fall style. The meditative 'W.B.' (2000) uses 'A Song of Liberty' with shards of *The Marriage of Heaven and Hell* (1790), earlier detectable in 'Ed's Babe' (1992) (Duff 2021, p.76). Though far from the first musician to find inspiration in Blake's illustrated texts (Roberts

2016), Smith's life had pertinent parallels. Both spent much of their lives in distinct locales and found inspiration in supernatural experiences. These started in youth and were closely linked to their environment, with Blake recalling a vision of a tree filled with angels on Peckham Rye (Ackroyd 1996, p.23) whereas Smith remembers speaking in tongues on a childhood holiday to Rhyl (Middles & Smith 2003, p.29), and "saw a monster on the roof" near his Prestwich flat ('Psykick Dance Hall' 1979). Both Blake's reaction to industrialisation and Smith's to post-industrialisation embraced visionary E.S.P. as one aspect of a doggedly independent creative mind-set. They employed novel production methods, sometimes suffering accusations of madness from uncomprehending peers. Both negated critical opinion, while expressing hostility to more commercially accepted orthodox contemporaries. Blake dismissed Joshua Reynolds' "simulations" as overly literal products of a "vegetative eye" (Williams 1998, p.20), whereas Smith offered similarly quotable insults: see Kate Bush, Bono, Sonic Youth, Mumford and Sons, etc. (Serota 2018). Even in a final interview, Smith explained much contemporary pop echoed music from when he was fifteen, "like Ed Sheeran . . . a duff singer songwriter from the 70's you find in charity shops" (Wray 2018). His E.S.P. reinforced personal subjectivity and buttressed an ability to resist prevailing social and artistic convention. For Smith, this process of mediumship as cultural resistance unlocked a working space, liberating psychic territory within which to construct The Fall.

Regardless of Smith's original intention, our human capacity for pattern recognition and desire for narrative connections means that even after Smith's death in 2018, listeners have continued to discover novel cases of lyrical precognition in contemporary events. For example, in 'Shake Off' (1998), Mark sang "You will end up eyeball injecting with Domestos or household products." We might consider this to foreshadow Donald Trump implying injecting disinfectant may cure COVID-19 infection (Noor 2020). "The evil of calvary and cavalry," 'Blindness' (2005), offers another uncanny Trump prediction. During his second impeachment hearing, Trump's lawyer David Schoen argued a tweet inciting supporters to "bring the *cavalry*" to the Capitol was a misspelling of the less plausible instruction to "bring the *calvary*" (Zurcher 2021). Retrospective confirmation bias no doubt, yet uncannily Smith also asks "When's curfew over?" as if foreseeing the coronavirus pandemic restrictions of the era, many years in advance. All this could suggest Mark's predictions extend far into the future, in the mode of a latter-day Nostradamus. More pre-cog predictions are sure to be unearthed, laying encoded within Smith's lyrics. Perhaps Smith even predicted these predictions in The Fall's earliest days with the lines "When I'm dead and gone, my vibrations will live on," 'Psykick Dancehall' (1979).

OUTRO

A plethora of psychology research finds psychic phenomena cannot be substantiated and are simple coincidences deemed significant because of cognitive errors and bias. Social surveys indicate supernatural beliefs became less fashionable since the 1970s whereas conspiracy theories gained ground. Supernatural beliefs may be groundless, but we cannot dismiss their significance to The Fall. The pre-cognitive, possibly prophetic, aspect of the work has been emphasised by Smith, fans, family, musicians, biographers, and journalists, reinforcing Fall mythos, and resurfaces in hitherto unseen manifestations after his death. E.S.P. was personally significant to Mark E. Smith's worldview. At times he considered it as dangerous, seeking to close it out, while at best, Smith's precognition offered a creative strategy for assembling incongruent elements, allowing redefinition and reinvention, while strengthening rebuttal of expectation and categorisation. E.S.P. opened a transliminal subjective space for Smith's project: The Fall's own room to live. Smith's writing remains a rich repository from which fresh prophecies will emerge, offering new facts, both tenuous and compelling, as future listeners engage with the matter of The Fall.

> *Ghosts are rising, coming down, it's a return.*
> *He's coming backward . . . and spirit-like, new facts emerge.*
> —('Second House Now', 2017)

REFERENCES

Ackroyd, Peter. 1996. *Blake*. London: Minerva.
Annotated Fall. n.d. "The Annotated Lyrics." Last updated 3 November 2021. http://annotatedfall.doomby.com/pages/the-annotated-lyrics/.
Bacon, Francis. 1620. *The New Organon and Related Writings*. (Ed. Fulton H. Anderson 1960). New York: Liberal Arts Press.
———. 1628. *The Novum Organon: Or a True Guide to the Interpretation of Nature*. Translated by G. W. Kitchin 1855. Oxford: Oxford University Press.
BBC. 2007. Frank Skinner TV interview, *BBC Culture Show,* unedited version U-tube video, 57:30. March 2007. Accessed 15 April 2019.
BBC News. 2003. "Music fan Choked on Vomit." 20 November 2003. http://news.bbc.co.uk/1/hi/england/3224860.stm.
Belfast Telegraph. 1982. "The Waite Way: Terry Faces the Cameras." 7 August 1982. https://www.britishnewspaperarchive.co.uk.
Blackmore, Susan. 1992. "Psychic Experiences: Psychic Illusions." *Skeptical Inquirer* 16: 367–76.

Blackmore, Susan, and Tom Trościanko. 1985. "Belief in the Paranormal: Probability Judgements, Illusory Control, and the "Chance Baseline Shift." *British Journal of Psychology* 76(4): 459–68. doi:10.1111/j.2044-8295.1985.tb01969.
Blake, William. 1790. *The Marriage of Heaven and Hell*. (*William Blake: The Complete Illuminated Books*. Ed David Bindman 2001). London: Thames and Hudson.
———. 1804. *Milton a Poem*. (William Blake: The Complete Illuminated Books. Ed David Bindman 2001). London: Thames and Hudson.
Bracewell, Michael, and John Wilde. 1992. "Mark E. Smith." *Frieze* 4.9.92.
Bramah, Martin. 2016. *The Story of Dragnet*. http://thefall.org/news/pics/MartinBramahsStoryofDragnet.pdf.
———. 2019. "Album By Album: The Fall." *Uncut*, July 2019: 92–94.
Braswell, Gregory S., Karl S. Rosengren, and Howard Berenbaum. 2012. "Gravity, God and Ghosts? Parents' Beliefs in Science, Religion, and the Paranormal and the Encouragement of Beliefs in Their Children." *International Journal of Behavioral Development* 36(2): 99–106.
Bressan, Paolo. 2002. "The Connection between Random Sequences, Everyday Coincidences, and Belief in the Paranormal." *Applied Cognitive Psychology* 16(1): 17–34. doi:10.1002/acp.754.
Channel 4. 1986. Jools Holland TV interview with Mark E. Smith. *The Tube*. 5 December, 1986. Video, 3:05. https://www.youtube.com/watch?v=efeSo884qDA.
Collings, Austin. 2021. *Gods Fox—Don Montgomery*. London: Pariah Press.
Crosthwaite, Paul. 2016. "Trauma and Degeneration: Joy Division and Pop Criticism's Imaginative Historicism." In R. Carroll and A. Hansen (eds.), *LitPop: Writing and Popular Music*, 125–40. Farnham: Ashgate.
Deleuze, Gilles, and Félix Guattari. 1977. *Anti-Oedipus: Capitalism and Schizophrenia*. Translated by Robert Hurley, Mark Seem, and Helen R. Lane. New York: Viking.
Dick, Philip. K. 1959. *Time Out of Joint*. Philadelphia: Lippincott.
———. 1977. *A Scanner Darkly*. New York: Doubleday.
Duff, Graham. 2021. *The Future's Here To Stay*. London: Strange Attractor Press.
Easlea, Daryl. 2010. *The Wonderful and Frightening World of The Fall—Omnibus Edition*. Sleeve notes BBQCD2066.
———. 2019. *Bend Sinister: The Domesday Pay-off Triad*. Sleeve notes BBQ2153CD.
Evrard, Renaud. 2014. "From Symptom to Difference: 'Hearing Voices' and Exceptional Experiences." *Journal of the Society for Psychical Research* 78(3): 129–48.
Fall Online Forum. n.d. "Precogs of Mark E. Smith." Last updated 23 May 2020. https://www.tapatalk.com/groups/thefall/pre-cogs-of-mark-e-smith-t30657.html.
Fisher, Mark. 2006. *Memorex for the Krakens*. 8 May 2006. http://k-punk.abstractdynamics.org/archives/007759.html.
Ford, Simon. 2003. *Hip Priest: The Story of Mark E. Smith and The Fall*. London: Quartet.
Gallup. 2005. "Three in Four Americans Believe in Paranormal." https://news.gallup.com/poll/16915/Three-Four-Americans-Believe-Paranormal.aspx.
Gecewicz, Claire. 2018. *'New Age' Beliefs Common among both Religious and Non-religious Americans*. https://www.pewresearch.org/fact-tank/2018/10/01/new-age-beliefs-common-among-both-religious-and-nonreligious-americans/.

Goddard, Michael and Benjamin Halligan, eds. 2010. *Mark E. Smith and The Fall: Art, Music and Politics*. Farnham: Ashgate.

Gray, Stephen J., and David A. Gallo. 2016. "Paranormal Psychic Believers and Sceptics: A Large-Scale Test of the Cognitive Differences Hypothesis." *Memory & Cognition* 44(2): 242–61.

Guardian. 1985. "Dangerous Mission for Terry Waite." *Guardian*, 15 November 1985. https://www.theguardian.com/theguardian/2013/nov/15/terry-waite-hostage-beirut-lebanon.

Haraldsson, Erlendur. 1985. "Representative National Surveys of Psychic Phenomena: Iceland, Great Britain, Sweden, USA and Gallup's Multinational Survey." *Journal of the Society for Psychical Research* 53: 145–58.

Herrington, Tony. 1996. "Mancunian Candidate." *The Wire*, September 151: 26–31.

Houtkooper, Joop M., and Erlendur Haraldsson. 1997. "Reliabilities and Psychological Correlates of Guessing and Scoring Behavior in a Forced-choice ESP Task." *Journal of Parapsychology* 61:119–34. http://dx.doi.org/10.1177/0165025411424088.

Johnson, Ben. 2018. "Helen Duncan, Scotland's Last Witch." Historic-UK.com, https://www.historic-uk.com/HistoryUK/HistoryofScotland/Helen-Duncan-Scotlands-Last-Witch/.

Josephson-Storm, Jason A. 2017. *The Myth of Disenchantment*. Chicago: University of Chicago Press.

Kaj, Riad. 1987. "A magazine Reported Friday that Hostage Negotiator Terry Waite . . .," United Press International Archives, 30 January 1987. https://upi.com/4562550.

Kaufman, Gil. 1998. "Fall Singer Arrested for Attacking Keyboardist Girlfriend." M.T.V. News, 4 October, 1998. https://www.mtv.com/news/151403/fall-singer-arrested-for-attacking-keyboardist-girlfriend/.

Lachman, Gary. 2014. *In Search of P. D. Ouspensky: The Genius in the Shadow of Gurdjieff*. Wheaton, IL: Quest.

Liverpool Echo. 1985. "Terry Waite, Holds Up Two Buckets to Symbolise the Search for Water in Sudan." 22 February 1985. https://www.britishnewspaperarchive.co.uk.

Lowe, Richard. 1987. "Crisp Smith." *LM*, January: 24–25. https://pitchandputtproductions.blogspot.com/2013/11/mark-e-smith-interview-from-1986.html.

Markovsky, Barry, and Shane R. Thye. 2001. "Social Influence on Paranormal Beliefs." *Sociological Perspectives* 44(1): 21–44. JSTOR, www.jstor.org/stable/10.1525/sop.2001.44.1.21.

Martin, Gavin. 1986. "I do always try to be nice." *New Musical Express*, 30 August 1986: 10–12.

Marvin, J. Neo. 1981. "The Fall (Unpublished, 1981)." http://jneomarvin.com/interviews-of-our-times/the-fall-unpublished-1981/.

Mattson, Mark P. 2014. "Superior Pattern Processing Is the Essence of the Evolved Human Brain." *Frontiers in Neuroscience* 8: 265. doi:10.3389/fnins.2014.00265.

Meyer, Werner T. 1986. "Zinc on the Move: Advancements in Coatings and Castings Keep the Metal Competitive." *SAE Transactions* 95: 826–34. www.jstor.org/stable/44725437.

Middles, Mick. 1987. "The North Will Rise." *Underground*, November: 22–23.

Middles, Mick, and Mark E. Smith. 2003. *The Fall*. London: Omnibus.

Mock, Geoffrey. 2009. "Synchronicity at Duke." *Duke Today*, 23 March 2009. https://today.duke.edu/2009/03/rhine.html.
New York Times. 2006. "Marcinkus, of Vatican Scandal, Dies." *New York Times*, 21 February 2006. https://www.nytimes.com/2006/02/21/world/europe/marcinkus-of-vatican-scandal-dies.html.
Newcastle Journal. 1980. "Iran Mercy Flight Hope." 27 December 1980. https://www.britishnewspaperarchive.co.uk.
———. 1985. "New Cyclone Fear." 30 May 1985. https://www.britishnewspaperarchive.co.uk.
News of the World. 1997. "Diana Dead." 31 August 1997: 1.
Noor, Poppy. 2020. "'Please don't inject bleach': Trump's Wild Coronavirus Claims Prompt Disbelief." *Guardian*, 24 April 2020. https://www.theguardian.com/us-news/2020/apr/24/trump-disinfectant-bleach-coronavirus-claims-reaction.
Park, Crystal L. 2010. "Making Sense of the Meaning Literature: An Integrative Review of Meaning Making and Its Effects on Adjustment to Stressful Life Events." *Psychological Bulletin* 136(2): 257–301. doi:10.1037/a0018301.
Pauwels, Louis, and Jacques Bergier. 1971. *The Morning of the Magicians*. Translated by Rollo Myers. St. Albans: Mayflower (Granada).
Poulou, Elena. 2021. "My Television Is Always On . . .," in Mark E. Smith and Graham Duff *The Otherwise*. London: Strange Attractor Press.
Powers, Albert R. 3rd, Megan S. Kelley, and Phillip R. Corlett. 2017. "Varieties of Voice-Hearing: Psychics and the Psychosis Continuum." *Schizophrenia Bulletin* 43(1): 84–98.
Reading Evening Post. 1985. "Waite Helps Drug Charge Yachtsman." 2 April 1985. https://www.britishnewspaperarchive.co.uk.
Reformation Post, The Pseud Mag. n.d. "Terry Waite Sez." Accessed 27 November 2021. https://sites.google.com/site/reformationposttpm/fall-tracks/terry-waite-sez.
Roberts, Chris. 2016. "William Blake: His Influence on Rock Musicians." *Louder Than War*, https://louderthanwar.com/william-blake-his-influence-on-rock-musicians/ [published 28th July 2016; accessed 27.11.21].
Schmeidler, Gertrude R. 1945. "Separating the sheep from the goats." *Journal of the American Society for Psychical Research* 39: 47–49.
Serota, Maggie. 2018. "Mark E. Smith's Best Insults". *Spin Magazine*, 24 January 2018. https://www.spin.com/2018/01/mark-e-smiths-best-insults/.
Simpson, Dave. 2009. *The Fallen*. Edinburgh: Canongate.
Sinker, Mark. 2001. "Cardinal R. Totale's Scrapbook." In *Excavate! The Wonderful and Frightening World of The Fall*, ed. Tessa Norton and Bob Stanley, 2021: 187–204. London: Faber.
Smith, Mark E. 1986. "Heroes, part I: His Influences." *Melody Maker*, 27 September 1986: 33.
Smith, Mark E, and Austin Collings. 2009. *Renegade, The Lives and Tales of M. E. Smith*. London: Penguin.
Smith, Odran. 2009. "The Fall Online—Fall News." 30 December 2009. https://thefall.org/news/2009-12-30.html.
Smith-Start, Brix. 2016. *The Rise, The Fall, and The Rise*. London: Faber.

Sunday Mirror. 1997. "Diana Dead." 31 August 1997: 1.
Thalbourne, Michael A., and Peter S. Delin. 1994. "A Common Thread Underlying Belief in the Paranormal, Creative Personality, Mystical Experience and Psychopathology." *Journal of Parapsychology* 58(1): 3–38.
Thompson, Dave. 2003. *A User's Guide to The Fall*. London: Helter Skelter.
Van Prooijen, Jan-Willem, Karen. M. Douglas, and Clara De Inocencio. 2018. "Connecting the Dots: Illusory Pattern Perception Predicts Belief in Conspiracies and the Supernatural." *European Journal of Social Psychology* 48(3): 320–35. doi:10.1002/ejsp.2331.
Waite, Terry. 1993. *Taken on Trust*. London: Hodder and Stoughton.
Whitson, Jennifer A., and Adam D. Galinsky. 2008. "Lacking Control Increases Illusory Pattern Perception." *Science* 322, 5898, 115–17. doi:10.1126/science.1159845.
Wilkinson, Roy. 1988. "The Bug.Eyed Pop Goblin." *Sounds*, 2 January 1988: 12–14.
Williams, Nicholas M. 1998. *Ideology and Utopia in the Poetry of William Blake*. Cambridge: Cambridge University Press.
Wiseman, Richard, and Caroline Watt. 2006. "Belief in Psychic Ability and the Misattribution Hypothesis: A Qualitative Review." *British Journal of Psychology* 97(Pt 3): 323–38.
Wooffitt, Robin, and Simon Allistone. 2005. "Towards a Discursive Parapsychology: Language and the Laboratory Study of Anomalous Communication." *Theory & Psychology* 15(3). doi:10.1177/0959354305053218.
Wray, Daniel D. 2018. "Mark E. Smith—the Final Interview: 'I can clear a pub when I want to.'" *The Guardian*, 25 January 2018. https://www.theguardian.com/music/2018/jan/24/final-interview-with-mark-e-smith-the-fall-people-still-cross-the-road-from-me.
Wright, Mic. 2019. "Remembering Mark E. Smith: The Complicated Politics of The Fall's Genius Leader." *The New European*, 24 January 2019. https://www.theneweuropean.co.uk/brexit-news-remembering-mark-e-smith-the-fall-s-genius-leade-40742/.
Wright, Peter. 1987. *Spycatcher*. Victoria, Australia: Heinemann.
Yallop, David. 1984. *In God's Name: An Investigation into the Murder of Pope John Paul I*. London: Jonathan Cape.
Zurcher, Anthony. 2021. "Trump Impeachment: Key Takeaways from Defence Case." *The Guardian*, 12 February 2021. https://www.bbc.co.uk/news/world-us-canada-56048654.

Chapter Five

'You can leave me on the shelf'
The Death of The Fall and Mark E. Smith
Martin Myers

"IS IT ALRIGHT IF I SPLIT?" (SMITH, 1994)

The death of Mark E. Smith, lead singer of The Fall on January 24, 2018, was largely anticipated by fans. Whilst the precise details of his deteriorating health were not made public, the evidence of his physical condition was readily apparent throughout the group's 2017 performances. In addition, many scheduled events were cancelled at the last minute including an American tour.

In a strange turn of events, Smith's death had been over-anticipated by the BBC the previous year, when his passing was prematurely announced on his sixtieth birthday. The BBC Music twitter feed tweeting a photograph of a suitably dour-looking Smith and the message 'RIP Mark E. Smith' accompanied by a sad-faced emoji (@bbcmusic 2017a). Realising their mistake, a second tweet appeared an hour or so later with the same photograph and an updated, upbeat message 'Happy 60th Mark E. Smith', this time accompanied by an altogether more celebratory party popper emoji (@bbcmusic 2017b) (fig. 5.1). Inevitably, the BBC's gaffe caused a degree of hilarity among Fall fans at the time, one that was hopefully also shared by The Fall and Smith himself. Whilst Smith is not the only celebrity to have their passing announced before their actual death and it seems unlikely he personally was the origin for the BBC's inaccurate tweet, this particular chain of events felt very much as though it was another typical moment in The Fall's narrative.

Smith's presumptive death notice echoed earlier occasions when Smith and The Fall seem to align with strange and uncomfortable events, and these often appear intrinsic to their body of creative work. It falls within a consistent pattern of sometimes well-documented, sometimes anecdotal

Figure 5.1. @bbcmusic tweets on Mark E. Smith's 60th Birthday

events that over time have assumed the status of a well-rehearsed folklore of Smith and The Fall. Very often, these moments are framed within a broadly humorous understanding of Smith's outrageousness: sacking studio engineers for ordering a salad, or being investigated by the Royal Society for the Prevention of Cruelty to Animals for attacking squirrels with a 'professional set of hedge-clippers' (Greenhill 2008; *M.E.N.* 2010; Schonfeld 2018). On other occasions they may be related to darker themes within numerous accounts of his psychic powers[1] (Ford 2003; Smith 2008; Goddard and Halligan 2010). Beyond being funny or unsettling, these accounts also identify Smith's agency with his seemingly deliberate generation of discomfort, amongst musicians in the group, with journalists, record labels, and within his body of work, as a form of practice.

The misreporting of his death was simply another instance in which The Fall, and Smith in particular, navigated around and generated a succession of such moments of discomfort. The timing of his death following a clearly traumatic year dealing with illness intensifying the sense of the BBC's bad taste. Unlike moments that appeared deliberately conceived by Smith, the death notice appeared to be an unplanned occurrence. Sitting within the anticipated world of The Fall, the forms of discomfort it mirrored signal overlaps of *heimlich*, 'the homely', and *unheimlich*, 'the unhomely', identified by Freud (2003) in his essay *The Uncanny*. In Freud's account the alignment of unhomely circumstances rooted within understandings of homeliness are identified in multiple contexts including language, behaviours, folktales, and personal recollections. In all cases, he argues that a particular form of frightening experience emerges because it is linked to what is well known, domestic, and homely. This chapter draws upon Georg Simmel's account of the *stranger* (Simmel, 1971; Myers 2010) to locate The Fall and Smith's presence within the music industry as a particular form of outsider producing uncomfortable work in which the local, domestic setting is deliberately deployed to enhance and intensify the work's discomfort. Simmel's *stranger* is a figure readily recognisable within local settings but somehow simultaneously a representative of a distant, unimaginable, and alien culture. Smith and The Fall often appeared bound by a localised White, working-class culture, geographically situated within a handful of streets and pubs in Prestwich. Despite drawing upon this local knowledge to produce an intelligent and literate counter-narrative to the 'high' culture of metropolitan elites, they also dallied with the cultural production techniques of these same elites; for example, happily engaging in modern ballet or avant-garde theatrical productions[2]. Smith often appeared to deploy such ambiguities as a strategy to produce an unsettling, often antagonistic body of work that retained the capability to unsettle fans' expectations and generate discomfort. By doing so, drawing upon the potential for exaggerating Simmel's account of the stranger (Myers 2015), as a creative process. It is potentially within those discordant features of unsettling or unexpected narratives, that the attraction of The Fall was most consistently maintained. From the most banal perspective, The Fall were rarely boring; more significantly fans found themselves drawn into a distorted, though disturbingly, real version of the world. In this sense, Freud's account of the uncanny also has a particular resonance identifying an underlying account of particular forms of fear as central to Smith's vision(s); and perhaps more disturbingly the impression they happened spontaneously (as in the BBC tweet) around The Fall.

Smith's death, like the death of any celebrity, has the potential to confirm, derail, or transform the pre-existing narrative of their life's work (Braudy 1997; Barry 2008; Rojek 2001, 2012). In Smith's case this intertwines both his personal reputation and life history with that of The Fall and the extensive body of work produced by the group. It raises the spectre of whether The Fall are/were a collective entity, a fractured collective entity, or a singular project masterminded by Smith. When Smith passed away, did The Fall also pass away, and if so, what is left behind? The chapter explores the significance and impact of Smith's death by posing a new question: What does the death of the *stranger* look like?

'YOU DON'T BREAK RULES, YOU DON'T FOLLOW THEM'

The Fall's last gig in November 2017 at the Queen Margaret Union (QMU), Glasgow, saw Smith wheelchair bound and clearly very ill but still committed to delivering a type of performance that fell within expectations of The Fall. The first song, 'Wolf Kidult Man', opened with just the group onstage and Smith physically absent but singing in the wings. Smith appeared midway through the song in a wheelchair lifted to the stage; his partner, Pamela Vander, then wheeled him to the front of the stage from where he continued to perform. One reviewer noted 'a swirling of sorrow and admiration' in the mixed emotions of fans encountering Smith, whose body was bloated and constrained within a wheelchair and a sling, but concluded, 'he is demonstrating courage and commitment to his work; these shows should not be regretted as a tragic spectacle but cherished as portraits of defiance and endurance' (Ross 2017, p.17). This commitment was evident in Smith's last public message to his fans apologizing for the last-minute cancellation of a subsequent gig in Bristol, which he blamed on his personal desire, against advice and against the odds, to continue performing (Smith 2018).

The QMU performance and other 2017 performances revealed much of Smith's personal ambivalence towards working within the music industry. On the one hand, he was the epitome of a rock-legend, seemingly determined to die on the road with his boots on; and yet at the same time, these gigs were like many other Fall gigs with little or no acknowledgement of the audience or their obvious appreciation and adulation of the man and the music. The fragility of Smith's body throughout 2017 seemed both indicative of his mental strength in the face of illness, but also something matter of fact and barely worth a mention. It was not the first time, for example, that Smith performed in a wheelchair; in 2009, following a hip injury he also took to the stage in a wheelchair. Fall performances have consistently established themselves in a context of ordinary work-a-day events (the group wearing the same clothes onstage and off, for example [Edge 1989]), and at the same time as intense outpourings of creativity.

The QMU performance highlighted how despite maintaining a distance from the music industry, Smith (inevitably, given his entire adult life has been spent working within that industry) is adept at performing rituals that suggest a *habitus* closely aligned within its field (Bourdieu and Wacquant 1992). Bourdieu's alignment of relationships between individual characteristics, traits, and learned behaviours (*habitus*); the rules within which social spaces operate and organize themselves (field); and the resources available and economies in which to compete for their acquisition (different forms of capitals) present possibly the most convincing sociological account of the dynamics between individual agency and social structuring. Smith seemingly (and particularly noticeably in the context of his celebrity death) unpicks elements of these relationships.

The collective and social nature of Smith and The Fall, of individual singer and individual musicians, emerges in the relational spaces of the personal within 'social practices and representations, or fields as they present themselves in the form of realities perceived and appreciated' (Bourdieu and Wacquant 1992, p.127). Field in the circumstances of the QMU gig might be considered a range of related but also discrete, potential fields including the 'music industry', 'The Fall', and also more specifically the 'dying celebrity performance'. Within each field it often appears Smith does not play by the rules of the field. This might appear within behaviors that work against the accumulation of useful forms of capital (deliberately producing work that derails easier access to economic capital or alienating social relationships within his social networks). It is also apparent in some of The Fall's appropriation of cultural capital outside or beyond the necessities of performing the role of a White, working-class group from the north of England, a role Smith never relinquished. So, for example, the production of work that falls within a register of high cultural capital (*avant-garde* plays produced within elite metropolitan art spaces or work within the field of modern ballet, for example) appears contrary to both the regime of successful practice of The Fall and simultaneously not a transformative development of standing or status. Smith and The Fall can obviously, and should, be read as an intellectual project that transgresses the rules and boundaries of working-class cultural production. In doing so, clearly sticking two fingers up to the intellectual limitations of the middle-class and middle-class cultural production. However, this leaves open the question of why bother? The energy expended in competing for and acquiring capital, particularly cultural capital, seems to be wasted in terms of value if it is not being transferred into a broader strategy of advancement such as acquiring greater economic capital or status. Whilst this could be understood within a Bourdieusian framework as unacknowledged complicity within a dynamic range of behaviours in which agency is severely restricted by the social structure (Bourdieu 1990), this does not entirely add up. Another perspective is that Smith worked against the widely understood rules of social structure by reimagining the rules of the field. By doing so, producing work that sits at odds with its surroundings (work that in Bourdieu's [2007] sense might lead to an alternative iteration of *habitus clivé* as a breakdown or dislocation between individual habitus and environment). Practice that can be understood as unsettling because, in its echoes of Freud and Simmel, it locates distant forms of knowledge within local understandings. Unusually this appears apparent not just in the body of recorded work but also in Smith's 'practical mastery' (Bourdieu 1990) of the day-to-day physical activities of the group such as live performances.

Smith's own performing rituals may appear odd in comparison to many performers who are in the position to draw upon a back catalogue of forty years of work; but the performances suggest a practiced repetition of actions. This has been a feature of live performances which were consistently framed within a pattern of recognisable rhythms and traits including often delayed starts; set lists based around the most current releases and little regard for performing the greatest 'hits'; Smith performing with his back turned or from off-stage; both little direct acknowledgement of the audience but matched by open invitations to participate by passing a microphone to audience members; a lot of microphone 'business' including Smith using multiple microphones seemingly chosen and discarded at random; two microphones used simultaneously; trails of microphone leads strewn across the stage in a random spider-web following Smith's onstage manoeuvres; and finally, what Eleni Poulou described as 'live mixing' (BBC 2005), that is much fiddling with the onstage amplifier settings of musicians during performances.

Performances by The Fall therefore remain distinctive, which we might anticipate with any performer who maintains a long-standing presence, but they also maintained an everyday workman-like quality. They were events within industry standards but often falling short of industry expectations. The delayed starts both building expectation but also winding up less happy tensions, the sense of an iconic performer subdued by a lack of direct engagement or even willingness to appear onstage[3]. Within these ambivalent moments of the relational context of Smith's work within the field of the music industry, it becomes apparent that whilst that relationship is maintained over time, it is also founded on Smith's own abilities to act as grist. In this sense, the rules of the field are actively challenged, even if they are only being shaped within a wider over-arching context in which the music industry adapts and works in relation to an individual performer.

The last song on The Fall's final album, 'Nine Out of Ten', hints at an attitude in which Smith's approach makes sense and, perhaps against the grain of The Fall adopting industry standards, harks back to Smith's own intellectual project. As noted by 'The Annotated Fall' website, the lyric 'you don't break rules, you don't follow them' echoes a reference to William Blake (see also chapter 11 by Kieran Cashell in this volume), one that appeared almost forty years previously in 'Before the Moon Falls':

> I must create a new regime or live by another man's
> Before the moon falls
> Before the moon falls
> I must create a new scheme and get out of others' hands
> Before the moon falls
>
> ('Before the Moon Falls', *Dragnet* 1979)

Both songs suggest a minor theft, borrowing, or adaptation of Blake's description of Los, slave-driving his Spectre to build a New Jerusalem in the shape of an aesthetic London:

I must Create a System or be enslv'd by another Man's.
I will not Reason & Compare: my business is to Create.

(Blake 1966, p.629)

Los representing the 'human imagination working, against great impediments, in the world of time and space' (Essick 2003, p.259) and the Spectre being workman-like but having antagonistic qualities including skills and dispositions, social networks, and materials for production necessary for the generation of creative work. However, the ability to create and the conditions in which that might occur are simultaneously intertwined with 'the resistance of matter to mind and personal entanglements that thwart creative acts. The "othering" or reification of the Spectre and his assumption of an independent will shifts him from the productive to the destructive ends of these spectra' (Essick 2003, p.259). The Spectre appears as a useful flagship for the agentic individual unwilling to be subsumed within an overwhelming structure.

Smith's creative energies seem directed not at breaking the rules, but rather at reimagining rules in which his creative work is produced. His is a *habitus* pushing against, but also engaged and complicit within its social world. It is not that The Fall have to somehow challenge the expectations of the music industry; that would be a waste of energy that could be better focused on producing another form of industry. Whilst it is often stated, and seems obvious, that Smith maintained his distance from the mainstream of the music industry, he also consistently generates distance between The Fall and other alternative or independent challengers to the mainstream. The Fall's creative output consequently belongs in a creative space produced by themselves. It avoids competition because it never sits in direct comparison to other artists. It simultaneously avoids being immediately recognizable by other agents within the industry despite Smith's performance of comparable behaviours and traits that do clearly belong there. The QMU performance is one in which Smith remains ever the workman-like creator of a brand of rock music within the rules of its own making. The exceptional circumstances of his extreme ill-health highlight much of the recognisability of the process and also his difference from other musicians. Within the context of live performances, Smith creates moments that echo the role of the stranger; he is both representative of something from far away and bound by its own rules whilst also at ease with the local conventions. It is worth noting The Fall's solid work-rate, touring every year in the UK and abroad throughout their career. As an outsider, Smith brought his work into play and into the local context of the stage all the time.

'THE DEAD CANNOT CONTRADICT, SOMETIMES THE LIVING CANNOT.' ('NEW FACE IN HELL')

A little over two months after the QMU gig, the news broke that Mark Smith had passed away. His death sparked a wide range of media interest and he possibly appeared to be a larger celebrity at that moment than previously in his lifetime. With time, however, that interest waned, leaving a new space open in which the memory of Smith would begin to assume its new post-Smith context.

A number of common tropes have been identified in understandings of celebrities, and the narrative arcs of their careers, and these are often cemented in the public reaction to their deaths. One commonplace narrative is that of witnessing celebrity destroyed, in particular the investment in supporting the rise to success of a celebrity that later turns in on itself with an equal or greater force following the celebrity's fall from grace (Braudy 1997; Wenner 2013). Variations on a theme include the sports narrative in which 'either a road to sporting success or a road to redemption [follow] a fall from grace and a problematic period in a celebrity's sporting life' (Palmer 2016, p.169). The arc of a rise and fall of a celebrity can also be confused within broader social identarian politics. C. Brick (2021) notes how the White, middle-class perspective of *Guardian* journalism created a specifically racially orientated context in which to lambast Kanye West's fall from grace for supporting Donald Trump. Similarly, M. Williamson (2010) identifies the different expectations accorded celebrities dependent on their gender and the consequent impact that has on their fall from grace.

The impact of death on a celebrity reputation is significant in part because it is a moment in which there is a literal fall from grace in which 'the dead cannot contradict' ('New Face in Hell'). E. Barry (2008) suggests that death opens up the likelihood of a number of possibilities, which like the narratives of rise and fall, seem programmed into public expectations of how celebrity deaths are framed within obituaries and other posthumous accounts. These include the granting of a 'lasting fame' and/or a focus on the ordinariness or lack of exceptionality that underscored the *real* lives of dead personalities. At its most extreme, C. Rojek describes 'celebrity supernova' as 'the death of an individual whose fame is so immense that their existence frames the character of the age' (2012, p.1). One such celebrity supernova, the death of Michael Jackson, highlights the impact death has on reputation. The singer's long-standing sullied reputation began an immediate rehabilitation, reimagined as an 'overwhelmingly positive image of Jackson as an irreplaceable superstar, a loving father, an admirable humanitarian and, in jaw-dropping irony, one of the greatest victims of media muckraking and character assassination' (Rojek 2012, p.7).

Placing The Fall within the patterns of celebrity behaviours and outcomes is problematic; it could feasibly be argued Smith was not even a celebrity as such. Comparable examples within the temporal, geographical, and music industry landscapes of Smith and The Fall might include the untimely death of Ian Curtis and his sanctification within Manchester music lore (Curtis 2005; Middles and Reade 2009) or the radio DJ John Peel whose death sparked an extraordinary outpouring of collective grief in which Peel's frankly quite extraordinary narrative arc was often reduced to his domestic status as a 'national treasure' (Stonehouse 2004, p.31) or 'Grumpy Old Man' (BBC 2004). Smith's death has clearly not been accorded the status of 'celebrity supernova', but a consequential reimagination of his reputation seems a potential outcome of the revaluation of his work. On past evidence this is likely to be driven by the reductionist tendencies of the media when it comes to describing Smith, The Fall, and their output within a handful of neat *clichés*. This was neatly satirized in 'The Fall Press Kit: a resource for bastard lazy journalists', which identified a handful of tropes and key words that could be randomly slotted into any article about The Fall ('cantankerous', 'sacked musicians', 'Granny on bongos', etc). Noticeably this is a trend that has multiplied and mutated with more media interest and even academic scholarship (Bewes 2018; Wilkinson 2020). It will prove difficult not to pick up any text on The Fall in the future that does not also refer to 'autodidact', 'football management', 'always the same always . . .', and so on. The *clichés* admittedly flag up some truths, but it will be disappointing if the last word on what The Fall were was mired in the vernacular of media accounts that have essentially remained unchanged in over thirty years.

Smith's death should possibly be understood differently to many of the classic tropes of narrative arcs of celebrity or the consequences of death. Specifically, The Fall have often appeared not to follow a narrative arc as such. Whilst their musical career included consistent appreciation of their artistic endeavour, this was often against a backdrop of equally consistent criticism. A case could be made to suggest their commerciality peaked in the mid-1980s; and, although it could be argued Smith personally stepped in to undermine such success and hence almost fulfill the narrative of a rise and fall, this tends not to ring true. The Fall simply carried on with their work, suggesting their progress can be understood in a more linear fashion. They continued to produce work, to play gigs, to attract attention, to please some fans and lose others as the ongoing regime. The lows, commercial, artistic, and personal, were generally ridden out; similarly commercial and artistic highs seemed often slightly sidelined as another moment in the narrative rather than the culmination of success. In part this appears connected to another characteristic of The Fall: their longevity.

The Fall, unusually in comparison to many other bands of the same age, never officially disbanded or even unofficially spent time in a hiatus. This tends to re-emphasise the absence of troughs and peaks in their career. There was never a need for The Fall to be rediscovered because they never go away. In part the reformation of bands with more striking narratives of a rise and fall is often premised on the basis of reselling their 'hits', that is, of returning to a moment in which they were at their most successful. One striking observation of The Fall's commercial practice has been the tendency to never rely on playing their hits (arguably Marc Riley broke with the band for precisely this anti-commercial stance [Ford 2003]). Against the trends of other artists with a significant back catalogue, The Fall did not come onstage with a view to playing the entirety of a most successful or most well-loved album. One rare, overt attempt at such a commercially orientated approach seemingly appeared in the 2002 Blackburn gig recorded for a DVD release (*A Touch Sensitive*), which despite including genuine 'hits' ('Victoria', 'Telephone Thing', 'Hit the North') was amply padded out with less well-known material of the time ('Two Librans', 'Cyber Insekt', 'Bourgeois Town') and material that although probably popular with long-standing fans did not necessarily broaden their appeal ('To Nkroachment Yarbles', 'Mere Pseud Mag. Ed.').

The distance between The Fall and other musicians is reflected in an ambivalent relationship to geographical space. Smith has stated, 'I'm not a particular patriot', whilst in the same breath suggesting bands should, but often tend not, to be 'true to their roots' ('Perverted by Language bis', 1983). This ambivalence between an attachment to the local and a distancing from geographical belonging has been at the heart of the strangeness that characterizes The Fall (Myers 2010). It can be understood in terms of Simmel's *stranger* with the freighting of distant forms of knowledge (cultural capital that does not belong or psychic knowledge from an unknown realm, for example) in terms of a local landscape. Despite being local, Smith and The Fall represent themselves also as alien and distant. The same patterns of overlaying the alien within the local highlights the troubling, unsettling form of fear associated with Freud's account of the 'uncanny' (Freud 2003; Fisher 2016). Despite seemingly emerging from similar backgrounds or sharing characteristics that might align with other bands or other musicians, there has often appeared to be a consistent and deliberate policy of unsettling such connections. Their initial appearance as an entity could easily be framed within canonical accounts of the 1970s Manchester music scene in which a handful of like-minded outsiders and visionaries attended the Sex Pistols' 1976 gigs at the Lesser Free Trade Hall (Ford 2003; Witts 2010). These included the founding members of Joy Division and New Order (Peter Hook and Bernard Sumner), Morrissey and Mick Hucknall, Buzzcocks (who also played support at the second gig), and Tony Wilson founder of Factory Records.

Witts (2010) argues this mythologizing account has always over-egged the reality of a city in which a vibrant underground music scene was likely to produce significant musical offerings—a view confirmed in Paul Hanley's (2017) discussion of events, groups, promoters, and recording studios that shaped the city's music production. It also places too great an emphasis on a single event causing a chain of events in which Factory Records revitalized the heart and soul of Manchester by means of a far-sighted strategy that recognized the cultural significance of Madchester and later Britpop. Significantly many of the major players have themselves made clear just how chaotic and unplanned Factory's business plans were. Smith (2008) meanwhile has actively downplayed the significance of the Pistols gig and broadly distanced himself from the scenes engendered by its spectators. Noticeably, The Fall never signed to Factory and with the exception of a videotape released on the Factory subsidiary Ikon ('Perverted by Language bis') did not release any product through the label. More generally The Fall have seemed broadly uncomfortable with the labels that tended to be assigned to their peers in the mid-1970s including contemporaneous nomenclature such as 'punk' or 'new wave' and later reimagining's such as 'post-punk' or 'indie' (Smith 2008). The various categories that might include The Fall within a broad homogenous grouping of the local (a Manchester band) or like-minded collective (post-punks) are actively sidelined. The rules of social solidarity and fitting-in are actively ignored in favour of making up new rules; pushing against the field of the Manchester Music Scene or the field of the UK Music Industry reflecting the same desire to reinvent the rules of creation.

One example of The Fall's characteristic push against social solidarity can be seen in the reaction to the narrative that they are a 'John Peel' band, specifically that The Fall were Peel's favourite band. Following Peel's death, many musicians and non-musicians were drawn into the social practices associated with venerating a well-loved celebrity. Smith disappointed some viewers anticipating The Fall would be part of the veneration of Peel when he and Michael Bradley of the Undertones were interviewed by Gavin Esler following Peel's death. Bradley and Smith are obvious candidates for such an interview because of their work within Peel's two favourite groups, both of which were actively supported in his broadcasting career. Smith's comments about Peel have regularly noted how little contact they had over the years and, when called upon by Newsnight to comment upon the deejay's demise, Smith immediately restates this whilst delivering a chaotic, unsentimental, and obtuse piece to camera (BBC 2004). The appearance of Smith on Newsnight was both necessary because of the DJ's well-known pronouncements about how significant The Fall were in his eyes but also engendered another typical moment of discomfort. The death of Peel played out across the media in a reverential way that identified Peel's iconic, well-loved national profile, one that intensified as presenter of the regular BBC Radio 4 Saturday morning programme, *Home Truths*, in which ordinary people recounted extraordinary stories about their lives and experiences. Smith gurning to camera (he later noted this was caused by problems with false teeth and the BBC's confusing audio links via an earpiece [Smith 2008]) suggests he and Peel kept themselves at 'arms distance' and notes that he admired Peel for that approach and his 'objectivity'. It is an approach that falls outside of the traditions of commenting on a recently deceased celebrity, national treasures underscored by a final, slightly combative challenge to Mark Esler: 'OK. Am I allowed to speak now?' Esler is running with the expectations of celebrating the nations' favourite DJ, but Smith is doing something else. Despite some of the perceptions of his performance, it does seem apparent that he is making no attempt to be disrespectful about Peel but rather simply providing an honest account of their relationship that does not embellish his feelings out of respect for the recent death of the DJ. It seems likely that Smith would fully understand the expectations of this moment but played the interview out instead within his own rules.

Understanding the Fall's sense of otherness, Fisher equates a moment of The Fall's output to the production of work that falls within understandings of the grotesque and the weird (Fisher 2010, 2016). In particular Fisher extracts the technical specifics of what constitutes the weird and the eery from Freud's (2003) essay *Das Unheimliche*, or, The Unhomely. Whilst Freud endlessly folds together his diverse evidence of what constitutes the unhomely back into the essay, forcing the reader to immerse within a literary sense of the unhomely; Fisher precisely draws out differences. In this analysis Fisher's timeline of The Fall's 'greatest work' (Fisher 2010, p.95) beginning with 'Specter vs. Rector' from the 1979 album *Dragnet* and concluding with 'Hex Enduction Hour' in 1982 is presented as evidence of the grotesque and the weird. Fisher highlights the out-of-placeness of The Fall's output at the time evidenced in their sonic soundscapes; the mad, disjointed narratives of Smith's work; and also in the crude and disturbing artwork from records. In this analysis The Fall's otherness is framed in their (and potentially their audience's) 'fascination for the outside, for that which lies beyond standard perception, cognition and experience' (Fisher 2016, p.8).

Where Fisher's account seems questionable is firstly in the significance accorded a compressed moment in time; the usefulness of the period 1979–1982 appears to be to identify a line of thought through which to unpack Freud's essay rather to understand The Fall. And, perhaps more significantly, the break with Freud's account of the *unheimlich*, in which there is a conflation of the meaning and sensation of the homely and the unhomely; discarded in order to reach a specific understanding of the weird and the grotesque. This seems to lose something in Freud's account of what constitutes the particular forms of the strange that he is interested in (i.e., the 'uncanny' or more accurately the unhomely, *unheimlich* in the original) and its clear resonance within work produced by The Fall in which there is a conflation of both aspects of the homely and the unhomely. Perhaps most noticeably when Freud moves away from the original discussion of the linguistic overlap between *heimlich* and *unheimlich* to discuss elements of folktales and stories he expends some effort in discussing the importance of repetitions and doubles in his understanding of what constitutes the strange. This obviously resonates with one canonical understanding of The Fall and Mark E. Smith in which their musical and conceptual roots are determined by 'repetition, repetition, repetition' ('Repetition', 1978). Though as Bewes (2018) notes, repetition is portrayed in a highly ambiguous context on the 1978 song and one that perhaps does not align with subsequent imaginings of The Fall's work. Bewes also notes that often it can be impossible in Smith's work, 'to distinguish the inflections of irony from those of earnestness within the same phrase' (2018, p.127).

"MY VIBES WILL LIVE ON": THE LOCAL AND DEATH

Some of the more immediate responses to Smith's death worked within the generative frameworks of The Fall's own output; in particular, the 'weird' quality identified by Fisher (2016) materialised in some local DIY tributes. Whilst fans responded to the deaths of George Michael or David Bowie with similar unplanned public shrines that drew upon collective memorializing, those for Smith appeared more personal, odder, and at one with the aesthetics of The Fall. They seemed less easily absorbed within a collective shared grief that might find an immediate, recognisability in the broader public imagination. Often, they made very specific references to the relationship between the local and something more alien. A handwritten notice gaffer-taped to the wall of Bargain Booze, a local off-licence, quoted Smith: 'I WROTE ABOUT WHAT WAS AROUND ME. BUT SOME PEOPLE ARE SO DAFT THEY DON'T UNDERSTAND THAT WRITING ABOUT PRESTWICH IS JUST AS VALID AS DANTE WRITING ABOUT HIS INFERNO' (fig. 5.2). A similar DIY approach was used when taping photographs of Smith to lampposts in Prestwich. At the same time, a stencil of Smith and the tagline 'This Nations Saving Grace' appeared on the Cheshire landmark, White Nancy, and on Twitter, singer-songwriter Badly Drawn Boy posted a photograph of Smith's false teeth (left in Badly Drawn Boy's car after he had been mistaken for Smith's taxi driver).

Mainstream media obituaries catalogued Smith's achievements within some well-established tropes including his 'unusual combination of poetic

Figure 5.2. Photograph posted on Twitter by @Orwell_fan_fan (Robert White)

sensibility and belligerence' (*The Telegraph* 2018); 'poet, satirist and misanthrope' (*The Guardian* 2018); 'working-class autodidact from Prestwich' (*New Statesman* 2018); and 'cranky, uncompromising genius' (*The Washington Post* 2018). In addition, almost all managed to squeeze in a reference to high staff turnovers, 'always different, always the same', the sacking of salad-eating studio engineers, sole permanent member and curmudgeonly. In terms of a narrative arc, Smith's death suggested something less momentous than a reimagining or reframing of his status; if anything, the linearity of The Fall seemed to be restated within the same readily identifiable *clichés* that have defined years of media coverage. Unlike the bestowal of lasting fame or sanctification of a star's ordinariness (Barry 2008), Smith's death in many ways seems to simply restate existing knowledge.

Finally, there has been a distinctly lackluster attempt to capitalise on The Fall as a commercial enterprise. This has included the release of multiple live CDs (largely freely available bootlegs); the publication of a scrapbook of Fall memorabilia (Norton and Stanley 2021); at least one cheaply edited, quickly thrown together, cash-in anthology of quotes (Anonymous 2018); at least one genuinely exceptional, brilliant memoir (Hanley 2019); and, a co-authored film script for an unmade horror film (Smith and Duff 2021).

The Fall always avoided the pitfall of becoming another old punk cabaret act, but this required Smith's discomfiting presence in the flesh. Following his death, a certain orthodoxy emerges in which The Fall are consumed less ambiguously; as discussed previously, the *clichés* reveal some truths. However, they also disguise the creative energies Smith deployed within The Fall and the deliberate generation of forms of discomfort that informed his body of work. The power of this discomfort in reality far exceeds the descriptions of 'curmudgeonliness' or 'belligerence' because, like Los in Jerusalem, Smith was engaging in the struggle to generate a creative body of work outside of the usual rules of engagement. The work trades on being able to replicate an alien vision of the world within a very local landscape. In many ways the particularity of this local landscape, the streets of Prestwich, for example, further exaggerates its strangeness in the eyes of metropolitan elites with an invested interested in the value of high cultural capital; not least because the metropolitan in this context is invariably London, not the northwest, not Manchester. Smith produced a body of work that constantly disturbed through its exaggerated strangeness. A further exaggeration can be unpicked within Smith's self-identification as local and rooted to a particular local geography, whilst at the same time he was a well-travelled global citizen clearly at ease in unfamiliar landscapes (Smith and Middles 2003). Walter Benjamin's description of the 'storyteller' echoes something of Simmel's stranger noting the potency of voices that are local and also those that are well travelled but suggesting the 'figure of the storyteller gets its full corporeality only for the one who can picture them both' (Benjamin 1986, p.84). The base materials of Smith's work (narratives, anecdotes, cut-and-pasted media, etc.) often appear alien and out of place as they are worked into more local contexts. In doing so, Smith endlessly replays accounts of the alien as local, the unhomely overlapping the homely. Unusually this seems not just to be a reflection of the body of his creative work but also a much broader swathe of all the activities around The Fall including live performances, business arrangements, and band management. In this respect, the death of Smith is also the death of The Fall; to maintain the unsettled set of relations in which the creative work can be produced requires the continuing struggle against the rules of the field. Without the presence of Smith, The Fall itself becomes defunct raising the question of whether the music, the creative output, maintains its value and potency if it is not being marshalled within the continuing routines of the group. Without Smith as a corporeal presence actively fostering the strangeness of The Fall, (e.g., without a new story emerging of Smith attacking squirrels with a 'professional set of hedge-clippers'), without the routines of live performances and regular record releases, what remains is the creative work without context. In some respects the death of the stranger is a moment of relief for the locals: they no longer are burdened by their discomfort or disturbed by an alien presence. More comforting, if the desire remains in place to view The Fall's output as disquieting and difficult, is Freud's mishmash of anecdotes and folktales embedding unhomely knowledge within a wider cultural framework? This suggests the sense in which the creative output becomes imbued with local and domestic knowledge embedded in shared cultural knowledge and still capable of being as unsettling as Mark Smith in the flesh. More generally though, new product and new writing about The Fall are unlikely to find much more than a dampened memory of what was strange and disturbing and exhilarating.

NOTES

1. One striking moment of the 2008 *Messing Up the Paintwork* conference at the University of Salford was the contribution by Alan Wise, long-time associate, promoter, and manager of The Fall. Wise suddenly appeared to falter during his descriptions of Smith's domestic life including the waft of Eleni Smith's soup-making permeating their home. He cut his talk short explaining he was under 'psychic attack' from Smith! (Wise 2008).

2. Smith's play *Hey! Luciani: The Times, Life and Codex of Albino Luciani* was performed at the Riverside Studios, Hammersmith, in December 1986. Starring Smith, The Fall, performance artist Leigh Bowery, and the ballet dancer Michael Clarke, the play revolves around a cryptic account of the death of Pope John Paul I. The Fall collaborated again with Michael Clarke in 1988 providing the music and performing in the avant-garde ballet *I Am Curious, Orange*. The ballet was performed at multiple venues including London's Sadler's Wells.

3. It is worth noting that Smith's initial off-stage vocals at the QMU gig was not a novel experience for fans of The Fall and not solely associated with health constraints; Smith would often wander backstage or behind a backdrop whilst continuing to sing.

REFERENCES

Anonymous (2018). *Messing Up the Paintwork: The Wit and Wisdom of Mark E. Smith*. London: Ebury Press.

Barry, E. (2008). From Epitaph to Obituary: Death and Celebrity in Eighteenth-Century British Culture. *International Journal of Cultural Studies*, 11(3), 259–75.

BBC (2004). John Peel: Obituary. http://news.bbc.co.uk/1/hi/entertainment/3955369.stm, accessed 26 October 2021.

BBC (2004). Newsnight. 25 October 2004.

BBC (2005). The Fall: The Wonderful and Frightening World of Mark E. Smith. 21 January 2005.

Benjamin, W. (1986). Illuminations (Vol. 241, No. 2). Random House Digital, Inc.

Bewes, T (2018). 'Mark E. Smith, 1957–2018'. *Radical Philosophy* 2.02.

Blake, W. (1966). *Collected Writings*. Oxford: Oxford University Press.

Bourdieu, P. (1990). *In Other Words: Essays towards a Reflexive Sociology*. Stanford, CA: Stanford University Press.

Bourdieu, P. (2007). *Sketch for a Self-Analysis*. Cambridge: Polity Press.

Bourdieu, P., and Wacquant L. (1992). *An Invitation to Reflexive Sociology*. Cambridge: Polity Press.

Braudy, L. (1997). *The Frenzy of Renown: Fame & Its History*. New York: Vintage.

Brick, C. (2021). Calling Out Kanye: Reflections on Post-racial Celebrity and the (Neo) Liberal Media. *Celebrity Studies* 12(1), 159–61.
Curtis, D. (2005). *Touching from a Distance*. London: Faber and Faber.
Edge, B. (1989). *Paintwork: A Portrait of The Fall*. London: Omnibus Press.
Essick, R. N. (2003). Jerusalem and Blake's final works. *The Cambridge Companion to William Blake*, 251–71.
Fisher, M. (2016). *The Weird and the Eerie*. London: Repeater Books.
Ford, S. (2003). *Hip Priest: The Story of Mark E. Smith and The Fall*. London: Quartet Books.
Freud, Sigmund ([1919] 2003). *The Uncanny*. London: Penguin.
Goddard, M., and B. Halligan (eds.) (2010). *Mark E. Smith and The Fall: Art, Music and Politics*. Farnham, UK: Ashgate Publishing, Ltd.
Greenhill, S. (2008). *Veteran Rocker Mark E. Smith Faces RSPCA Probe for Chopping Up Rare Red Squirrels with Hedge-clippers*. MailOnline 9, April 2008. https://www.dailymail.co.uk/news/article-558348/Veteran-rocker-Mark-E-Smith-faces-RSPCA-probe-chopping-rare-red-squirrels-hedge-clippers.html, accessed 10 December 2021.
Guardian, The (2018). Mark E. Smith Obituary: The Fall's Driving Force Was Poet, Satirist and Misanthrope. 25 January.
Hanley, P. (2017). *Leave the Capital*. Pontefract: Route.
———. (2019). *Have a Bleedin Guess: The Story of Hex Enduction Hour*. Pontefract: Route.
M.E.N. (*Manchester Evening News*) (2010). Fall Man in Squirrel Probe. *Manchester Evening News*, https://www.manchestereveningnews.co.uk/news/greater-manchester-news/fall-man-in-squirrel-probe-949861, accessed 8 September 2021.
Middles, M. and Reade, L. (2009) *The Life of Ian Curtis: Torn Apart*. London: Omnibus Press.
Myers, M. (2010). The Fall, Mark E. Smith and 'The Stranger': Ambiguity, Objectivity and the Transformative Power of a Band from Elsewhere. In *Mark E. Smith and The Fall: Art, Music and Politics*. London: Routledge.
———. (2015). Researching Gypsies and Their Neighbours: The Utility of the Stranger. In *Researching Marginalized Groups,* edited by Kalwant Bhopal and Ross Deuchar (pp. 227–40). Routledge.
New Statesman, The (2018). Mark E. Smith: A Sudden End to Forty Years of Prole Art Threat. 25 January.
Norton, T., and B. Stanley (2021). *Excavate!: The Wonderful and Frightening World of The Fall*. London: Faber.
Palmer, C. (2016). Drinking, Downfall and Redemption: Biographies and 'Athlete Addicts'. *Celebrity studies* 7(2), 169–81.
Rojek, C. (2001). *Celebrity*. London: Reaktion Books.
———. (2012). *Fame Attack: The Inflation of Celebrity and Its Consequences*. A&C Black. London: Bloomsbury.
Ross, P. (2017) The Fall at Queen Margaret Union, Glasgow: a triumphant portrait of courage and commitment. *The Telegraph 05.11.17*
Schonfeld, Z. (2018). 29 Truly Excellent and Typically Weird Stories About Mark E. Smith. *Newsweek*, https://www.newsweek.com/mark-e-smith-fall-nations-saving-grace-post-punk-790172, accessed 8 September 2021.

Simmel, G. (1971). *On Individuality and Social Forms.* Chicago: University of Chicago Press.
Smith, M. E. (1994). Mark E. Smith in Conversation with Michael Bracewell at the Institute for Contemporary Art, 8 March 1994. Personal archive.
———. (2008). *Renegade.* London: Viking Books.
———. (2018). A Message to All, to All. *Fall News*, 30 November. https://thefall.org/news/2018-01-24.html, accessed 14 December 2021.
Smith, M. E., and G. Duff (2021). *The Otherwise: The Screenplay for a Horror Film that Never Was.* London: Strange Attractor Press.
Smith, M. E., and M. Middles (2003). *The Fall.* London: Omnibus Press.
Stonehouse, C. (2004). From Hippy DJ to National Treasure: John Peel 1939–2004—The Gentle Passion that Stretched from Cult Rock at Midnight to Family Values at Breakfast Time. *The Express*, 27 October.
Telegraph, The (2018). Mark E. Smith: Lead Singer of Mancunian Band Whose Abrasive Exterior Concealed a Poetic Sensibility. 25 January.
Washington Post, The (2018). Always Different, Always the Same: Mark E. Smith of the Fall Was a Cranky, Uncompromising Genius. 25 January.
Wenner, L. A. (ed.). (2013). *Fallen Sports Heroes, Media, and Celebrity Culture.* New York: P. Lang.
Wilkinson, D. (2020). Mark E. Smith, Brexit Britain and the Aesthetics and Politics of the Working Class Weird, *Open Library of Humanities* 6(2). doi: https://doi.org/10.16995/olh.535.
Williamson, M. (2010). Female Celebrities and the Media: The Gendered Denigration of the 'Ordinary' Celebrity. *Celebrity studies* 1(1), 118–20.
Wise, A. (2008). Speech to Messing up the Paintwork conference, University of Salford, 9 May 2008. Personal archive.
Witts, R. (2010) Building up a Band: Music for a Second City, in M. Goddard and B. Halligan (eds.), (pp. 31–45), *The Art and Politics of Mark E. Smith and The Fall.* London: Ashgate.

RECORDINGS

'Repetition' (1978). B side of *Bingo-Master's Break-out!* Step Forward Records.
'Before the Moon Falls' (1979). *Dragnet.* Step Forward Records.
'Spectre vs. Rector' (1979). *Dragnet.* Step Forward Records.
'New Face in Hell' (1980). *Grotesque: After the Gramme.* Rough Trade.
'Nine Out of Ten' (2017). *New Facts Emerge.* Cherry Red.
Hex Enduction Hour (1982). Kamera.

DVDS

Perverted by Language bis (1983). IKON Videos: IKON 8.
A Touch Sensitive (2003). Secret Films.

Chapter Six

Dead Beat Descendant

Mark E. Smith's Life, Death, and Mourning as a Cult Hero (with Unlikely Peer Robert Forster of The Go-Betweens Used as a Support Act for Contrast and Shade)

John Fleming

This chapter focuses on and crossfades between Mark E. Smith (as revealed in *Renegade*, published in 2008) and Robert Forster (as revealed in *Grant & I*, published in 2016). Singers' forays into autobiography or memoir expose their literacy and lives to the scrutiny of a second test. My scope is informed by a real-time observation of their musical and lyrical paths, and a parallel appreciation of the stage-set of their contemporaneous pop culture. The two men were born just months apart but their aesthetic outputs and legacies are very different. Their complexity and quality arguably earn them two similar spaces in the cult firmament.

"Book reviewers—they are very evil. I think the book world is a crappy world. It's an evil world. It asks a lot more of you and gives you a lot less. Have you seen what book reviewers are like? . . . People like Ballard are embarrassed to be in the prize lists." Mark E. Smith, singer of The Fall, said this in a video interview in the 1980s. Smith died on January 24, 2018. With The Fall, he released thirty-two albums in forty-one years. His comment is an irate, jaded counterpoint to an innocent and awestruck line from Cattle and Cane about "A world of books / And silent times in thought", sung by Grant McLennan, Robert Forster's songwriting partner in The Go-Betweens. McLennan died on May 6, 2006. Forster worked with him on nine Go-Betweens albums in the eighteen years the band were active. McLennan and his death feature heavily in Forster's book.

The day the music—or a singer—dies, some flickering fanbase needle gets stuck in a groove; in the confused private loyalty of public mourning, there is a cultish, collective loss. There is the stark realisation there will be no more tunes. This is the run-out groove, the white-noise limbo of a dust-clogged needle stuck in the infinity rut at the end of side two: the train has finally jumped the tracks, the shared trek for fan and artist is over. For like writers, directors, actors, and others, singers are heroes. Articulate warriors of ideas and emotion, they do battle for us, winning our affections, forging an influential bond that we carry in what we might as well call the soul. Behind the record sleeve is a cacophony that speaks to us, a world we subscribe to, a place where we come dangerously close to belonging. These kingdoms of culture can be durable. They can last decades if the singer continues to create. We get to know and like this kingdom—we take partial refuge within its moat, within the spiralling groove of records, within the coil of tape, within whatever geometry dictates digital iterations. With music, we witness a world changing: the evolving age and maturity of the artist run in some lip-synced parallel with our own. Singer and fan both spin through the years and get older at the same rate: 16, 33, 45, 78 . . .

Mark E. Smith died in late January 2018, aged sixty, from lung and kidney cancer. He was a hard drinker and heavy smoker. Obituaries framed him as a pugnacious word master, as a scruff exemplar of the north of England, as a fascinating and prolific tyrant. Without compunction, he bullied and hired and fired five dozen band members in his constantly mutating group, The Fall. Grant McLennan died at forty-eight of a heart attack in 2006. Obituaries framed his death as that of a poet. His musical collaborator, Robert Forster, writes generously and lovingly about him in his autobiography, portraying him as a dear friend and songwriting partner.

The high profile and mass adulation of a David Bowie, Leonard Cohen, or Prince ensure they will be globally missed. Elvis Presley lives forever. Joe Strummer and Ian Curtis do too. But the cult singer, the Mark E. Smith or Grant McLennan or the still-very-much-alive Robert Forster, lives on an edgier altar—their output and popularity may wax and wane, and they may fade from the general purview. However, for their fans, their footprints are always there. Deep and indelible. When the artist returns with a new album, their fans are reactivated. Dusty but robust circuit-wiring fizzles and burns with the memory of faded zest; output in the later stages of a career re-energises a sympathetic, now mature affection, one willing to overlook possible diminution of excellence. When the hero is back, they are back. They get a hero's welcome. They are preachers and gods, illuminators of the way: they give you words and tunes to feed your brain, to touch your heart, to whistle in your daylight and use as torches in the dark. The Fall produced an album pretty much every year of their career; The Go-Betweens brought out albums more sporadically, with gaps of several years, and a recent Robert Forster solo release was seven years in the making.

Curators of pop culture often live by the crass aesthetics of a Fitch or Standard & Poor's, functioning as ratings agencies that reduce complex works to a pecking order of X amount of asterisks out of five. But this can stop when the artist dies. Then, mean-hearted, faculty-flexing reviewers often free themselves to read their own mortality. The death of a pop star begets obituaries and memorial plays on late-night radio. It gets Facebook pages full of heartfelt memory and framed appreciation. The shared culture of fandom ratchets up a gear: a period of international mourning is implicitly declared. People take to social media and post links to favourite songs. They offer anecdotes about how their life was shaped by the singer's work. The entire oeuvre becomes a structure on which they hang their sentient lives. The day the music dies, people overlook immediate bonds with family and friends, they look away from real-world links with loved ones whose health may be precarious. Excavating deep within, they project outwards some stored fear of inevitable loss onto the dead hero, onto the star. For days and weeks, the artist's gifts permeate the ether, flowing from one fan's heart and memory bank to the next, to collective post-death applause. Genuine tears may well up and be shed: for the godstar is dead and we are forced to realise the mediated hero was a mere mortal. And grief gets caught in a dark cage that lingers over the loyal audience. Fans who once found their vision of the world coded into timeless songs now, in the passing of the musician and singer, perceive their own inevitable decline.

Comparison is of dubious value. Books, music, and paintings are best not bullied into graphs, or twisted into learning curves from which to discern a trend. It is too easy to construct comparative timelines to cut like motorways through difficult terrain. But let's pitch two greats against each other. Let them share the same bill. Wordy musician versus wordy musician: Mark E. Smith and Robert Forster are two maverick talents who mean a lot to many literate and conceptual music fans across the four decades since the late 1970s. At first glance, Smith and Forster are Lancashire chalk and Antipodean cheese—stylistically, culturally, and creatively. The late Fall man was from Manchester; the living Go-Between is from Brisbane. The Fall man was urban and professed a hatred and fear of the countryside; the Go-Between is from a city but there is a greater sense of the rural in The Go-Betweens' aesthetics and lyrics. The Fall man was a tyrant, a dictator; the Go-Between was a collaborative partner. The Fall man was malevolent, an autodidact; The Go-Between is agreeable and made it to college. They can each be termed literate and charming. Both men were born in 1957 (Smith entered the world just 16 weeks before Forster). Neither made it onto the radar of popular acclaim (Smith was a proud saboteur of commercial success; Forster is a wistful regretter who has failed thus far due to bad luck). Both wrote autobiographies (Smith published *Renegade* in 2008; Forster published *Grant & I* in 2016). This sketch of their overlap is not a grading exercise: the comparison of the two men here is not a proxy talent show or ranking of who may or may not be top of the pops. Autobiography and music is their essential link, but so too is mortality: just as Mark E. Smith's sad death now hangs over The Fall's collective output, Grant McLennan's untimely passing shapes understanding of The Go-Betweens and weighs emotionally on songwriting partner Robert Forster's book of memory.

> Your sister picked me up at the station / She told me they'd taken you in, the word was it was just observation / I thought here we go again / Danger in the past / So I went and I saw you / We walked through the hospital grounds / I took your hand and I told you: never show your problems in a country town / Danger in the past / We had friends / We had friends that didn't make twenty-five / I knew a genius in a bedroom who couldn't walk outside (Robert Forster, *Danger in the Past*)

Forster was one of two singers in The Go-Betweens—the band was a type of splendid Simon and Garfunkel for the new wave age. Words like "literate" and "crafted" were used so often about them that at times The Go-Betweens could appear sanitised, scoured of real life, and dunked into some Antipodean sheep dip by bookish folk trying to prove that song lyrics could be lucid, tender, poetic, and literary.

The Go-Betweens entered obscure pop consciousness in the late 1970s, a two-headed hydra of guitars and ballpoint pens. Migrants to London, they were thoughtful and gentle signifiers for a mythic Australia not yet branded with *Neighbours*, one associated more with *Skippy*, with Nicolas Roeg's *Walkabout*, with Aboriginals, Ayer's Rock, and a TV entertainer called Rolf Harris. At the end of a decade that ranged from Mick Jagger in *Ned Kelly* (1970) to *Picnic at Hanging Rock* (1975) and years ahead of *Crocodile Dundee*, The Go-Betweens arrived in London with their lyrical verses.

In the same 1970s, British TV beamed out spangled Saturday entertainment extravaganzas such as *The Generation Game* with Bruce Forsyth, his glamourous assistant and members of the public; *Sale of the Century* with Nicholas Parsons, matching his 'n' hers sheepskin carcoats and the musical clues of gifted organist Peter Fenn (early Fall members Una Baines's and Yvonne Pawlett's keyboard sound strangely seemed to suggest his dinky tinklings, especially Pawlett's playing on the first Fall LP *Live at the Witch Trials*, and indeed Baines's work on *The Greatest Hit* [*Money Mountain*] when she played with Fall co-founder Martin Bramah in The Blue Orchids). TV was a mush of ice skating, snooker, and *Pot Black*, *Roobarb*, *Crown Court*,

Jokers Wild, How, Magpie, John Craven's Newsround, Blue Peter, and Open University programmes about signal testing. And there were hours of the test card. Jokes were raucous and often racist. Curvy assistants were stage props for an overall ideology of fang-collared nylon shirts and flares. Tuxedoed entertainers such as Jimmy Tarbuck, Les Dawson, and Bernard Manning wore the frilled shirts of bingo masters: on-screen they held microphones as though onstage. Prior to and parallel with punk, much of TV's entertainment looked like it was lifted straight from whatever show was running in the seaside theatre at the end of the nearest pier.

> Two swans in front of his eyes / Coloured balls in front of his eyes / It's number one for his Kelly's eye / Treble-six right over his eye / A big shot's voice in his ears / Worlds of silence in his ears / All the numbers account for years / Checks the cards through eyes of tears / Bingo-Master's Breakout! / A hall full of cards left unfilled / He ended his life with wine and pills / There's a grave somewhere only partly filled / A sign in a graveyard on a hill reads / Bingo-Master's Breakout (Mark E. Smith and The Fall, *Bingo-Master's Breakout*)

When The Fall released their first LP, *Live at The Witch Trials*, in 1979, the voice of Mark E. Smith—whether singing or talking—sounded like an anti-London weapon. The danger of his Manchester accent was quite distinct from the dense, literary ambition of his words and phrases; its danger was distinct too from the prevailing sneer of take-control-of-the-means-of-production punk and post-punk. In a pre-MTV, pre-YouTube world, visual identity was vested in record sleeves, concert posters, *Top of the Pops*, *The Old Grey Whistle Test*, and occasional photographs in the *NME* (*New Musical Express*), *Sounds*, or *Melody Maker*. Music leaked from tinny portable cassette players, from overly trebled passing car radios, from the hi-fi systems of record shops walked past. The Fall did not belong to this world of pop music: you'd find them eventually on late-night radio, on shows such as John Peel's, which were safe from the easy access of daytime radio. But they were still only starting off. *Witch Trials* was recorded in a single day. Despite a vaguely conceptual front cover, inspection of the reverse side reveals the crude design triumph of someone with weekend access to a photocopier and a typewriter on which to reproduce copybook biro verbal doodlings. The artwork is all poorly printed photographs, a hotchpotch of parish newsletter and punk fanzine. But amidst the rough package, the tracks—laid down with the cost-effective route precision of a taxi passenger unable to look out the window lest they avert their fearful eyes from the fare meter—are astonishing. Like a new form of elocution branded onto a new form of orchestration, a new sound, and its new delivery system—and Mark E. Smith's vision—had arrived.

In such dowdy circumstances as those prevailing in Ireland[1] and the UK in the late 1970s, a band had to live more vividly in your imagination; the mastery was mined in the music itself, not connoted by any effort at style. With The Fall, there would never be a star system or glamour, there would be no veneer of stylish escapism; instead, there would be the cracked, warped Formica of kitchen tables and bar counters, there would be recognisable urban magic realism as The Fall's sturdy musicians and their ringleader drained pint glasses that wobbled when returned to uneasy resting places on the flaking plywood beneath that Formica. In 1979 or 1980, in a record shop on Liffey Street, Dublin, that was crammed with listless weekend delinquents, I asked to hear *Live at the Witch Trials*, ahead of purchasing it for the sale price of £1.50. The dandified punk behind the counter selected track three on side one, 'Rebellious Jukebox', remarking that this was his favourite Fall song: its angular scales and tuneful runs struck me forcefully that day as mathematical and colourful. Across hundreds of listens in the forty-odd years that have elapsed since, the strange arithmetic of that Mark E. Smith/Martin Bramah composition still computes perfectly. That first listen reset some clock, it conjured up some new world; it recalibrated my ears and expectations of music and synchronised me with what previous generations would have called its beat. This was something rich and verbal, something dangerous and nasty, something poetic and vivid and angry. In a heightened and word-sharp contemporaneous world of Elvis Costello, The Jam, XTC, The Stranglers, Gang of Four, Joy Division, Magazine, and even The Sex Pistols, The Fall worked at another hyperactive level of phrase and music: the tunes and lyrics were enduring and mystical, with dragnets of meaning, vortexes of fragments, and phrases of syntax that mesmerised. It felt like psychology, it felt like sociology, it felt like literature, it felt like cultural studies, all those disciplines poisoned together in a toxic brew: it felt like first-class honours for a cheat. It felt like sincere satire, it felt like the menace of art, it felt like a jumble of newsworthy surreal headlines, maybe like what Smith might later allude to with the song title 'Prole Art Threat'. When I eventually saw proper photos of The Fall, they were scrawny young people whose physiques I read as emaciated signposts for the north of England. But these signposts pointed in the same general direction as the parallel streets of a hungry, frazzled, hopeless Dublin in which the gaslight glimmer of the punk new wave had also recently ignited: under its low-watt glow, the first healthy gasps were drawn through the lungs of The Atrix, The Radiators, Chant! Chant! Chant!, DC Nien, and many others. Images of the magnificent Joy Division had dour and disaffected industrialism dripping off them, and Magazine, Costello, and The Stranglers had a cool glamour. But The Fall looked like truants: they were unemployed young folk hanging around on street corners, badly dressed, an unwitting gang waiting for hours at a bus stop. The aesthetics of rough, word-scrawled, album-cover artwork looked less a choice and more a message of cut-price necessity. The riches were reserved for the complex tunes within. Welcome to the already wonderful and frightening world of The Fall.

> The tables covered in beer / Showbiz whines, minute detail / It's a hand on the shoulder in Leicester Square / It's vaudeville pub back room dusty pictures of / White-frocked girls and music teachers / The beds too clean / The waters poison for the system / Then you know in your brain / LEAVE THE CAPITOL! / EXIT THIS ROMAN SHELL! . . . It will not drag me down / I will leave this ten times town / I will leave this fucking dump / One room, one room/Hotel maids smile in unison / Then you know in your brain / You know in your brain / LEAVE THE CAPITOL / EXIT THIS ROMAN SHELL / Then you know you must leave the capitol / I laughed at the great god Pan (Mark E. Smith and The Fall, 'Leave the Capitol')

From the other side of the world, Robert Forster, his then girlfriend Lindy Morrison, and his pal Grant McLennan fell for the industrial lure of the English capital. London was necessary for them if their band The Go-Betweens was to graduate beyond its early stages of evolution, college idealism, and DIY releases back home in Brisbane. They arrived in London for the first time in late 1979. After some faltering years and several returns back Down Under, in early 1983, a little ahead of their second LP, they released the single 'Cattle and Cane'. It was a stunning tale of bucolic boyhood innocence.

The week it came out, its line "His father's watch / He left it in the shower" was praised by Orange Juice singer Edwyn Collins as guest singles reviewer in the *NME*. The song and its lyric conjured up a strong essence of childhood, universal but born of the spaces and prairies of Australia ("I recall a schoolboy coming home / Through fields of cane / To a house of tin and timber / And in the sky / A rain of falling cinders / From time to time the waste / Memory wastes"). From their forthcoming album at the time, *Before Hollywood*, the song included a line that would map the literate co-ordinates of The Go-Betweens: "I recall/A bigger brighter world/A world of books/And silent times in thought."

Grant McLennan wrote and sang this lyric. Ten years after his death, his surviving songwriting partner, Robert Forster, performed it live onstage in Whelan's[2] in Dublin, in a respectful and touching homage ahead of the publication of his cunning ventriloquist autobiography named after his friend (*Grant & I*). In the book, he describes 'Cattle and Cane' as a "song that . . . twinned the beat of the city with country childhood visions".

From the start there was something reflective and overtly emotional about The Go-Betweens. The words and musical moods were sculpted and refined and they whittled generally towards some poetic, lyrical, sentient truth. But they avoided being mawkish and the band was allied to the angularity and edge of punk. The tenderness seemed to reside mainly in McLennan: he was the half of the band who would write 'Batchelor Kisses' ("Hand, hands like hooks / You'll get hurt / If you play with crooks. / Your hand, that's all he took / The world opened up/For your looks") and 'The Wrong Road' ("The ghosts in the next room hear you cough / Time drags on Sundays spent in Mayfair / With all your riches, why aren't you there? / The wind acts like a magnet / And pulls the leaf from the tree / And the town's lost its breath / I took the Wrong Road round"). McLennan appeared for some time to be the main force. But all the time the other player was Robert Forster: he was more of a cypher, a vague energy field of the gangly, playful, and camp. A gent draped in the garb of satire, he was the second pillar of The Go-Betweens: he stood onstage, a dandy staring into the middle distance, a mild-mannered mockery of rock 'n' roll in his performance but plenty of poetics in his heart.

> Don't stare at the heavens / For guidance or reason or even rhyme / Don't stare at the heavens / Hoping to find the movement of time / It's not on my mind / But I know that there's someone / To turn on the rain (Robert Forster, 'Turn on the Rain')

His book *Grant & I* is both an autobiography and a biography: Forster is writing about his own life, using his relationship with McLennan as a personal benchmark. The title snipes at marriage deference—along "the wife and I" lines. There's also a signal twang of *Withnail and I* (the Bruce Robinson-directed 1987 film about two failed actors in London) in the sense of it being an exploration of an artistic duo. Both singers brought out solo records while the band was defunct (from 1989 pretty much right through to 2000 when they reformed). The Go-Betweens' lack of progression towards commercial success and their deepening cult acclaim and general pop obscurity had yielded the smart gag that when they did reform they could do so as The Australian Go-Betweens. (This was a reference to their being linked to London as well as their distant home Down Under, and the tribute band mania of which a band called The Australian Doors once seemed to be leading purveyors.)

Forster's memoir is indeed his own autobiography. He writes of boyhood and parents, of hope and the emergence of his seedling identity. There are the usual tales of first guitars and of listening to the radio, of the glamour of music entering a young heart and mind. But it is named for his dead songwriting partner. This is Laurel writing about Hardy. Or vice versa. This is Forster writing about himself by writing about McLennan. It is a book about friendship and its trauma, about partnership and the fear of betrayal. It is about creative co-operation and insecure competition, about mutual respect between complicit rivals. It is about taking on the world with delicate articulations about that world, the way all young wordy rebels imagine they will.

In one plotting of their shared early pathway, Forster recalls nervously telling McLennan the name he posited for their band as they drive over a bridge in Brisbane in 1978: "The band, however long it lasted, would be a contest and configuration of our wills. And be the stronger for it. I drew breath and, as evenly as I could, said, 'The Go-Betweens'." Poignantly, and rather triumphantly too, Forster notes that, thirty-two years later, some 500m from that same river crossing, a new bridge would be opened, named for their band. A respectful act by the nomenclature office of civic structures and an outstandingly clever semantic play: "The Go-Betweens Bridge". Cross it if you will.

Some years later in London, when he is working for a stint in St Mary's Hospital in Paddington, Forster comes across a medical file for Nicolas Roeg (who made the outback-set *Walkabout* in addition to *Don't Look Now* and *The Man Who Fell to Earth*). "On my last day of work there, I snuck out a rogue Roeg X-ray under my coat," he confesses. "It's as close as Grant and I ever got to the British film industry" (Forster 2017, p.67). The anecdote offers insight into two young men's shared artistic dream and the potential scale of literate ambition in a city such as London; it also reveals the drab off-stage difficulty of trying to make ends meet.

Grant & I was published amid expectations of at least passable literary ability. At best, something brilliant was possible. Forster does not fall short. He does not attempt to violate his dead friend with easy psychoanalysis. Rather, he observes McLennan's character and makeup through his evolving precarious lifestyle and situation. Nor does he self-aggrandise the hedonism that often attends a life in the arts. Drink and substance excess is portrayed as a casual lifestyle choice the way it is for the many fans who have never attended a gig sober. Music and drink have always made their own melody. And vignettes of The Go-Betweens enjoying alcohol or spliffs all seem very par for the course. It comes as a shock that Forster has contracted hepatitis from the sharing of dirty needles, an illness that fills him with his own intimations of mortality. "I was a dabbler, never owning a needle and always having someone else shoot me up, which wasn't helping me now. Heroin and amphetamine use was an occasional social thing with friends; a lot of people did it, and no one would have known, had not an undetected blood virus been dancing between us all. . . . My last emotion as I sat in the doctor's rooms was to curse myself for having been weak-willed enough to take drugs. They'd come and got me, like a hand coming through a curtain in a horror movie. I walked out thinking I had five years to live" (Forster 2017, p.273). His potentially fatal diagnosis comes long before his shock at the death of Grant McLennan. It all seems many years and a long way from the childhood innocence of 'Cattle and Cain' and that line, "His father's watch / He left it in the shower".

Mark E. Smith had his own take on watches in an early or mid-1980s interview, whose exact source details have slipped from my memory and exceed my internet research skills. Talking about a period of declared urban mystic energy when he worked on Manchester docks while forming the band in 1977, he says something along the lines of "That was a very psychic time. A lot of the lads down the docks, their wristwatches kept exploding." The image could not be further from The Go-Between's pastoral, filial-paternal capture of a little boy's fears around careless water damage to the timepiece he borrowed from his father but left in the shower. But Smith's exploding wristwatch is maybe even more vivid—a type of magical realism breaks through his industrial, dockside Manchester. No fields of cattle or fields of cane, more like the clanking sounds of machines breaking, of factories malfunctioning, of shop-floor accidents, all building into a symphony of wharfside negative energy. Ships unloaded ideas from overseas: cargoes of concepts and forces that could push a person to breaking point. Exploding watches: they sit like statues on the jagged Fall landscape of bingo halls and loading bays, as does perhaps William Burroughs's ticket that similarly exploded.

Mark E. Smith led The Fall from 1977 to 2018: forty-one years. From a pulpit in the margins, the group delivered dozens of albums—at a rate of almost one a year, not counting live recordings and various compilations that testify to malicious brand mockery (*50,000 Fall Fans Can't Be Wrong*). The group was of course named for the novel by Albert Camus. Smith ran it like a dictator: a talented despot capable of great kindness and extreme cruelty as he hired and fired some sixty-plus recruits over the years. For some reason he insisted The Fall was a "group" not a "band", the difference alluding to its collective and shape-shifting nature. Loyal bassist Steven Hanley describes his traumatic two decades in the band/group in his own excellent memoir *The Big Midweek: Life Inside The Fall*. It reads fascinatingly like the prison notebook the title suggests, detailing the paranoid control exercised by the domineering Smith and the death-row jail in which the constantly-on-the-verge-of-being-fired members do their time. Revered as the essential sound of The Fall with his deft, catchy, rumbling basslines until he could take no more and left in 1997, Hanley bandages his real scars as a human being for long enough at the end of the book to honourably thank his erstwhile tormentor for the "opportunity and unique life lessons" he has given him (Hanley and Piekarski 2014, p.446).

Smith's autobiography came out in 2008—just as his and The Fall's thin, angular, early music is the spiky antithesis of The Go-Betweens' refined songcraft, this work stands in a different corner of the culture boxing ring to

Forster's book. The *Renegade* hardback edition features a rare, studio-posed shot of Mark E. Smith standing in front of what looks like a blackboard. Suited, he stares at the camera, a cigarette in his hand. On the right of the image are lengths of gaudy gaffer tape holding the backdrop in place. By his feet is a plugboard to feed the studio lights. A sweeping brush just out of his reach frames the shot: it is an image of an image being taken. This is not a tedious reminder of deconstruction or an unnecessary reference to the media being the message or anything overt like that. (Such an approach has been second nature even for the most banal exhibits of mainstream pop culture for decades now and has always been a genetic part of the perceptual alloy in which The Fall's brilliance gleams.) Rather, it betrays a type of approach which devalues sheen, which ruptures veneer, which channels the raw and direct: it declares an aesthetic which is almost ugly in its condition. This is not Smith slumming it; this is Smith continuing to refuse to package himself, especially when accorded approval by establishment publishers Penguin/Viking. That's the real package: Mark E in a decent suit with a cigarette in hand looking like a football manager, a snooker player. An NHS inspector. A civil servant. There is nothing intentionally glamourous about him. An intensity yes. Question: Does he look literary? Answer: It is a book cover.

Smith writes of running his group like a foreman on a building site. He tries people out for a day. His management style and training programme for recruits reminds of a recurring *Beano* or *Dandy* gag of the 1970s about the job spec for a litter warden. Applicant asks question: "What do I do?" Gag's punchline: "Don't worry, son. You'll pick it up as you go along." In a BBC documentary, *The Weird and Frightening World of Mark E. Smith* (2005), he explains how his grandfather was the foreman at a factory. He used to stand outside prison on Friday and, as the men were being released, he'd pick out some and offer them a start. This is how Smith approached his own band. A musician's prospects were a function of how well they fitted in with his plan; their career in The Fall was subject to Smith's destructive creativity and often-malicious whim. You could get in trouble for eating lettuce.

> This road that we're on / We've travelled so far / Do you see the light / Of the horsebreaker star? (Grant McLennan, 'Horsebreaker Star')

Throughout *Grant & I*, Forster writes affectionately of McLennan: "He was a country boy who could only live in the city, he was a city boy who knew that part of his true self belonged in the country . . . who knew he was different not only to his fellow students but to most of his family. And maybe he lacked a little love. He took refuge in academic achievement, which flowered into grander passions. And he needed a skin to protect that boy fired with enthusiasm, one that took the form of an arrogance, never checked, which attracted and repelled those he encountered" (Forster 2017, p.331). And later: "I woke the morning after his death with him telling me two things. The first that I must put on paper everything that had happened to us, write our adventures down, which was the moment this book was born. The second was more abstract: Go to the biggest place of worship you know and think of me" (Forster 2017, p.333). The words are contemplative and considered. Forster has reflected on the value of friendship and his debt to his departed pal. He knows the vital role they played in each other's lives and is trying to recollect it in later-life tranquillity.

Smith takes a more sceptical approach when writing of his group on tour in the U.S.: "Three days in and they've got faces like vexed tomatoes, their skins flaking sci-fi style: burnt to fuck. They were an embarrassment; not only to me and the wife and The Fall fans but to their whole generation" (Smith 2008, p.2). That band later walks out on him in New York after a mid-show on-stage punch-up. "It was inevitable," Smith writes. "There was something in the air there. I knew it was coming. They'd been acting like irked union members for weeks" (Smith 2008, p.6).

Smith knowingly recounts the twisted fun of his childhood and looking after his sisters while his parents were out in a control game he called "Japanese prison camp"—"Today, we'd probably get investigated by the social services" (Smith 2008, p.14). Rarely photographed without a beer in one hand and a cigarette in the other, he writes, as idea-laden as ever, "I started smoking when I was about sixteen. I don't think you need it really before then. . . . We used to write our names on walls and garages with Capstan Full Strength cig-ends; they were that strong, like black chalk; better than a pen" (Smith 2008, p.18).

Smith often rounded on interviewers when asked about his writing process: he would reply to their question by making the rather fair point that he should not be expected to give away his trade secrets. One another occasion, he revealed to a reporter that the mysterious technique behind his musical collaboration with his group involved him whistling the melody down a phone line so the lads could work out the music. In *Renegade*, he volunteers an amusing home decor tip for creatives everywhere: "If you want to get your work done, if you want to be an artist, it's a good first step to avoid clutter. I only have three chairs in the house, for instance; one for the wife, one for me, and one for a guest. No more. One guest at a time—that's my philosophy. You don't want your house turning into a hippy commune" (Smith 2008, p.140).

A learned literacy surrounds The Go-Betweens, serving as an external credential. It infuses both Forster's and McLennan's lyrics with the expectation of poetic form. They almost appear to be men of letters, and there is a sense of unseen reserves of knowledge and bursting bookshelves. Mark

E. Smith comes across as a different kettle of fish, wrapped in amusing knowing obnoxiousness (shot through with jokey charm if you were not the subject of his wrath). An avid reader, he appears to just know things. While they both wear their learning lightly, Forster's appears acquired whereas Smith's seems innate. While Forster may be studied and insightful and donnish and may aspire most productively to the poetry of poets and of classic songwriters such as Bob Dylan and The Byrds and Big Star, Smith is filled with a magpie essence. Stark street intelligence emanates from his face. He professed a fondness for H. P. Lovecraft, Phillip K. Dick, and Wyndham Lewis. Something of his tapping into urban energy and its detail links Smith more to post-war writers—to the early Pinter and Osborne and Joe Orton—than to songwriters such as Ray Davies of The Kinks or any of The Beatles. You could probably place him on some ley line that runs through Lou Reed, Captain Beefheart, and Frank Zappa, but the idea of any direct influence is farcical as Smith ripped things into his own personalised shreds. The impression is he has not so much savoured books as seen right through them; he has read into them and filleted them. He compounds his literacy into stabbing commentary—he is not the reservoir of book learning; he is the leak in the dyke. What he does with literature is a process of mutation, not of respect. He funnelled his literary talent into lyrics which work as headlines and parodies of note dictation, and much of his work reads like poetic instruction booklets. The cover of *Slates* (1981) declares, "Cost: two pounds only u skinny rats". This is a million miles away from The Clash's *London Calling* cover sticker announcing the price for the CBS double album to be a fiver. While The Clash were brilliantly and idealistically engaging in an effort at erosion of capitalism, Mark E. Smith and The Fall were pimping their underground product via a mockery of transaction itself.

Grotesque (After the Gramme) is The Fall's third album and it came out in 1980. The song 'English Scheme' is probably about working-class emigration: "The clever ones tend to emigrate / Like your psychotic big brother / Who left home / For jobs in Holland, Munich, Rome / He's thick but he struck it rich. . . . You got sixty-hour weeks / And stone toilet back-gardens / Peter Cook's jokes / Bad dope, check shirts / Lousy groups / Point their fingers at America / Down pokey quaint streets in Cambridge / Cycles our distant spastic heritage". Another tune is 'The Container Drivers': "Grey ports with customs bastards / Hang around like clowns / The containers and their drivers / Bad indigestion / Bad bowel retention. . . . Communists are just part-time workers / And there's no thanks / From the loading bay ranks." Industry and the supply chain have seldom made such excellent subjects for songs.

Another tune on that album is called 'Pay Your Rates', and yet another is 'The North Will Rise Again' in which Smith imagines a future insurrection. In the spoken-word prelude, he recounts how one morning he hears music on the radio: "The song was *English Scheme*. Mine. They'd changed it with a grand piano and turned it into a love song. How they did it I don't know. DJs had worsened since the rising. Elaborating on nothing in praise of the track with words they could hardly pronounce, in telephone voices." The record refers to itself as part of some future scenario of upheaval.

What emerges from the *Grotesque* songs is a fresco of Britain at the close of the 1970s and the start of the 1980s—one that is more psychological than sociological. It is a world of daily activity described in terms of underlining ideas. There is no nostalgic portraiture, no indulgence. The songs—like The Fall's work at its best—are not stories but amalgams of thoughts around what might occasionally be a theme. Of this album, Smith remarks in *Renegade*: "I wrote about what was around me; that was the whole point—to get down the experiences, scenes, people, etc. But some people are so daft they don't understand that writing about Prestwich is just as valid as Dante writing about his inferno" (Smith 2008, p.86). Of the next album, *Hex Enduction Hour* (1982), he writes, "I wanted an album to be like reading a really good book" (Smith 2008, p.115).

> The rabbit killer left his home for the clough / And said goodbye to his in-fertile spouse / Carried air rifle and firm stock of wood / Carried night-site telescope light / A cemetery overlooked clough valley of mud / And the grave-keeper was out on his rounds / Yellow-white shirt buried in duffle coat hood / Keeping edges out with mosaic colour stones (Mark E. Smith and The Fall, 'Jawbone and the Air Rifle')

Forster mentions The Fall twice in his autobiography. The first reference is to seeing them play in London's Electric Ballroom. The second one is when, in April 1980, after arriving in London late the previous year, he and McLennan travel up to visit Edwyn Collins in Glasgow to record a single with Postcard Records. In awe of Orange Juice and the associated band, Josef K, Forster writes that he loved this "whiplash pop, miles away from the doom of the Joy Division imitators or the rumble of The Fall" (Forster 2017, p.76). Perhaps unsurprisingly, there is no mention of The Go-Betweens in Smith's autobiography. He does, however, have this to say about their homeland Down Under: "Kids start saving up to go to Australia when they're about seven, harbouring notions of the *Neighbours* life before they can even chew their food properly. It's time to eradicate this idea that by getting away you'll find yourself or walk into a glorious new existence. People who think like that just want rid of themselves. Where you're living is in your head" (Smith 2008, p.88).

Forster is very smart and his personality is endearing. This shines in his engaging and honest prose. On being a schoolboy, he writes, "I was enjoying my new role as raffish, lanky lord of mischief, willing to endure censure or detention for the sake of a quip, liked by the younger teachers, an enigma to the ancient and stern with my high grades and attention-seeking behaviour" (Forster 2017, p.16). He went to university and transferred from law to literature but, despite a deep appetite for books, found it hard to settle. He summarises his attitude as this: "My problem was that literature instilled a creative impulse in me, not an academic one" (Forster 2017, p.20).

Smith's experience of education is geoculturally and sociologically different, harking back to a post-war British world of self-improvement in which people attended college at night to better their minds with a view to getting ahead. Apart from grammar school selection, Smith's potential was not fostered by the state system. While he took an evening class in A-level literature when he started his first job, the theme of many Fall songs mocks students and the university-educated, many of whom loved the group. "Degrees have a way of warping people," he writes. "It's not good for people to spend that amount of time at university. . . . They get so distanced from the real world they haven't a fucking clue what's needed. It's a luxurious prison, almost" (Smith 2008, p.99).

It would be a mistake to appraise the literary merit of singers on the basis of books they write. The punch and kick and warm pulse of autobiographical words on a page are one thing: they may be read for information or insight into some personal world the singer has impaled upon memories that appeal. Smith and Forster both recount enlightening tales of life in their bands. They both merit the publication of their books by virtue of their fans' curiosity about their touring and recording careers, and their interest in the songs that have touched their hearts and minds. Both *Renegade* and *Grant & I* are essential insights into the psychology and experience of two outstanding men. They are little histories of the world, of great nutrition to music fans who often wonder how things are for their artistic heroes, and who are often oblivious to the mundane circumstances in which their artists actually live. To parse singers' autobiographies or their lyrics for proof of literary ability is a misguided task. The songwriter's art hides nowhere—it lurks out in the open, rollicking in the raw weave of multi-dimensional music, in the clanging sculpture of tunes, in the honing of melodies and verses and choruses, in the refusal to do any of this, and in the choice to parade sharp words and glistening ideas in ramshackle ways. The real art of Mark E. Smith and Robert Forster resides in their very different recorded output and contrasting live performances; it lives in their worlds of words. Their art is a cocktail of sound and vision which delivers literature and poetry and noise, both rough and polished. It pours magnificently from Forster as he stares off over the Whelan's crowd in May 2016 with a self-deprecating thespian smile while playing guitar and singing 'Danger in the Past' with the lonely ghost of his dead friend Grant McLennan living in his and his audience's hearts; it is there when The Go-Betweens play a joyous outdoor lunchtime gig in Trinity College Dublin in May 1985, and they are all glamourous and together and still alive. The art is there when The Fall play the TV Club in late 1984 and Mark E and his then wife Brix Smith talk generously afterwards with a young man whose mind has been reeling for days with the hypnotic mystery of their just-released 'Disney's Dream Debased' song. The art is there in August 2004 when an angry audience in CrawDaddy[3] waits for Smith to come onstage, the band already two hours late and just starting to play an extended instrumental as their singer is nowhere to be found. It looks like it might get nasty, but he suddenly appears to rapturous applause and instant crowd forgiveness. The art is there every time he tampers with on-stage amps to sabotage the sound-desk mix. It is there whenever he wanders off to the side of the stage and slumps on the floor to continue warbling one of his hundreds of lyrics into what may be the wrong microphone. And it is there when a sadly disfigured Mark E. Smith plays a final gig in a wheelchair, far from books and studio time and tours and fights and firing his musicians, a sick and dying man persisting in his brilliant lyrical art.

NOTES

1. See chapter 12 from Michael Murphy in this volume for more details.
2. Whelan's is an intimate rock venue on Wexford Street, Dublin.
3. CrawDaddy was a music venue on the site of the POD nightclub on Harcourt Street, Dublin. Both have ceased to exist.

REFERENCES

Forster, Robert. 'Danger in the Past', track on *Danger in the Past* (Beggars Banquet, 1990, LP).

Forster, Robert. 'Turn on the Rain', track on *Songs to Play* (Universal Music Australia, 2015, LP).

Forster, Robert. *Grant & I: Inside and Outside The Go-Betweens* (Omnibus Press, 2017).

Hanley, Steve, and Olivia Piekarski, Olivia. *The Big Midweek: Life Inside The Fall* (Route, 2014).

McLennan, Grant. 'Horsebreaker Star', track on *Horsebreaker Star* (Beggars Banquet, 1994, double LP).

Smith, Mark E. *Renegade: The Lives and Tales of Mark E. Smith* (Viking/Penguin, hardback 2008).

The Fall. 'Bingo-Master's Breakout' (Step-Forward, 1978, seven-inch EP).
The Fall. 'English Scheme', track on *Grotesque (After the Gramme)* (Rough Trade, 1980, LP).
The Fall. 'The Container Drivers', track on *Grotesque (After the Gramme)* (Rough Trade, 1980, LP).
The Fall. 'Leave the Capitol,' track on *Slates* (Rough Trade, 1981, 10-inch EP).
The Fall. 'Jawbone and the Air Rifle', track on *Hex Enduction Hour* (Kamera, 1982, LP).
The Go-Betweens. 'Batchelor Kisses', track on *Spring Hill Fair* (Sire Records, 1984, LP).
The Go-Betweens. 'The Wrong Road', track on *Liberty Belle and the Black Diamond Express* (Beggars Banquet, 1986, LP).
The Go-Betweens (McLennan/Forster). 'Cattle and Cane' (Rough Trade, 1983, seven-inch single).

Chapter Seven

"What's a computer?"
Intuition Meets the Science Law in a Complete Fall Lyrics Corpus

Matt Davies

> *Eloquent people talk about The Fall. Clever writers spin The Fall into extended essays.*
> *People study The Fall . . . they do . . . at college!*
> *Mark: 'That's fucking disgusting. They should be shot.'*
> *People scrutinise Fall lyrics and spin deeper and deeper into literary theory.*
> *Which is to miss the point.*
> *Hugely.*
> *Better really . . . better to listen . . . then go and have a drink.*
>
> —(Smith & Middles 2003, p.278)

This chapter outlines experiments with the Wmatrix software programme in identifying significant semantic categories and thematic patterns in a corpus of the complete Fall lyrics. It was a work-in-progress while Fall frontman and lyricist Mark E. Smith was alive and still adding to his prolific lyrical output.[1] Now that there is a semblance of completeness to the corpus, it may make sense to try and establish a Fall lyric road map.

It would be a fool's errand to claim that this is anything much more than a cursory, mainly decontextualised, list of things (correct or incorrect) which the reader can use to make further investigations. There is no analysis of individual songs (each one could constitute a chapter in its own right), most of the examples are taken out of context, and there is little consideration of music and performance. But given that discussions around lyrics in most of the burgeoning literature on Mark E. Smith and The Fall tend to focus largely on *individual* songs or LPs, I would suggest that the results outlined here may contribute a modicum of further insight into some of the more consistent preoccupations of one of the music world's most inventive wordsmiths across several decades.

When Mark E. Smith passed away on 24 January 2018, after forty-two years at The Fall's helm, it was no coincidence that central to the tributes and obituaries were references to Smith's capacity for ingenious, distinctive, and inimitable lyrical composition. A. Sweeting, in *The Guardian* (2018, January 25), for instance, claimed that "Smith's work defied categorisation, combining [. . .] elements of satire, social commentary, grumbling misanthropy and an abiding enthusiasm for cunning wordplay". D. Kelly, in *GQ Magazine* (2018, January 25), refers to Smith's "gritty, angular tunes backdropping cascades of words that flitted between Hogarthian social observation and surrealist dreamtalk". And C. Welsh, in *Factmag* (2018, January 25), states that "Smith was first and foremost a storyteller whose wry, absurdist vision was informed by the literary canon as much as his observations of daily life."

Previous to this, M. Fisher (in Goddard & Halligan 2010, p.95) claimed some of the Fall's earlier work "bears comparison with the great works of twentieth-century high literary modernism by James Joyce, T. S. Eliot and Wyndham Lewis" in terms of its innovation. Fisher and other Fall pundits commented on how once exposed to Fall songs, it is almost impossible to avoid imposing order and meaning on them and equally futile reaching any firm conclusions. Former band member Brix Smith-Start (2016, pp.143–44) recorded hearing 'Slates' (1981) for the first time (not long before she met Mark E. Smith and soon joined the band) and wrestling obsessively with the meanings of the lyrics:

> Because I couldn't understand all the words, my mind filled in meanings particular to me. The music dragged up my own subconscious thoughts in an effort to make sense of what was being sung. [. . .] The songs were infectious in a way that I had not experienced before. They were intellectually contagious. I found myself thinking deeply about them for days, trying to make sense of it. [. . .] I was desperate to understand what was being said, what the songs were about, not realising that part of the power of the music was the precise effect it had in the brain of the listener.

Similarly, Ford (2003, pp.xii–xiii) asserted that "The Fall becomes the very language you think through. Its corpus provides an inexhaustible stream of neologisms and buzz-words, trigger phrases that you can't just shake off".

Perhaps the most succinct characterisation of the desire for understanding and the simultaneous inevitability of failure—much like Stewie Griffin's 'squiggly line in my eye fluid' poem in *Family Guy*—is Doran's (2011) declaration that "[t]hese songs happen in the corner of your eye—when you turn your head they vanish, or else assume a form that can't be described in (other, inferior) words."

So, although the results outlined below maybe considered an ineffectual attempt to drag the songs away from your peripheral vision towards the centre, the results of computer-generated patterns do at least confirm some personal intuitions and provide some avenues for additional investigation. The disclosure by the software that the words 'man', 'head', and 'face', and the semantic category ANATOMY AND PHYSIOLOGY, are deemed consistently significant throughout the Fall lyrical output, may be bland findings to some, but there's enough here for it to be worth the effort. If they leave you a little surprised, even if not slapping revelation right in your eyes, I deem it a success.

"BECAME A RECLUSE AND BOUGHT A COMPUTER"—WMATRIX AND CORPUS-BASED TEXT ANALYSIS

The thematic patterns identified in Fall lyrics generated for this chapter derive from the corpus analysis and comparison functionality of Wmatrix (Version 4), an online software service hosted by Lancaster University, UK (see Rayson 2008). Users upload their chosen text file, and Wmatrix assigns each of the words to one of twenty-one major semantic domains. These include, for instance, SOCIAL ACTIONS, STATES & PROCESSES, and THE BODY AND THE INDIVIDUAL. Each of these is further sub-divided into more discrete categories such as RELIGION AND THE SUPERNATURAL and CLOTHES AND PERSONAL BELONGINGS, which sit inside the former and latter main categories, respectively. Like most corpus linguistic software, it creates word lists ordered by frequency, as well as concordance lists (key words in their context). But more importantly it generates *keywords* and *key semantic categories* as judged against reference corpora which are built into Wmatrix. The reference corpora are just under one million words in size and consist of samples from the 100-million-word British National Corpus. The comparison generates ranked lists which establishes words and semantic categories deemed significant in the user corpus—because of their heightened frequency—compared to the BNC reference corpus. For a number of important reasons—including the arbitrary nature of the reference corpus, and lexical polysemy (many words have more than one meaning)—the results have to be treated with caution, necessitating a manual examination of examples in context, as this chapter shows.

There is precedent, in the field of literary stylistics, for using Wmatrix to validate intuitions about individual or groups of texts and to potentially open up new ways of thinking about them. In an early trial, the pioneering corpus linguist Geoffrey Leech used the software to reinforce his knowledge of "deviant" or "key" features in the 3,130 words of Virginia Woolf's short story 'The Mark on the Wall'. His aim was to "see whether the empirical basis of stylistic analysis could be put on a sounder footing by using an objective, empirical method of text analysis" (Leech 2008, p.162). He concluded in the affirmative, asserting that Wmatrix helped him notice "more relevant features" and encouraged him to be "less influenced by personal preferences or as to which features of style to highlight" (p.177).

Walker (2010) also took advantage of the semantic comparison tool function of Wmatrix to examine the 73,469 words of Julian Barnes's 1991 novel *Talking It Over*, which is told from the perspective of nine first-person narrators. The generation of key concepts for each narrator, compared externally to the BNC samplers, and internally (compared to the novel as a whole) provided new insights into their unique styles and preoccupations which would have been very time-consuming, if not impossible, without computer assistance. Similar to Leech, B. Walker's study "produced empirical data that supported my intuitions, as well as those of various critics [. . .] and [. . .] offered new, interpretively relevant information" (p.386). He also notes that the software helped to identify themes within the text and locate important sections which may have been missed if studied manually.

More recently, there have a been a trickle of publications which employ Wmatrix to investigate song lyrics. H. Motschenbacher (2016) studies the lyrics of 388 Eurovision Song Contest songs delivered in English from 1999 to 2013 (constituting 93,881 word tokens and 3,447 word types) and compares them to a reference corpus of 280 German chart songs (also delivered in English) to show how the former constructs a discursive world embracing "transnational European values" in "a world in which future orientation and universality/eternity" are prevalent. M. Brindle (2018) uses Wmatrix to examine 795 lyrics from thirty-five male blues singers recorded between 1920 and 1965, comparing the pre-WWII period (1920 to 1941) to those recorded from 1945 to 1965. One of the conclusions of the study is that "the portrayal of women as objects of desire or a means of obtaining sexual gratification for the male speaker within the lyric appears to be a central motif of blues lyrics in both the pre- and post-war era" (although clearly not exclusive to the genre) (p.33). The study also notes the limitations of examining a body of lyrics across a range of artists rather than individual ones.

Whereas the studies summarised above are based around using Wmatrix to analyse individual works of fiction and assortments of lyrics produced by a multitude of writers, the uniqueness of *this* study is predicated on the fact it centres on words recorded by one band—The Fall—composed mainly by one person and constituting more than 80,000 words in 457 songs recorded over a forty-one-year period. There are very few popular music lyricists whose work would merit this kind of scrutiny.

Building the corpus of Fall lyrics was a significant challenge, much more so than having an 'oven-ready' digitised short story or novel to upload. So, the next section summarises some of the key decisions made in collating (and editing) this nebulous lexical mass, followed by a selective snapshot of some 'results'. The tentative nature of the analysis is based on the unavoidable restrictions imposed by the quantity and quality of the Fall's lexical treasure trove, and how the thematic patterns suggested by the software correlate with the subjective standpoint of the analyst and their previously accumulated knowledge of The Fall when investigating these results. In other words, my own Wmatrix-generated revelations may come as little surprise to those Fall fans whose dogged obsessiveness already provides them with superior insight into over four decades of lyrical ingenuity, but hopefully some of it is revelatory.

"THESE ARE THE WORDS OF COMPLETE DISORIENTATION"—THE FALL'S LYRICAL QUAGMIRE

So, in the decades before compiling the lyrics corpus, my first exposure to The Fall was as a teenager hearing 'Rowche Rumble' played by the band's champion, DJ John Peel, as Number 40 in his 1979 Festive 50, a listener's poll of their all-time favourite tracks. My interest duly piqued, I acquired their back catalogue (four singles, two studio LPs, plus the mostly live 'Totale's Turn'), and like, I suspect, many of my equally intrigued contemporaries, made mostly vain attempts to decipher the words delivered in Smith's Salfordian/quasi-U.S. drawl. This was further hampered by: a combination of deliberately muddied production values; a slurred or growled vocal delivery often hidden behind or overlaid with various megaphone, lo-fi tape-recording sound effects or buried in the mix behind a wall of drums and guitars; and—in the pre-Google age—obscure cultural references often impossible to navigate. For instance, versions of 'Spectre vs. Rector' were available on the second LP *Dragnet* (October 1979), live LP *Totale's Turn (It's Now or Never)*, and the *Live in London 1980* Chaos cassette tape released early 1982, none of which shed clear light on the content of the mesmeric incantation delivered a multitude of times by Smith as a pseudo-chorus throughout the eight minutes or so running time of the song. What sounded to me at the time, but I could attribute little meaning to, was "Elmore James, be bored be bored! Let's settle this alone. Van Greenway aah come on [. . .] such hatred

J... Jason", interspersed by even more obscure grunts and vocal tics, decades later appears to be—thanks to the invention of the internet and a committed coterie of Fall 'translators'—this likely interpretation, according to *The Annotated Fall* website:

> M.R. James, viva[n]t viva[n]t
> Yog Sothoth, Ray Milland
> Van Greenway, R. Corman
> Sludge hai choi, choi choi son

The mantra contains references to horror writers (M. R. James, Peter Van Greenaway), fictional beings (Yog Sothoth, an 'outer God' in H. P. Lovecraft's *Cthulhu Mythos*), film director Roger (R.) Corman, actor Ray Milland who took lead roles in two Corman directed films, a Vincent Price chant in a Corman-directed adaptation of a Lovecraft story ('vivat . . . vivat'), and an unrecognisable phrase ('sludge hai choi'), which is at least helpfully hidden in plain sight on the back of the *Dragnet* album cover in handwritten capitals underneath the declaration 'IVANT AR CORMAN'. These deductions show the lengths to which Fall devotees have gone to impose meaning on four short lines and it encapsulates the impossibility of determining the definitive road map of the Fall's lyrical corpus in a completely coherent and cohesive fashion.

However, a combination of my own listening practices, the collective detective instincts of those contributing to fan sites (notably *The Fall online*, *The Flickering Lexicon*, *The Annotated Fall*, and *Reformation*), the growth in published works on Smith and the Fall (Ford 2003; Thompson 2003; Simpson 2009; Goddard & Halligan 2010; Norton & Stanley 2021; Pringle 2022) including several by former band members (Hanley & Peikarski 2014; Smith-Start 2016; Wolstencroft 2017; Hanley 2020) and those co-written or sanctioned by Smith himself (Smith & Middles 2003; Smith 2009) led to the collation of some *pre*-Wmatrix conclusions about Fall lyrical content. None of these I would be foolish enough to claim have not been discussed elsewhere.

For instance, regardless of the often densely obscure nature of Smith's lyrical musings, several themes and motifs seem transparent, many of these the target of scorn and disdain: the music industry (including musicians and producers); trends and 'trendiness'; nostalgia; the culture of celebrity; curtailment of various freedoms; drugs and alcohol; grotesque physical forms and figures combined with mental and physical decay or disorders; the nature of imagination and inspiration; the detrimental effects of technology (e.g. computers, touch screen phones, and tablets); and psychic or spiritual 'precognition' (which Smith had, at various times, claimed to possess).

Many songs consist of compressed or fragmented stories of spiritual possession, time travel, loners, and outsiders dealing with paranoia and government interference. These narratives wear on their sleeves the influences of H. P. Lovecraft, Phillip K. Dick, M. R. James, Colin Wilson, William Blake, William Burroughs, and Hunter S. Thompson, some of whom are explicitly cited or named in the songs themselves. B-movies and early TV sci-fi shows such as *The Twilight Zone* are also referenced.

Smith name-checks a cavalcade of real historical and contemporary figures including William of Orange, Pope John Paul I, Queen Victoria, the poets Lord Byron and William Blake, the singers Dolly Parton and Damo Suzuki, serial killer Harold Shipman, businessman Richard Branson, a Fall tour bus driver ('Noel's Chemical Effluence'), and even members of the band themselves—'Craigness', 'The Quartet of Doc Shanley', 'Xmas with Simon', '(Jung Nev's) Antidotes'.

Many of the songs centre on a gallery of (mainly male) *fictional* characters who are either named in the song title—'Ed's Babe', 'Cowboy George', 'Fiery Jack', 'Nate will not Return', 'Arid Al's Dream'—or more commonly defined by specific traits or functions—'The Man whose Head Expanded', 'Carry Bag Man', 'Green Eyed Loco Man', 'Paranoia Man in Cheap Sh*t Room', 'Wolf Kidult Man', 'Bingo Master's Breakout', 'Senior Twilight Stock Replacer', 'The Container Drivers' and 'The Mixer'. Several of the characters are alter-egos or personas adopted by or directly about Smith himself—'Roman Totale', 'Hip Priest', 'Big New Prinz', 'The Dice Man', 'Marquis Cha Cha', 'Mark'll Sink Us' 'Edinburgh Man', 'Last Commands of Xyralothep via M.E.S.' and '50-Year-Old Man'.

Some of the more obvious *stylistic* idiosyncrasies which I'd assimilated before some of them were augmented and verified by the corpus linguistic software include: intertextual references to lyrics in other songs within and between LPs (e.g., "I should have listened to New Face in Hell" on 'I'm into CB') and paratextual scribbles on LP covers (see reference to 'sludge hai choi' above); a preoccupation with numbers and (often incomplete) lists (e.g., 'Last commands of Xyralothep via M.E.S'[2]); a willingness to play with language by inventing neologisms (e.g., 'corporatulent') and non-standard spellings in song titles (e.g., 'Kurious Oranj'); and a liberal use of regional dialects and English vernacular including a veritable and often humorous use of caustic, aggressive, and vitriolic taboo language and insults to rival Shakespeare.

Although some of the above may provide a modicum of new insight for the uninitiated, it would be surprising if much of it opened up new vistas of lyrical awareness for the diehard fan.

WHAT IS THE KING SHAG CORPUS?
NOT DIGGING REPETITION

So what constitutes a corpus of Fall lyrics? From a corpus linguistic perspective, on a simple level, a corpus "merely refers to a body of electronically coded text" (Baker 2006, p.26) around which a boundary has been placed for research purposes with a view to counteracting investigator bias (or confirming intuition) by applying a number of empirically verifiable techniques.

However, unlike much popular music, the Fall's lyrics were rarely reproduced on record sleeves or anywhere else other than on unofficial sites. The exceptions are the two Smith-authorised books containing lyrics of some of their earlier songs (Smith 1985; 2008) which comprise only a very small proportion of the hundreds of songs attributed to them. Even then, some of these 'official' lyrics seem not to consistently accord with what occurs on official releases, whilst the numerous official and bootlegged recordings of their 1,632 live performances (up to and including 4 November 2017—see 'The complete gig list' on the *Reformation* website) illustrate that Smith constantly amended his lyrics in performance.

So, the content of my corpus relies to a large extent on the astonishing work undertaken by contributors to Fall fan websites name-checked in the last section. This network of devotees, whose patience in transcribing and determining the exact lyric, includes comments, and at times passionate discussions, on most songs, which have aided in refining an understanding of the lyrics and indeed clarifying what words Smith articulates[3].

It is also important to note that there are at least two noteworthy precedents for Fall lyric corpus-building. The first was part of a Fall-themed art exhibition called *Paintwork#2* which ran for two weeks at the SW1 Gallery in London in May 2009. Amongst the more conventional paintings was a piece entitled 'Eighty-five thousand, nine hundred and ninety-nine words: Every word spoken or sung by Mark E. Smith on The Fall's studio recordings (in alphabetical order)'. This consisted of laminated printouts, in varying font sizes, of exactly what the title suggests. This corpus artwork was likely generated by using the existing online fan transcriptions available at the time and feeding them into a computer programme to generate an alphabetical list of every word. The top of one printout reads, for instance, "rabbit's rabbit-killer rabbits rabbit rabbit rabbit rabbit rabbit rabbit rabbit rabid Raccoons Raced Raced raced races" with clearly no intention of placing the words in any context other than to emphasise in a unique, decontextualised fashion the lyrical virtuosity in Fall lyrics.

The second bears a closer relationship to corpus linguistic techniques and complements the approach of this study, albeit with a different function. *The*

HEAD [133]

I'm an ill head [1]	Printhead	1979	Dragnet
How my head increases [1]	Printhead	1979	Dragnet
Pumpkin head escapes [4]	Pumpkin Head Xscapes	1992	Ed's Babe
Head through a blue haze [1]	Rebellious Jukebox	1979	Live at the Witch Trials
Your head explodes if you try on it [1]	Recovery Kit	2003	The Real New Fall LP
Your head explodes [1]	Recovery Kit	2003	The Real New Fall LP
Head sparkles [1]	Return	1992	Code: Selfish

Figure 7.1. A screenshot for 'head' from *The Flickering Lexicon*

Flickering Lexicon website—'Dannyno's Concordance to the Song Lyrics of The Fall'—provides a version of concordance lists containing every word, arranged alphabetically, used in a 99,124-word corpus of the texts of 493 songs up until June 2014. A concordance list is built around a word chosen by the researcher (or interpreted by the corpus software as important), and is usually then presented in a list accompanied by a roughly equal number of characters on either side of it to assist in an interpretation of its contextual meanings.

Although the concordance formatting on *The Flickering Lexicon* website does not necessarily accord with that used in conventional corpus linguistic studies—that is, with the key word aligned in the middle of each row—its arrangement offers useful additional information: the number of times the word is used in the corpus overall and in each of the same formulations (the number in square brackets); the string of words in which it appears contextually in the song; the title of the song each example occurs in; and the recording it appears on (LP/single/EP) with its year of release. See, for instance, figure 7.1, which is a screenshot taken from *The Flickering Lexicon* for the word 'head', the subject of analysis later in this chapter.

Figure 7.2 consists of the first ten examples of Wmatrix-generated concordances for the word 'head' in my data. Importantly, for this study, because

```
m looking for the real thing , yeah    Head    through a blue haze Waiting for the
other , Sister Why did you put your    head    in ? Reach or preach It 's all a dim
0 Black windows And smokey holes My    head    is full of lead And the beer is so w
ge It 's what we needed I 'm an ill    head    My face increases How my head increa
n ill head My face increases How my    head    increases Real problems , biz So how
ed , roundhead , army career , grim    head    If we was smart we 'd emigrate NEW F
p bottles and comics stuffed by its    head    Fuck it , let the beard grow I 'm to
ite a freak on a train Warts on his    head    and chin Boy , was I getting so vain
p all your allowance of experiences    Head    filled with a mass of too-well-known
ad a Joker Hysterical Face Her back    head    's full of skriking kids There 's no
```

Figure 7.2. A Wmatrix screenshot of a concordance list for 'head' from the data for this study

the lyrics are arranged in order of release, it provides an opportunity for a chronological distribution analysis to ascertain whether there are *patterns* of word usage clustered in particular time periods or spread significantly evenly over the whole time span.

The awareness that "Fall fans love lists" makes the *Flickering Lexicon* website a crucial resource for anyone interested in lyrical inventiveness in popular music[4]. And although website architect 'Dannyno' suggests rather too modestly that "the sensible concordance-compiler would not touch this project with a barge-pole", we have both independently had to consider similar dilemmas about what to include in our respective corpora. Where we diverge is largely down to the *aims* of our specific projects rather than any conflict about the nature of the lyrics.

For instance, *The Flickering Lexicon* includes a crucial outline of how choices are made in determining what counts as a legitimate Fall song lyric, declaring that there is "no consistently credible [. . .] definitive edition of Fall lyrics, even those which are Smith-approved" and citing Smith himself (in Smith & Middles, pp.271–72) explaining how he was never completely satisfied with the lyrics and that "lyrics change shape and meaning all the time". Although Mark E. Smith was responsible for the vast majority of song lyrics, several of them involved collaborations with other band members, especially Brix Smith-Start, and a small proportion of Fall songs were cover versions and/or adaptations of songs written and recorded by other artists, such as 'Victoria' (The Kinks—Ray Davies), 'Rollin' Dany' (Gene Vincent), 'Lost in Music' (Sister Sledge—Edwards/Rogers), and 'I Can Hear the Grass Grow' (The Move—Roy Wood). Smith also produced solo material and collaborated with other artists for whom he wrote the lyrics. My corpus closely matches that of *The Flickering Lexicon* in that it consists of lyrics delivered by Mark E. Smith as the Fall's singer, including cover versions (some of which are adapted for Smith's own purposes or are thematically congruent with other Fall lyrics), but *excluding* other Smith projects. All songs given an official studio release are incorporated, including exclusive radio sessions (mainly DJ John Peel) tracks, and official live releases which do not have a studio equivalent. The discrepancy in the number of songs—457 here and 493 in *The Flickering Lexicon* (which stops at 2014)—can be accounted for by the fact that the latter includes reworking and remixes of the same songs as separate entities and some obscurer non-official bootlegged live recordings. My corpus includes just one version of each song to ensure the statistics are not overly skewed by repetition.

Further to this point, the methodology that informs my approach—relying as it does on statistically based semantic keyness judged against reference corpora—necessitates further consideration of what constitutes a 'lyric' given that often phrases and lines are repeated to conform to the constraints and conventions of their delivery, such as the length and structure of the song and the nature of the musical accompaniment. Given that the concept of 'repetition' is closely associated with the band, a point of contention has been to what extent the number of times that a word or phrase is repeated adds any significant meaning to a song. For instance, although the pleasure derived from listening to The Beatles' 'I Want to Hold Your Hand' may derive partly from the repetition of that line in the song, it would be foolish to attach special semantic significance to the fact it is repeated eleven times, as opposed to say sixteen or eight, other than it fits the verse/chorus structure and the conventions of the length of traditional pop songs, partly driven as they were, by the limits of what a 7-inch vinyl single could contain on one side. Similarly then, although The Fall lyrics are far denser and with a much richer vocabulary than most of their pop/rock music counterparts, many of the songs contain repeated elements, the number of which it is difficult to assign credible meaning, not without endless debate!

So, to maximise the authenticity of the semantic significance categories generated by Wmatrix, which relies on statistics for these results, I have distilled the lyrics down to some kind of lexical 'essence' by manually removing all repeated lines, individual phrases, and the same word chanted consecutively to fit the rhythm and length of the song. 'Big New Prinz', for instance, has been condensed from 238 to 34 words so that the repeated lines "check the record, check the guy's track record' / 'rock the records' / 'he is not appreciated", appear just once in the corpus. There is inevitably some element of subjectivity in this refinement process presenting as it does a number of conundrums. Smith was adept, for instance, at subtly altering, shifting, or removing words within recurrent phrases creating a tension between repetition and transformation (aptly described in the phrase by DJ John Peel, which is the name of this volume). As a result, the decision was made to include all variants of a similar pattern in the corpus with the assumption that each variation counts as a different conceptual unit. So, although the song 'Frenz' is edited down from 135 to 65 words, it still contains the word 'friends' eight times in formulations such as "my friends ain't enough for one hand, my friends don't amount to one hand [. . .] my friends don't add up to one hand [. . .] my friends don't count up to one hand, my friends cannot count on one hand". Similarly in 'Dog is Life', 'dog' appears in singular, plural, and in compounds, twenty-three times in the edited version, but in each case appearing in a different modified noun phrase in a stream of consciousness homage to that animal's cultural connotations: "Dogs pet dogs dogs rapacious wet dogs, owner of dogs slow-witted dog owner, owner of rabid dog saving fare for tunnel, Euro-dream of civil, civil liberation for dogs [. . .]

mutt citadel dog-eye mirror hypnotic school slaver and learn rot from dog on grass and over nervous delicate dog [. . .] dog the pet-owner owner blistered hanging there death dog, Plato of the human example and copier dogmaster pet mourner, dog is life". The reduced number of instances of 'dog(s)' from one song may still inflate the significance of the semantic category in which it appears (in this case LIVING CREATURES: ANIMALS, BIRDS, ETC.), so it is essential that the analyst manually checks individual cases in context in order to register discrepancies[5].

The unedited corpus consists of 84,703 words and the editing process has removed 23,983 of these, resulting in a kind of distilled 'super-text' or 'macro-text', a condensed composite of 60,720 words (or 'tokens'), comprising 10,756 'types' (individually distinct words). The data is organised in chronological order of release, which is important for assessing the diachronic distribution, as the analysis below shows. Song titles are included in the data and capitalised.

"I REALLY THINK THIS COMPUTER THING IS GETTING OUT OF HAND"—FREQUENCY VS. KEYNESS

This next section considers the importance of distinguishing between *frequency* and *significance* (or *keyness*) and gives a brief overview of the key words and key semantic categories in the corpus, as generated by Wmatrix. This is followed by a more detailed analysis of a limited (given the size of the corpus) number of examples.

Baker (2006, p.121) asserts that compiling a raw frequency list—the most frequently occurring lexical items in rank order—is often an important first step in an analysis, but also has its limitations. In the Fall corpus the most frequent words used were, unsurprisingly, grammatical function words. At the top is 3,054 instances of 'the' (representing 5.03% of all the words in the corpus). This is followed by 'I' (1,732—2.85%), 'and' (1,553—2.56%), 'a' (1,392—2.29%), 'you' (1,142—1.88%), and 'in' (1,006—1.66%). At this stage it would be foolish to attach any significance to these determiners, pronouns, conjunctions, and prepositions until their *keyness* can be gauged in relation to other corpora, and there is no space here to do so, although they should not be ignored.

So Baker (2006, p.148) also claims that "[w]hen used sensitively, *key*words can reveal a great deal about frequencies in texts which is unlikely to be matched by researcher intuition".

Figure 7.3 shows the top ten keywords, revealing that 'man' tops the list, and is therefore deemed highly significant along with other nouns such as

"What's a computer?" 131

	Item	01	%1	02	%2		LL
1 Concordance	man	211	0.35	333	0.03	+	513.55
2 Concordance	my	498	0.82	2354	0.24	+	473.21
3 Concordance	his	257	0.42	1243	0.13	+	236.88
4 Concordance	life	100	0.16	181	0.02	+	224.64
5 Concordance	the	3054	5.03	37283	3.79	+	207.36
6 Concordance	me	408	0.67	2861	0.29	+	202.87
7 Concordance	city	36	0.06	6	0.00	+	171.04
8 Concordance	in	1006	1.66	10563	1.07	+	152.85
9 Concordance	head	73	0.12	149	0.02	+	151.88
10 Concordance	your	403	0.66	3250	0.33	+	145.44

Figure 7.3. A Wmatrix screenshot of the top ten keywords in the Fall corpus

'life', 'city', and 'head'. Other words of potential interest below the top ten are 'TV' (11th), 'dream' (15th), 'soul' (17th), 'heart' (20th), and 'brain' (22nd). It is worth noting that 'man' is the first *noun* to appear in the *frequency* list (36th most frequent) constituting 0.35 percent of all the words in the corpus, therefore seeming to confirm its significance.

Before I demonstrate the necessity of a contextual analysis of 'man' to secure the credibility of the statistical data, it makes sense here to provide a snapshot of what Wmatrix reveals about *semantic categories*. Frequency provides little insight, telling us that the top category—DISCOURSE BIN—comprises 24.78 percent (15,046) of all the words in the corpus. This is a dumping ground for grammatical function words, of which 'the' is the most frequent. Second is the category PRONOUNS—13.46 percent (8,171 words)—followed by EXISTING, consisting mostly of forms of the verb 'to be' such as 'is' and 'was'—3.57 percent (2,166 words).

However, the semantic-*keyness* lists generated provide potentially valuable insight into Mark E. Smith's lyrical preoccupations. Figure 7.4 is a screenshot of the top twenty most significant categories.

	Item	01	%1	02	%2		LL	LogRatio	
1 List1	Concordance Z99	1426	2.35	5684	0.58	+	1665.85	2.02	Unmatched
2 List1	Concordance B1	1066	1.76	3703	0.38	+	1439.54	2.22	Anatomy and physiology
3 List1	Concordance S9	360	0.59	1106	0.11	+	545.97	2.40	Religion and the supernatural
4 List1	Concordance L2	406	0.67	1727	0.18	+	440.07	1.93	Living creatures: animals, birds, etc.
5 List1	Concordance L1+	106	0.17	51	0.01	+	411.08	5.07	Alive
6 List1	Concordance K2	229	0.38	586	0.06	+	404.80	2.66	Music and related activities
7 List1	Concordance W2	69	0.11	0	0.00	+	392.47	11.13	Light
8 List1	Concordance Z2	589	0.97	3541	0.36	+	390.85	1.43	Geographical names
9 List1	Concordance W3	241	0.40	699	0.07	+	384.45	2.48	Geographical terms
10 List1	Concordance O2	642	1.06	4156	0.42	+	373.45	1.32	Objects generally
11 List1	Concordance O4.3	357	0.59	1718	0.17	+	331.27	1.75	Colour and colour patterns
12 List1	Concordance B2-	250	0.41	959	0.10	+	304.63	2.08	Disease
13 List1	Concordance A1.1.2	186	0.31	524	0.05	+	304.14	2.52	Damaging and destroying
14 List1	Concordance S2.2	344	0.57	1829	0.19	+	277.43	1.61	People: Male
15 List1	Concordance E3-	228	0.38	959	0.10	+	250.43	1.94	Violent/Angry
16 List1	Concordance L3	170	0.28	564	0.06	+	240.09	2.29	Plants
17 List1	Concordance W1	125	0.21	300	0.03	+	232.04	2.75	The universe
18 List1	Concordance M1	1244	2.05	12692	1.29	+	212.89	0.67	Moving, coming and going
19 List1	Concordance L1-	150	0.25	501	0.05	+	210.48	2.28	Dead
20 List1	Concordance O1.1	216	0.36	1117	0.11	+	181.41	1.65	Substances and materials: Solid

Figure 7.4. A Wmatrix screenshot of the top twenty key semantic categories in the Fall corpus

Several categories in the upper reaches were unsurprising, such as RELIGION AND THE SUPERNATURAL[6] (3rd most significant), MUSIC AND RELATED ACTIVITIES (6th), and GEOGRAPHICAL NAMES (8th).

However, there were several intriguing categories which signal thematic concerns in Fall lyrics which would have been harder to foresee. These include ANATOMY AND PHYSIOLOGY (2nd), LIVING CREATURES: ANIMALS, BIRDS, ETC. (4th), LIGHT (7th), GEOGRAPHICAL TERMS (9th), and COLOUR AND COLOUR PATTERNS (11th). The much vaguer category label UNMATCHED, which is first in the list and much more significant than may appear on the surface, is explored in the next section.

THE LEAGUE OF MANY-HEADED 'MEN'

But let's start with a commentary on the 14th most significant semantic category—PEOPLE: MALE, largely accounted for by the presence of the ubiquitous 'man' at top of the keyword list constituting 61 percent of the words in this category.

The fact that 211 instances of 'man' occur in 60,720 words (0.34 percent frequency) seems trivial unless we start to burrow down into their contextual and distributional realms. One danger is that statistics can be skewed by the clustering of the same word around a small group of similar-themed songs. For instance, by far the most frequent item in the LIVING CREATURES category is 'dog', which appears thirty-three times (after editing) along with eight instances of its plural—6th in the list. However out of the forty-one instances of 'dog(s)', twenty-one of these unsurprisingly occur in 'Dog is Life/Jerusalem'—whereby (as discussed in the section on the editing process above) various types of dogs (and their owners) appear in a stream of consciousness list. The distribution of the word is therefore a lot more modest than first appears and significant only to a minority of songs. As it happens, this does not hugely misrepresent the high-ranking of the LIVING CREATURES category (see Appendix 2).

So, a manual analysis of a concordance list for 'man' is necessary to ascertain the extent to which the appearance of that word is significant throughout the Fall's oeuvre. Figure 7.5 is a concordance list screenshot of examples 20–39 which represent twelve songs arranged chronologically (from May 1980 to March 1982) from *Totale's Turn* ('That Man') taking in two more studio LPs (*Grotesque*, *Hex Enduction Hour*), an extended EP (*Slates*), two singles, and two tracks not available on any official studio recordings (John Peel session track, 'C 'n' C-Hassle Schmuck' and the live version only of 'Session Musician').

```
eat THAT MAN That man loves you That   man   cares for you That man loves a heathe   20
oves you That man cares for you That   man   loves a heathen He came down from Acc   21
tle . In Darlington , helped a large   man   on his own chase off some kids who we   22
nd Of RT XVII And was an opportunist   man   Come , come hear my story How he set    23
sticks The fall had made them sick A   man   with butterflies on his face His brot   24
he people ask me How I wrote Plastic   Man   Life should be full of strangeness Li   25
yes . If I were a communist , a rich   man   would bale me . The opposite applies    26
  close season A quiet dope and cider  man   But during the season Hard drug and c   27
PROLE ART THREAT Pink press threat !   MAN   WITH CHIP : I 'm riding third class o   28
rt threat Safehouse , safehouse tone   MAN   WITH CHIP , That clan has gotten away   29
Sex with no drugs Be able to make a    man   Be able to trust your man Hassle , Ha   30
to make a man Be able to trust your    man   Hassle , Hassle Schmuck Everything yo   31
d cameras in the clothes dummies . A   man   came up to them He wanted sex in the    32
hat you cast out will hit back And a   man   will find he has to deny his Ours is    33
the crack Met a 54 year old dustbin    man   And '48 he 'd been in Jerusalem Sold    34
ouse Was a replica dartboard And the   man   on the floor Sorta went out of window   35
nd put it on " So around the mad kid   Man   on the first floor said " I just look   36
t species All the O 's cross country   Man   super shag-artists You mind tellin me   37
Scotch island To make you a bit of a   man   " The rabbit killer did not eat for a   38
back to the family And be their own    man   The people want what they know He '11   39
```

Figure 7.5. A Wmatrix screenshot of examples 20–39 from a concordance list for 'man'

Unlike the clustering of 'dog' in one song, this sample is representative of a relatively even distribution of 'man' across forty-one years. It occurs in 103 different songs, 22.5 percent of all the songs in the corpus. Figure 7.6 is a distribution pattern of 'man' (generated by the *Antconc* corpus software), where the black lines indicate instances of 'man' reading chronologically from left to right. Each of the thirty-two albums (and many singles), apart from *Levitate* (1997), is represented.

A detailed examination of each example would need more than this chapter to do it justice[7], so all I can do here is draw attention to some patterns.

One of the disadvantages of Wmatrix is that it assigns each word to one semantic category only, and therefore cannot account for the polysemous nature of words such as 'man' which are not always nouns referring to adult males. So only manual analysis can ascertain which meanings are in operation, in order to confirm or reject the significance of words flagged up by the software. There is one example, for instance, of 'man' used as a verb—"dark glasses on Western Union **man** the gates" ('Disney's Dream Debased'). There are a maximum of eleven uses of 'man' as an informal

Figure 7.6. A distribution pattern for the word 'man' from 1977–2017, reading chronologically from left to right

direct address moniker such as 'you got ta watch your wallet, **man**" ('Crew Filth'). However, these instances are few and far between as the other 199 examples open a window onto a gallery of male misanthropes and outcasts—central and peripheral, specific and general, first person ("I'm a **man**") and third person ("that **man**").

It is helpful to subdivide these into the following categories:

PHYSICAL/MENTAL ATTRIBUTES: "average **man**", "dice **man**", "strange **man**", "stupid **man**", "large **man**", "plastic **man**", "**man** whose head expanded/diminished", "**man** with butterflies on his face", "**man** [who is] tall and twisted back", "**man** [who is] extremely lazy", "**man** [who] was made up of twisted pitch", "serious **man**", "roly-poly **man**", "little **man**", "paranoid **man**", "**man** who pretends he knows it all", "broken like the other **man**", "balding **man**", "bearded **man**", "blind **man**", "joyous **man**".

AGE: "54-year-old dustbin **man**", "mid-30s **man**", "50-year-old **man**", "**man** of 49", "young **man** at the age of 19"; "old **man**".

GEOGRAPHICAL/ETHNIC CHARACTERISTICS: "semite **man**", "Shepherd's Bush **man**", "Edinburgh **man**", "country **man**", "Ibis-Afro **man**", "Hittite **man**", "cheap English **man**".

OCCUPATION/ROLE: "ex-worker **man**", "gas-board **man**", "Mr Sociological Memory **man**", "carrier bag **man**", "junk **man**", "session **man**", "operator **man**", "computer **man**".

Other men are defined by SPATIAL LOCATION in relation to the narrator or characters in the songs, using prepositional phrases, such as "**man** on my/your trail", "**man** on the first floor", "**man** at the bar", "**man** from down south", "**man** in digs with me", "**man** outside in the bucketing rain".

There are also anonymous men, often pre-modified by the indefinite article ('a') or a demonstrative pronoun ('that') and characterised by their actions: "a **man** came up to them", "a **man** laid down his life for you", "a **man** cries in pain", "that **man** loves you".

'Man' is used occasionally in a more generic sense: that is, not referring to a specific character in the lyrics, for instance, "the feast of **man**" (Xmas), "the spirit of **man**", "all that is foul in **man**"; "a **man** should not have to do this", "what keeps a **man** pushing on", "trust your **man**", "a **man** will find he has to deny his", "every **man** wants to be what he is not".

The panoply of male names and functional role labels (some generic) in song titles, in addition to the use of the word 'man' (or 'men') itself, are an indicator of the importance of (mainly) male characters in Fall songs and this clearly merits further investigation, beyond the scope of this chapter:

Table 7.1. Song titles containing "man" and functional role labels

Song titles containing 'man'/'men': 'Diceman', 'That **Man**', 'How I Wrote "Elastic **Man**"', 'The **Man** Whose Head Expanded, 'Carrier Bag **Man**', Edinburgh **Man**', 'Paranoia **Man** in Cheap Sh*t Room', 'The League of Bald-Headed **Men**', 'Junk **Man**', Secession **Man**', 'Mad.**Men**-Eng.Dog', 'Ibis Afro **Man**', 'Green Eyed Loco **Man**', 'Wolf Kidult **Man**', '50 Year Old **Man**', 'Stout **Man**', 'Hittite **Man**', 'Wise Ol' **Man**, 'O! ZZTRRK **Man**'

Song titles containing occupational (or other functional) role labels: 'Black Monk Theme', 'Bingo Master's Breakout', 'Cab Driver', 'Dr Buck's Letter', 'Das Katerer', 'Early Life / Real Life of the Crying Marshall', 'Early Days of Channel Fuhrer', 'Hey! Student', 'Hip Priest', 'Mere Pseud Mag Ed', 'New Puritan', 'Oswald Defence Lawyer', 'Petty Thief Lout', 'Rainmaster', 'Riddler', 'Senior Twilight Stock Replacer', 'Solicitor in Studio', 'Spectre vs Rector', 'The Ballard of J Drummer', 'The Container Drivers', 'The Knight, The Devil and Death'.

"FED WITH RUBBISH FROM DISPOSAL BARGES"— DON'T DISCARD THE TRASH

There is also a significant number of specific male names (see below) which appear in another category, that are deemed to be the *most* significant by Wmatrix—UNMATCHED—but unlike the DISCOURSE BIN, which encompasses a mishmash of unclassifiable lexical clutter, this collection of 1,426 words (1,075 types) verifies Sweeting's (2018) (and many others') reference to Smith's "abiding enthusiasm for cunning wordplay". As the category label signifies, it is a repository for all the words not recognised by the software (2.35% of the whole corpus) and it could be tempting to dismiss it as full of irrelevant typos, contractions, and elisions (e.g., "outta'", "waitin'", "coulda'"), abbreviations ("cig", "meth") and unfamiliar proper nouns (e.g. "Muzorewi", "Stacey", "Bonjela", "Rowche"). However, a further examination reveals the extent to which Fall songs exhibit a stream of imaginative neologisms, brand names, non-standard spellings, archaisms, and other obscure lexis, and draw on a range of vernacular and colloquial English (mostly northern UK dialect), signifying a consistent creative playfulness with the language arguably unequalled in contemporary song writing.

Smith creates neologisms (new words) through several related and sometimes overlapping processes recognised in linguistics as 'compounding' (joining two whole words together such as 'pop-stock', 'scareball'), 'blending' (merging partial sections of two or more words, e.g., 'corporatulent',), 'affixation' (the addition of unusual prefixes or suffixes onto familiar words, e.g., 'unguilty', 'pleasurelicious', 'blindlessly'), and word class conversion (using suffixes to transform a word from, for example, a noun to an adjective as in 'teletubbied' or a preposition to a noun, such as 'outsidedness'). The compression of several word fragments into one can generate novel concepts so that in the line from 'Kicker Conspiracy'—"[t]heir guest is a Euro-State magnate, **corporatulent**"—Smith blends the words 'corporate' (relating to a large company) and 'corpulent' (obese) to signal his disgust at the bloated state of UK soccer management in the early 1980s.

Some other noteworthy examples in context include:

- "He no longer denies or hides his **enfondness** for mech." ('Recipe for Fascism")
- "**Paralytis**, I'm telling you" ('Systematic Abuse')
- "**Extramentally** drawn" ('Mexico Wax Solvent')
- "The last statement with no name proved **diversible** to the authorities" ('Is This New')
- "Soundtracks, soundtracks **melched** together, the light, the lights above you" ('I am Damo Suzuki')
- "But do not make your **enig-noise** public" ('Last Commands of Xyralothep via M.E.S.')
- "Time of the **vulperines**, time of the wolverines" ('Service')
- "You're history, you've quit **existation**" ('Blood Outta Stone')
- "The lyrics of Hey Jude, he was **victuous** trembling" ('Assume')

Several song titles include neologisms which embed elements of more familiar words, such as 'I Feel **Voxish**', '**Spinetrak**', '**Hexen** Definitive—Strife Knot', 'Open the **Boxoctosis** #2', and '**Amorator!**'

Other words, which to the uninitiated, may also seem like Smithisms, are actually obscurities listed in the *Oxford English Dictionary* (*OED*), demonstrating the breadth of the Fall corpus lexicon. Alongside archaisms such as "thyself", "deploreth", "forsooth", and "verily" are:

- "All the streets are blue and **beshadowed** today" ('On My Own')
- "It's a curse, and am not **unguilty** of using it" ('It's a Curse')
- "Horseshoes **splacking**, swallows hay cart, cart horse" ('Dktr Faustus')

In this last example, the *OED* defines 'splack' as "[w]ith a sound suggestive of splashing and smacking", a rare usage of which there is one just citation, from E. M. Forster's 1971 novel, *Maurice*: "Mr London and Mr Featherstonhaugh dived **splack** into the water lilies".

Other UNMATCHED items include a range of colloquial, vernacular, and regional Englishes which contribute to the realism, grittiness, and in some cases, humour in many Fall songs, confirming Smith's reign as the 'slang king'. Regional northern UK English includes "kecks" (trousers), "mithering" (bothering, worrying), "youse" (regional plural 'you'), and "skriking" (crying). More general colloquialisms (often insulting epithets) include "swizz" (swindle), "crapheads", "asslickers", "spliffhead", "smartass", "cack-head", and, of course, the legendary (Hey there) "fuckface" from 'The Classical'.

In addition, UNMATCHED confirms Smith's tendency to name-check contemporary brands and companies, which lends the songs an additional aura of social realism. These include: "Curly Wurly", "Spangles", "Chocolate Treets" (UK confectionary); "Stuvyesant", "B & H", "555s", (cigarette brands); "Prozac", "Trimidine", "Rowche", "Monocard" (prescription drugs/drugs companies), "ZTT", "Regal Zonophone" (record labels), "Vimto" (a Manchester-based blackcurrant drink), and "Domestos" (household disinfectant).

Non-standard spellings of common words are a characteristic of many song titles including 'Underground **Medecin**', '**Kurious Oranj**', '**Frenz**', 'Big New **Prinz**', Mountain **Energei**', 'Mike's Love **Xexagon**', 'Pumpkin Head **Excapes**', '**Tuff** Life Boogie', '**Psykick** Dancehall', 'Cyber **Insekt**', '**Happi** Song', 'Everything **Hurtz**', and 'Pittsville **Direkt**'.

A significant number of the other words in UNMATCHED name-check a range of mostly real, historical, and contemporary characters, including the former prime minister of Zimbabwe Rhodesia (as it was then called) Bishop Muzorewa, the legendary nineteenth-century machine-smashing leader Ned Ludd, poet Lord Byron, and singers Dolly Parton and Captain Beefheart.

Smith's fascination with names (mostly male)—real and fictional—is signalled by the number of song titles which include them, including several self-references and to members of the band. This reinforces the significance of the preoccupation with MEN discussed earlier in the chapter:

Table 7.2. Song titles referencing male names

'(Birtwistle's) Girl in Shop', 'Arid Al's Dream', 'Cary Grant's Wedding', 'Cowboy George/ Gregori', 'Craigness', 'Disney's Dream Debased', 'Ed's Babe', 'Haf Found Bormann', 'Hands Up Billy', 'I am Damo Suzuki', 'I'm Ronny the Oney', 'I'm Frank', 'Impression of J. Temperence', 'Ivanhoe's Two Pence', 'Janet Johnny and Jame's,' Last Commands of Xyralothep via MES', 'Ludd Gang', 'Mark'll Sink Us', 'Marquis Cha Cha', 'Mike's Love Xexgaon', 'Mister Rode', 'Nate Will Not Return', 'Muzorewi's Daughter', 'No Xmas for John Quays', 'Noel's Chemical Effluence', 'Rollin' Dany', 'Sir William Wray', 'Stephen Song', 'Terry Waite Sez', 'The Quartet of Doc Shanley', 'Tom Raggazzi'.

UNMATCHED also logs a range of geographical names not recognised in the 8th most significant category—GEOGRAPHICAL NAMES—many of which would be familiar to those living in the Manchester/Salford/Lancashire regions of the UK such as Cheetham (Hill), Salford, Chorlton(ite), Piccadilly, Victoria Station, Deansgate, Corporation Street, Arndale (Shopping Centre),

Ramsbottom, Castleford, Rochdale, Bury, Prestwich, Accrington, and Marsden. Add these to the 342 different types of words in the GEOGRAPHICAL NAMES category and confirmation is provided of the importance of *place* in the Fall songs. The list below is just a sample:

Table 7.3. A selection of place names in Fall song lyrics

Abu Dhabi, Bournemouth, Basingstoke, Bath, Berlin, Birmingham, Bolton, Bradford, Brisbane, Bristol, Buxton, Chicago, California, Cambridge, Camden, Chelsea, Chile, China, Chiswick, Cologne, Cumbria, Dallas, Damascus, Darlington, Edinburgh, Flanders, Florida, Glastonbury, Hamburg, Hampshire, Hampstead, Hebden Bridge, Hollywood, Hounslow, Iceland, Istanbul, Italy, Japan, Jerusalem, Kensington, Kentucky, L.A., Leeds, Mesopotamia, Mexico, Midlands, Milan, Montreal, Munich, New York, Newcastle, Newquay, Norway, Oxford, Portugal, Paraguay, Paris, Poland, Portsmouth, Prague, Rome, Russia, Salem, Skegness, Soho, Spain, Stamford Bridge, Stoke, Sudan, Surrey, Sweden, Switzerland, Texas, Thailand, Turkey, Vatican, Venice.

As an interesting aside, the semantic category in 9th place—GEOGRAPHICAL TERMS—provides what may be surprising to some (given The Fall's urban roots), a variety of topographical imagery including twenty-eight instances of "hill(s)", seventeen of "valley", fifteen of "mountain(s)" plus "desert", "bog", "forest", "landscape", and "volcano". Water-features in landscapes are also prominent—"sea", "beach", "waves", "tide", "creek", "lake", "river", "whirlpools", "canal", "cove", "shore", "lagoon", "oceans", "lochs", "surf", and "bay".

"I'M THE 'HEAD' WRANGLER"— A CORPUS OF BODILY FUNCTIONS

From a personal perspective, the most unpredictable significant 'key concept' category generated by Wmatrix is ANATOMY AND PHYSIOLOGY, although the logic of its significance becomes apparent after further scrutiny. Ranked second, it comprises a cornucopia of words related to body parts, functions, and states—237 different word types expressed 1,066 times (1.76 percent of the whole corpus), including, in rough order of frequency (with conflation of, e.g., singular and plural), the following:

Table 7.4. Words appearing in the ANATOMY AND PHYSIOLOGY category, in frequency order

back, head(s), face(s), eye(s), hand(s), heart(s), brain(s), blood, hair(s), hip, tear(s), feet/foot, born, sleep(ing), mouth(s), shoulder(s), arm(s), breath, neck, bone(s), ear(s), body, shit, chest(s), nose, leg(s), finger(s), sweat, tired, tooth/teeth, flesh, forehead, nerve(s), skin, dick, eyelids, lips, suck, chin(s), spit(s)(ting), veins, stomach, birth, breathe, gut(s), arse, cry(ing), throat, knees, numb, liver, fist, elbow(s), bosoms, lap, mitts, beard(s), spleen, skull, bald(ing), sperm, ankle(s), skinny, shivered, genes, piss, nimble, spine, faeces, orgasm, kidney(s), muscular, bowel(s), hard-ons, unborn, thighs, lung(s), belly, jowls, flabby, diaphragm, ticker, gulping, womb, belched, blink, adrenaline, unconscious, aerobic, inhaled, wrist, drool, skeleton, armpit, retina, facial, slumber, cranium, freckles, limb(s), knee, septum, rectum, alopecia, cuticles, foetus, visage, pee, jaw, eyeball, palm(s), moustache, scalp, metamorphosis, waist, frown, wince, inhale, complexion, lick, marrow, muscle, sputum, palm, fringe, pouting, skeleton, ectoplasm, snout.

In a similar way that 'man' has several related meanings, it was necessary to generate a concordance list of the highest frequency words in this category—'back' (81) and 'head' (68)—and manually check each one to determine whether in their context they have meanings other than those specifically related to physiology. And indeed, doing so for 'back' reveals that the word is rarely used in the anatomical sense.

Figure 7.7 is a representative sample of twenty, showing that apart from "was annoyed at skin-patch on **back**" ('Bremen Nacht'), most examples of 'back' are used in the broader spatial and temporal sense, and potentially over-emphasising the prevalence of bodily references. These include "**back** of the exhaust clip" ('2X4'), "put the Curly Wurly **back**" ('Slang King'), "suddenly **back** on its own" ('Vixen'), "I don't make passes from the **back**" ('Entitled'), "why don't you bog off **back** to Xanadu" ('Glam Racket'), and "regardless of the look-**back** bores" ('It's a Curse').

The concordance list for 'head', however, offers a very different and much more satisfying picture. A configuration is produced which demonstrates a

```
 's a new fiend on the loose On the    back   of the exhaust clip Clipped on rich     20
 ific time frame Redhead skinny with   back   leg-brace He danced behind a singer     21
  trendy wretch BLACK saucers at the   back   of your neck Interruptions , from th    22
 o take , had to put The Curly Wurly   back   Slip away at court or him and his bl    23
  Create company Green is starboard ,  back   Left is port , there Old continental    24
   had taken her a long time Suddenly  back   on its own To sit , friendless &; al    25
  ing See the people holding from the  back   Hat-boaters tilting Got nice pink bu    26
     mean to you ? You take her from the back We 're so respectable But I 'm entit    27
 you ? I do n't make passes from the   back   Is it something usual ? To be so ent    28
 ( Manacled to the system ) From the   back   third eye psyche , the reflected mir    29
 t Was then annoyed at skin-patch on   back   Then I did myself acquit On Bremen N    30
 ck collar sends East German refugee   back   switch and crap pathetic Of earth-li    31
 ITE LIGHTNING In North Carolina way   back   in the hills Lived my pappy and he h    32
    Glittering beach Johnny he replied back   With me you struck a pact ZV day Fiv    33
 ig fat foot on my knee bone And the   back   of my is in my septum IMMORTALITY Yo    34
   left me but you will find your way  back   To that black barren land that bears    35
 ere or other Why do n't you bog off   back   to Xanadu in Ireland Glam Rick Do n'    36
    's burden Operation Mind-Fuck Look back   bores Bach and Wagner All you really    37
 lways crap , regardless of the look   back   bores . Waiting for you . PARANOIA M    38
  with a garden vegetable Take a look  back   Rear-view mirror : it 's all behind     39
```

Figure 7.7. A Wmatrix screenshot of an extract from the concordance list for 'back'

highly significant use of the word in its *physiological* sense, spread relatively evenly crossing five decades, although tailing off in the 2010s. If we discount a few uses of 'head' in its broader metaphorical and adjectival senses, for example, "bottles and comics stuffed by its [bed] **head**" ('How I Wrote "Elastic Man"') and "to find their **head** clown" ('Over! Over!'), we are left with an intriguing picture. Table 7.5 shows each use of 'head' in chronological order, in context. Note that the standard concordance list view has been adjusted so that each example includes the full clause in which 'head' occurs, along with the title of the song and year of release. This shows that 'head' occurs in fifty-seven individual songs over twenty-nine different years. It appears on songs on twenty-six LPs, eight singles, and three exclusive John Peel Radio show sessions.

Table 7.5. A 40-year chronology of 'head'

Context	Song	Year
Head through a blue haze	*Rebellious Jukebox*	78
Why did you put your **head** in?	*Mother Sister*	78
My **head** is full of lead	*Various Times*	78
I'm an ill **head**	*Printhead*	79
My face increases, how my **head** increases	*Printhead*	79
roundhead, army career, grim-**head**	*English Scheme*	80
bottles and comics stuffed by its **head**	*How I Wrote Elastic Man*	80
Warts on his **head** and chin boy	*Fit and Working Again*	81
Head filled with a mass of too well-known people	*Just Step Sideways*	82
Head's full of skriking kids	*Joker Hysterical*	82
There's a bayonet beside my **head**	*Marquis Cha Cha*	82
Man whose **Head** A: knew about politbureau facade	*Neighbourhood of Infinity*	83
Goes with you down, and pats your **head**	*Hexen Definitive – Strife Knot*	83
The man whose **head** expanded / diminished	*The Man Whose Head Expanded*	83
Sounds like my **head** trying to unravel this lot	*The Man Whose Head Expanded*	83
I'm the **head** wrangler	*Words of Expectation*	84
Hit him on the **head** with a 2 by 4	*2 by 4*	84
His **head** was full of icy calm	*Pat Trip Dispenser*	84
It was a thing with a **head** like a spud ball	*Stephen's Song*	84
feared beer was making a sludge of my **head**	*Couldn't get Ahead*	85
By the way I hang my **head** you can see I'm afraid	*Ghost in my House*	87
Pivot your legs, shake your **head**, take an easy breath	*Sleep Debt Snatches*	87
Hold the grip, make a mark on your **head**	*Sleep Debt Snatches*	87
When in town I keep **head** down	*Carrier Bag Man*	88

Context	Song	Year
Candelabra lions **head** Via butchers display too.	*The Steak Place*	88
Head down the steak place	*The Steak Place*	88
When he sees CIA shot flying over **head**	*Oswald Defence Lawyer*	88
Oswald's **head** added on a commie tie	*Oswald Defence Lawyer*	88
My **head** swooned	*Twister*	88
I caught the side of my **head** on a protruding brick chip	*Jerusalem*	88
Make out your **head** is in a bell	*Dead Beat Descendant*	89
Do not fret, rest your **head**	*Xmas with Simon*	90
Look at the glass, turn your **head**	*You Just Haven't Found It Yet*	91
Impulses crowd your **head**	*You Just Haven't Found It Yet*	91
You're into the top shackle mental saw-down of your **head**	*You Just Haven't Found It Yet*	91
He turns his **head** and smiles at me	*The Mixer*	91
But still this creature raised its fury **Head** sparkles	*Return*	92
How can you smell your own **head**?	*Return*	92
It's hard to extract the brains from the **head** of a minor executive	*Time Enough at Last*	92
My **head** dip dip dipping	*Everything Hurtz*	92
One had brown spectacles on his **head**	*Crew Filth*	92
Pumpkin **head** escapes	*Pumpkin Head Xscapes*	92
Puts his **head** down when girls pass in the street	*Paranoia Man in Cheap Sh*t Room*	93
And at my **head**, one who laughs at nothing	*Service*	93
Your heart was still in marble and your **head** was reckoning	*Reckoning*	94
You're gonna get it through the **head**	*Hey Student*	94
Keep your **head** down for the moment	*City Dweller*	94
I watch your **head** expanding	*Glam Racket / Star*	95
I got zero tolerance My **head** full	*Don't Call Me Darling*	95
Head loaded people avoid bad luck	*Powder Keg*	96
He cannot find 3 points below the **head** and shoulders	*Shake Up*	99
His **head's** a little weary	*Hand's Up Billy*	00
Get on a bus, Keep **head** down	*Bourgeois Town*	01
Sat opposite a politician with his **head** held down	*Bourgeois Town*	01
I need a long regular bed and a feather pillow for my **head**	*Loop 41 Houston*	03
How can you leave your money and guilded land, Your **head** explodes	*Recovery Kit*	03
My **head's** attracted to magnetic wave of sound	*I Can Hear the Grass Grow*	04

(continued)

Table 7.5. **Continued**

Context	Song	Year
Put your **head** down to the ground and listen to your mind	I Can Hear the Grass Grow	05
To find their **head** clown It was shut by the EC	Over! Over!	07
Put a stocking over his **head** and you couldn't tell the difference	Insult song	07
Or impress your dipshit **head**	My door is never	07
Her **head** hurts	The Wright Stuff (	07
You've got your **head** in water	Systematic Abuse	07
I'm an inferior product man, They call me 'Bad **Head**'	50-year-old man	08
My mind is a blank My **head** is spinning	Funnel of Love	10
And makes your hair silver H CO CO2 Rat 's **head** Cosmos 4 awaits	Cosmos 7	11
Cosmos rat 's **head** Four eyes	Cosmos 7	11
There he stands Homogenous bone and **head** Homeric cogs of steel	Fol de Rol	17

All I can do here is provide a cursory and subjective overview of thematic trends suggested by the role 'head' plays in Fall songs. The examples in Table 7.5 illustrate how 'head' is used as a motif metaphorically to symbolise various states of mind. Several of the references to 'head' are as a metaphor for the mind as an overloaded container, dangerously close to bursting, indicated by references to 'full'/'filled', 'increases', 'crowd', 'loaded', 'expanded', 'explodes'. Given the ubiquity of 'man' and 'head' in the corpus, it is worth pointing out here that perhaps 'The Man Whose Head Expanded'—about a paranoid man who believes a soap opera writer plagiarises his lines—encapsulates some of the key themes in Fall songs. In its more literal sense, 'head' is used symbolically in a downwards position to represent negative emotions such as shame or fear expressed by characters in the songs, or to describe physical aspects of the head deemed distasteful by the songs' personas, such as "sat opposite a freak on a train, warts on his **head** and chin" ('Fit and Working Again').

It is apt then that 'face' is the third most frequent word in the ANATOMY AND PHYSIOLOGY category, which occurs eighty-five times when also counting 'faces' and 'faced'. Apart from the rare times it appears as a verb (e.g., "why don't you **face** up to it?" in 'Black Roof'), 'face' complements 'head' in the signification of unflattering ('grotesque') physical attributes and related subject matter.

Table 7.6. Examples of 'face' in the Fall lyrics corpus

And the crap in the air will fuck up your **face**	**Face** a mess covered in feathers
You can see their ugly **face** lines	And sick red-**faced** smile
An old Jew's **face** dripping red	French fries spread on her **face**
Gets out of the bath with a dirty **face**	Joker Hysterical **Face**
Hey you horror-**face**!	The nurses climbed up, our **face** paled
Just stupid **faces** looking bad	Crows feet are ingrained on my **face**
My **face** is slack	Try to wash the black off my **face**
A man with butterflies on his **face**	Two-**face**, boat-race disgraced
His brother threw acid in his **face**	His **face** is full of ex-cruelty

And if we add to this, words listed above from the categories JUDGEMENT OF APPEARANCE: NEGATIVE, and DISEASE, we have further confirmation (if any was needed) of the extent to which mental and physical ugliness and decay permeates the Fall's lyrical landscape (see below):

Table 7.7. Words generated by WMatrix in the JUDGEMENT OF APPEARANCE: NEGATIVE, AND DISEASE category

JUDGEMENT OF APPEARANCE: NEGATIVE
horrible, mess, filth, dirt(y), trash, ugly, hideous, disgusting, desolate, nasty, unclean, wreck, vulgar, wretched, rotting, junk, unutterable, crummy, shitty, muck, grubby, ogre, hellish, stooped, horrid, mouldered, macabre, abhorrent, pained, rancid, obnoxious, gory, poxy, bedraggled, scruffy, vile, decay.

DISEASE
mad(ness), plague, sick(ly)(ening)(ness), pain, hurry, crazy, insane, disease(s)(ed), paranoia(d), fever, ill(ness), cold, bug, scratch(ing), hurt(s), exhausted, anthrax, cancer, fracture, sore, scar(red), psychosomatic, spastic(s), neurotic, addiction, burn(s), psychotic, boils, indigestion, weariness, cripple, nauseous, wart(s), zits, hangover, itch(es), amnesia, infertile, germ(s), infect(s)(ion), patients, ailing, bruise(s), tonsillitis, rabid, blistered, deranged, jaded, pneumonia, psoriasis, tinnitus, cough, vomit, rash(es), schizophrenic, injury, paralytic, limp, herpes, scabies, retarded, lame, retched, asphyxiation, short-sighted.

"WHAT DO YOU MEAN 'WHAT'S IT MEAN? WHAT'S IT MEAN'"? OPENING THE BOX ...

Charlatan's frontman Tim Burgess asserted on BBC's *Newsnight* on the announcement of Smith's death that "every lyric is just pure gold really" and joked that on the occasions they met, Smith "could be quoting Nietzsche one minute and scrounging a cigarette the next". The creative interplay between Smith's literariness and his ability to use the vernacular contributes to the defamiliarised vision of the world around him that is hard to pin down, much like the refrain in 'Spectre vs. Rector' and the squiggly line at the corner of your eye. If this study has revealed anything, it is the aptness of the oft-cited line from 'Psykick Dancehall' (1979): "When I'm dead and gone, my vibrations will live on" in that all computer-generated list-making and pattern spotting can achieve is to open the goddam box and lead to further debate and head-scratching. Tensions have always been at the heart of The Fall's lyrics, and our abilities to make sense of them—between difference and similarity, obscurity and clarity, intuition and science—reflect this.

List lovers can ogle the content of the RELIGION AND THE SUPERNATURAL and LIVING CREATURES: ANIMALS, BIRDS, ETC. categories in the Appendices and scratch around the floor for further elucidation. Before doing so, perhaps you should heed the ominous warning from 'Glam Racket':

> You post out sixty page computer printouts
> On the end of forests
> All the above will come back to you
> And confirm you as a damn pest.

APPENDICES

Appendix 1: Words appearing in the third most significant semantic category—RELIGION AND THE SUPERNATURAL in rough frequency order—360 examples from 137 types:

Table 7.8.

God, soul(s), Christmas(tide), holy, spectre(s)(al), hell, priest, rector, ghosts(s), spirit(ual), witch(craft), heaven, devil, reformation, troll, puritan, mystic(s)(ism), fate, vampires, psychic, church(es), satan(ic), jew(s)(ish), altar, pilgrim, elf, clergy, exorcise(d)(ist), hobgoblin(s), gremlins, papa, bless(ed), elves, Jehovah, purgatory, Christianity, Lucifer, demon, haunting, missionary, prayer, vicar, miracle(s), myth(ical), new-age, gnome(s), reincarnate, psalm, rite, heathen, monk(s), friar, preacher, religion, ritual, archbishop, prophet, Methodist, Easter, bishop(s), pray(ed), fairies, omen, Muslims, Baptists, haunted, chapel, rev(erend), Jesuits, legend(s), superstitious, divine, magic, Valhalla, god(s), worship, familiars, benediction, angel, Parson, holy spirit, halo, coven, quaker, werewolf, shrine, ominous, sermon, saint(s), orthodox, bible, hydra, Jehovah's Witnesses, redemption, parish, temple, celestial.

Appendix 2: Words appearing in the fourth most significant semantic category—LIVING CREATURES: ANIMALS, BIRDS, ETC.—406 examples from 161 types, sub-categorised manually into various types:

Table 7.9.

Insects – fly, insect, bees, aphid, midges, spiders, moths, ladybird, fleas, cockroaches, parasite, gnat, butterflies, bluebottles, tarantula	**Fish and other marine life** – shark, sardines, oyster, whale, squid, goldfish, frogs, pike, trout
Domestic pets/ farmyard animals – dog, cat, rabbit, horse, mutt, lamb, fox, poodle, kitten, hog, pussy, bunny, hen, bull, feline, goat, piggies	**'Exotic' animals** – monkey, baboon, snake, yak, lizard, hippo, elephant, alligator, camel, jackal, tiger
	Birds – kiwi, vulture, hawk, crows, chicken, pigeon, swans, duck(ling), cuckoo, dove, ostrich, ibis

Appendix 3: A Wmatrix-generated word cloud of the key semantic categories:

Alive   Anatomy_and_physiology   Cause&Effect/Connection   Change   Closed:_Hiding/Hidden
Clothes_and_personal_belongings   Colour_and_colour_patterns   Comparing:_Unusual   Constraint   Crime
Damaging_and_destroying   Darkness   Dead   Degree   Disease   Drama,_the_theatre_and_show_business
Drinks_and_alcohol   Emotional_Actions,_States,_And_Processes_General   Evaluation:_False   Evaluation:_Bad   Evaluation:_Unauthentic   Evaluation:_True   Exceed;_waste   Expected   Failure
Farming_&_Horticulture   Fear/shock   Flying_and_aircraft   Food   Foolish   Furniture_and_household_fittings   Games   General_appearance_and_physical_properties
Geographical_names   Geographical_terms   Happy   Inability/unintelligence
Information_technology_and_computing   Judgement_of_appearance:_Negative   Light
Living_creatures:_animals,_birds,_etc.   Location_and_direction   Long,_tall_and_wide
Medicines_and_medical_treatment   Mental_actions_and_processes   Mental_object:_Conceptual_object   Moving,_coming_and_going
Music_and_related_activities   No_constraint   No_change   No_knowledge   Objects_generally   Open:_Finding:_Showing
Other_proper_names   Parts_of_buildings   People   People:_Male   Personal_relationship:_General   Personal_names   Personality_traits
Plants   Psychological_Actions,_States_And_Processes   Putting,_pulling,_pushing,_transporting   Quantities_etc.   Relationship:_Intimacy_and_sex
Religion_and_the_supernatural   Residence   Sad   Sailing,_swimming,_etc.   Selfish   Sensory:_Sound
Sensory:_Taste   Shape   Size:_Big   Smoking_and_non-medical_drugs   Sound:_Quiet   Sound:_Loud   Substances_and_materials:_Solid
Substances_and_materials_generally   Temperature:_Cold   Temperature:_Hot_/_on_fire   The_universe   The_Media:_TV,_Radio_and_Cinema   Time   Time:_General
Time:_Old;_grown-up   Time:_New_and_young   Time:_Ending   Time:_Beginning   Unethical   Uninterested/bored/unenergetic   Unmatched   Unseen   Unused   Unwanted
Vehicles_and_transport_on_land   Violent/Angry   Warfare,_defence_and_the_army:_weapons   Weather

NOTES

1. This chapter is an updated version of several presentations on the Fall lyrics corpus, including one given at the Louder than Words Festival, Manchester, on 16 November 2014, on a panel with Steve Hanley and Simon Wolstencroft (to launch their books), Fall sleeve notes writer Daryl Easlea, chaired by music journalist and author Mick Middles. At that point the corpus was unfinished.

2. If there is such a thing, I would argue 'Last commands of Xyralothep via M.E.S.' is one of the most archetypical Fall lyrics. Discuss!

3. Pringle's You Must Get Them All: The Fall on Record (2022, pp.14–19) gives a thorough overview of these dedicated platforms as well as an ambitious attempt to review every song.

4. For anybody wanting instant access to an alphabetical list of individual Fall words in context, *The Flickering Lexicon* is an invaluable resource. See here: http://dannyno.org.uk/fall/flickeringlexicon.htm.

5. I must emphasise that I am fully aware of the unsubtlety of this editing process and the method has been occasionally challenged at academic conferences, but I stand by it until offered a more robust and convincing way of building a lyrics corpus of one artiste.

6. See Appendix 1.

7. Readers can consult *The Flickering Lexicon* for all instances of 'man' (and 'men') in the corpus.

REFERENCES

Baker, P. (2006). *Using corpora in discourse analysis*. Bloomsbury Academic.

Bridle, M. (2018). Male blues lyrics 1920 to 1965: A corpus based analysis. *Language and Literature*, 27(1), pp. 21–37. https://doi.org/10.1177/0963947017751757

Dannyno's Concordance to the Song Lyrics of The Fall. *The Flickering Lexicon*. http://dannyno.org.uk/fall/flickeringlexicon.htm

Fisher, M. (2010). 'Memorex for the krakens': The Fall's pulp modernism'. In Goddard, M. and Halligan, B. (eds). (2010). *Mark E. Smith and The Fall: Art, Music and Politics*, pp. 95–110. Ashgate Publishing Limited.

Ford, S. (2003). *Hip Priest: The Story of Mark E. Smith and The Fall*. Quartet Books Limited.

Goddard, M. and B. Halligan (eds). (2010). *Mark E. Smith and The Fall: Art, Music and Politics*. Ashgate Publishing Limited.

Hanley, P. (2020). *Have a bleedin guess: The story of Hex Enduction Hour*. Route.

Hanley, S. and O. Piekarski. (2014). *The Big Midweek: Life inside The Fall*. Route.

Kelly, D. (2018, January 25). Mark E. Smith was a rogue and rascal—and very funny, too. *GQ Magazine*. http://www.gq-magazine.co.uk/article/mark-e-smith-was-a-rogue-and-a-rascal-and-very-funny-too

Leech, G. (2008). Work in progress in corpus stylistics: A method of finding 'deviant' or 'key' features of texts, and its application to 'The Mark on the Wall'. In Leech, G. (2008), *Language in Literature: Style and foregrounding*, pp. 162–77, Routledge.

Motschenbacher, H. (2016). A corpus linguistic study of the situatedness of English pop song lyrics. *Corpora*, 11(1), pp. 1–28. DOI: 10.3366/cor.2016.0083

Norton, T., and B. Stanley. (2021). *Excavate! The Wonderful and Frightening World of The Fall*. Faber.

Parkes, T. (2018, January 24). The Fall and Mark E. Smith as a narrative lyric writer. *The Quietus*. http://thequietus.com/articles/03925-the-fall-and-mark-e-smith-as-a-narrative-lyric-writer

Pringle, S. (2022). *You must get them all: The Fall on record*. Route.

Rayson P. (2008). From key words to key semantic domains. *International Journal of Corpus Linguistics* 13(4), pp. 519–49. DOI: https://doi.org/10.1075/ijcl.13.4.06ray

Simpson, D. (2009). *The Fallen.* Canongate Books.
Smith, M. E. (1985). *The Fall lyrics*. Lough Press.
———. (2008). *vII*. Lough Press.
———. (2009). *Renegade: The lives and tales of Mark E. Smith*. Penguin.
Smith, M. E. and M. Middles. (2003). *The Fall*. Omnibus Press.
Smith-Start, B. (2016). *The rise, the fall, and the rise*. Faber & Faber Ltd.
Sweeting, A. (2018, January 25). Mark E. Smith obituary: the Fall's driving force was poet, satirist and misanthrope. *The Guardian*. https://www.theguardian.com/music/2018/jan/24/mark-e-smith-obituary
The Annotated Fall. *Annotated Fall*. http://annotatedfall.doomby.com/
The Complete Gig List. *Reformation*. https://sites.google.com/site/reformationposttpm/Home
The Fall Discography. *The Fall Online*. http://www.thefall.org/discography/albums.html
Thompson, D. (2003). *A User's Guide to The Fall*. Helter Skelter Publishing.
Walker, B. (2010). Wmatrix, key concepts and the narrators in Julian Barnes's *Talking It Over*. In McIntyre, D. and Busse, B. (eds.), *Language and Style*, pp. 364–87. Palgrave Macmillan.
Welsh, C. (2018, January 25). Mark E. Smith was the supernatural priest of post-punk. *Factmag*. http://www.factmag.com/2018/01/25/mark-e-smith-the-fall-tribute/
Wolstencroft, S. (2017). *You can drum, but you can't hide*. Route.

Chapter Eight

Searching for the Right Word or Phrase that Would Put a Chill Up the Spine

A Corpus-based Discourse Analysis of Mark E. Smith's Lyrics

Elaine Vaughan, Brian Clancy, and Eoin Devereux

WORDS OF EXPECTATION

Once described by Simon Reynolds (1996) as "a kind of Northern English magic realism that mixed industrial grime with the unearthly and uncanny, voiced through a unique, one-note delivery somewhere between amphetamine-spiked rant and alcohol-addled yarn," The Fall, in its myriad of manifestations—but always led by Mark E. Smith—were one of the most intriguing, influential, and prolific post-punk groups in British popular culture. This is evidenced in the group's unique sound, aesthetic, and in the often complex narratives and themes contained in Smith's sometimes obtuse lyrics (see Parkes 2018). As a northern English working-class auto-didact, Smith eschewed conventional approaches to song-writing, recording, and performance. Indeed, we would argue that many of his songs force us to call into question our very expectations of what constitutes a 'song' in terms of structure, content, and delivery. Smith was, for all intents and purposes, a prose writer who recorded and performed songs atypically. Traditional song structures (Intro/Verse/Chorus/Bridge) were regularly ignored; lyrics routinely resisted usual narrative and linguistic expectations and were delivered through a mixture of spoken word and singing. Live performances sometimes witnessed cross-referencing to other Fall lyrics and other spontaneous outbursts. The wide range of influences Smith drew upon, including his northern working-class upbringing; his psychic experiences of pre-cognition; his in-depth knowledge of literature and film (see Smith and Duff 2021) have already been well documented (see, for example, the chapters by Smith and Devereux, Lawley and Cashell in this volume) and it is not our intention to rehearse them in this chapter. In examining Smith's songcraft, we do not engage in a close reading of a particular song or investigate fan reception of songs. Rather, we adopt an interdisciplinary research approach which focuses on the discourse(s) present in the lyrics of The Fall *via*, in the first instance, an investigation of patterns and irregularities in the linguistic characteristics of the lyrics themselves. We do this by blending macro-level, thematic analysis of the lyrics, with more micro bottom-up corpus-based analysis; the corpus-based approach to discourse analysis is elaborated later in this chapter. Given Mark E. Smith's evident love of words and of wordplay we hold that it is entirely fitting that we focus on a more systematic analysis of his lyrics.

SYSTEMATIC (ABUSE?)

Our purpose is to explore what ballast, if any, a different type of empirical perspective can add to systematic observation of intra- and intertextual thematic characteristics of lyrics. In essence, our open-ended research question could be expressed as 'what would happen if we did *that* (corpus-based analysis) to *this* (the lyrics of The Fall)'? Apart from an important contribution by Davies (2019) to the University of Limerick symposium on The Fall from which the present volume grew, to our knowledge there is no other study within the diverse and dynamic universe of academic study of The Fall that utilises this type of approach. Matt Davies's (see chapter 7) analysis differs from our own as it uses a corpus processing and analysis platform called WMatrix (Rayson 2008, 2009) to investigate key semantic domains in a complete corpus of the lyrics of The Fall, which prioritises lexical content, or words with dictionary meanings. By contrast, in our work, we sample from the group's output, selecting the lyrics of the first five studio albums and comparing them with those of the final five. We include both lexical and grammatical items in the analysis and argue that by doing so, we can claim to capture at least some of the unconscious selections of the writer, whilst acknowledging that lyrics are essentially *crafted*. They can be created consciously or in flow, over shorter or longer periods of time, as the result of an individual or collaborative creative process; they are pondered, distilled, drafted, redrafted—and where The Fall are or were concerned are infinitely mutable in Smith's act of live performance. Smith's hybrid vocal delivery mixing singing and spoken word, using two different microphones, using a megaphone, changing amp settings for other group members, as well as on-stage banter and 'ranting' are all examples of his playfulness as a performer (for an elaboration of the latter, see, Nickas and Planck's (2021) *Slang King: M.E.S. on Stage, 1977–2017*. For our analysis, the selection of *this* over *that* is as interesting to us as the more visible and identifiable deployment of techniques such as a 'deviant' spelling like *psychkick, frenz,* or *Prole Art Threat*, which play with homophony and phonematic equivalences (cf. Kreyer and Mukherjee 2007) to create lyrical worlds and meanings. We contextualise our blended approach in our discussion below of relevant work and concerns within the sphere of popular music and popular culture, and how linguists have approached lyrics as linguistic data, before articulating how we collected and analysed the selections of Mark E. Smith's lyrics examined in this chapter.

LINGUISTIC ANALYSIS OF LYRICS

From a language and literature perspective, West (2019, p.4) suggests that, on the whole, the language-based elements of how song lyrics work as pieces of text, and their integral role in the "whole multimodal experience" of a song, has been largely absent in the otherwise thriving field of research that explores the social and political contexts of popular music and culture. The present study builds on work that focuses on salient features in the lyrics of popular songs, whether more generally (e.g., Murphey 1992; Tlili 2016), or with a focus on a close interpretation of a specific instance of the output of a particular artist e.g., Power, Dillane and Devereux's (2012) analysis of *Interesting Drug* by Morrissey, or Morini's (2013) work on *Running up that Hill* by Kate Bush. Linguistic interest in (mainly) pop lyrics is often described as predicated on their impact factor—the ubiquity of our exposure to the language and patterns of pop music, and the interesting position they occupy on the written-to-spoken cline: while not spontaneous, and often fixed in writing, many pop lyrics are more oral than written in nature; while oral in nature, they are nevertheless often fixed in writing, or published, and they are written to be sung (see also Werner 2012). The primarily linguistic or language-based research on lyrics is exemplified by, for example, work by Johnson and Larson (2003) which looks at metaphors of musical motion in the work of The Beatles, showing essential connections between conceptions of physical and musical motion. Kreyer and Mukherjee (2007) use findings from the Giessen Bonn Corpus of Popular Music (GBoP) to discuss, amongst other things, metaphors typical of pop songs, including those relating to love. Based on the Top 30 Albums in the US charts, their corpus of 176k words allows them to identify the 'metaphorical superstructure' LOVE IS AN UNPLEASANT THING: it hurts the body and soul. Connected sub-metaphors such as HEART within this superstructure can indicate both vulnerability (hearts can be stabbed, tortured, bruised) and toughness (hearts can be made of ice, or stone). As becomes evident in reviewing the linguistic literature on lyrics, much of the research focuses on the genre of pop. Given that datasets aim for substantial coverage of 'typical' examples of lyrics, most linguistic studies aiming to characterise the genre itself take a pragmatic, commonsense approach and sample from, for example, the top-selling albums in the U.S. or UK charts (e.g., Werner 2012). This sort of approach, whether with smaller datasets or larger ones, has foregrounded innovative or 'deviant' spellings or 'non-standard' grammar, perhaps best alternatively viewed as those that are standard within specific varieties; see Olivo's (2001) work on spelling conventions in rap music, and Werner's observations on double-negatives ('won't let nobody hurt you') and increasing use of *ain't* in his corpus of pop lyrics.

Linguistic analysis of lyrics via corpus building and analysis has gained some momentum with linguistic analysis on corpora of lyrics such as the GBoP (Kreyer and Mukharjee 2007) and collections such as the Blues Lyrics collected at the University of Regensburg (BLUR), which contains 8,000 song transcripts (Miethaner 2005). These focus on themes of sociological and anthropological work from a linguistic perspective, for example, Kreyer's (2015) work on representations of gender in the GBoP, or work by Alim (e.g., 2006) and Pennycook (e.g., 2003, 2007) on the language of hip hop culture and its global spread. Still other recent work has focused on the discursive construction of 'Europeanness' in lyrics of songs entered in the Eurovision Song Contest, from a comparative, critical, and corpus-based perspective (Motschenbacher 2016). Some variational sociolinguistic work considers singing styles and accents of specific bands or types of music: Simpson (1999) builds on the work of Trudgill (1983) which had examined the phenomenon of British singers affecting American accents in their performances, comparing this with the changing trends of the late 1970s, 1980s, and 1990s away from this sort of delivery. Beal (2009) focusses on the characteristics and potential language-ideological impact of the Arctic Monkey's use of Sheffield English in their performances, arguing that it taps into and indexes a type of authenticity which is in keeping with their musical style (indie) and persona. Specific music genres are also discussed. Cheung and Feng (2019) analyse the high-frequency lexical items in a corpus of lyrics of over a thousand heavy metal songs, showing them to be characterised by fear of death and darkness (the top five items are *death, fear, darkness, flesh,* and *human*), and using appraisal theory (Martin and White 2005) as a prism for their analysis they show, amongst other things, how the genre discursively challenges religions, speaks of alienation, and condemns injustices, as well as the counter-discourses of resistance to authority present. Kreyer and Mukharjee (2007, p.36) also connect particular items which are semantically related to death, pain, and blood to gothic rock, and suggest that they could be construed as 'primed' (cf. Hoey 2005) for use in this genre (much like they appear to be for heavy metal as Cheung and Feng 2019 shows). All of these observations of lyrics and style from a (socio)linguistic perspective pertain to the lyrical output of The Fall, which is replete with 'deviant' spellings, linguistic innovations, and condensed, complex, and gnomic world-building. In order to sample from the prolific output of The Fall, we compiled a corpus of lyrics from the first and last five studio albums recorded, using as a basis the lyrics available online from the site *The Annotated Fall* (http://annotated-fall.doomby.com).[1] The complementary perspectives generated allow for an alternative, fine-grained analysis of the linguistic construction of identity and place in Mark E. Smith's lyrics.

TO NKROACHMENT: YARBLES—DATA AND METHODOLOGY

The data for this chapter is twofold. First, we used the lyrics of both the first and last five albums of The Fall to form a corpus (hereafter referred to as the First/Last Fall corpus). A *corpus* (pl. *corpora*) is a principled collection of texts that are stored in an electronic format to facilitate analysis using specifically designed computer software. As The Fall never published official versions of lyrics in sleeve notes, and due to Mark E. Smith's propensity to alter lyrics when performing live (as part of his on-stage 'live-mixing'), the lyrics used to form the corpus were downloaded from *The Annotated Fall*. This allowed us to 'fix' a version of the lyrics of the songs and analyse them using the corpus software. This is not the place to dispute the validity of the lyrics or the interpretation of their meaning; rather its purpose is to illustrate what might be done with a key aspect of The Fall's creative output when viewing it from an alternative methodological perspective, thereby adding to the methodological canon utilised by the Centre for the Study of Popular Music and Popular Culture. Thus, allowing for the existence of other versions of lyrics in a live setting, the first five and last five albums (First/Last Fall corpus) form a representative sample of Mark E. Smith's work consisting of 104 songs and a corpus size of 19,628 words. This is illustrated in table 8.1:

Table 8.1. Description of the corpora employed

First/Last Fall corpus	
Total word count = 19,628 words	
First Five Fall	Last Five Fall
Live at the Witch Trials (1979, Step Forward)	*Your Future Our Clutter* (2010, Domino)
Dragnet (1979, Step Forward)	*Ersatz GB* (2011, Cherry Red)
Grotesque (After the Gramme) (1980, Rough Trade)	*Re-Mit* (2013, Cherry Red)
Hex Enduction Hour (1982, Kamera)	*Sub-Lingual Tablet* (2015, Cherry Red)
Room to Live (1982, Kamera)	*New Facts Emerge* (2017, Cherry Red)
Word count = 11,146	Word count = 8,482

The second treatment of the data involves dividing the First/Last Fall corpus into two subcorpora. The first of these, as illustrated in table 8.1 consists of the first five albums recorded by The Fall, which we have called the First Five Fall corpus (hereafter First Five). This corpus is 11,146 words in size and consists of fifty songs written over a four-year time frame. The second subcorpus, Last Five Fall (hereafter Last Five) is 8,482 words in size, consisting of fifty-four songs spanning a seven-year period. Organising the data in this way allows us to ask two very broad questions regarding the song lyrics of The Fall:

1. What functional language patterns characterise the lyrics of The Fall, and what might this contribute to their interpretation?
2. To what extent do these patterns change over time?

Most modern corpora, especially written corpora such as those consisting of song lyrics, are large corpora. For example, the MusiXmatch corpus, employed later in this chapter, is 55 million words in size. However, smaller corpora such as the First Fall/Last Fall corpus are unproblematic, when, as outlined in question one here, researchers focus on functional rather than lexical items. Functional items that are the focus of this chapter, such as personal pronouns, or demonstratives, are commonly found in the most frequent items in most corpora, both spoken and written. In addition, small corpora have proven to be suitable and extremely useful for the investigation of functional items. This is due to an iterative approach to the data, outlined in the methodology section, that is not possible when using larger corpora (see, for example, Clancy and Vaughan 2012; Vaughan and Clancy 2013).

The methodology employed for the chapter can be broadly described as corpus-based discourse analysis, and more specifically has become a corpus-pragmatic one. This approach harnesses the ubiquity of linguistic pragmatic phenomena, for example, personal pronoun usage (items such as *you*, *we*, and *they*) or demonstratives such as *this*, *that*, *these*, and *those*, all small polysemous and polyfunctional items common to everyday usage which are nonetheless complex in their interpersonal and contextualisation properties.

CORPUS PRAGMATICS

Corpus pragmatics is a relatively recent development at the intersection of the fields of corpus linguistics and pragmatics, and a growing number of studies are emerging that illustrate the benefits of this synergy (see, for example, Adolphs 2008; Romero-Trillo 2008; O'Keeffe et al. 2011; Aijmer and Rühlemann 2015). Corpus pragmatics makes use of specifically designed computer software to analyse corpora. Through the use of software tools, in this chapter *word frequency lists*, *keyword lists*, and *concordance lines* are all analysed, the more traditional, 'horizontal' qualitative approach to linguistic analysis is integrated with the more 'vertical', quantitative approach to corpus linguistics (Aijmer and Rühlemann 2015). *Word frequency lists*, the starting point for most corpus researchers, appear visually as a list of all the types (unique word forms) in a corpus in order of their frequency of occurrence (highest frequency first). Corpus word frequency lists are, however, a rather raw measure of comparability, based on the potential of a word form rather than its actual function. Therefore, many corpus studies recommend that frequency analysis be complemented through the use of other concordancing tools. This chapter employs both the *keyword* and *concordance line* tools. Keywords are used to ascertain whether an item (or items) under scrutiny occurs with statistically significant frequency relative to a larger, comparable corpus (see below). Concordance lines, on the other hand, present a search item, or *node*, in the centre of the co-text, the words that occur to the left and to the right of the node. The use of these tools constitutes a bottom-up approach to corpus pragmatics where the starting point for the analysis are corpus frequency counts and then concordance lines are explored atomistically. Studies such as this one represent a highly iterative approach to the study of pragmatic phenomena, and here it is applied to the lyrics of The Fall.

FINDINGS AND DISCUSSION

First/Last Fall Corpus: Frequency Differences

As previously mentioned, the first stop for corpus analysis is the word frequency list, which is generated quite quickly by corpus linguistic software. A word frequency list, in general, appears visually as a list of all the word forms in a corpus (highest frequency first), coupled with the number of occurrences of each word (*Frequency* column) as demonstrated in table 8.2. This word frequency list has been generated using *WordSmith Tools* (Scott 2021). The musiXmatch (MXM) dataset is a c.55-million-word corpus of song lyrics (see http://labrosa.ee.columbia.edu/millionsong/musixmatch). Table 8.2 compares the frequency counts for the top twenty-five most frequent words in the First/Last Fall corpus with those in the MXM corpus.

Table 8.2. Top 25 most frequent words in the MXM and First Fall/Last Fall corpora

N	Fall	Freq.	MXM	Freq.
1	the	935	I	2,078,808
2	I	615	the	1,863,782
3	and	478	you	1,744,257
4	a	476	to	1,067,578
5	of	356	and	1,055,748
6	you	322	a	974,499
7	in	311	it	821,152
8	to	297	me	771,755
9	it	284	not	735,396
10	for	228	in	626,410
11	's	202	my	611,942
12	**he**	**187**	is	595,735
13	is	186	of	540,064
14	on	161	that	474,535
15	**they**	**136**	do	470,946
16	n't	131	your	463,681
17	was	129	on	419,354
18	my	121	am	407,827
19	**this**	**121**	**we**	**393,787**
20	do	117	are	381,331
21	your	115	all	361,511
22	'm	113	will	357,386
23	no	113	for	334,143
24	me	103	be	330,613
25	his	99	no	315,665

He Is Not Appreciated

Table 8.2 shows that there are many commonalities between the two frequency lists, for example, as in many corpora of spoken language, *I* occurs more frequently than *you*. This supports previous findings that show that frequency lists for song lyrics are dominated by first- and second-person pronouns (see, for example, Werner 2012). In terms of differences, *he* occurs in position 12 on the First Fall/Last Fall frequency list but does not occur in the top twenty-five items in the MXM corpus. In addition, *this* in position 19 on The Fall frequency list does not occur in the twenty-five items in the MXM list. It is also interesting to note the presence of second-person plural *they* (position 15) in First Fall/Last Fall, and the first-person plural pronoun *we* (position 19) in the MXM list.

To further investigate these frequency differences, due to the two datasets being of unequal size, it is necessary to normalise the frequency counts. Normalisation involves a simple mathematical calculation that allows two corpora of unequal size to be compared. The process of calculating the number of occurrences of *he* per 100,000 words in the First Fall/Last Fall corpus, for example, involves the calculation 187/19,885 × 100,000. This gives us a result of 941 occurrences per 100,000 words. Similarly, if we apply this process to the MXM dataset, we can determine that *he* has 261 occurrences per 100,000 words (143,897/55,163,335 × 100,000). Therefore, *he* is more than 3.5 times more frequent in First Fall/Last Fall than in MXM. The comparative, normalised frequency counts for *he*, *this*, *we*, and *they* are presented in table 8.3.

Table 8.3 demonstrates that the normalised frequencies support the findings from table 8.2 in that *he*, *this*, and *they* are more frequent in All Fall, whereas *we* is more frequent in the MXM corpus. The first-person plural pronoun *we* is commonly associated with the creation and maintenance of in-group identity, solidarity, inclusion, and closeness (see, for example, O'Keeffe 2006; Rühlemann, 2007), and it might be that Smith is less interested in this than, say, a more traditional pop song as represented in the MXM corpus. Instead, Smith appears more preoccupied with personal pronouns that represent a third person—*he* and *they*. In contrast to *we*, *they* is commonly associated with the other or not-group. Similarly, the demonstrative *this* has been associated with the creation of an oppositional, confrontational, or independent stance (Strauss 2002). Therefore, in order to further explore the hypothesis

Table 8.3. The comparative frequency of occurrence of **he, we, they** and **this** normalised per 100,000 words

	The Fall	MXM
he	941	261
this	609	451
we	402	714
they	684	309

that Mark E. Smith creates a masculine, confrontational, not-group identity in his song lyrics, *he, they,* and *this* are explored in more detail.

SUBLINGUAL TABLET: CONSTRUCTING THE IDENTITY OF THE FALL THROUGH THE USE OF FUNCTIONAL LINGUISTIC ITEMS

The process of generating concordance lines using computer software is central to the analysis of any corpus. It is common practice to use corpus analysis software to search a corpus for a particular word, part of a word, or a phrase. What is characteristic of concordance lines, is that the search item, or *node,* is presented visually in the centre of a concordance line surrounded by a number of words on either side, referred to as the *co-text.* This visual presentation is called the Key Word in Context or KWIC format. Figure 8.1 illustrates a random sample (random samples can be generated using the corpus software) in KWIC format for *he* as a node word. Given that these concordance lines represent the use of *he* in the First Fall/Last Fall corpus, a detailed examination yields a number of elements that can be associated with Smith's creation and maintenance of a definite identity for The Fall. Smith primarily indexes three groups through his use of *he*. The first of these is the music business and uses *he* to refer to, for example, *Gibbus Gibson* (line 1); *Tony Wilson* (line 7), and *Simon 'Ding' Archer* (line 17). Smith also uses *he* to refer to himself, for example, *Hip Priest* (line 11) and *Hittite Man* (line 19). Linked to this identity

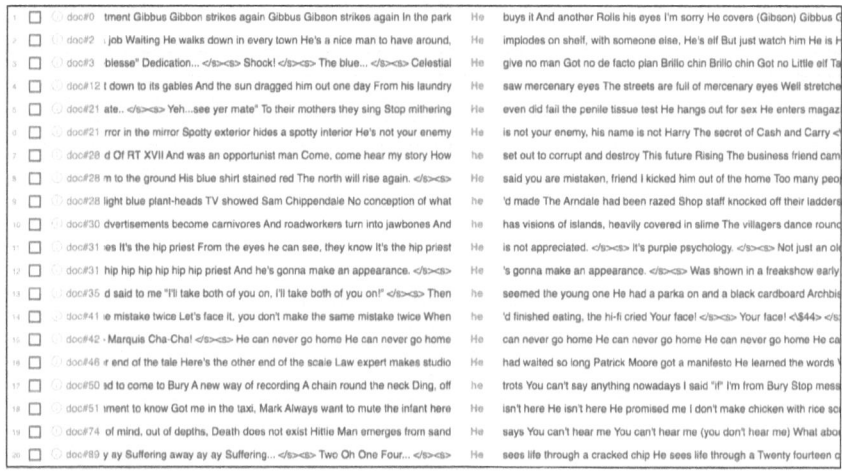

Figure 8.1. Random sample of twenty concordance lines for *he*

category is the influences on Smith's song writing represented by *he*—for example, the Germanic influence is evident in *he = Brillo* (line 3) and *he = Marquis Cha-Cha* (line 15), and H. P. Lovecraft's influence may be seen in the *he = Rabbit Killer/hunter* (line 9) allusion. Finally, the third category is Smith's use of *he* to refer to society. *He* refers to both mainstream society, for example, *he = elf* (line 2), *he = neighbour* (line 14), *he = lawyer* (line 16), and also outsiders such as *he = mad kid* (line 13). These identity categories are prevalent throughout Smith's song writing and it is interesting to explore the language that surrounds Smith's use of the third-person pronoun *he*. In relation to the music business, we see *corrupt and destroy* (line 7), which might suggest a negative connotation or attitude. Similarly, in relation to mainstream society the verb *implode* (line 2) is visible. When Smith refers to himself and his influences, the language is again negative on occasion, for example, *not appreciated* (line 11). The concordance lines featuring *they* and *this* offer further evidence of Mark E. Smith's attitudes and stances towards the music industry, himself, and his influences and society in general.

In further exploring Mark E. Smith's creation of identity and his stance towards his preoccupations, attention now turns to a detailed look at the third-person plural pronoun *they*. Figure 8.2 illustrates a random sample of twenty concordance lines with *they* as the search item. The concordance lines in figure 8.2 echo much of the identity creation associated with *he* in figure 8.1. The difference in the use of *they* lies in the fact that the pronoun serves to further 'other' the elements referred to and, therefore, gives some insight into Smith's attitudes towards them. As with his use of *he*, Smith references

Figure 8.2. Random sample of twenty concordance lines with *they* as the search item

other musicians and the music industry in general in lines 1, 7, 9, and 14 and 18. The language associated with the use of *they* in the surrounding co-text is negative—*mithering* (line 7), *imitate* (line 9), *snotty and offensive* (line 14), and *ask for creative money* (line 18). It is also possible that Smith uses *they* in relation to his personal health. The *they = magicians* (line 6) who *take your heart out with a sharp knife* may be a reference to undergoing surgery and *they = doctors* (line 20) may be an allusion to his chances of survival, or not, *nine out of ten*, from cancer. In this case, the language is largely positive. Finally, mainstream society is portrayed negatively, for example, where *they = a drudge nation* and *they = human trash* (line 12). Mark E. Smith also uses *they* to refer to outsiders in society; *they = young black men* (line 10), which portrays them linguistically as a socially isolated grouping.

THIS NATION'S SAVING GRACE

The final functional item to be explored in this section is the demonstrative *this*. Demonstratives are 'primarily used to orientate the hearer in the speech situation, focussing his or her attention on objects, locations or persons' (Diessel 1999, p.93). In this way, demonstratives act as instructions to the hearer/listener. Demonstratives have a variety of pragmatic functions in that they are used interpersonally by a speaker to focus a hearer's attention for a variety of reasons. For example, demonstratives can be used to convey speaker emotion—*this/these* can be used to signal a more positive and involved attitude, whereas *that/those* can be used to signal a more detached and possibly critical attitude. The choice of demonstrative used by the speaker is one based on the degree of importance attached to the information being provided. For this reason, the function of *this* is often associated with involvement devices which focus a hearer/listener's attention on information that is discourse 'new', and therefore, requires a high degree of focus as this information has not been previously shared (see Strauss 2002; Rühlemann 2007). *This* functions as both a demonstrative determiner, *This song means . . .*, and a demonstrative pronoun, *This is not a song about. . . .* This analysis focuses on the use of *this* as a demonstrative determiner given that this function of *this* is the more frequent (Strauss 2002). Therefore, *this* functions as a high focus marker in that "the entity being referred to remains in the discourse in the form of a full NP [noun phrase]" (Strauss 2002, p.150). Figure 8.3 illustrates the use of *this* as a demonstrative determiner, *this + noun phrase*, in the First Fall/Last Fall corpus.

Searching for the Right Word or Phrase that Would Put a Chill Up the Spine   161

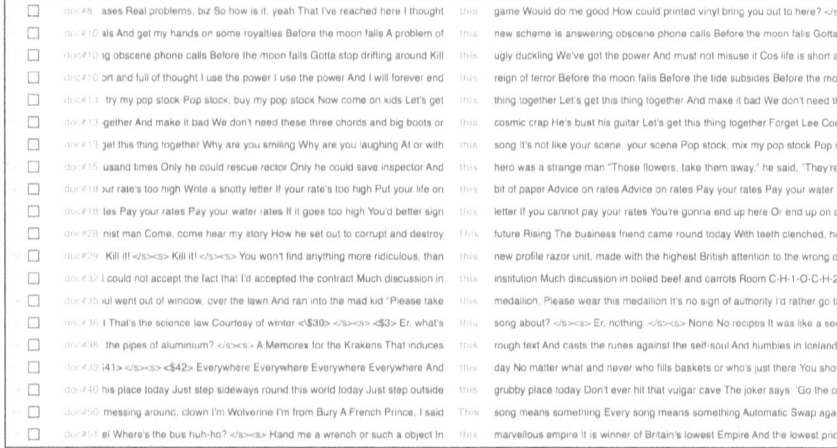

Figure 8.3.   Random sample of twenty concordance lines with *this* as the search item.

The process of marking an item as high focus and therefore, important new information for the hearer/listener can be illustrated using two examples of *this* from figure 8.3. Lines 2 and 8 demonstrate the use of *this* by Smith after the first mention of a noun phrase. In both extracts (1) and (2), Smith moves from the indefinite article *a (new scheme)* and *a (hero)* and replaces *a* with *this* in subsequent mentions (all in bold).

(1)
I must create **a new scheme**
And get out of others' hands[2]
Before the moon falls
I could use some pure criminals
And get my hands on some royalties
Before the moon falls
A problem of **this new scheme**
Is answering obscene phone calls
Before the moon falls ('Before the Moon Falls', 1979)

(2)
Comes **a hero**
Soul possessed a thousand times
Only he could rescue rector
Only he could save inspector
And **this hero** was a strange man
"Those flowers, take them away," he said,
"They're only funeral decorations" ('Spectre vs. Rector', 1979)

The change in determiner from the indefinite *a* to the demonstrative *this* acts as a signal that the noun phrase *scheme* and *hero* are now the topic focus of the song in that it establishes "major discourse participants in the universe of discourse" (Diessel 1999, p.98; see also Strauss 2002). Smith uses the change from *a* to *this* to emphasise the importance of what he is saying and to mark topic persistence. This, in turn, focuses the attention of the listener. There is also an argument to be made that writers employ *this* in order to ensure that the focus on a topic is successfully achieved and is easy to track (see Himmelmann 1996).

Many of these instances are examples of the use of *this* to focus speaker attention by drawing on situational knowledge about the wider context. Smith is consistently sharing this information throughout his lyrics, through his use of functional items such as *he* and *they*. However, through his use of *this*, he marks topics as high-focus items and, therefore, demands that the hearer pay attention. Again, Smith focuses the hearer's attention on the music business. For example, in line 1, *this game*; line 3, *this ugly duckling*; line 4, *this reign of terror*; and line 6, *this cosmic crap*. It is apparent that the lexical items immediately surrounding *this*, are not positive ones. This observation, then, builds on the allusions made by pronouns *he* and *they*, but furthers the negative connotations by marking them as the focus of attention through the use of *this*. Similarly, line 9, *this bit of paper*; line 12, *this new profile razor unit*; line 13, *this institution*; line 14, *this medallion*; and line 18, *this grubby place*, all focus the hearer's attention on society in general. Smith uses *this* to portray mainstream society in a negative light. *This bit of paper* refers to the Poll Tax, a time of great unrest in the UK; *this new profile razor unit* to the meaninglessness of consumerism; *this institution* (*institution* arguably conveys connotations of *lunacy/insanity* in The Fall's lyrics (see chapter 13 by David Meagher and John McFarland for an elaboration); and *this grubby place* to the UK; and finally, *this medallion*, which may be a reference to the getting of a 'medal' for sobriety. High frequencies of the use of *this* have been associated with stances of 'opposition, confrontation, separateness or independence' (Strauss 2002, p.144).

FALLING THROUGH TIME: LINGUISTIC PATTERNING IN FIRST FIVE VS. LAST FIVE

In attempting to ascertain whether the topical preoccupations of Smith, and by extension the music of The Fall, changed over time, we now turn our attention to an analysis of the First Five and Final Five subcorpora. As detailed in table 8.1, the First Five subcorpus is 11,146 words in size and consists of the first five albums released by the band. In contrast, the Last Five subcorpus is 8,482 words in size and consists of The Fall's final five albums. As in the previous section, the first analytical step is to generate word frequency lists and these results are shown in table 8.4.

Table 8.4 demonstrates that the top ten most frequent items in both subcorpora consist of the same linguistic items, albeit with some differences in

Table 8.4. Top 25 most frequent words in the First Five and Last Five corpora

N	First Five	Freq.	Last Five	Freq.
1	the	594	the	341
2	a	294	I	324
3	I	291	and	204
4	and	274	a	182
5	of	199	of	157
6	in	176	you	146
7	you	176	to	144
8	it	166	in	135
9	to	153	it	118
10	for	129	for	99
11	's	125	**he**	**87**
12	is	104	is	82
13	**he**	**100**	's	77
14	**this**	**98**	on	69
15	on	92	n't	63
16	**they**	**86**	do	58
17	was	75	me	57
18	'm	72	was	54
19	no	69	my	52
20	my	69	man	51
21	n't	68	all	50
22	your	65	**they**	**50**
23	his	65	your	50
24	out	62	get	49
25	do	59	with	45

the rank order. These top ten most frequent items are similar to many spoken corpora, the absence of the item *that* being the exception. The results also show the presence of *he* and *they* (bold and shaded) in both subcorpora, with relatively small frequency differences. This provides further empirical evidence that throughout Smith's career his lyrical world continued to be a masculine one, characterised by the creation of oppositional others such as the music industry and mainstream society (for example, sometimes the focus was on London/southern England, the British middle class, and the Labour Party). One of the main differences between the two frequency lists in the context of this chapter is the absence of *this* from the Last Five most frequent items (*this* is in position 14 in the First Five corpus). In order to account for this frequency difference, another corpus tool, the keyword list, is employed here.

A keyword list is a list of words that occur with unusual and statistically significant frequency, or not, in a 'target' corpus relative to a reference corpus (Baker 2006; Scott and Tribble 2006). Due to the statistical nature of the results, keyword lists are not only indicative of unusual frequency, but also of saliency in a corpus. In other words, keywords are associated with 'aboutness'. Aboutness items are generally lexical items in the form of nouns, verbs, or adjectives. In addition, the statistical measure of significance indicates that an item's presence on a list is not due to chance, but to the "author's (conscious or subconscious) choice to use the word repeatedly" (Baker 2006, p.125). Table 8.5 illustrates the top fifteen positive keywords (those with high frequency in comparison to the reference corpus) for the First Five and Last Five subcorpora. In this instance, in order to generate the keyword lists, in the First Five, the Last Five was the reference corpus and vice versa.

The results show that, in addition to aboutness items, there are also commonly used functional items, and *this* appears on the First Five keyword list (position 10). As discussed, *this* is commonly used to flag information that is 'new' to listeners, attaching a high focus to the accompanying noun phrase, thereby demanding attention. It is possible that, in the first five albums, Smith was establishing the identity of the group and, therefore, felt the need to signal what was important, to create the outgroups, to mark the group as confrontational, independent, and beyond categorisation. Having succeeded in doing this, it might be that the maintenance of this identity was not necessary in the later years of the group, as represented by the Last Five items, leaving Smith to concentrate on other concerns. It can also be seen that the First Five keyword list contains other functional, commonly occurring items such as *behind*, *yeah*, *but*, and *who* that do not feature in the Last Five list. This points towards a less dense lyrical style in the early albums.

Table 8.5. Top 15 positive keywords in the First Five and Last Five subcorpora

N	First Five	Last Five
1	hip	troll
2	choi	facebook
3	pop	ay
4	stock	pledge
5	muzorewi	unseen
6	daughter	suffer
7	ba	change
8	behind	year
9	nazis	de
10	**this**	quit
11	yeah	shake
12	face	wray
13	park	stop
14	but	help
15	who	slippy

Returning to aboutness words, the keyword list is indicative of the changing world of Smith in the years between the albums. In common with many of the results presented in this chapter, the world of Mark E. Smith and The Fall in the First Five is concerned with the music industry, and a reference to this occurs as *pop* (position 3). The keyword list for the First Five also contains reference to Smith himself in the form of his shamanism—*hip* (position 1), *choi* (position 2), and *behind* (position 8)—and his wider-reading *Nazis* (position 9), *face* (position 12), and *park* (position 13). Mainstream society also receives a mention with reference to *Muzorewi* (position 5). In contrast, the Last Five keywords appear more concerned with technological advances such as social media, illustrated by the occurrence of *troll* (position 1) and *Facebook* (position 2). However, the Last Five results suggest that Smith had two, more pressing concerns. One of these is related to the passage of time. The keyword list indicates that *change* (position 7) and *year* (position 8) are more statistically frequent in the Last Five. This passage of time has led to ill-health, and there are aboutness words that show Smith's deteriorating health situation—*unseen* (position 5), *suffer* (position 6), *quit* (position 10), *shake* (position 11), *stop* (position 13), and *help* (position 14).

THESE ARE THE WORDS OF SUCCESS EXPECTATION

Interviewer: Have you ever thought of putting in the lyrics?

Mark E. Smith: No, I don't believe in it. I think that's another thing that's wrong with rock 'n' roll at the moment—the consumer is getting everything on a plate. [. . .] And like, why should people have lyric sheets—it's a waste of fucking time. [. . .] I don't like lyrics for people to read. I like lyrics to go with music. I'd be a fuckin' poet wouldn't I? I wouldn't write like I write, if they were meant to be read. *It's like some of the new stuff that the band's going to do soon—there's no lyrics actually in it. Most of them are like sounds, sort of sub-words.* (Fall Fanzine, in Norton and Stanley 2021, p.96) (Emphasis added)

This chapter evidences the potential that a linguistic approach holds for the analysis of contemporary song lyrics. It provides a micro and macro examination of Mark E. Smith's use of specific words. In doing so, it offers the first empirical and systematic account of Smith's lyrical preoccupations on ten Fall studio albums and the degree to which these changed over time. Given that Smith's voice(s) (and by extension his delivery of specific words) was an essential part of The Fall's distinctive sound, a close scrutiny of his linguistic choices adds to a deeper understanding his work. While many of Smith's song lyrics do not lend themselves easily to a straightforward textual or thematic analysis (as in, this song is primarily about X and was influenced by Y) our use of a corpus-based discourse analysis approach provides an alternative set of keys to unlock their linguistic patterns. This chapter has shown how it is possible to track the prevalence of particular words (e.g., *he*, *this*, and *they*) in Smith's lyrical canon and how their use and frequency compares with song lyrics, more generally. We have shown how it is possible to trace Smith's changing preoccupations through such an analysis and how the words he used (consciously and unconsciously) reveal a consistent oppositional stance. We can, of course, only speculate as to what Mark E. Smith might make of our examination of his lyrics using these particular methods. However, given his interest in and use of William S. Burroughs's strategy of 'cut up' writing, his invention of new words, his idiosyncratic and sometimes subversive use of words, we would like to think that he might appreciate this forensic and systematic examination.

NOTES

1. *The Annotated Fall* is a resource for Fall fans and for academic researchers. While we have used it to draw down lyrics, it also contains layers and layers of fan

interpretations of lyrics and their likely origins. Songs are organized both alphabetically and by album. In addition to annotation, entries also allow for fan comments.

2. Based, presumably, on William Blake's line, "I must create a system or be enslaved by another man's'.

REFERENCES

Adolphs, Svenja. 2008. *Corpus and Context: Investigating Pragmatic Functions in Spoken Discourse*. Amsterdam: John Benjamins.

Aijmer, Karin, and Christoph Rühlemann, eds. 2015. *Corpus Pragmatics: A Handbook*. Cambridge: Cambridge University Press.

Alim, H. Samy. 2006. *Roc the Mic Right: The Language of Hip-Hop Culture*. London: Routledge.

Baker, Paul. 2006. *Using Corpora in Discourse Analysis*. London: Continuum.

Beal, Joan C. 2009. "'You're not from New York City, You're from Rotherham': Dialect and identity in British indie music." *Journal of English Linguistics* 37, no. 3: 223–40.

Blake, William. (1804–1820). *Jerusalem: The Emanation of Great Albion*. The William Blake Archive. www.blakearchive.org, last accessed June 24, 2022.

Cheung, Joyce Oiwum, and Dezheng (William) Feng. 2019. "Attitudinal Meaning and Social Struggle in Heavy Metal Song Lyrics: A Corpus-based Analysis." *Social Semiotics* 31, no. 2: 230–47.

Clancy, Brian, and Elaine Vaughan. 2012. "'It's lunacy now': A Corpus Based Pragmatic Analysis of the Use of 'Now' in Contemporary Irish English". In *New Perspectives on Irish English*, edited by Bettina Migge and Máire Ní Chiosáin, 225–46. Amsterdam: John Benjamins.

Davies, Matt. 2019 "'What's a computer?': WMatrix and the Distilled Lyrical Art of Mark E. Smith and The Fall." Paper presented at *Always Different, Always the Same: A Symposium on The Fall*. 7 November 2019, University of Limerick, Ireland.

Diessel, Holger. 1999. *Demonstratives: Form, Function and Grammaticalization*. Amsterdam: John Benjamins.

Himmelmann, Nikolaus. (1996). "Demonstratives in Narrative Discourse: A Taxonomy of Universal Uses." In *Studies in Anaphora*, edited by Barbara A. Fox, 205–54. Amsterdam: John Benjamins.

Hoey, Michael. 2005. *Lexical Priming: A New Theory of Words and Language*. London: Routledge.

Johnson, Mark L., and Steve Larson. 2003. "'Something in the Way She Moves': Metaphors of Musical Motion." *Metaphor and Symbol* 18, no. 2: 63–84.

Kreyer, Rolf. 2015. "'Funky fresh dressed to impress': A Corpus-linguistic View on Gender in Pop Songs." *The International Journal of Corpus Linguistics* 20, no. 2: 175–204.

Kreyer, Rolf, and Joybrato Mukharjee. 2007. "The Style of Pop Song Lyrics: A Corpus-linguistic Pilot Study." *Anglia* 125, no. 1: 31–58.

Martin, James R., and Peter R. R. White. 2005. *The Language of Evaluation: Appraisal in English*. New York: Palgrave Macmillan.

Miethaner, Ulrich. 2005. *'I can look through muddy water': Analysing Earlier African American English in Blues Lyrics (BLUR)*. Frankfurt a. M.: Peter Lang.

Morini, Massimiliano. 2013. "Towards a Musical Stylistics: Movement in Kate Bush's 'Running Up That Hill'". *Language and Literature* 22, no. 4: 283–97.

Motschenbacher, Heiko. 2016. "A corpus linguistic study of the situatedness of English pop song lyrics." *Corpora*, 11, no. 1: 1–28.

Murphey, Tim. 1992. "The Discourse of Pop Songs." *TESOL Quarterly* 26, no. 4: 770–74.

Nickas, Bob, and Nicholis Planck. 2021. *Slang King: M.E.S. on Stage with The Fall*. London: Tenderbooks.

Norton, Teresa, and Bob Stanley, eds. 2021. *Excavate! The Wonderful and Frightening World of The Fall*. London: Faber and Faber.

O'Keeffe, Anne. 2006. *Investigating Media Discourse*. London: Routledge.

O'Keeffe, Anne, Brian Clancy, and Svenja Adolphs. 2011. *Introducing Pragmatics in Use*. London: Routledge.

Olivo, Warren. 2001. 'Phat Lines: Spelling Conventions in Rap Music.' *Written Language and Literacy* 4, no. 1: 67–85.

Parkes, Taylor. (2018). https://thequietus.com/articles/03925-the-fall-and-mark-e-smith-as-a-narrative-lyric-writer, last accessed June 24, 2022.

Pennycook, Alastair. 2003. "Global Englishes, Rip Slyme and Performativity." *Journal of Sociolinguistics* 7, no. 4: 513–33.

———. 2007. *Global Englishes and Transcultural Flows*. London: Routledge.

Power, Martin, Aileen Dillane, and Eoin Devereux. 2012. "A Push and a Shove and the Land Is Ours: Morrissey's Counter-hegemonic Stance(s) on Social Class." *Critical Discourse Studies* 9, no. 4: 375–92.

Rayson, Paul. 2008. "From Key Words to Key Semantic Domains." *International Journal of Corpus Linguistics* 13, no. 4: 519–49.

———. 2009. "Wmatrix: A Web-based Corpus Processing Environment." http://ucrel.lancs.ac.uk/wmatrix/, last accessed May 15, 2022.

Reynolds, Simon. (1996). *The Sex Revolts: Gender, Rebellion, and Rock 'n' Roll*. Cambridge: Harvard University Press.

———. http://reynoldsretro.blogspot.com/2018/01/rip-mark-e-smith-me-and-others-on-fall.html, last accessed June 24, 2022.

Romero-Trillo, Jesús, ed. 2008. *Corpus Pragmatics: A Mutualistic Entente*. Berlin: Walter de Gruyter.

Rühlemann, Christoph. 2007. *Conversation in Context: A Corpus-driven Approach*. London: Continuum.

Scott, Mike. 2021. *WordSmith Tools Version 8.0*. Liverpool: Lexical Analysis Software.

Scott, Mike, and Christopher Tribble. 2006. *Textual Patterns: Keywords and Corpus Analysis in Language Education*. Amsterdam: John Benjamins.
Simpson, Paul. 1999. "Language, Culture and Identity: With (Another) Look at Accents in Pop and Rock Singing." *Multilingua* 18, no. 4: 343–67.
Smith, Mark E, and Graham Duff. (2021). *The Otherwise: The Screenplay for a Horror Film That Never Was*. London: Strange Attractor Press.
Strauss, Susan. 2002. "*This*, *That* and *It* in Spoken American English: A Demonstrative System of Gradient Focus." *Language Sciences* 24: 131–52.
Tlili, Zied. 2016. "A Critical Chronotopic Approach to Lyrics of Top-ranking Popular Songs in the UK." *Critical Discourse Studies* 13, no. 2: 228–46.
Trudgill, Peter. 1983. "Acts of Conflicting Identity: The Sociolinguistics of British Pop Song Pronunciation." In *On Dialect*, edited by Peter Trudgill, 141–60. Oxford: Basil Blackwell.
Vaughan, Elaine, and Brian Clancy. 2013. "Small Corpora and Pragmatics." In *Yearbook of Corpus Linguistics and Pragmatics: New Domains and Methodologies*, edited by Jesús Romero-Trillo, 53–73. Berlin: Springer.
Werner, Valentin. 2012. "Love Is All Around: A Corpus-based Study of Song Lyrics." *Corpora* 7, no. 1: 19–50.
West, David. 2019. "Introduction: The Challenges of the Song Lyric." *Language and Literature* 28, no. 1: 3–6.

Chapter Nine

I Am Damo Suzuki Lost in Music (Dub)

Mike Glennon

> *I always thought the pure essence of rock and roll was a completely non-musical form of music. Rock and roll is surely not a 'music' form. I hate it when people say, 'Oh but the production's so bad on it and I can't hear the lyrics properly.' If they want all that then they should listen to classical music or Leonard Cohen—who's nothing but 'poetic'. I'm not about that. Writers like that are too serious and precious about their 'craft' as they call it. There's no fire or danger there, because they've thought all of it out.*
>
> —Smith 2009, p.115

The work of Mark E. Smith and The Fall displays a conscious and consistent disregard for many of the conventions and dictates of pop and rock music. It displays, also, an inclination towards working methods which subvert or discard practices which are often considered central tenets of pop and rock practice, or of music industry mechanics. These inclinations are evidenced through a degree of conscious disdain for conventional production standards and techniques, for lyrical narrative or legibility and, perhaps most famously, for the sanctity of the band (Smith once notably declared that, "if it's me and your granny on bongos, then it's a Fall gig") (Robinson 1998, pp.50–52). They include, also, a rejection of the esteem afforded to musical virtuosity, or instrumental prowess, and of the notion of fixed and final form with regard to musical works and recordings. These characteristics may be related to Smith's belief, as expressed above, that rock and roll, in its purest form, is, "a completely non-musical form of music," (Smith 2009, p.115) which eschews poetry, production, and perfect craftsmanship. This chapter explores these tendencies within the work of The Fall, within the music of CAN, within dub reggae, and within some of Mark E. Smith and The Fall's dance-related creative excursions.

Connections between CAN, one of the key acts associated with the krautrock scene of 1970s Germany, and The Fall are well documented.[1] CAN's impact upon Smith and The Fall is most explicitly acknowledged on The Fall's homage to former CAN vocalist Damo Suzuki ('I Am Damo Suzuki') on *This Nation's Saving Grace* (1985). This chapter explores CAN 's conscious rejection of musical virtuosity, conventional songcraft, and fixed-form and their embrace of elements such as repetition, improvisation, collage, and fluid form. It connects these with similar tendencies within the work of The Fall. Links between The Fall and dub practice are perhaps less immediately apparent. Dub is a sub-genre, or hybrid, of Jamaican reggae music which flourished during the 1970s and within which conventional reggae pop songs were reworked and reimagined by artists such as King Tubby or Lee 'Scratch' Perry, across multiple abstracted 'versions'. Kindred tendencies, however, can be identified, for example, in Smith's frequent engagement in what he referred to as a process of, "live dubbing" (Stubbs 2007, p.32), both onstage and in the studio, adjusting the settings on musician's equipment during performance, thereby "opening the trapdoors of chance and opportunity" (Stubbs 2007, p.32). Further connections between The Fall and dub practice and aesthetics are explored later in this chapter. The Fall's cover of Sister Sledge's 'Lost in Music' on *The Infotainment Scan* (1993) (as referenced in the title of this chapter) is one of multiple excursions into the domain of dance and dance music. This chapter will explore how Smith and The Fall's dance-based collaborations, and in particular those with avant dance ensemble the Michael Clark Company and German electronica duo Mouse on Mars facilitated further excursion beyond conventional pop and rock territory into forms including theatre, ballet, and installation.

Political and philosophical dimensions may also be identified within the interrelated creative strategies touched upon thus far: the rejection of fixed and final form or function, of product form, or of production standards. In order to further explore the implications of these actions, this chapter begins with a consideration of Theodor Adorno's writing on reification as it relates to music.[2] This provides a mechanism through which to explore various organisational structures which seek to 'fix,' control, or formulate the form, content, and format of music so that it functions more efficiently as a commodity. The chapter goes on to explore how such mechanisms are dismantled within the work of CAN, King Tubby (and dub practice more broadly), and within Mark E. Smith and The Fall's dance-related collaborations. In doing so, it places Smith's 'non-musical' music within a broader aesthetic, political, and philosophical context.

REIFICATION AND THE RENDER OF
MUSIC SAFE FOR CONSUMPTION

Mark E. Smith, in the quoted passage that opens this chapter, expresses scorn for numerous inclinations which he equates with a particular notion of musicality. Smith is contemptuous of expertly produced records with perfectly legible lyrics, of the master poet/songwriter, and of the meticulously crafted, serious, and esteemed masterwork. He equates rock and roll, in its purest form, rather, with risk, danger, spontaneity, non-musicality, and a disregard for formal dictates. Smith expresses such a disregard across his entire body of work and consistently employs numerous creative strategies which mess with the 'rules' of the form and which seem to have been devised in order to find ways to make things new, unfamiliar, strange, non-musical, open-ended, or unexpected. This is clear, for example, in the manner with which he approaches his own vocals and lyrics: often obscuring his voice by singing through a loudspeaker, recording to dictaphone or cassette recorder, pushing his vocals away from narrative territory to a point where they take on a more textural or rhythmic function. It is evident in his tendency to obscure his lyrics through the omission of certain key words so that new meaning or unexpected juxtapositions (new facts perhaps) emerge. It is apparent, also, in his refusal to allow his lyrics to be presented in printed form lest, it would seem, their form become fixed in the process, and their continued creative capacity diminished. Similar tendencies, as will be demonstrated, exist within the work of CAN, within dub practice and within aspects of dance music culture. Each displays a certain disregard for musicality, virtuosity, or musical hierarchy, for fixed-form and fixed formulae. In seeking to explore these tendencies and to examine what common thread or ideology they represent across the work of The Fall, CAN, and within dub and dance music culture, it is insightful, I suggest, to draw upon Adorno's concept of reification as it relates to music. This provides a means of exploring why, on the one hand, a particular ideal of music might proliferate and why, on the other hand, artists such as Smith may be driven to actively work in opposition to such ideals.

Adorno utilises the term 'reification' to describe various processes through which music is organised and standardised, its content and form dictated by predetermined criteria. Principally, processes of reification are administered by the music industry, in order to improve music's efficiency as a product. Music, Adorno states, "has allowed itself to be intimidated economically . . . [by] . . . the superior power of the music industry" (Adorno 2002, p.392). This, in turn, impacts upon all aspects of musical life. How music is made, performed, and received is all dictated, if not entirely, then at least to a degree, by criteria designed to improve music's performance, not as music, art, or activity, but as commodity.

To reify, in a literal sense, is to make into a thing, to render the immaterial material, the intangible tangible. Smith's aversion to presenting his lyrics in printed form, thus, may be viewed as resisting a process of reification wherein fluid associations and imagery are translated into fixed and final form. The act of recording a piece of music may also constitute a process of reification. That which previously existed, only in the moment of performance is now given a more permanent and tangible form. For Adorno, recording places a full stop of sorts upon the work featured therein. It shuts it off from future reinterpretation and development and dictates future performance, "making the recording a reference point" (Hegarty 2007, p.181). Adorno writes that:

> Perfect, immaculate performance in the latest style [thus] preserves the work at the price of its definitive reification. . . . The performance sounds like its own phonograph record. The dynamic is so predetermined that there are no longer any tensions at all. (Adorno 1991, p.39)

Frederic Jameson, meanwhile, offers a concise summary of reification as it functions within Marxist thought more broadly, stating that:

> The theory of reification describes the way in which, under capitalism, the older traditional forms of human activity are instrumentally reorganised and "taylorised," analytically fragmented and reconstructed according to various rational models of efficiency. (Jameson 1979, p.130)

The factory assembly line serves as a classic example of reification in this sense. The act and actions of assembly are fragmented into individual tasks. Certain tasks and actions may then be mechanised and automated. The need for human expertise is minimised and commercial efficiency is enhanced.

Musical examples of such restructuring models of efficiency might be the format and structure of the pop song, designed, it may be said for ease of distribution and consumption, to fit the confines of popular formats or broadcast media. Another example, perhaps, is the tendency that Smith highlights towards an ideal of 'perfect' production. Common examples within contemporary rock or pop production include an inclination to 'fix' vocal performances using the now ubiquitous Auto-Tune software which allows producers and studio engineers to re-pitch precise moments of performances so that they attain an ideal of perfect pitch and performance. The quest for production perfection may also be demonstrated by reference to the digital production technique of quantisation which allows for the temporal repositioning of micro-musical material so that it is 'perfectly' in time.[3] More recently it is the activity of listening itself that has been reorganised and reconstructed to deliver maximum efficiency and profit. Spotify, for example, neatly categorises "seven key audio streaming moments for marketers to tap into"—working, chilling, chores, gaming, partying, driving—and advises that "for marketers, this is a chance to reach millennials through a medium they trust and see as a positive enhancer or tool" (Spotify for Brands 2019). In this example then, the act of listening is analysed, fragmented, and reorganised into a range of categories that fit the models, demographics, and product categories of brands and advertisers. Listening is transformed from process to product. Music is simply the content that facilitates the process. Each of these examples illustrates how the form and content of music, or of the activity of listening to music, is, as Jameson puts it, "analytically fragmented and reconstructed," (Jameson 1979, p.130) so that it functions more efficiently as commodity. The analyses that follow will demonstrate how CAN, King Tubby, elements of dance culture, and, indeed, The Fall devise and implement a range of creative strategies that subvert and resist such tendencies to fix and formulate the form of music.

CAN

The musicians who would come to constitute CAN were, prior to their coming together as a creative unit, unlikely proponents of the non-musical form of music that Smith views as the essence of rock and roll. Each brought considerable individual pedigree to the table when they came together in 1968. They were veterans, variously, of classical music, free jazz, and the avant-garde. Keyboardist Irmin Schmidt, for example, studied composition with both György Ligeti and Karlheinz Stockhausen and was a noted soloist and conductor. The playing style Schmidt embraces on early CAN recordings, however, could hardly be further away from the world of distinguished classical piano recital. Schmidt's contributions to the band's debut album *Monster Movie* (1969) often consisted of two or three note organ parts or of single sustained tones: to call them riffs seems too grand a term. Bass player Holger Czukay also studied under Stockhausen and served in numerous jazz combos. As a member of CAN, however, Czukay embraced a more primitive palette than his academic training afforded him access to. Czukay's playing often employed simple and forceful repetition. In the band's later years, Czukay would abandon conventional instrumentation entirely, performing with short wave radios or morse code keys. Drummer Jaki Liebezeit, meanwhile, was a veteran of the European free jazz scene. In CAN, however, his jazz chops are kept under wraps and Liebezeit develops a style of playing equal parts concerned with stasis and continued propulsive momentum: the funky and machinic sound of the motorik beat, now synonymous with the krautrock era. The final member of the core CAN quartet was guitarist Michael Karoli, a former student of Czukay's and, in his own words, "the only one who thought he was going to make rock music" (Harrison 2012). The members of CAN, thus, brought experience, training, and skill aplenty to the table, but set their virtuosity aside, deciding instead that repetition and "primal monotony" (Reynolds 2019, p.176) were where it's at.

This inclination towards the primitive and repetitive was bolstered by the arrival of original vocalist Malcolm Mooney in August 1968, thus completing CAN's original lineup. Mooney's arrival in the band annihilates "any notions that CAN might remain rooted in academia" (Harrison 2012). Rather, the "aggressive strangeness" (Fallowell 2021) of CAN's early phase explodes into being with his arrival in the band. Mooney, a New York–born painter, moved to the microphone with CAN and pushed the band, via the rhythm and drive of his improvised performances, into more primal terrain. 'Butterfly', recorded sometime between Mooney's arrival in August 1968 and the end of that year, illustrates the intensity of the creative explosion that followed and the forceful primitive repetition that characterises early, Mooney era, CAN. Schmidt, Czukay, and Karoli lock into a dissonant two-chord motif (perhaps punk's fabled three chords were overly ornate in hindsight). Liebezeit maintains a sparse, repetitive pattern. Mooney free associates. Predetermination, songcraft, and 'perfect' performance are disregarded and tension is embraced.

Mooney's tenure in the band was brief and in 1970 he was replaced by Damo Suzuki. In the Suzuki era the band would arrive at what we now probably recognise as the 'classic' CAN sound—carving out the common ground between Stockhausen, James Brown, and The Velvet Underground. It is territory in which much of the most vital and innovative music of the twentieth century to that point seems to exist in one space. This period of CAN is perhaps best exemplified by their 1971 double album *Tago Mago*, wherein musique concrete, tape music, electronics, funk, rock, and improvisation inform an album that sounds unmistakably like CAN. Mark E. Smith would later say of *Tago Mago* that "it formed my skills listening to it" (Young and Schmidt 2019, p.370). 'Oh Yeah' from the album illustrates something of what the band were at, at this point. It is funky but is not funk. It's trippy but is not psychedelic. It's repetitive but no two bars are the same. It is recognisably related to rock music but has few of its recognisable traits—a verse, a chorus, song structure, intelligible lyrics, or, indeed, a clearly identifiable language. 'Oh Yeah' also demonstrates one of CAN's principal working methods—a combination of spontaneous composition and studio collage. In a live context this meant that tracks were never played the same way twice and rather became "live remixes in which the original themes, riffs and melodies were barely recognisable" (Schmidt 2012). The notion of live remixes, as will be discussed later, would also become a characteristic of live performances by The Fall. In the studio, CAN's spontaneous compositions were the raw material for collages which subsequently constituted their album tracks. Lengthy improvisations were cut, edited, and rearranged or multiple versions were spliced together. Michael Karoli recalls of 'Oh Yeah's' creation that "we had made a rhythm tape, so we played the tape backwards and played on it, and Damo sang, and then we turned it back around, so the whole dub is going backwards" (Young and Schmidt 2019, p.146). The final piece, thus, consists of multiple components reversed and cut together, different temporalities overlaid and woven in and out of one another as Liebezeit's rhythms and Suzuki's vocals phase between forward and reverse momentum. It is a potent illustration of CAN's creative methodology wherein live improvisation and studio-based techniques of collage and composition merge and where conventional notions of narrative or songcraft are suspended.

'Oh Yeah' also provides the template for Smith's homage to CAN on 'I Am Damo Suzuki'. Smith's vocal phrasing on the track is noticeably based upon Suzuki's on 'Oh Yeah'. Karl Burns's drums, equally, seem to pay homage to Jaki Liebezeit's work on 'Oh Yeah'. The song's central chord sequence, meanwhile, as noted by The Annotated Fall website, quotes a recurring CAN motif:

> The descending changes that form the main theme of the song, however, do not come from "Oh Yeah," although they are, fittingly, a recurring pattern in Can's work, spanning several years: they first first appear on "Don't Turn the Light On" from Soundtracks, and the same descending chord figure appears in "Gomorrah," and later in "Bel Air" and "Midnight Men," and a similar pattern appears in "Hunters and Collectors."[4]

Smyth's lyrics, meanwhile, adopt a cut-up collage aesthetic incorporating multiple CAN references into their flow: name-checking, for example, the band's base city of Cologne, their track 'Vitamin C,' Schmidt and Czukay's former mentor, Stockhausen, and their *Soundtracks* album. It is notable, perhaps, that Smith does not choose to pay homage to CAN through the conventional form of the cover version (despite the large number of cover versions that appear across The Fall's catalogue). Rather, 'I Am Damo Suzuki' embraces the spirit of CAN's composition as collage aesthetic, folding elements of the band's work and history into a new original work.

CAN's working methods, as outlined above, display much of what Mark E. Smith identifies as the pure essence of rock and roll. Most explicitly, perhaps, their rejection of their own virtuosity chimes with Smith's concept of a 'non-musical' form of music. Collectively the quartet arrived at a musical approach that might be likened to a kind of reverse engineered punk. Where the musicians of the punk and post-punk eras rejected the need to acquire a high level of musical mastery, the members of CAN brought experience, training and skill aplenty to the table but left it there deciding instead that repetition and monotony were where it's at. CAN's embrace of spontaneous composition, of studio collage, and of live reconstructions, meanwhile, serves as methods through which to circumnavigate the predictable, predetermined, or "perfect, immaculate performance" (Adorno 1991, p.39) that Adorno identifies as emblematic of the reified musical work, designed to function efficiently within the marketplace. Similar processes of avoiding fixed form and of subverting the 'rules' or conventions of musical form occur within dub reggae.

DUB

The line that may be drawn between The Fall and dub is perhaps less clear than that which connects them with CAN. There is, however, Smith's previously referenced inclination for 'live dubbing' both in concert and in the studio. Smith is on the record referencing Big Youth's *Natty Cultural Dread* as one of his favourite albums[5] while links between reggae, dub, and the broader punk and post-punk movements are well documented. The Fall also worked with the UK dub producer Adrian Sherwood on the 1981 *Slates* EP and on 1990's *Extricate* LP. Something of a dub aesthetic can also be heard in the minimalism of some of The Fall's soundscapes. A track like 'Frenz' from *The Frenz Experiment* (1988), for example, with its pared back bass, drums, and vocals sound exists, it may be said, somewhat within a dub lineage. Mark Fisher, meanwhile, describes 'Hip Priest' from 1982's *Hex Enduction Hour* as being "like dub, if it had been invented in drizzly motorway service stations rather than in recording studios in Jamaica" (Fisher 2021, p.165). The incorporation of elements of 'Hip Priest' into 'New Big Prinz' and 'Big New Priest' in 1988 also demonstrates an engagement with open-ended form that is central to dub-practice and that exists in opposition to the notion of reification. The fact that a phrase or motif has been recorded or published in one work, for example, does not imply that its creative capacity has now expired and that it cannot reappear elsewhere in somewhat altered form.

This tendency towards multiple iterations of works is central to dub. Dub derives its name from shorthand for the process of doubling or duplicating. Its very etymology, thus, places it in opposition to the notion of a single, definitive performance, recording, or listening experience. Dub replaces this notion with that of multiple versions, or dubs, of existing works, hybrid variations that frequently abstract the language of popular song or question the 'rules' that govern it. Material is cut up, rearranged, recombined, and relocated. It is subject to processes of electronic manipulation and sonic abstraction. The background frequently shifts to the foreground with bass and drums often taking precedence over vocal and melodic material. The dubs or 'versions' that result frequently position rather conventional source material in decidedly more avant-garde and abstract terrain. Within the work of The Fall, a single recording might constitute such a hybrid collage, with multiple versions of a track collapsed into one. Fisher (2021), for example, refers to 'Spectre vs. Rector' from 1979's *Dragnet* as, "a palimpsest, spooked by itself—[wherein] at least two versions are playing out of sync" (Fisher 2021, p.153). For Fisher, The Fall's "palimpsests" are, "a deliberate refusal of the 'coffee table' aesthetic Smith derides." For David Toop, the dub mixer "unpicks music in the commercial sphere" (Toop 1995, p.115) and treats it as though it were, "modelling clay rather than copyright property" (Toop 1995, p.118). In each instance thus, we may say that there is a subversion of recorded music's product status. Dub's hybrid variations refuse to allow recorded music to exist purely as a product, nor to acknowledge its status as inviolate intellectual property and instead, reignite its creative potential. The Fall's hybrid palimpsests refuse to adhere to the notion that a recording should seek to represent an ideal or perfect version of a piece and instead foreground multiple versions at once in a form of fragmented collage.

Some of the techniques by which dub abstracts the language of pop music can be illustrated by reference to one of the form's best-known works, 'King Tubby Meets Rockers Uptown', a King Tubby dub of Jacob Miller's 'Baby I Love You So'.[6] The track's dismantling of the established form and conventions of popular song is perhaps most explicit in its removal and fragmentation of vocals and, by extension, of narrative. Miller's vocals are largely removed and where retained, are cut into fragments of two or three words. Hints of the narrative remain but principally these fragments are repurposed as tonal, timbral, or rhythmic elements. They are displaced in the stereo spectrum, right panned as opposed to centred in the mix, as per Miller's original and as standard in popular music production. They are further manipulated by distortion and delay and are lowered in the mix, disrupting the hierarchical priority usually assigned to vocals. The vocal harmonies which introduce both versions are, in Tubby's dub, similarly cut and displaced. Only the second of their two iterations is retained and only, it would seem, a background layer that does not contain the melodic resolution of its counterpart. What serves, in 'Baby I Love You So', to introduce the singer and the melodic material is, in its dub, abstract colour that lacks either introduction or resolution. The track, as such, deploys multiple strategies that push vocal material (and, by extension, the overall piece) into unexpected and unconventional terrain.

The instrumentation of 'King Tubby Meets Rockers Uptown' similarly breaks with convention, norm, and established hierarchy. The guitars and keyboards that punctuate 'Baby I Love You So' are dissolved in a manner not unlike the vocal treatment. The latter are removed entirely, the former remaining, as per vocals, in fragmented and heavily manipulated form. The background shifts to the foreground and the principal components of the soundscape are bass, drums, melodica, and Tubby's dub manipulations. It is an instrumental combination that is unconventional in any musical form to which dub might be said to be related: reggae, jazz, pop, rock, soul, or funk. 'King Tubby Meets Rockers Uptown', thus, disregards the road map by which a listener may be more used to navigating a popular music or reggae recording and through which, by extension, it is presumably rendered more palatable for consumption. In doing so, it arguably forefronts the recording's capacity to function, not as commodity, but as artwork.

DANCE

The multiple excursions made by Mark E. Smith and The Fall into the world of dance and dance music span much of the spectrum of what may be covered by these terms. Arguably, the most extensive and substantial of these collaborations were those with Michael Clark's avant dance ensemble and Smith's collaboration with the German electronica duo Mouse on Mars on the Von Südenfed project. The former culminated in the ballet and album *I Am Kurious Oranj* (1988) while the latter yielded the *Tromatic Reflections* album in 2007. These collaborations are dealt with in greater detail below. Other notable examples include collaborations with Coldcut on the tracks 'I'm In Deep' (1989) and 'Telephone Thing' (1990). The former track (featured on the duo's 1989 album *What's That Noise?*) placed Smith's vocals within an acid house landscape and anticipates many of the rock/dance crossovers that would follow in the '90s (such as Leftfield and Lydon's *Open Up*). *What's That Noise?* also featured a track named 'My Telephone' with vocals by Lisa Stansfield which caught Smith's ear and which he reworked with The Fall as 'Telephone Thing' (with Coldcut returning on production duties). Smith told the *NME* (*New Musical Express*) in 1990 that:

> Their 'Telephone Thing' was a misjustice to the tune. That single was a flop and it was rubbish. You see, they compose all their shit on machines, so I got the band to learn it, played naturally. So it's very different indeed. (Collins 1990, pp.24–26)

Rather than Coldcut adding dance beats and pulses to a Fall track, The Fall reverse-engineer Coldcut's sampled and programmed textures and the resultant collaboration exists in more of a hybrid space wherein multiple iterations of a piece coexist. Smith also collaborated with Gorillaz on the track 'Glitter Freeze' (2010) and with less widely known acts such as D.O.S.E, Inch, and Ghostdigital. As previously stated, however, it is arguably the Michale Clark and Mouse on Mars collaborations which are the most substantial of these excursions into dance, both for the quantity of output they produced but also for the manner in which they open pathways into new modes of expression encompassing forms such as theatre, ballet, and installation.

Smith's association with dancer/choreographer Michael Clark and the Michael Clark Company ensemble began when Clark started to stage performances to recordings of The Fall's work. Clark recalls that:

> 'New Puritan' (Peel version) felt like a clarion call for me to begin my own dance company. I went to see the band on the outskirts of London with the express intention of asking Mark if he would allow me to use the Fall's music for my work . . . the band began coming to see performances of my early work. When they were in the audience, they would refuse to allow anyone to leave the theatre. A strong bond was forged . . . new work emerged. (Clark 2021, p.xi)

In 1984, Smith and Clark collaborated on *Le French Revolting* for the Paris Opera Ballet under the directorship of Rudolf Nureyev. Clark went on to encourage Smith to write the play *Hey! Luciani: The Life and Codex of John Paul 1* (1986), staged at London's Riverside Studios and featuring Smith and performance artist Leigh Bowery.[7] Their most complete collaboration would come with 1988's *I Am Kurious Oranj*, a full live performance collaboration between The Fall and Clarke's ensemble. Clarke would later recall that 'Fall fans, who would never have chosen to go anywhere near a ballet, were exposed to my work, and vice versa' (Clark 2021, p.xi). The piece served, thus, not only to enable the band and ensemble to venture beyond their prescribed terrain but, rather, facilitated a similar process of discovery and exploration amongst their respective audiences.

Another of Smith's more extensive dance-related collaborations was his partnership with electronica duo Mouse on Mars as Von Südenfed for 2007's *Tromatic Reflexxions* album. This collaboration also led to what would go on to constitute Smith's final released recordings (at the time of writing), three collaborations with Mouse on Mars's Jan St. Werner released on Werner's 2020 album *Molocular Meditation*. These pieces again demonstrate the capacity that dance and electronic music offered Smith to move outside the world of music and rock and roll. They also offer further demonstration of non-musicality and of Smith's disdain for the music industry and for the capacity of commerce to dictate to creativity. The album's title track is a twenty-minute, "experimental listening environment & surround sound composition . . . [comprising part of] . . . a bespoke light and sound environment," commissioned by Manchester's Cornerhouse Centre for Contemporary Visual Arts and Independent Film. The piece surrounds Smith's spoken word contributions with a range of electronic pulses, patterns, and oscillations. The album's closing track, 'VS Cancelled', meanwhile features a recording of Smith reading aloud a letter from Domino Record's Jonny Bradshaw wherein he announces, to Werner, the label's decision not to proceed with a second Von Südenfed album:

> I'm terribly sad for us that the market is beating us down. We cannot dictate it anymore with our hard work. Also, on a personal level, it's hard cos I passionately love the VS music and the experience of working with Andy, Mark and yourself. Yours, Jonny.[8]

Certain lines elicit scornful laughter from Smith: "I'm in Switzerland at the moment. . . . I told you times were tough" (see note 8). Werner, again, creates a somewhat abrasive electronic environment of harsh pulses and clanging percussive hits with which to surround Smith. As a final entry within a lengthy and prolific recording career it is a somewhat minor and superfluous piece. Simultaneously, however, it is representative of elements which are central to Smith's work and persona and which have been the central focus of this chapter: a disregard for prevalent notions of musicality or production, for how a musical work should be constructed and a contempt for the capacity of music to be intimidated by commerce.

CONCLUSION

Collage, repetition, spontaneous composition, dissonance, the accentuation of imperfection, open-form, a rejection of virtuosity, the erasure of narrative, abstraction, and displacement. These are some of the techniques discussed herein employed by The Fall, by CAN, and by dub mixers such as King Tubby that consciously push music away from predictable and prosaic pathways wherein, to paraphrase Adorno, the record seeks to present an idealised version of the performance, and subsequent performance seeks to perfectly reproduce the record. Music, in such circumstance, "intimidated economically . . . [by] . . . the superior power of the music industry" (Adorno 2002, p.392) functions according to an efficient formula of ever more perfect production and reproduction. More in time, more in tune, and more efficient in the marketplace. Smith's 'non-musical' music, and the various creative methodologies it employs, may be seen thus, not as a lasting allegiance to a garage or punk rock sense of DIY or a predilection for lo-fi production but rather as a conscious determination not to allow himself, his music, or music more broadly to be intimidated artistically, aesthetically, or economically by the (seemingly) superior power of the music industry.

NOTES

1. CAN were an innovative and experimental band formed in Cologne in 1968 and often cited as prominent exponents of the German krautrock scene of the late 1960s and 1970s (along with acts such as Cluster, Faust, and Neu). The band's work fused influences from sources including funk, garage rock, and experimental composition. CAN have been cited as an influence and inspiration by key members of the punk and post-punk movements including Mark E. Smith and John Lydon. Their work has been covered by acts including The Jesus and Mary Chain and Radiohead and has been sampled by acts including A Tribe Called Quest and Tyler, The Creator.

2. For more on Adorno's writing on reification, see Theodor Adorno, "On the Fetish Character in Music and the Regression of Listening," in *The Culture Industry: Selected Essays on Mass Culture*, ed. J. M. Bernstein (London: Routledge, 1991), 26–52.

3. Quantisation is a process within digital music processing wherein material is transformed so as to be placed on beat. Wikipedia defines quantization as, 'the studio-software process of transforming performed musical notes, which may have some imprecision due to expressive performance, to an underlying musical representation that eliminates the imprecision. The process results in notes being set on beats and on exact fractions of beats'. https://en.wikipedia.org/wiki/Quantization_(music). Accessed July 14, 2020.

4. "I Am Damo Suzuki," *The Annotated Fall*, http://annotatedfall.doomby.com/pages/the-annotated-lyrics/i-am-damo-suzuki.html. Accessed July 17, 2021.

5. https://thequietus.com/articles/08568-the-fall-mark-e-smith-record-collection

6. King Tubby was one of the key innovators of dub helping to develop and popularise the form in the early 1970s.

7. Smith's script centered on the mysterious death of Pope John Paul 1—born Albino Luciani—in 1978.

8. Excerpted from lyrics of "VS Cancelled," by Jan St. Werner (feat. Mark E. Smith) on *Molocular Meditation*, Editions Mego, 2020.

REFERENCES

Adorno, Theodor. "On the Fetish Character in Music and the Regression of Listening," In *The Culture Industry: Selected Essays on Mass Culture*, edited by J. M. Bernstein. London: Routledge, 1991.

Adorno, Theodor. "On the Social Situation of Music." In *Essays on Music*, edited by Richard Leppert. Berkeley: University of California Press, 2002.

Clark, Michael. "Foreword." In *Excavate!: The Wonderful and Frightening World of The Fall*, edited by Tessa Norton and Bob Stanley, xi. London: Faber, 2021.

Collins, Andrew. "Funky, Cold, Modern-ah," *New Musical Express*, January 25, 1990, pp. 24–26. http://thefall.org/gigography/90jan25.html

Fallowell, Duncan. CAN: Soundtracks, sleevenotes. https://www.spoonrecords.com/archive/critiques.html, 2021.

Fisher, M. (2010) 'Memorex for the Krakens': The Fall's Pulp Modernism. In *Mark E. Smith and The Fall: Art, Music and Politics*. London: Routledge.

Harrison, Ian. *CAN: The Lost Tapes*, sleevenotes. Spoon Records, 2012.

Hegarty, Paul. *Noise/Music: A History.* New York: Bloomsbury Academic, 2007.

Jameson, Frederic. "Reification and Utopia in Mass Culture." *Social Text*, No.1 (Winter, 1979).

Reynolds, Simon. *Rip It Up and Start Again: Post-Punk 1978–1984.* London: Faber & Faber, 2019.

Robinson, John. "Narky Mark." In *NME* (February 7, 1998), 50–52. http://thefall.org/news/980222.html#nme

Schmidt, Irmin. *CAN: The Lost Tapes*, sleevenotes. Spoon Records, 2012.

Smith, Mark E. *Renegade.* London: Penguin, 2009.

Spotify for Brands. "UNDERSTANDING PEOPLE THROUGH MUSIC: Millennial Edition." https://www.spotifyforbrands.com/en-US/insights/millennial-guide/

Stubbs, David. 'Shotgun Wedding'. In *The Wire*, Issue 279 (May 2007).

The Annotated Fall. "I Am Damo Suzuki," http://annotatedfall.doomby.com/pages/the-annotated-lyrics/i-am-damo-suzuki.html, 2021.

The Quietus. 'From Rock's Backpages: Mark E. Smith Shows Us His Record Collection'. https://thequietus.com/articles/08568-the-fall-mark-e-smith-record-collection, 2012.

Toop, David. *Ocean of Sound.* London: Serpent's Tail, 1995.

Young, Rob, and Irmin Schmidt. *All Gates Open: The Story of CAN.* London: Faber & Faber, 2019.

Chapter Ten

Remembrancer/Rememorator/Amorator!

The Remainderer *EP and the Roots of The Fall's Late Obscurity*

Samuel Flannagan

"Never forget, remembrance is worth nothing," gargles Mark E. Smith on the title track of *The Remainderer* released in 2013 (02:20–02:24). It is an EP carrying the familiar Smithian maxim that while other groups are looking backwards, The Fall is only concerned with its ongoing present. I argue that the EP also stands as a testament to the effectiveness of the group's late aesthetics, and reveals that rather than an unravelling of Smith's talent, the final decade of The Fall represents a self-aware and intentional embracement of obscurity, and an artistic evolution akin to those of many preeminent literary modernists.

THE FALL'S WORKING-CLASS MODERNISM

The Fall's fundamental resistance to nostalgia and remembrance must be read differently now, in light of Mark E. Smith's death on 24 January 2018, and the outpouring of appreciation that it triggered. Critics in the music press, fellow musicians, and former collaborators paid their respects with a double sense of astonishment: that such a prolific creative force had come to an end, but also that it had been able to sustain itself for so long. Fundamentally, The Fall as an ongoing practice of musical creation maintained a level of productivity with repercussions for how we must approach the music itself. Through the impression of relentless productivity, The Fall establishes its identity, the position from which it is able to subvert and challenge the very systems in which it is necessary to operate. In practice, this meant an unwavering adherence to a self-enforced, forward-looking creative mind-set in which the commitment to the latest work, and works in process, takes precedence over the songs that came before them. Live, The Fall's set lists were populated with titles that had yet to be released, the lyrical and musical forms of which would be altered noticeably by the time they received studio treatment. Where other veteran groups performed greatest hits accumulated over the course of their careers, The Fall operated differently, with an anti-nostalgic outlook that remained subversive of the typical jouissance of reminiscence found in the association of pop music with youth, with specific time and place, and also with changing trends within the industry itself.[1] The Fall always produced, and seemingly produced whatever they liked, but it would be a notable occurrence if The Fall revisited an original song that had been released prior to their most recent album cycles. Such a show of productivity affects our reading of the songs as texts. In *Mark E. Smith and The Fall: Art, Music & Politics* (2010), Michael Goddard and Benjamin Halligan describe The Fall's state of constant "becoming," a robust presentist attitude towards creation that evades modernity's need for classification, quantification, and commodification, which differentiated, for so many fans, the feeling of following The Fall from that of other groups of a similar ilk. But to engage with the music of The Fall is also to enter into a world of paratexts and intertextual allusions. The aforementioned debuting, live, of works-in-progress is an ongoing demonstration of song as a palimpsest, obscuring access to an imaginary definitive version of the song, yet heightening the listener's sense of the poetic selection function of language across disparate versions, which are unified by title and a shared musical atmosphere. Titles matter in The Fall: as well as adding to the aesthetic value of the lyrics, titles take on the role of signifiers beyond individual recorded texts, as unifying signs for the mental constructs of associated meanings that the listener accumulates not only within a single recording but across several versions of the same song. The nature of this fragmentary accumulation of material is central to the identification of the group's aesthetic, and to the argument that The Fall, as a forty-year process of musical creation, is comparable to modernist texts of early twentieth-century literature. In *Modernism: An Anthology*, Lawrence Rainey offers a panoramic assessment of the debates surrounding the use of the term, and describes the waning influence of the term 'postmodernism', as 'modernism' is increasingly liberated from its traditional historical definition, that is, the hegemonic canon of Western literature in the first half of the twentieth century. Rainey demonstrates how the boundaries of the term are still very much open to debate; however, he does identify some of the innovative aesthetics associated with modernism as a process, and the posture of modernism as follows:

> Multiple and unsteady points of view, stream of consciousness, illusionism with a self-consciousness of formal structure, collage, montage, juxtaposition, a dis-

play of raw medium (language, sound), a unified but lost order beneath apparent fragmentation. . . . Whatever literary modernism was, it was impatient with or overtly hostile to received conventions. . . . Modernism, with all its machineries of extremism, was anything but eager to resolve the experience of wonder/ horror into the ready comprehensibility of spatiotemporal and logical-casual connectedness. Quite the contrary. Its antinarratival aesthetics constituted an unprecedented rupture with a major strand, perhaps the major strand, of post-Renaissance aesthetics in the West. (Rainey 2011, pp.xxv–xxvi)

To argue that The Fall should be identified as a working-class modernist practice is timely, not just because of the recency of Smith's death, but also because it comes at a time when the modernist canon is being remapped, to include otherwise neglected and excluded forms of modernism across a range of media. The inaugural *Modernist Legacies and Futures* conference at NUI Galway on 17 and 18 May 2019, at which a shorter version of this paper was first presented, is a testament to how the boundaries of modernism are shifting both temporally and formally. If, following Bob Dylan being awarded the Nobel Prize in Literature, we are to embrace the assertion that forms of modernism will continue to emerge up until the present day, then the "hostile," "extremist" nature of The Fall's aesthetics, working in antithesis to the accepted norms of popular songwriting and the pop music industry in general, appear self-evidently modernist.

The group's modernist aesthetic takes the form of unconventional textual and paratextual practice, identifiable at the most basic level by their exploitation of the relationship between recorded music and its sleeve art, and in a more esoteric manner regarding the identification of definitive lyrical formations. The music of The Fall exudes newness yet maintains key idiosyncrasies which render it utterly recognisable. The group's most prominent champion, BBC Radio 1 DJ John Peel, uttered possibly the most famous epithet concerning the music of The Fall: "They are always different; they are always the same" (quoted in O'Hagan 2005). Peel's description serves to encapsulate the increased appreciation one has of a Fall song, as text, when taken as part of an ongoing process, a process that undergoes significant evolution, particularly in terms of Smith's lyricism and the dynamism of the poetics on display, while maintaining the key principles of composition and production that mean The Fall is always recognisably The Fall. Despite the famously high turnover of musicians who have served in The Fall and contributed to Smith's singular vision, the fact that these principles and identifying characteristics are more often than not present in the music of The Fall, in addition to Smith's unmistakable voice, means that to encounter a song by The Fall is to enter into play with an aesthetic site that is at once familiar and unpredictable, grounded, yet open.

THE CHARACTERISTICS OF "FALL SOUND"

It is for this reason that we may approach the music of The Fall—or "Fall Sound," as Smith came to label it—in terms of a literary-artistic practice, and insist that any worthwhile critical evaluation, if it is to examine the songs as texts of cultural and literary value, must take into account the intertextual continuities—those of content, style, and procedure—that we can identify throughout their catalogue, existing as a part of and apart from the social and cultural environments in which the texts were made.

Smith's vocals have little to offer in terms of melody, clarity, or traditional musical ability. The source of their effectiveness lies elsewhere, first and foremost through the interplay of Smith's unpredictable style of delivery and the relentlessness of the abrasive musical arrangements which underpin it, as well as his voice's capacity for being misinterpreted. An obituary in the *Village Voice*, published the day after his death, explained it thus: "any pairing of repetition and Smith's voice creates Fallness, a complexity wrought from what should not be enough, but is" (Frere-Jones 2018). 'Complexity' encapsulates well the aesthetic experience of encountering many of The Fall's songs, and is suggestive of the heightened mode of listening that we are invited to adopt in the effort to make meaning out of often esoteric lyricism, a "flickering lexicon," as Smith utters in "R.O.D." (00:40–00:45), sustained by repetition.

Repetition has been a key component of "Fall Sound" since the group's formation, and the release in 1978 of "Bingo-Masters Break-Out!" carrying the B-side, ""Repetition," which expounds the group's commitment to the "three are's, repetition, repetition, repetition" (01:40–01:51). The text can be read as a musical manifesto, that also serves to establish the oppositional and combative posture that would continue to characterise the artist-recipient relationship until the very end: "You don't love repetition. . . . We dig it, we dig it, we dig it, we dig it" (02:30–02:33, 03:30–03:35).

While repetition remains the central characteristic of "Fall Sound" throughout much of the group's discography, Smith's lyricism and delivery undergo a significant evolution, accompanied by the increasing adoption of sonic, lyrical, and performative practices that purposefully distort and disrupt the listener's automatic instinct to make traditional sense of aural texts. The mighty late-period track "Auto Chip 14–15" describes the experience of being a twenty-first-century Fall listener by describing a character who "sees life through a broken glass window" (06:15–06:27), a line that is also tellingly self-referential; elsewhere, Smith references a "cracked mirror" (03:12–03:14).

Two examples of this destabilising instinct serve to demonstrate Smith's early embrace of the unreliability of his method of transmission and the purposeful disruption of meaning-making I argue is central to the aesthetic intentionality of late-period Fall. The first can be found on the A-side of the 7-inch single "How I Wrote 'Elastic Man,'" released on 11 July 1980. The narrative of "How I Wrote 'Elastic Man'" is a familiar portrait of an artist, a writer, whose rise to prominence is accompanied by, in turns, unwanted praise, imposter syndrome, and writer's block, in which sycophantic "empty brains" continually approach the dejected narrator to misguidedly enquire about his prior creative fecundity (01:54–02:19).

However, the central aesthetic device contained in "Elastic Man" relies upon paratext, and the intertextual relationship that exists between the song's title, as given on the record sleeve in characteristically scrawled handwriting, and the content of its repeated vocal refrain. Because as would be revealed eventually in 1985, five years after the single's release, Smith does not utter the title of the song at all. The refrain is in fact: "How I wrote 'Plastic Man'" (*The Fall Lyrics*). It is only here, with direct reference to the lyric book, that we can be sure of the utterance, and identify the McGurk effect[2] of which we have become the unwilling victim. This example is relevant to this reading of The Fall as it plainly demonstrates the group's early adoption of subversive means of drawing attention to the textuality of the recording, and the aesthetic potential to affect and distort perceived meaning. What we witness here is an awareness of paratextual and medial effects, and that of the singer's own voice and its capacity to be misinterpreted, being purposefully exploited to aestheticise the song's otherwise linear narrative. The device positions the listener adjacent to the character of the sycophant—both 'fans'—made aware of their own capacity for misunderstanding and misinterpretation. And it is an early example of "Fall Sound" making emergent in the mind of the listener a state of heightened aesthetic awareness, and the distortion of text affected by paratext.

"Spectre vs. Rector," released on the *Dragnet* LP in 1978, is a narrative piece, employing overt allusions to M. R. James and H. P. Lovecraft, which tells the gothic tale of a rector's possession by an evil spirit. Over a grinding, distorted instrumental, Smith's chorus vocal takes the form of a demonic chant, evoking the names of writers, Hollywood figures, and creatures from the horror genre. The exact lyrical contents of the chorus have long been debated in fanzines and music forums, a debate which has not ceased since the official publication of the lyrics in 2008, for reasons we shall explore. The website *The Annotated Fall*, which undertakes the Sisyphean task of pinning down definitive transcriptions of the group's studio recordings, offers the following as of March 4, 2022:

> M.R. James vivant vivant
> Yog Sothoth Ray Milland
> Van Greenway R. Corman
> Sludge hai choi choi choi son (*The Annotated Fall* 2022)

As an example of the kind of fandom-inspired detective work that goes into developing the texts on the *Annotated Fall* website, circumstantial evidence is given on the site for the inclusion of Ray Milland, for example, as a line he utters in the film *The Premature Burial* (1962), directed by R. Corman, is elsewhere paraphrased: "Those flowers, take them away . . . they're only funeral decorations" (03:24–03:31).

When the official lyrics to the song were finally published in 2008, their contents were notably different from what the fans had pieced together:

> M.R. James live on live on.
> You suffered grief ere long,
> Than grimly, ah! come on.
> Sludge hatred T.T. son. (*vii* unnumbered, 2007)

Unlike in the example of "How I Wrote 'Elastic Man,'" the printed lyrics of "Spector vs. Rector" offer little in the way of meaningful revelation and in fact further muddy our attempts to pin down the definitive text. Even leaving aside that the phonemes uttered on the actual recording would be hard pushed to accommodate such an interpretation, the temptation to side with the author on this particular debate is shattered by reference to the record's cover art, which contains paratextual material that seemingly supports the fan-made transcription (*Dragnet*, back cover). Whether the handwritten block lettering on the lower half of the back sleeve to the record on which "Spector vs. Rector" was first released corresponds entirely to what is chanted in the song's chorus or not, it, like the title of "Elastic Man," works to suggest a certain auditory interpretation of its content, which the later official lyrics would seek to erase. The realisation that, thirty years after the song's release, its author would apparently seek to obfuscate its semantic content, attempting to maintain the opacity and mystery of the lyrics, holds important implications for our understanding of The Fall's aesthetic objectives, and those of its principal lyricist. To engage with "Fallness" is to establish one's own capacity to subjectively sublimate meaning amidst a site of chaos which at once offers up and obscures the materials through which the listener accumulates a mental construct. This offering of material is frequently complicated by the presence of paratexts that seem to promise clarification, a skeleton key to the recordings as literary texts, but which instead frustrate as often as they elucidate. Some of The Fall's most famous record sleeves, such as those of *Slates* (1981), and *Hex Enduction Hour* (1982), perform this constructive/destructive function, and the direct influence of Wyndham Lewis's *Blast* can be seen in each. In "The Name and Nature of Modernism," Malcolm Bradbury and James McFarlane characterise "the great works of Modernism" in terms of their ambiguous images: the city as a new possibility and an unreal fragmentation; the machine, a novel vortex of energy, and a destructive implement; the apocalyptic moment itself, the blast of explosion which purges and destroys—images, like Forster's Marabar Caves, which are potentially a synthesis of all possible experience, globally conceived, or of the empty multiplicity and anarchy of the world. It is the image of art holding transition and chaos, creation and de-creation, in suspension which gives the peculiar concentration and sensibility of Modernist art—gives it . . . its "Janus-faced quality." (Bradbury et al. 1983, p.49)

The Janusian aspect of The Fall is characterised by Smith's purposefully disruptive impulses, which as well as the devices already mentioned include mistitling, lo-fi recording, and ambiguous, misleading pronunciations—that include growls, slurs, wheezed exhalations, and rattles in the throat and chest—which work in opposition to his highly declarative and evocative assertions of significant images. Like punk and proto-punk, which served as the musical and performative template for the group's early style, The Fall is inherently parodic of popular music by their subversion of the media they have adopted; an invasion of a medium that is being perverted to accommodate newly made forms, bent to new purposes, and made to reveal its textuality. In stark contrast to typical pop fare such as, for instance, The Beatles' "Love Me Do" (1963), in which the universality of theme is offered up for passive reception of the song's emotional content, The Fall at their most effective provide curated sites built upon sustained and sustaining musical atmospheres that grow hypnotic in their dissonant deployment of repetition, but which through their angularity remain inhospitable to audience passivity.

The confrontational aspect of The Fall—that is ever-present in their music and which was characterised in Smith's early lyricism with the employment of direct insult and audience abuse[3]—becomes more cerebral, more aesthetic in its effects, as we progress through their discography. In 1983, The Fall released their sixth studio album *Perverted by Language*, the second track of which, the vivid and mysterious "Garden," represents a high point in the group's aesthetic functionality. We will explore the exact workings of the song after briefly outlining how theorists have approached unravelling the similar aesthetics of literary modernism. In *The Fictive and the Imaginary* (1991, trans. 1996), the literary theorist Wolfgang Iser explores Samuel Beckett's late short fiction piece "Imagination Dead Imagine" as a site of text play that invites the activation of conscious meaning-making while it simultaneously subverts and assaults it, rendering consciousness "helpless" in the face of unsubstantiable mimesis. Iser redefines the concept of mimesis beyond the traditional Aristotelian notion of a purely representational phenomenon. Iser instead sees mimesis as an imaginative process that diversifies and grows more dynamic in its own processuality—a definition more suitable to the temporal aspect of engagement with literary texts. Iser states:

> [F]or mimesis as a process reference must be continually diversified, so that the resulting dynamism will produce a referentiality that will allow action to become present. (Iser 1996, p.290)

In aesthetic texts such as Beckett's which invite imaginative text play, Iser identifies the potential for "changeability," a "game of transformations" which occurs in the mind of the imagination of the receiver. *The Fictive and the Imaginary* is an ambitious theoretical work of literary anthropology, and the multifaceted concept of text play and its implications are examined in many ways. However, the following summary from Ben De Bruyn encapsulates Iser's approach:

> Beckett supposedly shows that we can only capture the imaginary as such if we minimize the conscious part of our mental activity, and thereby ensure that it does not instrumentalize the creative potential of the imaginary. However, since every act of consciousness, including writing, inevitably shows a certain intentionality, we can only conjure up the imaginary by using and then undermining our forms of speech. In other words, Beckett's self-undermining style is able to present the imaginary because it unsettles the intentional character of straightforward forms. Iser repeats this argument in a related analysis of Walter Pater's work: the imaginary can be truly seen only if we disrupt its ability to function, and this effect can best be obtained by a specific, suggestive style, which incites 'the recipient's imagination' and produces a sequence of readerly images. . . . Iser draws attention to works such as those of Beckett . . . because they reflect self-consciously upon the workings of the imagination, and both evoke and revoke their fictional images. (De Bruyn 2012, pp.181–82)

In his discussion of why such openness of text should prove so effective, Iser comes helpfully close to aligning it with the underlying emotional ennui that characterises much of what we would call "modernism," when he quotes a passage from Roger Caillois's book *Der Krake*:

> If a mystery can stir, if the unusual can grip, if poetry is possible, then perhaps this is because of the complex, confusing correspondences into which the unity of the cosmos has disintegrated. Everything that reminds us of this unity calls forth within our feelings agreement and good will, an ab initio approving echo and longing for unanimity. (Caillois, trans. in Iser 1996, p.240)

For The Fall, it is the exploitation of this longing that becomes the central tenet of what many consider to be their classic period in which sonic sites of text play allow for fractured yet fruitful imagining, whereby the fantastic is never quite permitted to ossify among the mundane. "Garden" is built on a chiming two-note lead guitar part, with added reverb bleeding the repeated notes into one another, and textually appears to contain all the identifying tropes of "Fallness." Smith utters a succession of interrelated gnomic images and phrases, syntactically broken descriptions of scenes that are offered syntagmatically; the song opens:

> The first god had in his garden
> From the back looked like a household pet
> When it twirled round was revealed to be
> A three-legged black-grey hog (00:33–00:55)

This is later echoed by:

> The second god lived by mountains that flowed
> By the blue shiny lit roads
> Had forgot what others still tried to grasp
> He knew the evil of the phone (05:28–05:47)

Meanwhile, the selective-poetic function is foregrounded by a sequence of substitutions. The refrain, "Garden, Garden," transforms, through "Godzone! Godzone!" (03:09–03:13) into "Shotgun! Shotgun!" (04:50–05:00). The uniformity of the delivery of the refrains creates the need for similitude, extending the religious association of the word "garden" created by the "god" of the first line to include "shotgun," its inherent violence, and the prior melding of pagan and Judeo-Christian imagery in direct relation to modernity. The modern also shares imaginative space with the religious with the placement of the telephone, and, later in the midst of what might potentially represent a religious vision, an incongruously placed lift shaft:

> He's here
> He's here at last
> I saw him
> I swear
> He's on the second floor
> Up the brown baize lift shaft
> He's here
> He's here at last
> I saw him
> I swear (06:13–06:30)

"Garden" is flooded with images of misidentification, miscategorisation, false perception, and the deceptive exploitation of direct communication. The "evil of the phone" lyric is offset after the fourth syntagmatic fragment, by the abrupt introduction of a lo-fi, sliced-up tape recording reading a comedic letter purporting to be from "On the Buses" actor Reg Varney, whereby "explosive charges, left to me by a dead sailor from Bury" are wired up to destroy a ringing telephone (03:35–04:02). The tape serves to subvert the high-flown tone that has been achieved by the spatial assemblage of images, interrelations, and transformations, while also adding to it, connecting it to the real, a connection that disturbs and dissipates any risk of the song's disparate contents convalescing into a closed imaginative whole.

After revealing the appearance of the black-grey hog, Smith intones, "see what flows from his mushy pen" (00:57–01:07). The initial base image of the runoff from a hog's pen, if it gains ground in the imagination at all, is supplanted by the image of the pen as a writing implement, a metonym for the creative act. "Mushy pen" is later transformed into "slushy pen," a transformation of a self-referentially unstable image, and an encapsulation of the song's intentionality (02:37–02:47).

"BETWEEN THE PHRASES"

When The Fall takes off, we are dragged with them, through sonically sustained atmospheres, assailed by image fragments and ideas, imaginative possibilities that cannot be fulfilled, exhilarated by an experience that eludes definitiveness. Beckett's process of distillation, his taking away of as much material as possible, is mirrored by the evolution of the music of The Fall, an increased awareness that the imagination of the reader/listener will fill the spaces aired between the fractures. A line from "Garden" appears self-referential in this context: "The best firms advertise the least" (05:00–05:06). There is this salient quote from Beckett's posthumously published *Dream of Fair to Middling Women*:

> The experience of my readers shall be between the phrases, in the silence, communicated by intervals, not the terms, of the statement, between the flowers that cannot coexist, the antithetical (nothing so simple as the antithetical) seasons of words, his experience shall be the menace, the miracle, the memory of an unspeakable trajectory. (p.138)

This is what a song from The Fall provides, but rather than "between the phrases, in the silence," it can be found between the phrases, *amongst the noise*, where, among the drone of post-punk repetition, our imaginations are left to savour and multiply the meanings that flourish from Smith's cryptic lyrical formations. The insinuation of our failure to cohere concrete meaning is that we are not as clever as we think.

If "between the phrases" are found the spaces in which the fictive activates the imaginary, as Iser would claim, then it is important to highlight the increasingly spatial nature of Fall songs in the second half of their career. Where "Garden" has some sense of disembodied, unexplainable unity, later recordings push listeners farther out to sea, culminating in something approaching a Dadaist posture of disregard for the form itself, in which the form is still present, but abused as a socio-political act. For example, the single "Sir William Wray," from 2012, is populated with semantically empty monosyllables such as "wa wa wa" and "gish gish gish," and was described around the time of its release on the album *Re-Mit* as "anti-lyric" (*Radcliffe and Maconie* 2013).

The following year *The Remainderer* was warmly received by critics and fans, who appreciated The Fall's recent return to prolificness, with Kevin Perry writing in the *NME* (*New Musical Express*):

> As if putting out an album almost every year for three and a half decades wasn't enough, Mark E. Smith's productivity is now so high that The Fall have released this EP as a 'bridging point' between May's 'Re-Mit' and next year's scheduled 31st studio album. With a work ethic like that, it's no surprise Smith can't contain his contempt for any band who've taken a few years off and recently reformed. (Perry 2013)

The EP in question is useful for scholars today in overcoming certain unhelpful narratives concerning the late period of The Fall as a creative practice. The problem we face in attempting to establish a discourse around the cultural impact of The Fall, and Mark E. Smith in particular, is that the inevitable caricature—which seems to have come into being during the tumultuous "Mad Mark" period of the late 1990s—often overshadows the work itself. There are obvious comparisons to be drawn between Smith and Hunter S. Thompson, the subject of the 2005 song "Midnight in Apsen," whose conflation with the semi-autobiographical Raoul Duke meant that his antics invariably became more of a draw than the literature that he produced in his later years. The same might be said for Mark E. Smith, while such overshadowing of the work itself has perpetuated the false assumption that in his later years Smith was an artist in creative decline. For scholars today attempting to establish a critical consensus concerning the cultural impact of Mark E. Smith and The Fall, this gives pause for thought: that through unconscious neglect of the latter part of The Fall's discography we might perpetuate a distorted view of the work itself.

OBLIQUE TACTICS

I argue that *The Remainderer* EP may serve as a useful counterpoint to assumptions concerning the music produced by The Fall in its final form—the lineup that included Kieron Melling, Dave Spurr, and Pete Greenway, who were Smith's collaborators from 2008 onwards, as well as Eleni Poulou, who was a member of The Fall from 2002 until 2016—as it is possible to identify within its short running time a gamut of devices which, once revealed, demonstrate that the later period of The Fall, rather than being one of decline, sees the increased use of oblique aesthetic practices that heighten, reinforce, and reiterate the key anti-nostalgic themes identified in my opening quote. It is worth remembering Sasha Frere-Jones's description of "Fallness" quoted above: "a complexity wrought from what should not be enough, but is."[4] With the increasing abandonment of linear narrative, traditional structure, and conventional grammar and syntax, the evolution of Smith's lyricism means his avant-garde tendencies and idiosyncrasies are much more pronounced in his later work. In literary theory, this is expressed as a leaning away from the linear ordering of words, and a heightened activation on the poetic function of word selection. In *The Structure of Obscurity*, Randa Dubnick outlines the modernist writer Gertrude Stein's progression from her first to second 'obscure styles,' and how in her more challenging work such as *Tender Buttons*, she "combined words without regard for whether the mental constructs evoked by them mirrored referential reality" (Dubnick 1984, p.xvi). Take, for example, the following, which is uncannily reminiscent of Smith's late lyricism:

> Alas, alas the pull alas the bell alas the coach in china, alas the little put in leaf alas the wedding butter meat, alas the receptacle, alas the back shape of mussle, mussle and soda. (Stein 1914, p.53)

In interpreting Smith's later lyricism we face many of the same challenges that Stein scholars have faced for the last one hundred years:

> Much misunderstanding of Stein's work is based either on underreading—seeing too little meaning in her work and regarding it as empty words—or on overreading—insisting on finding discursive meaning where none exists. Both erroneous approaches reflect a rejection of obscurity. But as D. C. Yalden-Thompson said, "It is precisely Stein's obscurity which is the challenge to anyone who takes her seriously." (Dubnick 1984, p.xv)

However, Smith's growing impenetrability is combined with accompanying aesthetic practices, an accumulation of idiosyncrasies within the practice of creating Fallness, which further heighten, amend, and extend the intentionality behind releases such as *The Remainderer* EP.

The Fall's song titles are often eccentric. Songs such as "Mere Pseud. Mag Ed" and "To NK Roachment: Yarbles" contain their own semantic dynamism, often reading as micro poems themselves. In the later period of The

Fall, however, with songs such as "Dedication Not Medication" receiving wildly different lyrics across various formats, and the lyrical content of songs altering from performance to performance, the titles work as unifying signs, anchoring the fractured gleams of the disembodied song across multiple versions which, as we attempt to grasp at the definitive text scattered through the palimpsest, reinforce the sense of The Fall as a continuum, a practice, and that to engage with the music is not only to listen to individual songs, but to experience the ongoing phenomenon of "Fallness." Fall titles function as paratexts to the songs themselves, as part of the accompanying sleeve art, a refinement of the famous paratextual scrawlings on the cover of early releases like *Hex Enduction Hour*, the typed song-explanations of *Slates* and the semi-censored descriptions of Domino Records' "x-legged approach" on the back of *Your Future Our Clutter.*

For *The Remainderer*, the titles provide hermeneutic signals that sustain these themes through the adoption and alteration of arcane and obscure terms, governing our interpretations of Smith's lyrics and musical choices and exploiting the imagination's automatic insistence on creating coherence in the art we encounter. Smith's lyrics teem with references to memory, forgetfulness, the futility of fetishising the past, the relentlessness of time's passing, and the ossification of artistic practice.

"The frost covers up what the summer men made." ("Amorator!," 02:10–02:17)

"He's forgot how to break loose, become a tree." ("The Remainderer," 00:33–00:45)

The release of *The Remainderer* followed that of *Re-Mit* in 2013, with the title's prefix unusually separated from the rest of the word with a dash, the combination of "r" and "e" continue to be important for this EP. The title word "remainderer", which is a real word, seems to serve a dual function—first, to denote the bargain basement associations of the word itself, and second, to evoke a sense of waning, of diminishing returns when taken in the context of the EP as a broadside against reformed groups.

The word 'Remembrancer,' taken as a key term or source, seems to me to be of vital importance, though it is not enunciated by Smith in its conventional sense or found like this on the sleeve notes. There is a chance that Smith may have come across it in the work of eccentric poet George Wither, whose long poem *Britain's Remembrancer* is subtitled: "Containing a Narration of the Plagve Lately Past; A Declaration of the Mischiefs Present; And a Prediction of Ivdgments to come." It is not too much of a stretch to think of Wither, who was a pamphleteer, prolific poet, and satirist, as a proto-Blakean figure, though lacking the visionary quality. In an anthology containing selections of Wither's work, George Gilfillan wrote that "Wither was a man of real genius but seems to have been partially insane" (Gilfillan 1868, p.112). The denunciatory, sloganeering style of Wither certainly would have appealed to Smith.

There are further modernist parallels that arise here, namely, the creation of neologisms, and the transformation of words to create added meanings and shades of potential meaning, such as, in *Finnegans Wake*, the coining of the world "benefiction," simultaneously evoking benefaction, benediction, and fiction (Iser 1996, p.7). Here, the word "remembrancer" evokes its synonym, "memorator," which undergoes a transformation to achieve a new function. Smith coins the neologism of its opposite, "amorator," one who rejects the act of remembrance. For the title of track four, the word 'remembrancer' itself receives treatment: "the final "R" is amputated, capitalised, and held apart from the rest of the word, with inverted commas that seem to anticipate the vocalisation of the letter, which, spoken phonetically, is the vowel sound "ah."" This is a common sound in the Smithian repertoire of non-verbal vocalisations, and we can think of its tuneless deployment in the climax of "O.F.Y.C. Showcase" (03:40–04:20). However, in the context of the EP and its anti-nostalgic themes, the "ah" then functions as a motif, deployed sarcastically as a parodic intonation of nostalgic feeling.

What is created, then, is the manipulation of title terms which work as paratexts to the recordings themselves. It's worth noting here another alteration to the word "Rememberance", no longer "remembrancer", with the added "e" seeming to work as an indicator that some meddling has taken place not just with the word itself, but with the manner in which the word "remembrance" is being deployed. Such elements taken in combination establish the schema through which Smith's obscure symbolism—such as the frost vs. the summer men, as well as "You play in winter sun" ("Rememberance R," 03:58–04:09) and "In the castle, it is decay" ("Touchy Pad," 00:10–00:15)—might best be interpreted.

If the thematic resonance of such lines remains in doubt, "Rememberance 'R'" itself contains further aesthetic elements that suggest the continuity of the anti-nostalgic theme, culminating in a prose poem, delivered by long-term Fall collaborator Simon 'Ding' Archer, which makes abundantly clear the intended targets of the EP's multifaceted ire. Recurrent key phrases are given their fulfilled artistic extended meanings through their redeployment in this context: "running on remembrance" (05:06–05:09) as though it were fuel or a weak drug—we might note the presence of the title's superfluous "e"—but where this remembrance is accompanied by a naive forgetfulness on the part of "The Remainderer." It is perhaps indicative of my claim that this EP is an example of Smith's "second obscure style" that the monologue is not delivered by Smith himself. And this suggests yet another modernist parallel, concerning arrangement: not musical arrangement, but rather the EP's cohesive combination of lyrics, paratexts, and intertextual musical allusions. The following quote from Stephen Dedalus in *Portrait of the Artist* has often been identified as the manifesto of Joyce's early aesthetics, and the distance he attempted to establish between himself and the text's intentionality: "The artist, like the God of the creation, remains within or behind or beyond or above his handiwork, invisible, refined out of existence, indifferent, paring his fingernails" (Joyce 1992, p.252). As an artist occupying the "barrier between writer and singer" ("Printhead," 01:37–01:41), Smith cannot be expected to extricate himself from his work in such a way: Smith self-references in his music, and his vocal performance is crucial to our interpretation of his lyrics. But it is telling that in this case, when the lyrics are the most prosaic and straightforward, most direct, Smith steps out of the spotlight and gives the moment to Simon "Ding" Archer, whose monologue decries reformed bands explicitly and ensures Smith's lyrical and aesthetic choices coalesce around a thematic core, while Smith as aesthetic decision-maker operates the EP's more obscure machinery.

It is interesting to note here how fittingly the music on the track complements the monologue, performatively demonstrating a continuum in the history of The Fall: the use of lifted riffs from key Fall influences. As noted by reviewers and fans alike, "Rememberance 'R'" reworks the famous riff from The Stooges' 1969 track "I Wanna Be Your Dog." The influence of The Stooges and the use of this riff in particular, can be seen throughout the Fall discography, while Smith himself has kept The Stooges in general as a continuous touchstone.[5] In 1999, Smith performed a cover of "I Wanna Be Your Dog" live onstage as a guest of The Clint Boon Experience, and the riff recurred again in 2004 in the Peel Session version of *Fall Heads Roll*'s "Clasp Hands." The purpose of it here, then, is to remind the listener of The Fall's consistency as an ongoing practice of musical creation, consistent yet surprising, as described by Peel's famous epithet about the group. As we can see from this, The Fall never went away, and never returned to the limelight in an attempt to recapture a past moment which is irrevocable. ("The frost covers up what the summer men made.") Simultaneously, it demonstrates The Fall's evolution and constancy, through our intertextual familiarity with the riff's recurrence throughout The Fall's discography, and positions them in opposition to their targets. The insinuation is that "while you were away, we never left."

A similar effect is achieved on track five, "Say Mama/Race with the Devil." Though the track was arguably the least well received by fans and critics alike at the time of release, it deploys several devices that effectively perform a continuous thematic function. In this medley of two Gene Vincent covers from the late 1950s, the group seemingly plays it pretty straight, though Smith again signals the continuation of the theme by squeezing the phrase "Rememberance 'R'" into the end of "Say Mama." However, the change in the feel of the recording, the dynamics of the band, and the voice of Smith himself give away the fact that the second half of the track, "Race with the Devil," is not contemporaneous with the rest of the release. It is actually a bootleg recording of the track, performed especially on the occasion of John Peel's fiftieth birthday party in 1989. That the recording comes from an inherently nostalgic and elegiac occasion could have some relevance in light of *The Remainderer*'s overarching themes, but whether we find that convincing or not, the flashback's aesthetic function is to further what was previously shown by track four's idiosyncratic Stooges lift: that The Fall have always been here, plying their trade, creating Fallness, "always different, always the same." The placement, here, of a nearly twenty-five-year-old recording to make an oblique point about The Fall's productivity and consistency is not without precedent. The most obvious comparison in my mind is to the Beatles' "All You Need Is Love" (1967), which reminds the listener of the central theme of love in the band's discography to that point, by reaching back half a decade—a lifetime in pop music then—to fade out with the refrain from 1963's "She Loves You" (03:20–03:30). Like The Beatles in 1967, the juxtaposition of these two recordings obliquely says: "we've been doing this all along." In a tongue-in-cheek parodying of nostalgia, the segue between the two songs is achieved by sampling and looping the descending guitar intro from the original Peel recording, which comes to resemble a perverted version of the tonic scale that is familiar for its deployment in film and TV as an indicator of dream sequences and flashbacks (00:56–01:06).

"ALWAYS THE SAME"

While a critic attempting to fix concrete meaning to the lyrics of Mark E. Smith remains liable, like those of Stein, to fall into the hole of either underreading or overreading, the *Remainderer* EP reveals a host of other aesthetic devices are at work which offer a sense of thematic coherence unusual in The Fall's forty-year discography. We are used to the familiar idiosyncrasies of Fall Sound—the recurrence of lyrics across an album or across a longer period, such as "Unseen Knowledge, Unseen Footage, Unseen Facts" appearing on numerous tracks on *Your Future Our Clutter*, of "the crying marshall" referenced throughout the course of *The Marshall Suite*—but it is rare to find a release where such disparate aesthetic elements are combined to create a schema that leaves the listener in no doubt of *The Remainderer*'s themes and targets. In this instance, they are themes closely tied to The Fall's artistic and cultural identity.

It was a typically perverse move on Smith's part to downplay the EPs release, and suggest it was a collection of offcuts, saying, "that's why it's called the remainder" (*Annotated Fall*), debasing the quality and coherence of it as a self-contained release, opting to sabotage its position as a high-point of late-period Fall, and instead to draw attention to The Fall as an ongoing creative phenomenon. *The Remainderer* is a fine example of the effectiveness of late Fall aesthetics in all their impactful obscurity. A wonderful display of continuity, of the manifold aesthetic aspects of Fallness, a revisiting of sounds and themes from throughout the group's discography—including a reference, through "the tentacles of the old ones" (01:53–01:56), to H. P. Lovecraft, an evergreen influence on Smith first referenced in "Spector vs. Rector." Although repetition and Smith's voice are the base elements that constitute Fallness, by the twenty-first century the group had also accumulated an arsenal of oblique tactics and aesthetic practices, on full display here on this otherwise underappreciated release.

NOTES

1. An incomplete archive of set lists can be found at: https://sites.google.com/site/reformationposttpm/.
2. Simply, a perceptual phenomenon that sees the mischaracterisation of speech sounds. See McGurk et al. 1976.
3. "The difference between you and us is that we have brains," features in the "Intro" to the live album *Totale's Turns* (1980) (00:13–00:18).
4. Elsewhere, Frere-Jones made the claim that "Smith's contribution to rock lyrics has been to liberate them from the need to make sense, continuing Captain Beefheart's work" (Frere-Jones 2011).
5. It is worth noting, when thinking of the proximity of the influence of The Stooges to the music of The Fall, that it was present right until the very end; the encore of the final gig The Fall would ever play was a rendition of 2015's "Stout Man," a reworking of the Stooges "Cock in My Pocket."

REFERENCES

Beckett, Samuel, and Eoin O'Brien. *Dream of Fair to Middling Women*. Arcade, 1992.
Beckett, Samuel, and S. E. Gontarski. *The Complete Short Prose, 1929–1989*. Grove Press, 2010.
Blast 1, Ed. by Wyndham Lewis. BLACK SPARROW PR (CA), 1981.
Bradbury, Malcolm, and James Walter McFarlane. "The Name and Nature of Modernism" in *Modernism: 1890–1930*. Penguin, 1983.
Bruyn, Ben De. *Wolfgang Iser: A Companion*. De Gruyter, 2012.
Dubnick, Randa. *The Structure of Obscurity*. University of Illinois Press, 1984.

Fall, The. "Auto Chip 14–15." *Sub-Lingual Tablet*, Cherry Red, 2015.
Fall, The. *Dragnet*, Step-Forward, 1979.
Fall, The. "Fall Sound." *Reformation Post TLC*, Slogan, 2007.
Fall, The. "Garden." *Perverted by Language*, Rough Trade, 1983.
Fall, The. *How I Wrote 'Elastic Man'*, Rough Trade, 1980.
Fall, The. "O! Zzrttk Man." *New Facts Emerge*, Cherry Red, 2017.
Fall, The. "O.F.Y.C. Showcase." *Your Future Our Clutter*, Domino, 2010.
Fall, The. "Repetition." *Bingo-Masters Break-Out!*, Step-Forward, 1978.
Fall, The. "R.O.D." *Bend Sinister*, Beggar's Banquet, 1986.
Fall, The. "Sir William Wray." *Re-Mit*, Cherry Red, 2013.
Fall, The. "Spector vs. Rector." *Dragnet*, Step-Forward, 1979.
Fall, The. *The Remainderer*, Cherry Red, 2013.
Fall, The. *Totale's Turns*, Rough Trade, 1980.
Fall, The. *Your Future Our Clutter*, Domino, 2010.
Fisher, Mark. *The Weird and the Eerie*. Repeater Books, 2016.
Frere-Jones, Sasha. "Mark E. Smith's Mantras of Disdain." *Village Voice*, 25 January 2018, https://www.villagevoice.com/2018/01/25/mark-e-smiths-mantras-of-disdain/.
Frere-Jones, Sasha. "Plug and Play." *The New Yorker*, 6 November 2011, https://www.newyorker.com/magazine/2011/11/14/plug-and-play.
Gilfillan, George. *Specimens with Memoirs of the Less-known English Poets, vol. II.* William P. Nimmo, 1868.
Goddard, Michael, and Benjamin Halligan. *Mark E. Smith and The Fall: Art, Music & Politics*. Ashgate, 2010.
Iser, Wolfgang. *The Fictive and the Imaginary: Charting Literary Anthropology*. Hopkins University Press, 1996.
Hoelstrom, Troels, director. *It's Not Repetition, It's Discipline*. Ozit Dandelion, 2015.
Joyce, James. *A Portrait of the Artist as a Young Man*. Wordsworth Classics, 1992.
Mcgurk, H., and J. Macdonald. "Hearing Lips and Seeing Voices." *Nature* 264, 746–48 (1976), https://doi.org/10.1038/264746a0.
O'Hagan, Sean. "He's Still the Fall Guy." *The Guardian*, Guardian News and Media, 16 January 2005, https://www.theguardian.com/film/2005/jan/16/bbc.
Perry, Kevin. "The Fall—'The Remainderer' EP." *NME*, 22 November 2013.
Radcliffe and Maconie, BBC Radio 6, 6 May 2013, https://www.bbc.co.uk/sounds/play/p018pxfy.
Rainey, Lawrence S. *Modernism: An Anthology*. Blackwell, 2011.
Smith, Mark E. *The Fall Lyrics: Lyrik & Texte*. Lough Press, 1985.
Smith, Mark E. *Vii*. Lough Press, 2007.
Stein, Gertrude. *Tender Buttons*. Claire Marie, 1914.
The Annotated Fall. 2022. "How I Wrote Elastic Man." Last modified March 3, 2022, http://annotatedfall.doomby.com/pages/the-annotated-lyrics/how-i-wrote-elastic-man.html.
The Annotated Fall. 2022. "Spectre vs. Rector." Last modified February 26, 2022, http://annotatedfall.doomby.com/pages/the-annotated-lyrics/spectre-vs-rector.html.
The Annotated Fall. 2022. "The Remainderer." Last modified February 26, 2022, http://annotatedfall.doomby.com/pages/the-annotated-lyrics/the-remainderer.html.

Chapter Eleven

Linguistic Perversion
Ezra Pound and The Fall
Kieran Cashell

Negative, splenetic, borderline-nihilistic, the songs of The Fall have a semantic complexity atypical in the heritage of Anglo-American popular music. Arguably closer to Christopher Marlowe and William Blake[1] than revered lyricists like Leonard Cohen, Joni Mitchell, Bob Dylan, Jim Morrison, Morrissey, Patti Smith, or David Bowie (Smith 2008, pp.39 & 117; Middles 2003, p.272), The Fall's music is fundamentally grounded in language. Mark E. Smith's corpus of lyrics, album- and song-titles[2] (comprising an incomparable archive of typewritten and quasi-calligraphic content on record sleeves and inserts, press release flyers, gig posters, etc.[3]) constitutes, not so much a paratextual or 'minor literature,' in Deleuze's influential idiom, as an elaborate and irreverent interrogation of the English language itself (Deleuze 1975). Like Irish metafictional author Flann O'Brien, Smith mistreats syntax in a creatively subversive way: as a metamorphous medium for heuristic and corruptive rewiring, a logographic material wrung and wrought into unstable polysemantic slang anagrams.

> *HEXEN DEATH BUBBLE*—RESPECT-INDUCING HYPHEN
> Hexen School Keep Shtum Casting Runes EARN'D hexen-schule.
> Slogger Gelatine-Git Hacks
> Dream of Gibbous Synth-men or their BAGS.
> MOST HILARIOUS MAN-CRIED AT VIDEO
> load o bloody nowt—NEX REX Etc
> BREAK IN DOWN CURVE.
> <u>SAXON-GAELIC</u> <u>POOR-PROCESS</u>
> **CHUMMY LIFESTYLE**

In this transcription of the handwritten slang grimoires on the sleeve of *Hex Enduction Hour*[4] (1982), for example, we witness the English language gnarled and misshapen, distended to the limits of sense (while somehow remaining within the realm of legibility!).

This chapter examines the crucial role of language in enacting what Mark Fisher has called 'pulp-modernist' textual effects in the songs of The Fall. Text, I shall argue, constitutes the elemental medium of The Fall's most innovative musical achievements: it is precisely at the textual or semiotic discursive level, in other words, that this founding instance of the post-punk project is at its most radical, experimental, and provocative. Yet it is with specific reference to what I shall term *linguistic perversion*—perversion in the sense of *obstinate*, deliberately *difficult*, being unreasonable or *wrong* on purpose; *perversion* as in rejecting proper use, putting to improper use . . . even *abuse*; *perversion* as in deviance, aberration, abnormality[5]—that The Fall's most significant contribution to post-punk music culture can simultaneously be identified, exegeted, and understood. Proposing that the songs of The Fall constitute a polymorphous *perversion of communicative discourse*, I suggest that Smith's lyrics can be thematised as a form of neo-Vorticism (where Vorticism, defined as 'Imagism, animated, energized,' is further convulsed by Smith's offbeat, unhinged vocalisation [Stead 2016, 13][6]) and that therefore The Fall's 'quasimodernist' project (Haddon 2020) has a closer hereditary and aesthetic affinity with Ezra Pound (who characterised Vorticism methodologically as a 'verbal manifestation' of the era's 'accelerated grimace') than any of the canonical authors usually referenced in this connection.[7]

In their edited volume, Goddard and Halligan capture the complex and fine-grained textuality of Smith's songs with the observation that his lyrics contain rich 'lineaments of a rhizomatic, subterranean network of inferences and connotations, allusions and borrowings' (2010, p.12). And several critics have acknowledged the rich seam of literary allusion in the music of The Fall (Bracewell [1997]; Easlea [2005a, 2006]; Reynolds [2005, p.175]; Middles [2003]; Fisher [2018]; Goodall [2010]; McDonald [2010]; Goddard and Halligan [2010]; Laity [2019]; Penman [2021]; Sinker [2021]). Such 'writerly' practices of indirect reference and cryptic allusion imply a literary (as opposed to exclusively musical) genealogy—a heritage announced in the group's very name which is, again, not merely a name but, as everyone knows, itself an allusion (to Albert Camus's 1956 novel *La Chute*).

Yet, arguably, the name constitutes an intertextual reference to Dante *mediated through* Camus (*Inferno* Canto V ends with the line, 'And I fall as a dead body falls').[8] *La Chute* is an existentialist reimagining of the *Inferno* and, therefore, the relevant reference for Smith's group is the paragraph where Clamence compares the canalisation of the Dutch capital to the concentric structure of Dante's Hell: 'Middle class hell, of course, peopled with bad dreams' (Camus 1957, p.13).⁹ Regarding the genealogy of the name, Tony Friel, 'cofounder of The Fall' (Smith 2021, p.27) allegedly reading the novel at the time, suggested the title (Reynolds 2005, p.175; 2009, p.206). In his memoir, however, Smith claims that Friel preferred *The Outsiders* (after the earlier novel *L'Etranger*) (Camus 1946; Smith 2008, p.41) and only decided on The Fall with Smith's discovery of 'a 60s band [also] called The Outsiders' (p.41).

Aside from the obvious Camus reference, the songs of The Fall include oblique citation of Blake, Bram Stoker, Alfred Jarry, Wyndham Lewis, T. S. Eliot, Thomas Mann, Vladimir Nabokov, Allen Ginsberg, William Burroughs, and Norman Mailer, strong evidence, as Mark Goodall has indicated, that a 'range of European [and American] modernist texts have been devoured or at least scoured for inspiration by Smith' (2010, p.50). This evidence, however, is often submerged in the dank layers of the singer's more eccentric and outré preoccupations. Smith's interest in the occult and the necromantic is well documented: references to weird fiction and futurist horror genres—to fringe authors like H. P. Lovecraft, M. R. James, Dennis Wheatley, Aleister Crowley, Arthur Machen, Colin Wilson, Luke Reinhardt, Malcolm Lowry—proliferate in The Fall's oeuvre (Fisher 2010; Goodall, 2010; Penman 2021). And admittedly this (perhaps less nuanced) layer tends to occlude the canonical allusions under the skin of the Smith palimpsest.

Driven by an amphetamine-wired eclecticism, this skin secretes adrenalized traces of Marlowe (those high-astounding curses that bristle through the songs!) of Donne (Tempo House), of Dickens (City Hobgoblins); Hardy, Kafka, even Dostoyevsky appear relevant here (Penman 2021, p.41). Alert to the imperceptible prole menace in Harold Pinter's dialogue, the vocalist's capacity to spike a quotidian phrase with an undertone of malice is utterly Pinteresque. Even scat smidgens of Larkin can be detected in Smith's more jaundiced, gnomic stanzas (e.g., 'New Puritan,' 'The Classical,' 'Bill Is Dead,' 'New Face in Hell,' and especially, 'Living too Late').

All this is, admittedly, well known. But the effect of the collision of canonical and fringe in Smith's sullen art is less to elevate pulp than to *pathologize* the canonical. With the autodidact's instinctual feeling for the hysterical subtext under the numinous aura of whatever he misreads, Smith deploys the pulp augur to displace the extra-linguistic excess buried beneath the consecrated soil of the modernist text; it is precisely through this mediumistic exhuming of orthodox Modernism's suppressed Other that The Fall so vividly invoke those phobic spaces where kitchen-sink realism is convulsed by the noonday horrible.

POST-PUNK PULP-MODERNISM

In his contribution to Goddard and Halligan, the late Mark Fisher refers the 'modernist poetics' of The Fall explicitly to Barthes's concept of the 'writerly' (where meaning requires the productive intervention of the reader [Barthes 1974]) to argue that, if the intentionality of Smith's lyrics remains ultimately (and vexingly) opaque, where 'Everything [he sang or uttered] sounded like a quotation' (Fisher 2010, p.107), this shouldn't be regarded as a vulgar accusation of plagiarism or, worse, an admission of unintelligibility; acknowledgment of intertextual density (or irreducible opacity) does not imply meaninglessness. Unlike, for example, the ecstatic glossolalia of The Cocteau Twins' *Treasure* period,[10] Smith's lyrics are not abstract 'strings' of arbitrary vocalisation (Fisher 2010, pp.105–106). And yet, if paraphrasing The Fall's songs into vehicles of literal meaning is otiose (and pointless), it's equally impossible to 'stop making sense of them' (Fisher 2010, p.105). This is the mobius-strip of Modernism. A lyrical corpus that requires 'productive reading' to 'make sense,' Smith's songs constitute a paradigmatic example of Barthes's 'writerly text' (Barthes 1974, p.14).

This exegesis is indebted to Fisher's argument that postpunk culture constitutes a popular iteration of Modernism. Like the literary *avant-garde* of the early twentieth century, the post-punk project was motivated by a critical—sometimes even self-sabotaging—attitude of unreserved exploration, 'adventure,' experimentation (Reynolds 2005, p.xiv). Yet, it is the uncompromising *critical ethos* associated with Modernism that receives a reincarnating stimulus in the post-punk era when refracted through the anarchic punk animus. Wired by aggressive opposition to the inanity of mainstream pop convention, impelled by the 'constant orientation towards the new, and a hostility towards the outmoded, the already-existent, the familiar,' post-punk is recontextualised by Fisher as a late efflorescence of Modernism, reclaiming its unfinished critique from its institutionalised state (and from its recuperated academic status). This thesis is undoubtedly Fisher's most important and original contribution to music discourse: 'The principle behind post-punk', he argues, 'was the popular-modernist idea that you couldn't repeat things, you couldn't use forms that had become kitsch . . .' (Fisher 2016, p.11). Indeed,

> Part of what made this culture popular-modernist rather than populist was its embrace of difficulty. It didn't immediately make sense, references weren't explained to you, and you had to rise to that challenge if you wanted to engage with it. (Fisher 2016, p.14)

Citing the movement's specific challenges to conventional lexical intelligibility—its juxtaposition of incommensurable modes of discourse and its paratactical density, its disregard for accessibility, 'resistance to closure' and obsession with the intractable materiality of language—Fisher identifies a key affinity with the 'difficulties and compulsions' of early-eighties' post-punk culture where reflexivity, 'dissonance, obliquity,' appear again as criteria of originality and aesthetic innovation (Kleinzahler 2019, p.38). For Fisher (and others: Easlea, Reynolds, Laing) this post-punk 'modernist imperative' is epitomized by The Fall, 'the only group to survive the punk era with critical status undiminished and critical faculties intact' (Lee 2006, p.40).

In a recently republished three-part study republished in *K-Punk* (Fisher 2018), Fisher proposes that Smith's song-writing—precisely the way 'it foregrounds its own textuality and texturality'—is equivalent to any of the canonical works of 'high literary modernism' (2018, pp.326 & 324). Especially evident in the sequence of recordings from 1979 to 1982 (*Dragnet, Grotesque, Hex Enduction Hour*) The Fall's classic phase constitutes a paradigm instance of the post-punk restatement of Modernism. Describing the multi-layered, granular texture of the group's acoustic aesthetic as 'gnarled, collage cut-up, deliberately incomplete' (a tortuous form that 'haemorrhages' through the insert onto the album-covers and beyond) (Fisher 2018, pp.326 & 340). Fisher recontextualises The Fall with reference to T. S. Eliot, James Joyce, Wyndham Lewis (p.324; Bracewell 1997, p.182); and indeed, undeniably, Smith's songs, in a similar way to experimental Modernism, are embroidered and encrypted with erudite intertextual allusion in the tradition of the literary *avant-garde* of the previous century.

Yet it could be argued, equally plausibly, that The Fall enacts a corrosive subversion of Modernism. Smith's schtick of aggressive autodidacticism sabotages the formalist excesses of highbrow Modernism, profaning the pretentious elitism of lit-theory rhetoric with a feral vernacular, and undermining, in the process, assumptions about musical and aesthetic sophistication being the exclusive preserve of the 'privileged and formally educated' (Fisher 2018, p.324). This pertains to the splenetic proletarian animus—the 'White Crap that Talks Back,' the 'Destroyer of Romanticism,' the 'Prole Art Threat,' the vicious invective against 'intellectual half-wits,' 'academics,' 'students,' 'slates,' 'pseuds,' 'male slags'—associated with Smith's confrontational, agitative, anti-aesthetic (and, yes, *punk*) attitude.

Aware of his 'contempt for formal education' (Scott 2019, p.70), it is common practice to contextualise Smith's prole art anti-aesthetic with reference to Vorticism's Luddite tendency to valorise the amateur and shambolic above elegant design professionalism (Bracewell 1997); but Smith's neo-Luddite attitude, as Michael Bracewell notes, was mobilised specifically against the austere neoclassicist aesthetic of Factory productions and their Tschichold-influenced art director (pp.180–81). The anti-academic adoption of the amateur-shambolic in the post-punk phase of The Fall Mark Fisher terms 'Pulp Modernism,' identifying an avant-antiart style that, although continuous with modernist textual practice, incorporates the destabilising influence of dysfunctional genres such as weird fiction, grotesque realism, occult mysticism, horrorcore esoterica, and, onstage, theatre-of-cruelty-style vocalic hysteria. But pulp-Modernism is unique, Fisher maintains, because of the specific way it unearths the perverse 'doppelganger' of Modernism from its encrypted state in the monuments of official culture, thereby giving vent, through post-punk culture, to its latent ludic—and *cursed*—essence ('cast the runes against your own soul') (Fisher 2018, p.324); it achieves its textual effects by reappropriating the modernist text (already a xenomorphic palimpsest of allusion and vestigial quotation) and shredding it into a snarl of fragments before rendering it down into the grey 'witches' brew' of indecipherable grimoire and apotropaic hieroglyph. The new membrane formed from the resultant sublingual amalgam, Fisher suggests, resembles a kind of 'mystic pad on which stray psychic signals impress themselves.' Here a radically new choric space is generated, which, precisely because of its flat amorphousness, is freshly responsive to a 'multiplicity of mutually antagonistic voices.' The 'riot of voices' heard convulsing the central nervous system of The Fall's 'writer-ranter-chanter' warps through the rock-drill assault of *Dragnet, Grotesque, Slates*, and *Hex Enduction Hour*—where the vocalist sometimes seems possessed by an unquiet polyglottic force. The 'logorrhoeic disgorging of "slanguage"' Fisher calls this vocal spasming, where the heterogeneous 'voices [note the plural] . . . will often be reported speech, recorded in the compressed "telegraphic" headline-style Smith borrowed from the [Wyndham] Lewis of *Blast*' (Fisher 2018, p.328). The Fall, Bracewell agrees, 'could be seen as a vorticist Blast against the design-conscious professionalism and Mancunian elitism of Anthony H. Wilson's Factory Records' (1997, pp.180–81).

VORTICSM™ (EZRA POUND)

Many commentators, as noted, have acknowledged the relevance of Vorticism (as well as Imagism) for Smith's artistic identity (Bracewell, 1997; Easlea 2005a; Fisher 2010, p.109; 2018, p.341; Lee 2019; Norton & Stanley 2021; Bertolotti-Bailey 2021). But his iconoclastic attitude is routinely associated with the influence of (his 'hero') Wyndham Lewis, where Ezra Pound ought to constitute at least as salient a reference in any critical elaboration of The Fall's post-punk (or 'pulp') Modernism.[11] It is weird that the American poet—arguably as influential as Lewis—is rarely, if ever, mentioned in this connection. Although recognising that 'the intertextual methodology is crucial to pulp modernism,' Fisher, inexplicably, avoids Pound, afraid perhaps of the controversy associated with his name that has done much to discredit his achievement (and often considered sufficient to condemn anyone referring to him as an apologist for anti-Semitism).[12] Yet, despite this issue, I insist that Fisher's thesis of post-punk pulp-Modernism can be completely thematised only relative to the specificity of Pound's Vorticism. To appreciate the unusual semantic effects of Smith's writerly style, in other words, but also to do justice to 'the vertiginous experience of the songs and the distinctive jouissance provoked by listening to them' (Fisher 2010, p.105), Pound (a voice nullified in Fisher's essays) cannot be ignored.

More extreme (and convulsive) than the precious East Asian–inspired imagist school, Vorticism—a reference to French 'savage-messiah' sculptor Gaudier-Brzeska (Pound 1970; Ede 1931)—was committed to convulsing poetic language with a centrifugal, violent, almost 'demonic,' energy. Its objective was not simply to dynamize (or energise) the static image, however, but to incapsulate the thought '*process* through which the image was conceived and transmitted' (Albright 1999, p.4) and in this way to 'probe a spot on the brain which has not been de-sensitized' by overfamiliarity with rarefied aesthetic style (Ingham 1999, p.248) even if, in the process, poetic form is distressed to the 'limits of coherency' (Fraser 1960). Pound assimilated the effect to a mental gyroscope around whose 'radiant node' an eidetic 'cluster' of displaced fragments furiously whirl. This spiralling form with the enduring yet unstable image at the nucleus 'is what I can and must perforce, call a VORTEX, from which, and through which, and into which, [other] ideas are constantly rushing' (Pound 1970, p.92).[13]

Designed around 1984–1985, The Fall's ensign—a swirling time-tunnel maelstrom with the group's name stamped in its whorl—diagrammatically invokes the Poundian vortex. Reproduced, for example, on the (Claus Castenskiold–designed) sleeve for *The Wonderful and Frightening World*, C.R.E.E.P. (see also Victoria and the promotional flyer for C.R.E.E.P. which includes a nightmarish image of the "Creep" emerging from the vortex[14]), this graphic visualises the centrifugal sound of The Fall.[15] Capturing its dilating rhythmic arcs and the vertiginous density of its pulsating dynamics, The Fall's sonic vortex intensifies in frequency until sucked into the nucleus of silence—arguably the node of most violent perceptual intensity in the sound ('Silence', Pascal Quignard's epigram states, 'is to ears what night is to eyes' [2016, p.187]).[16] In fact, The Fall's music should be characterised as a sonic Poundian vortex precisely in that the auditory experience it stimulates probes cerebral regions not yet de-sensitised by generic, harmonic melody.

Ezra Pound, émigré poet, outsider iconoclast, didn't use English in the conversational, confessional mode that was becoming the dominant poetic address of the period; but as an 'observing alien,' his syntactical style, as Fraser observes, is characterised by 'very odd'—indeed *perverse*—juxtapositions of 'ironically formal, mandarin language and a kind of slanginess. . . .' But this 'mandarin-demotic' style has grammatical connotations 'not of unselfconscious assurance, like the true conversational style, but of very intelligent, and sometimes arrogant or aggressive, *unassurance*' (Fraser 1960, p.39). In Pound's poem 'The Garden', for instance, the prosaic phrase 'She would like someone to speak to her' is completed with the bombastic, precious, 'I will commit that indiscretion', and, in this confrontation, Fraser comments, the diction of the 'highbrow,' drawing on the 'deliberately informal' period idiom is conjoined with the grandiloquent construct to generate a peculiar 'self-critical irony' (Fraser 1960, 40) familiar to Fall fans. Compare the effect with lyrics such as, 'I do not like your tone'—from 'It's a Curse' on *The Infotainment Scan* (1993)—when completed with, 'It has ephemeral, whinging aspects,' the correlation with Pound's eccentric idiom is immediately apparent. Indeed, strikingly similar mandarin-demotic juxtapositions as those Fraser observes of Pound are evident throughout Smith's lyrics. And the technique is particularly emphatic on *Perverted by Language* (1983) which contains exemplary archaic-vernacular conjunctions, 'I grope about / And when I go out / My mind splits / My eyes doth hurt' ('Eat Y'self Fitter'); 'lickspittle Southerner' ('Smile'); 'But it made me hungry / For victuals I could not raise nor buy' ('I Feel Voxish'); 'Kickback art thou that thick?' ('Hexen Definitive / Strife Knot').

With specific reference to the paradigmatic vorticist text, *The Cantos*, Pound's encyclopaedic, aggressively erudite and formally intimidating, polylingual—*unfinished*!—epic poem, this analysis focuses on The Fall's sixth studio album *Perverted by Language* (1983), the title of which derives from Canto XIV:

> And the betrayers of language
> .....n and the press gang
> And those who had lied for hire;
> the perverts, the perverters of language,
> the perverts who have set money-lust
> Before the pleasures of the senses.

Perverted *by* language rather than '*of* language' spoken of in Canto XIV introduces a subtle but important grammatical modification implying that language is, in this case, the *agency* of perversion, not something done to language but something language—and Pound's language in particular—accomplishes. Smith's syntactical twist suggests that the effect Vorticism has on the prelapsarian reader is far from innocuous. Language perverts. Are we not convulsed, *corrupted* even, by Pound's promiscuous exhibitions of linguistic abnormality? 'And as for the original-sin racket . . . the hex-hoax,[17] / Aswins drawing the rain-cloud, / Fou-Hi by wood' (XCVI).

Weird. But listen to this: 'These fragments you have shelved (shored),' Canto VIII begins. And then comes the convulsive, '"Slut!" "Bitch!" Truth and Calliope / Slanging each other sous les lauriers: / That Alessandro was negroid. And Malatesta / Sigismund. . . .'[18] Addressed to Eliot[19] this canto personifies a dispute between historiography and rhetoric, a bitter antagonism between the demands of documentary veracity and the impulse of aesthetic form that runs right through Pound's epic and remains unreconciled when the poem finally burns out with the cry: 'I am not a demigod! I cannot make it cohere' (CXVI).

        From Canto CIV:
          'Said Yo-Yo:
            "What part ob yu iz deh poem ??"'

And, listen to this, from Canto LXXVII (composed in a maximum security U.S. 'Disciplinary Training Centre' near Pisa where Pound, arrested for treason after the war, was detained in an outdoor 'gorilla' cage illuminated 24/7 by klieg-lights):

      As Arcturus passes over my smoke-hole
         the excess electric illumination
         is now focussed
    On the bloke who stole a safe he cdn't open
             (interlude entitled: periplum by camion)
         and Awoi's hennia   plays hob in the tent flaps
            k-lakk.....thuuuuuu
                making rain
                    uuuh
2,   7,   hooo
            der im Baluba
   Fassa !   4 times was the city remade . . .

Language, functional medium of communication, transparent as it is pragmatic, in these samples, is convulsed by a deeper, disobedient force, an instinctual pulse, a pneuma of libidinous energy that 'pluralizes, pulverises, "musicates"' syntax, destabilising the passive reader's expectation of normality (Lechte 1990, p.132). This awakening to the polymorphic excess of language (language, we could say, as 'thingy'—a formulation Pound would appreciate) becomes paradigmatic for Smith's lyrical and writerly practice in *Perverted by Language*. Semantic (or lyrical) density, he realised, depends on the *abuse* of syntax. The following sample derives from the lyrics of 'Kicker Conspiracy' reprinted on the inner sleeve of *Perverted* and transcribed in Smith's characteristic typewritten zine-squib style, a polyphonic 'riot' of caps and lowercase, with supplementary biro-graffito additions.

> In the Marble Halls of the Charm School
> How Flair is Punished
> Under Marble Millichip, The F.A. Broods
> On how style can be punished
> THEIR GUEST IS A EURO-STATE MAGNATE
> CORPORATE-ULENT[20]

A good example of Smith's polysemantic rewiring "Corporateulent" is an ugly portmanteau conjunct invoking the image of a morbidly obese, morally bankrupt, institution. Reference to 'body mass' ('bulk,' 'fat') in the suffix when hyphenated with 'big business' exploits the shared somatic etymology of the words (L.: *corpus* body) to generate the perverse connotation.

PERVERTERS OF LANGUAGE

Announcing The Fall's return to Rough Trade two years after abandoning the label, 1983's *Perverted by Language* is characterised by sparse, parsimonious arrangements. The tectonic foundation remains heavily beat-based (compounded by the binaural double drum-kit structure). Skank subsonic bassline frequencies flesh out caesurae in the background centrifuge; while the foreground, inscribed with Scanlon's sharp repetitious staccato riffs, is further textured with Brix's frictionless guitar. Microphonic detail is added by atonal piano noise, primitive electronic keys, and Smith's violin-scraping. But the most significant element distinguishing this record, obviously, is the recruitment of Brix (Laura Elisse Salenger) into the ensemble. Brilliantly complementing the lead vocalist's soliloquised roaratorio (interrupted by semi-involuntary interjective and 'micro-vocables' [*Er*, *um*, *uh* and his signature end-stopped syllable *shwa*] indications of 'mouth in search of a voice') (LaBelle 2014, p.132), Brix's limpid singing style—female, American-accented, at once more distinct and more conventional than her husband's—introduces a melodic air-freshening luminosity into the sullen monologic tonalities of The Fall's sound.

Against the critical consensus that Brix 'ushered in the Commercial Fall Era,'[21] Siân Pattenden defends the unorthodox view that this phase (from 1983 on) represents the group's 'most avant-garde period' (2021, p.256). The introduction of Brix, she provocatively suggests, brought a new 'subversive presence' to The Fall 'fully involved, part of the art, a woman too, brandishing the phallic guitar object,' and it is simplistic (and chauvinistic) to dismiss Brix's contribution to the group (despite her influence on Mark's wardrobe!) as nothing more than 'a commercial agent' (2021, p.256).[22]

Recorded at Pluto Studios in Manchester[23] Fall percussionist Paul Hanley remembers the parsimonious arrangement giving the musicians a welcome flexibility to explore a more austere yet multi-layered sonic architecture; the 'simpler musical palette' enabled, he says, the creation of a dynamic sense of space, the result of which is an immersive receding soundscape that contrasts with the marshy foreground density of previous recordings. Produced by Steve Parker, it was the first album the group recorded with Brix (Smith's violin and spoken word Hotel Blöedel was sutured into the Banda Dratsing hook One More Time and a new sound was born). Their enigmatic vocalist, however, responded to the severe template, Hanley recalls, by authoring the most challengingly esoteric lyrical content of his career (Hanley 2017, p.176).[24] Notoriously taciturn when discussing his metier, however, the singer used to say things like, 'I'm not giving my secrets away to the fucking idiots in the BBC. Can you understand that?' (Newton 2005). Interviewed (with Brix) a year later (in connection with the release of *The Wonderful and Frightening World . . .* [1984]), Smith revealed that during the *Perverted* project he was paranoid that his writing was becoming 'too dense and complex.' Following a burst of creativity in 1982–1983 he started to worry that he was suffering from writer's block—his solution, he says, was to leave the record company. And this strategy worked: 'It was like, I'd rather retire than stay with Rough Trade!' (Smith in Irwin 1984, p.134).

If *Perverted by Language*, by consensus, signals a musical departure for The Fall, the album equally marks the consummation of an intense period of productive creativity. Following its release Smith resigned (definitively this time) from the record company. As the 2005 CD re-release (with supplementary tracks) clarifies, the final cut constitutes a judiciously edited sample of 1982–1983's extensive repertoire. Notwithstanding the contemporaneous Rough Trade single releases ('The Man Whose Head Expanded' and 'Kicker Conspiracy / Wings'), there was, as Easlea's commentary reveals, a veritable 'stockpile' of material available for the LP (2005). Live sets of the period (*Austurbaejarbio: Reykjavik Live* 1983) include the remarkable 'Look Know' (released as a single on *Kamera* in 1982) and 'Backdrop'. 'Pilsner Trail' was recorded but omitted from the track-list (see master notes for Rough 62.B); and, given the appearance of the lyrics on the inner sleeve, 'Kicker Conspiracy' was probably intended to be included on the record (or at least considered an element of the wider *Perverted* project). Indeed, retrospectively, there's a sense in which the selected content—which incorporates an eight-minute live track recorded in the Hacienda (Tempo House) as well as the duet 'Hotel Blöedel' (never performed live)—was strategically curated to generate a 'subject-rhymed' thematic coherence.[25]

A case in point, the song itself, 'Perverted by Language', designated the 'missing title track' by Easlea (2005), was not even recorded for the album and, unfortunately, the live version included on the expanded CD is overwhelmed by the dominant double-drum *bombarde*. Consequently, it's not possible to decode the lyrical content from the enveloped backgrounded vocal. And neither of the two inconsistent transcriptions available online appear to cohere with what Smith's vocalising nor, in text, seem characteristic of his writing style.[26] A missed opportunity for anyone interested in the Pound connection.[27] Yet this 'rag-bag'[28] vocal eclipsed by a '*tarabust*'[29] of propulsive, oppressive bastinado beats, it could be argued, paradoxically performs an appropriate response to Pound's 'Hell Cantos' (XIV–XVI), which as Daniel Albright observes, concern the degradation of language (coincidentally, 'language' is one of the few signifiers that emerge with any clarity in the performance[30]) where Pound 'mangles, spreads, unwrites, unspeaks, the texts and voices that need to be consigned to oblivion' (Albright 1999, p.78). Following the transcription on the Annotated Fall website, the editors refer to a comment on the Online Forum posted by one "ezra pound" that quotes from Canto XIV and goes on to observe that, as a fan of Wyndham Lewis (again!) Smith would have been familiar with Pound; to which "Zack" replies: 'If Perverted by Language is indeed a reference to Ezra Pound, that's a delightful pun since the song consists of little more than, well, pounding.'

LINGUISTIC PERVERSION: THE 'HELL CANTOS'

Perverted by Language references Pound at his most visionary. Yet Cantos XIV–XVI (the so-called 'Hell Cantos')[31] also contain the ugliest, most sordid, *scatological* passages of the work. Composed in a rancorous vernacular reminiscent of his treasonable wartime radio-rants, Canto XIV channels Dante to conjure a vision of Hell; but any semblance of the solemn architectonic of the *Inferno* ends there. Hell, in Pound's manifestation, is obnoxious quagmire. And noise. Unleashed in its full, malodourous, brown, crawling squalor, the Hell scene reeks from its leering pages:

> The stench of wet coal, politicians
> .... e and ..... n, their wrists bound to their ankles,
> Standing bare bum,
> Faces smeared on their rumps,
> wide eye on flat buttock,

>   Bush hanging for beard,
>   Addressing crowds through their arse-holes,
>   Addressing the multitudes in the ooze,
>   newts, water-slugs, water-maggots,
> [. . .]   Profiteers drinking blood sweetened with shit,
>   And behind them ...... f and the financiers
> [. . .]

The paradigm for Pound's vision of Hell is neither Homer nor Dante but Hieronymus Bosch. The orgiastic *Garden of Earthly Delights* (1480–1490) possesses that exact combination of hallucinogenic clarity and teeming detail captured in Cantos XIV–XVI. Although the poet must have been impressed by the scatological character of the Netherlandish painter's imagination (the panels are patterned with abundant motifs of defecation and regurgitation), ultimately, though Pound has appreciated (and this is the principal feature drawn attention to in this analysis) that Bosch's inferno is *aural* torment, a realm of pandemonium and noise, of 'acoustic suffering,' where colossal orchestral instruments are deployed as 'instruments of torture,' allegorised in the ear-slicing leitmotif; and where a screaming choir of the damned, conducted by a ceremonious demonic being, follows a musical score tattooed across a dead soul's buttocks (Belting 2018, p.38). Optical complexity and microscopic detail in Bosch's painting, indeed, double as pictorial equivalents for *noise* which spectators of the work experience vicariously in the 'auditory imagination' (Eliot 1953). The nude figure at the top of the lower third of the panel with the flageolet between his buttocks reappears in Canto XIV (line 66) as one of Pound's anonymised damned, 'frigging a tin penny whistle.'

In the realm of sludge, the damned wallow in cacophonous congress: legislators, plagiarists, philologists, bank-managers, capitalists, career-journalists, press-editors, bishops, the 'murderers of Pearse and MacDonagh', media tycoons, slum-landlords, industrialists, entrepreneurs . . . These 'betrayers of language,' are depicted in fiendish hallucinogenic detail: bent-double, like some Boschian nightmare, smelted into malformed anatomies, buttock-face amalgams, the damned heckle through flapping sphincters, 'fahrting through silk, / waving the Christian symbols . . .' It's not clear whether The Fall vocalist counts himself among Pound's condemned (his lyrics denigrate similar malefactors, Plagiarists, Idiots, 'Slates,' 'Male Slags,' 'Print-Heads,' 'Pseud-Mag-Editors,' Journos, 'Hacks,' 'Fuckfaces,' 'Intellectual Half Wits,' 'Dim-Wits'). But one thing is certain, revelling in the perversion of language, Smith, with Pound-like ambivalence, adds to the noisome chorus while simultaneously reviling it:

> Tight faded male arse
> Decadence and anarchy
> He said, he smiled . . .
>
> Smile!
> Meat animals

And:

> Sodomised by presumption . . .

'I intended cantos XIV and XV,' Pound wrote (to his father) in May 1925, 'to give an accurate picture of the state of England in the years 1919 and following. . . . The ang-sax race as a whole or a hole, very insensitive to rot and decomposition. Eng much worse than US. England insensitive to mental decay.' He also described this subsection of cantos to Wyndham Lewis, saying, '"Hell" is a portrait of contemporary England, or at least Eng. As she was when I left her.'[32]

Significantly, 'awareness of the stink, the rot, the shit dripping through the air is all the poet's and ours.' That self-consciousness is denied to the oblivious souls (but not to their observers) makes their condition, for readers, even more appalling (Kearns 1980, pp.62–63). Indeed, 'The real point about Pound's usurers . . . perverters of language etc.,' as Christine Brooke-Rose observes, 'is that despite the harm they do, the hell they create is here on earth.' This is the reason why, she says, they are depicted in such nauseating realism: seeing them 'chasing each other around, eating each other in a senseless circle but almost unaware of it' is both frightening and pitiful (Brooke-Rose 1971, p.221).

ENGLAND AS INFERNO

A stygian landscape of chimney stacks, derelict warehouses and mysterious black monoliths, Smith's vision of Hell is situated in the post-industrial North (of England). Above ground, no new Jerusalem can be built while under the anthracite fields, an eternal incinerator consumes the souls of the dead. Smith's Hell—*negative-Jerusalem*—like Pound's is, of course, modern English society. 'I wrote about what was around me,' he riffs in a frequently quoted passage from *Renegade*, 'that was the whole point: to get down the experiences, scenes, people, etc. But some people are so daft they don't understand that writing about Prestwich[33] is just as valid as Dante writing about his inferno' (Smith 2008, p.86). Kay Carroll (early Fall keyboardist and manager) remembers that the singer used to frequent the Forrester's pub in Prestwich (observing the local Dickensian grotesques) for inspiration.[34] Driven mad by ambivalence about his homeplace, North Manchester was both source of, and treatment for, Smith's morbid nostalgia, the Satanic industrial environment as pharmakon (toxin and antidote) so that, 'In the end,' comments Fisher, he cannot bring himself to leave, 'he is as afflicted by paralysis as Joyce's Dubliners' (Fisher 2018, p.104).

Designed and painted by Claus Castenskiold (presumably under Smith's direction) the lurid sleeve of *Perverted by Language* depicts Pound's vision of England as Hell ('utter decrepitude . . . the bog of stupidities'). With angular brushstrokes controlled by his signature iron-black outlines, the painter channels this infernal 'portrait of contemporary England' through the distortionist style of Weimar Dadaism (especially Otto Dix and Georg Grosz). Ejaculating their sputum from tumescent tongues onto an indifferent world, preacher-swindler, sleazy ratfink press-reporter—perverters of language—are modelled in purple and blue-black with facets of vermillion and bloodshot pink, acid-yellow, and caustic-green (intentionally rhyming with Suzanne Smith's palette for the cover of *Grotesque*[35]). One figure (in suit and tie) brandishes a rolled-up newspaper as bludgeon (it reads "NEWS: LIES"), while another, reclining left, bawls from grossly distended mouth, gesturing with index finger, an allusion to Canto XIV (lines 79–81): 'the drift of lice, teething, / and above it the mouthing of orators, / the arse-belching of preachers.' Vermin crawl in garbage containers and the windows of fire-trap tower blocks, inflamed by reflection, capture the inferno burning below. A line of Satanic high-tension pylons cuts through the Bosch-inspired skyline. Cooling towers pump out bilious fumes. Black beetles skitter out of the bin. Discarded scraps of windblown headline read: 'Daily-Rag Propaganda!'

Grounded in a substratum of compulsive metronomic rhythms, the opening track of the record announces the features that define its frugal aesthetic: 'Eat Y'self Fitter' perverts the vacuous slogan of a 1980s Kellogg's cereal advertisement—the elision (Y-apostrophe) abbreviating the phrase—to suggest that the words are consuming themselves. Thinning out through a process of verbal autophagy, the syntax is, reflexively, *eating itself*. All instruments on this track are (mis)treated percussively, pumping out an oscillating two-note parody of the call-response form: a vaudeville chorus answering the leader's acapella phrases.[36] 'He was the Manager? Eat Y'self Fitter! / Up the stairs Mister . . . Eat Y'self Fitter!' An electronic noise, possibly Casiotone VL1 (Easlea 2005b), but sounding suspiciously like an open tin whistle (and, given the kazoos used on *Grotesque*, it may very well *be* a whistle), encircles the repetitious two-beat 'syndrome' adding strokes of dissonant amateur abandon to the aural *melee*.

Originating in work contexts, the call-and-response pattern follows the repetitious rhythms of labour. And 'Eat Y'self Fitter' begins with an industrial reference (to the machine lathe), the mechanical rhythm of which determines the rotating tempo of the song. In call-response mode, incidentally, the controlling presence of the vocalist is emphatic: the motley choir acquiesces to the dominant voice directing the song. And Fisher's observations regarding Smith's imperious control of The Fall are relevant here, when he claims, for instance, that the group at this point had become 'zombie slaves of [Smith's] vision' (Fisher 2010, p.106). Particularly evident on this record ('Don't confuse yourself / With someone who has something to say')[37], Smith's dictatorialism is performed on this track with a carnivalesque reflexivity.

> He is the shaman-author, the group the producers of a delirium-inducing repetition from which all spontaneity must be ruthlessly purged. (Fisher 2010, p.106)

The 'perverters of language,' in this vortex of Hell, are reduced to a pantomime ring of subhuman entities, running around in a senseless circle, eating each other.

GARDEN OF UNEARTHLY DELIGHTS

'I don't pretend to understand' *Perverted by Language* percussionist Paul Hanley later admitted. 'Was "Garden,"' for instance, he asks, 'a treatise on the nature of man's relationship with God since expulsion from Eden, a sideways look at the dank underbelly of suburbia, or both?' Yet despite his confusion, the drummer rhapsodises Smith's lyric as 'incredible.' And immediately adds the simile, 'like Blake.'[38] . . . But if you tried to say anything, the first thing [Mark'd] say is, "What the fuck's it got to do with you?"'

Yet is this experience of uncertainty not structural to a song like 'Garden's' 'vertiginous' and 'libidinous' effects? Lyrical elision, Gavin Hopps observes, is paradoxically 'creative,' producing semantic gaps that seethe with excess, if ultimately equivocal, significance (2008, p.286). Hopps argues further that the intentional '*withholding* of meaning' can be crucial to the performance of the kind of 'apparitional play' of semiosis in a track like 'Garden' with its gnomic compositional structure 'loosely netted around holes and blanks' (Hopps 2008, p.286; Froula 2016, p.161). Listeners, placed in an analogous position to readers (of *The Cantos*), in fact, need to be prepared to 'make a set of personal hermeneutic decisions about the meaning and connection of its various elements' without being certain that any connections discerned between the gaps in its 'weird associative logic' are ever valid, definitive, or, indeed, intentional (Froula 2016, p.158). Respectful of this caveat, let us scrutinize this track more carefully.

Garden begins with a grim image.

Something hanging from a tree, slowly revolving, is disclosed as a three-legged hog. This opening tableau, reminiscent of a grainy scene from a Hammer horror, takes place in the pastures kept by the 'first god.' But Smith's lyric is equivocal; the scribe pauses twice to admire what's oozing from his 'mushy'—or 'slushy'—pen onto the surface of his new testaments. A spoken-word excerpt is inserted like a playback message in the middle of the song before the reading of the second testament: a new god, depicted in classical mode, beside a fountain. Smith's lyrics invoke Easter ('the bells stopped on Sunday when he rose') as the narrator excitedly annunciates the arrival of the messiah: a figure coming up an elevator (Jacob's Ladder) enters the ocular nucleus of sound (Hanley helpfully explains the brown baize reference)[39] as 'Garden' reaches its crescendo and the counter-melodies, entwined until this point, dramatically detach from each other and the dissonant thunder of a piano beaten like timpani palpably breaches the parameters of acoustic space. At which point the singer's hysterical screams become *white*—an acoustic space where noise and silence coexist.

'Jew on a Motor . . . BIKE!'

Interpolation of the 'dictaphonic' (Walker 2010) sample (a fragment in the strict philological sense) alongside other experimental vocal intrusions in the mix, gives the track the heterogeneous, cinematic texture of (a sound) montage.[40] The provenance of this audio-fragment is a satirical advice-piece performed by the vocalist on Greenwich Sound Radio (pirate station) sometime in 1983 entitled 'Mark E. Smith's Guide to Writing Guide'[41], recommending how to manage pestering and persistent phone-calls using hotwired remote-controlled explosive devices and signing off, *sincerely*, under the pseudonym Reg Varney.[42] This sample is followed by another spectral vocal interpolation, '(........ his ferry stopped at 'Pool port. revealed to be a spoilt slate with largesse resource. Wild Bill hick, shaves and charts at last, made the second god sad—he's coming up.)'[43]

Close listening reveals several further episodes of this interpolative soliloquised technique, engaged to interrupt homophonic uniformity/contextual coherence ('Do a dance here,' 'Jacob's Ladder,' 'The best firms advertise the least,' 'shotgun' . . .). Yet it's not that conventional compositional structure is completely rejected in 'Garden'—the song is haunted by the ghost of verse-chorus-bridge-chorus-crescendo form—but it is as if the vocalist is determined to deliberately sabotage the formula with his sub-vocal vivisections, doing everything, for example, to avoid repeating keywords (SHOTGUN! GODZONE!) in time to the melody when it shifts to the "chorus" section. As a result, the chorus refuses to be lyricised: it just allows for the (Lou Reed–type) off-beat spoken, repeated, 'Garden, Garden.'

Although Smith's target of perversion is Joni Mitchell's 'Woodstock' (first recorded by Crosby, Stills, Nash, and Young in 1970)—a psych reimagining of vintage hippy-fest as Eden[44]—I'm convinced that the key allusion in 'Garden', as in Pound's 'Hell Cantos', is Bosch's *Garden of Earthly Delights*. In the lower right of the Hell panel, for instance, a three-legged pig wearing a nun's veil is depicted inscribing a document with a reed-pen ('SEE what flows—from his slushy pen'); added to this, the centrepiece of the Eden panel where God creates Eve is dominated by a weird phallic fountain emerging out of an azure pool, again, evoked in the song: 'The second god, lived by a fountain that flowed, by the blue shiny lit roads.' Even the reference to the 'evil of the phone' resonates with the myriad images of acoustic torment in the Hell panel. If 'Garden', admittedly, cannot be considered a precise ekphrasis of Bosch's triptych, the lyrics (significant enough to be published, and framed, on the insert) plausibly constitute a key instance of Smith's Oulipian project to re-imagine the *Inferno* in contemporary suburban contexts (as in his memoir). Into this Boschian afterimage a series of disjunctive, impressionistic episodes is interpolated: Ian McCulloch arriving by ferry in the Liverpool docks;[45] Jacob's Ladder; Ben Hecht's pulp horror bestseller *Kingdom of Evil* (Hecht 1978) concealed under a German history text (a metaphor for Smith's pulp modernist intertextual method); and when the melody shifts to the chorus pattern, the cinematic montage is punctuated by the off-beat repetition of the one-word chorus '*GARDEN*', and its cognates, the random exclamations 'GODZONE! SHOTGUN!'[46]

The theology of original sin (elliptically: the "Fall") is closely identified with the motif of the lost paradisiac garden (Gen. 1:24–31). Garden and Fall, in this sense, have become thematically synonymous in Judeo-Christian tradition. But in The Fall's Garden the pastoral tableau merges with the apocalyptic vision of post-lapsarian Hell that informs *Perverted by Language*. Hanley's speculative searching therefore inadvertently identifies the relevant link. If, according to the cover of Hans Belting's 2002 study of the *Garden of Earthly Delights* Bosch depicts a 'vision of humankind in a paradise untouched by the fall,' 'Garden', candidly, offers that vision when *touched by The Fall*. Composed by one of Smith's 'half-mask' personae, 'The Man Whose Head Expanded,' the track glosses Adam's expulsion, apropos biblical hermeneutics, as prefiguration of Christ's agony in the Garden of Gethsemane (Matt. 26:36–46; Mark 14:32–42; Luke 22:39–46; Sinker 2021, p.199) and thus achieves a profane, borderline-heretical condensation of the two Testaments, starting with a corrupted vision of Eden in the shadow of the Fall and concluding with an absurdist Palm Sunday tableau (Matt. 21:1–11;

Mark 11:1–10; Luke 19:29–38; John 12:12–15): Christ (as Dylan Zimmerman—the second god [Sinker 2021, p.199]) entering 'Negative Jerusalem' (Chorazina, Woodstock)[47] on a motorcycle.[48]

In the ephemera reproduced on the album's insert (a repeated variant appears in the lyrics of Neighbourhood of Infinity) the vocalist hints (perhaps facetiously) that the surge of manic creativity driving the *Perverted by Language* project was associated with the application of 'cut-up technique literally to brain.' Application of auto-surgical techniques to brain (or self) implies a more biological, existentially invested—indeed *cerebral*—expansion of method than the semi-interesting ludic (or, if preferred, creative cul-de-sac) of Burroughs's Surrealist-inspired protocol (or, in Bowie's case, problem-solving programme to relieve creative block).

Here, arguably, Smith's reflexive references to the cut-up practices engaged for *Perverted*, suggest that we're dealing with a visceral or even *neurological* reinterpretation of the surrealist-inspired Burroughs-Bowie exquisite corpse technique.[49] And apropos the discussion of *The Cantos* it can now be proposed that, rather than the aleatory cut-n-paste technique popularised by Burroughs (with painter Brion Gysin [Naiman 2015]), what has been applied in this instance is Pound's vorticist method; this, I argue, is a more accurate way of contextualising the auto-surgical compositional practices (both semantic and acoustic) explored on *Perverted*; in other words, the album is the result of an experimental—yet systematic—application of the vorticist method (enacted paradigmatically in Pound's *Cantos*) to motivate lyrical ideation and compositional strategy. And to confirm this, the lyrics printed in characteristic manual typewritten inserts should be compared with Pound's typewritten manuscript pages (rather than, say, the cover of *Blast* magazine).

Pound insisted that his vorticist disruption of the opticality of the reading surface in *The Cantos*, although immediately an eidetic experience, was developed to have an acoustic effect, to evoke tonalities in the 'auditory imagination' (Eliot's concept for sensitivity to language that penetrates 'far below the conscious levels of thought and feeling, invigorating every word') (Eliot 1953, p.89). The typographic distortions of his poetry were intended to stimulate sensitivity to aural things 'addressed to the ear more than to the eye: the page layout is designed to influence the reader's perception of vocal tone.'

> All typographical disposition, placing of words on the page, is intended to facilitate the reader's intonation, whether he be reading silently to self or aloud to friends. (Pound, in Albright 1999, p.75)

Music, Pound later acknowledged, was the key to decoding the mysteries of his masterpiece: its apparently disjunctive elements, he revealed (to Passolini) in 1968, are related by great 'musical themes that find each other out' (in Crawford 2016, p.33). Early efforts were influenced by Dadaist-montage techniques, where composition was determined by deconstructionist practices and designed with satirical intentionality (Albright 1999, p.84). Later, however, the compositional paradigm for the Cantos evolved an auditory, non-sequential, contrapuntal structure, as in the fugue, a sonic 'texture,' Albright remarks, where 'all the musical material tends to be co-present' (1999, p.84). At this point Pound desired 'to hear the [heterogenous] voices in the Cantos, not as taking regular turns,' Albright observes, 'but as *sounding all at once*, in an overlapping vocal polyphony' (1999, p.82). From about the fifth Canto, the poet is increasingly spectral: his own voice nullified in the heckling that increasingly disrupts the monophony of the text. By the time we enter that 'modern hell of interfering voices' (Froula 2016, p.167) the cacophony is chronic, long-wave telegraphy in tempest, airwaves sputtering with hectoring fragments of transmission—phrases of music, scraps of monologue, snatches of argument—cackling in simultaneous bursts through the static before disappearing into white noise; so, Pound, according to Albright, 'attended to the many voices in the mixed-up soul, to the infernal and heavenly noises all jumbled up together within him' (1999, p.69).

CONCLUSION

Language is the medium of The Fall's most significant musical achievements. It is precisely at the semantic level, I have argued, that Mark E. Smith's founding contribution to the post-punk project has its most impressive cultural impact. Following Fisher's pulp-Modernism, Smith's writings were analysed as a form of neo-Vorticism with a structural affinity to the idiomatic poetic practices of Ezra Pound. But it is with reference to what I have termed the *perversion* of discourse (the disruption of communicative functionality through strategies of grammatical corruption, typographic and graphological auto-surgery, prodigal misspelling, textual, and, finally, vocal convulsion) that The Fall's most original, radical—indeed, visionary—contribution to music culture is identified and exegeted. Focusing on the group's sixth studio album, *Perverted by Language*, whose title derives from Canto XIV, I have demonstrated that Smith's experimental textural manipulation of the dynamics of aural space is an auditory equivalent of Pound's vorticist disruption of the opticality of textual surface in *The Cantos*.

This argument is not intended to diminish the founding contribution The Fall have made to avant-garde popular music culture. Rather, by focusing critical attention on the semantic content of the songs, I have attempted, following Fisher's pulp-modernist hypothesis, to explore the unexamined influence of Pound's Vorticism on Smith's song-writing practice and singing style. The erudite and ludic songs of The Fall push the English language (and its polymorphous vocal potentiality) to its outer limits. The visionary singer's knowing (and *reflexive*) mistreatments of syntax, grammar, and orthodox spelling have a provenance in Pound's privileging of the performative and oracular, graphic, and incantatory aspects of language over its discursive functional—communicative—aspects: Smith, like Pound, perverts language to generate mysterious, paratactical poetic effects; and, like Pound, Smith disrespects rhetorical conventions, but for the singer (as for the poet before him) English is *not* primarily a *medium* of communication but a physical substance to be manipulated into weird syntactical and graphic contortions of linguistic self-sabotage where the transparency of discourse is corrupted and transgressed into perverse semantic shapes that overflow all normative codes of meaning, convention, rhetoric, and style: 'I've kinda ran outta books, me . . . you could say I been perverted by language.'

NOTES

1. The Fall recorded 'Jerusalem,' the most celebrated of Blake's lyrics. Of 'Dog is Life / Jerusalem' performed as part of the *I am Curious, Orange* project and appearing on the subsequent album *I am Kurious Oranj* (1988).

2. Smith's gnomic titles constitute an essential element of The Fall's paratextual dimension.

3. On typography/quasi-calligraphy in The Fall's corpus, see Wilson (2010).

4. Combining reference to "Cessation" and "Initiation Rite," *Enduction* is an example of the reflexive and contorted criss-cross semantics of Smith's semiotic.

5. The Fall's (per)version of Blake's 'And did those feet . . .' (*I am Kurious Oranj* [BEGA 96] 1988) is a key example.

6. Pound was a founding member of both movements, coining the term "Imagist" to promote HD's poetic style, and developing the category of the Vortex out of frustration with the stagnation of Imagism around 1914 when appropriated by acolytes as a school formula. See Charles Altieri (in Stasi and Park 2016) and Hugh Witemeyer (in Nadel 1999).

7. Mimi Haddon's examination of classification in popular music culture concludes that 'post-punk' fans are distinguished from their ancestral punk aggressionists through prerogatives of complexity, intellectualism, and cultural progressiveness. Any structural cohesion post-punk can be considered to possess 'as a musical movement' is informed, she writes, by the orientation towards originality, a 'radicalism and stylistic eclecticism' that surpasses the lumpen expressionism of the punk rock paradigm (Haddon 2020).

8. 'The fall,' remarks Borges of Canto V, 'resounds through the repetition of the word *fall*' (1984, p.11). This interpretation is confirmed by the Penguin cover design reprinted in Penman (2021, p.40).

9. Several music-press reviewers have endeavoured to take seriously the eponymous Camus reference—some even elaborating potted exegeses of the novel in the effort to decipher the enigma of The Fall: 'The world view Clemence [sic] describes in the novel is a fall from innocence produced by a relentless unblinking clarity of perception, combined with an ungenerous lack of sympathy and forgiveness,' Angus McDonald pronounces, 'That Smith realised this persona would fit him perfectly . . .' (2010, p.148). And 'Smith's withering gaze' Simon Reynolds proposes, 'scanned the whole of society, and found only grotesquerie. In many ways he resembled the "judge penitent" of Camus's novel *The Fall*.' (Reynolds 2005, p.178). As late as 2021, you have Ian Penman referring to the character in Camus's novel, the 'judge-penitent,' as if this is self-evidently revealing. In *Renegade* Smith retains the right to the last word: 'I thought *The Fall* . . . a better book [than *The Outsider*]' (Smith 2008, p.41).

10. It's tiresome and unfair to repeatedly single out Elizabeth Fraser when rehearsing this argument (see Hopps 2008). An equivalent observation could be applied to the lyrical vacuity of Killing Joke, UK Decay, Echo and The Bunnymen, even The Birthday Party, The Jesus and Mary Chain, New Order.

11. Bertolotti-Bailey's (2021) essay on Lewis, Vorticism, and The Fall alludes in passing to Pound but never pursues or develops the connection any further, preferring to focus on Lewis (and cancel Pound from the historical narrative).

12. Jean-Michel Rabate confronts the widespread prohibition of Pound: his 'very name still emits sulphurous vapours for most [readers]' (2016, p.107). The best critical assessment of the problem of Pound's anti-Semitism is Wendy Flory's study, 'Pound and Antisemitism' in *The Cambridge Companion* (1999, pp.284–305). Also, Stead who argues that 'If we take a step back . . . and refuse to reduce Pound to an argument about anti-Semitism,' his poetic achievements become evident (Stead 2016). I accept, however, that it might not always be possible—or ethical—to take this 'step back.' The elderly Pound revoked his anti-Semitism as 'suburban prejudice'.

13. A transdisciplinary and militant aesthetic collective Vorticism was influenced by Cubism and Italian Futurism and, with co-founder (and editor of the agitprop journal *Blast*) Lewis attracted visual artists such as David Bomberg, Jacob Epstein, and Gaudier-Brzeska into its orbit. Epstein's sculpture *The Rock Drill* (1913–1914) is considered to embody the aesthetic codes of the collective.

14. The titular Creep, despite contemporary RT gossip, is not Morrissey. In interview, Brix replied to the allegation by claiming she assumed it was Morrissey's 'paranoia' that 'perpetuated the rumour' (Irwin 1984). Richard Skinner, following a call from Smith, was forced to issue a retraction on Radio One's programme *Round Table* that C.R.E.E.P. was not (about) Morrissey (Irwin 1984).

15. Reproduced on the cover of the recent *Excavate: The Wonderful and Frightening World of The Fall* (2021).

16. Which means, incidentally, that the vortex, described thus, resembles a record revolving on a turntable, track by track until the centre of silence. Try digitising that!

17. This quotation from Canto XCVI is selected because of Pound's use of 'hex.' Here hyphenated with hoax, "Hex" is a recurring signifier in Smith's personal lexicon, signifying, "spell" (OE) and "witch" in modern German, it is linked with a signifying family of terms: *Hex Enduction Hour*, *Witch Trials*, Hexan Schule, Hexan Definitive etc. (which demonstrate a special apotropaic, hermetic significance for Smith).

18. Cantos VIII–XI, the so-called Malatesta cycle of cantos, present a hagiography of Sigismundo Pandolfo Malatesta (1417–1468) *condottiere* of quattrocento Rimini and patron of the renaissance. Of Sigismundo's many quixotic projects, the most notorious is the architectural extension of the Chapel of San Francesco in Rimini (with original frescoes by Giotto) in honour of his wife. He commissioned Alberti to supervise the enclosing of the Franciscan church in an elaborate Romanesque marble shell which became known as the Tempio Malatestiano. But the ambitious multidenominational project was never completed and, very oddly, the building (obscuring the original Gothic church) is detailed in hierophantic and Zodiacal iconography. Malatesta's Tempio was condemned by Pope Pius II as a 'temple of heathen devil worshippers' in his encyclical recommending the excommunication of Sigismundo in 1461. Alec Marsh claims that the incomplete (but preserved) Tempio (a renaissance 'paradigm of modernism') is *The Cantos*'s 'best model' (2011, p.88). For Daniel Albright, with its 'filigree hiding in the gothic' the Tempio represents a 'stone metaphor for *The Cantos*' (1999, p.74). Contrarian-wise, Pound maintained that Malatesta's failures eclipsed all the achievements of the epoch. And here if I had space, I would have extended the discussion of The Fall's pulp-Modernism with a close analysis of the live track on *Perverted by Language* Tempo House with reference to the description of the construction of the Tempio in the Malatesta Cantos and thereby consolidate the Pound connection established in the essay.

19. The first line of Canto VIII is an intentional corruption of the penultimate line (in English) of *The Waste Land*: 'These fragments I have shored against my ruins' (l. 431). Pound recognised at this point that he needed to distance himself from Eliot and the bricolage style that had become synonymous with him (yet that he—Pound—had been instrumental in developing and promoting through his extensive and maieutic editing of *The Waste Land*—so extensive in fact that parts of Eliot's celebrated poem come close to collaboration: his intervention, according to Eliot himself, transformed the work from a 'jumble of good and bad passages' a 'sprawling chaotic' mess into a poem. Pound described his part in the process as like a midwife performing a 'Caesarean' section). Canto XVIII (which Alec Marsh argues is the true beginning of the poem) can be regarded as a response to Eliot's and his backhanded compliment in the epigraph of *The Waste Land*: *il migglior fabbro* (a reference to Dante's acknowledgement of Provencal troubadour Arnault Daniel in *Purgatory*, xxvi), i.e., the "better craftsman" (Southam 1968, p.136), a sobriquet which implies, conversely, the "lesser poet".

20. Many other instances could be enumerated, for example, "Hexan" (cf. spell; Ger., witch; six-sided) "Enduction" (hybridising references to cessation and inauguration).

21. Easlea (2005b) has identified this era as The Fall's 'gothic' period.

22. Incidentally, apropos the connection with Pound developed here, Brix has made some valuable and critically insightful comments; especially pertinent to Linguistic Perversion is her remark that, 'It was intellectual music. Like a musical Rorschach Test. The aural equivalent of looking at the ink blots, each time you'd make out a different shape or figure' (Start Smith in Peacock 2018, p.78).

23. The Pluto Recording Studios were run by two ex-members of Herman's Hermits.

24. Most of it was composed prior to Brix's recruitment.

25. On subject-rhyme in Pound's *Cantos*, see Albright (1999, p.82).

26. 'Perverted by Language' (doomby.com), http://annotatedfall.doomby.com/pages/the-annotated-lyrics/perverted-by-language.html.

27. Only played live on four occasions in 1983 (Easlea 2005b).

28. Pound intended the eclectic quotations of the *Cantos* to resonate with each other (as in the model of the fugue) and ultimately find a natural harmony in the complete text (Moody 2014; Yeats in Albright 1999, p.83); yet the gigantic poem, by his own admission, remained in the end, 'a shop-window full of various objects . . . [I] picked out this and that thing that interested me, and then jumbled them into a bag.' Revoking the attempt to establish a conventional narrative or aesthetic coherence, Pound at the end abandoned himself to the 'phalanx of particulars' accumulating in his bewilderness of ruins: 'the modern world / Needs such a rag-bag to stuff all its thought in' (*Three Cantos* [1919]).

29. *Tarabust*, an archaic term, retrieved and redefined by Pascal Quignard in *The Hatred of Music* (a study of 'the bonds between music and acoustic suffering'), refers to the 'drumming of obsession.' Belonging to a 'group of asemic sounds that disturb rational thought inside the skull' the *tarabust* 'awakens' what Quignard calls a 'non-lingusitic memory' (2016, p.38).

30. 'Between us the only thing that our ears agree on is "language" it seems.' 'Perverted by Language' (doomby.com), http://annotatedfall.doomby.com/pages/the-annotated-lyrics/perverted-by-language.html.

31. *Draft of XVI Cantos* (1925).

32. Letter to his parents, 1947. The Cantos Project—Cantos XIV–XV (Hell), http://thecantosproject.ed.ac.uk/index.php/a-draft-of-xvi-cantos-overview/the-hell-cantos.

33. On Smith's Prestwich, see Harwood (2021, p.21).

34. *Grotesque (After the Gramme)* (1980) is regarded as exemplifying this ambition.

35. Emphasising the connectedness of the two albums, Suzanne's nightclub scene on the sleeve of *Grotesque*, a postpunk *Walpurgisnacht* is the perfect visual rendering of her brother's vision.

36. Stewart Lee's brief review of the album in *The Wire* (2006) supports this reading: 'On *Perverted* the group channelled the twang of Link Wray into a vortex of vast, surreal mantras and dadaist call and response chants' (2006, p.43).

37. Hanley makes it clear that he believes this lyric from 'Hexen Definitive / Strife Knot' was directed at the group: 'You know nothing about it / It's not your domain. . . .'

38. How is Garden 'like Blake'? Hanley is probably thinking of 'The Garden of Love.' Track 1, Side 2 'Smile', is more Blakean, arguably, being a reimagining of Blake's poem 'The Smile'.

39. The walls of Pluto were coated in brown 'baize' for acoustic or soundproofing purposes.

40. Sinker discovers more interesting intrusive sub-threshold frequencies under close listening: 'right out at the edges of the stereo mix' there are percussive textures that make 'you think,' Sinker writes 'that someone's moving around in your flat' (2021, p.199).

41. Pound published similarly ironic tongue-in-cheek "guides" in mock-advisory mode: *The ABC of Reading* (1934) and *Guide to Kulchur* (1938).

42. British actor Reg Varney's (1916–2008) most notable role was cockney bus driver Stan Butler in the 1970s TV sitcom *On the Buses*.

43. Wild Bill hick refers to Frank Zappa who entered the UK top 40 for the first (and last) time in 1982 with his hit single 'Valley Girl' (an atypically commercial project for Zappa: it's in 4/4 time). His distinctive wacky (Bill Hickok–style) facial hair was newly trimmed for the occasion.

44. Recorded on the album *Déjà Vu* (1970). References to shotgun clinch the connection. Also, Neil Young is aware of The Fall's song—see his contribution to the exegesis on the Annotated Fall website.

45. Pat Reid's *Morrissey* refers to a 1983 interview with Ian McCulloch (Echo and the Bunnymen) in his home in Liverpool which mentions his pet hamster called 'Hieronymous' (sic) (after the singer's 'favourite painter') (Reid 2004, p.16). On the Annotated Fall website there's a contemporaneous quote from Smith referring to 'Garden's' critique of the 'prophet syndrome' in which he refers explicitly to Echo and the Bunnymen song 'The Cutter' (1983). 'Garden' (doomby.com), http://annotatedfall.doomby.com/pages/the-annotated-lyrics/garden.html.

46. These apparently arbitrary signifiers are intertextual allusions to Joni Mitchell's 'Woodstock', which contains the lyric: 'bombers riding shotgun.'

47. On the madcap sleeve-annotations of *Dragnet*, the reference to Chorazina, the birthplace of the antichrist (hence Negative Jerusalem), derives from M. R. James's tale "Count Magnus."

48. Dylan's motorcycle accident occurred in 1966. In Woodstock, New York.

49. On the use of cut-up as generative technique in Bowie's song-writing, see Naiman (2015).

REFERENCES

Albright, Daniel. 1999. "Early Cantos I–XLI." In *The Cambridge Companion to Ezra Pound*, edited by Ira B. Nadel, 59–91. Cambridge: Cambridge University Press.

Altieri, Charles. 2016. In *Ezra Pound in the Present*, edited by Paul Stasi and Josephine Park, 3–20. London: Bloomsbury.

Annotated Fall (website): 'Garden' (doomby.com), http://annotatedfall.doomby.com/pages/the-annotated-lyrics/garden.html.

Annotated Fall (website): 'Perverted by Language' (doomby.com), http://annotatedfall.doomby.com/pages/the-annotated-lyrics/perverted-by-language.html.

Barthes, Roland. 1974. *S/Z*. Translated by by Richard Miller. New York: Hill and Wang.

Belting, Hans. 2018. *Hieronymus Bosch: Garden of Earthly Delights*. New York: Prestel.
Bertolotti-Bailey, Stuart. 2021. In "Wyndham Lewis." *Excavate: The Wonderful and Frightening World of The Fall*, edited by Tessa Norton and Bob Stanley, 233–39. London: Faber & Faber.
Borges, Jorge-Luis. 1984. *Seven Nights*. London: Faber & Faber.
Bracewell, Michael. 1997. *England Is Mine: Pop Life in Albion*. London: Faber & Faber.
Brooke-Rose, Christine. 1971. *A ZBC of Ezra Pound*. London: Faber & Faber.
Butt, Gavin, Kodwo Eshun, and Mark Fisher. 2016. *Post-Punk Then and Now*. London: Repeater.
Camus, Albert. 1946. *The Outsider*. Translated by Stuart Gilbert. London: Penguin.
Camus, Albert. 1957. *The Fall*. Translated by Justin O'Brien. London: Penguin.
Crawford, Robert. 2016. "He was the Man." *London Review of Books*. 30 June, 31–33.
Dante Alighieri. 2002. *The Inferno*. Translated by Ciaran Carson. New York: New York Review Books.
Deleuze, Gilles (with F. Guattari). 1975. *Kafka: Toward a Minor Literature*. Translated by Dana Polan. Minneapolis: University of Minnesota.
Easlea, Daryl. 2005a. *The Fall: Hex Enduction Hour* (CD expanded edition commentary). Sanctuary Records Group.
Easlea, Daryl. 2005b. *The Fall: Perverted by Language* (CD expanded edition commentary). Sanctuary Records Group.
Easlea, Daryl. 2006. *The Fall: Dragnet* (CD expanded edition commentary). Sanctuary Records Group.
Ede, H. S. 1931. *Savage Messiah: A Biography of the Sculptor Henri Gaudier-Brzeska*. London: Gordon Fraser.
Eliot, T. S. 1953. *Selected Prose*. Edited by John Hayward. London: Faber & Faber.
Fisher, Mark. 2010. "'Memorex for the Krakens': The Fall's Pulp Modernism." In Goddard and Halligan (eds). *Mark E. Smith and The Fall: Art, Music and Politics*, 95–110. Farnham: Ashgate.
Fisher, Mark. 2016. "Introduction." In *Post-Punk Then and Now*, edited by Gavin Butt, Kodwo Eshun, and Mark Fisher. London: Repeater.
Fisher, Mark. 2018. *K-Punk: The Collected and Unpublished Writings*. Edited by Darren Ambrose. London: Repeater.
Flory, Wendy. 1999. "Pound and Antisemitism." In *The Cambridge Companion to Ezra Pound*, edited by Ira B. Nadel, 284–300. Cambridge: Cambridge University Press.
Fraser, G. S. 1960. *Ezra Pound*. London: Oliver and Boyd.
Frere-Jones, Sasha. 2021. "Perverted by Language: Mark E. Smith's Lyrical Stage Rants." *Bookforum* 28(3): 8–9.
Froula, Christine. 2016. "Ezra Pound and the Comparative Literature of the Present." In *Ezra Pound in the Present*, edited by Paul Stasi and Josephine Park, 135–72. London: Bloomsbury.
Gidley, Mick. 2016. "Ezra Pound and *The Listener*." *Times Literary Supplement*. April 15, 14.
Goddard, Michael, and Benjamin Halligan (eds). 2010. *Mark E. Smith and The Fall: Art Music and Politics*. Farnham: Ashgate.

Goodall, Mark. 2010. "Salford Drift: A Psychogeography of The Fall." In *Mark E. Smith and The Fall: Art Music and Politics*, edited by Michael Goddard and Benjamin Halligan, 41–53. Farnham: Ashgate.
Haddon, Mimi. 2020. *What Is Post-Punk? Genre and Identity in Avant-Garde Popular Music 1977–82*. Ann Arbor: University of Michigan Press.
Hanley, Paul. 2017. *Leave the Capital: A History of Manchester in 13 Recordings*. London: Route Publishing.
Harwood, Elain. 2021. "Jerusalem to Prestwich." In *Excavate: The Wonderful and Frightening World of The Fall*, edited by Tessa Norton and Bob Stanley, 17–24. London: Faber & Faber
Hecht, Ben. 1978. *Kingdom of Evil: A Continuation of the Journal of Fantazius Mallare*. London: Harcourt Press.
Hopps, Gavin. 2008. *Morrissey: The Pageant of His Bleeding Heart*. London: Continuum.
Ingham, Michael. 1999. "Pound and Music." In *The Cambridge Companion to Ezra Pound*, edited by Ira B. Nadel, 236–48. Cambridge: Cambridge University Press.
Irwin, Colin. 1984. "A Lot of It's About Nowt." *Melody Maker*, October 20, 34–35.
Kearns, George. 1980. *Guide to Ezra Pound's Selected Cantos*. New Brunswick, NJ: Rutgers University Press.
Kenner, Hugh. 1969. "Blood for the Ghosts." In *New Approaches to Ezra Pound*, edited by Eva Hesse, 331–48. London: Faber & Faber.
Kleinzahler, August. 2019. "Pound and Co." *London Review of Books*, 26 September, 37–38.
La Belle, Brandon. 2014. *Lexicon of the Mouth: Poetics and Politics of Voice and the Oral Imaginary*. London: Bloomsbury.
Laing, Dave. 2015. *One Chord Wonders*. London: PM Press.
Laity, Kathryn. 2019. "Spoiling all the Paintwork: Mark E. Smith's Playful Post-Punk Perturbations." *Always Different, Always the Same: A Symposium on The Fall*, Limerick Ireland, November 7 2019.
Lechte, John. 1990. *Julia Kristeva*. London and New York: Routledge.
Lee, Stewart. 2006. "The Primer: The Fall." *The Wire*, April (266): 40–47.
Lee, Stewart. 2019. "Hex Enduction Hour: By The Fall (1982)." *Q Magazine*, April, 66.
Marsh, Alec. 2011. *Ezra Pound*. London: Reaktion Books.
McDonald, Angus. 2010. "The Sound of The Fall, The Truth of This Movement of Error: A True Companion, An Ambivalent Friendship, and Ethic of Truths." In *Mark E. Smith and The Fall: Art Music and Politics*, edited by Michael Goddard and Benjamin Halligan, 147–56. Farnham: Ashgate.
Middles, Mick (and M. E. Smith). 2003. *The Fall*. London: Omnibus Press.
Naiman, Tiffany. 2015. "Art's Filthy Lesson." In *David Bowie Critical Perspectives*, edited by Eoin Devereux, Aileen Dillane, Martin Power. London and New York: Routledge.
Newton, Dione. 2005. *The Fall: The Wonderful and Frightening World of Mark E. Smith*. TV Film Documentary.
Norton, Tessa, and Bob Stanley (eds). 2021. *Excavate: The Wonderful and Frightening World of The Fall*. London: Faber & Faber.

Pattenden, Sian. 2021. "'I Want to Sell A Million': Use Value, Exchange Value and Woolworths - Twickenham, 1983–5." In *Excavate: The Wonderful and Frightening World of The Fall*, edited by Tessa Norton and Bob Stanley, 253–259. London: Faber & Faber

Peacock, Tim. 2018. "Lay of the Land." *Record Collector*, Issue 447, March 2018, 77–80.

Penman, Ian. 2021. "'Fugue" Is Not a Word I Would Normally Use, But . . .: The Fall and Repetition.' In *Excavate: The Wonderful and Frightening World of The Fall*, edited by Tessa Norton and Bob Stanley, 35–44. London: Faber & Faber.

Pound, Ezra. 1934. *The ABC of Reading*. eds. New York: New Directions.

Pound, Ezra. 1938. *Guide to Kulchur*. London: Faber & Faber.

Pound, Ezra. 1970. *Gaudier-Brzeska: A Memoir*. New York: New Directions.

Pound, Ezra. 1975. *Selected Poems*. London: Faber & Faber.

Pound, Ezra. 1986. *The Cantos*. London: Faber & Faber.

Quignard, Pascal. 2016. *The Hatred of Music*. Translated by Matthew Amos. New Haven and London: Yale University Press.

Rabate, Jean-Michel. 2016. "Ezra Pound and the Globalisation of Literature." In Stasi and Park (eds). *Ezra Pound in the Present: Essays on Pound's Contemporaneity*, 107–134. London and New York: Bloomsbury.

Reid, Pat. 2004. *Morrissey*. Bath: Absolute Press.

Reynolds, Simon. 2005. *Rip It Up and Start Again: Post-punk 1978–1984*. London: Faber & Faber.

Reynolds, Simon. 2009. *Totally Wired: Post-Punk Interviews and Overviews*. London: Faber & Faber.

Scott, Hayley. 2019. "The Fall." *The Wire* 428 October 2019, 70.

Sinker, Mark. 2021. "Cardinal R. Totale's Scrapbook: Torn Fragments of James, Machen and Lovecraft, Unpulped Among a Jumbled Trove of Songs by The Fall, Early and Also Late." In *Excavate: The Wonderful and Frightening World of The Fall*, edited by Tessa Norton and Bob Stanley, 187–204. London: Faber & Faber.

Smith, Mark E. 2008. *Renegade*. London and New York: Viking.

Smith, Mark. 2021. In *Excavate: The Wonderful and Frightening World of The Fall*, edited by Tessa Norton and Bob Stanley. London: Faber & Faber.

Southam, B. C. 1968. *A Student's Guide to the Selected Poems of T. S. Eliot*. London: Faber & Faber.

Stead, C. K. 2016. "Less of the Savage." *Times Literary Supplement*. April 15, 13.

The Cantos Project—Cantos XIV–XV (Hell), http://thecantosproject.ed.ac.uk/index.php/a-draft-of-xvi-cantos-overview/the-hell-cantos

Thorn, Tracey. 2015. *Naked at the Albert Hall*. St Ives: Virago.

Walker, Robert. 2010. "Dictaphonics: Acoustics and Primitive Recording in the Music of the Fall." In *Mark E. Smith and The Fall: Art Music and Politics*, edited by Michael Goddard and Benjamin Halligan, 77–86. Surrey: Ashgate.

Wilson, Paul. 2010. "Language Scraps: Mark E. Smith's Handwriting and the Typography of The Fall." In *Mark E. Smith and The Fall: Art, Music and Politics*, edited by Michael Goddard and Benjamin Halligan, 111–122. Farnham: Ashgate.

Witemeyer, Hugh. 1999. "Early Poetry 1908–1920." In *The Cambridge Companion to Ezra Pound*, edited by Ira B. Nadel, 43–58. Cambridge: Cambridge University Press.

Chapter Twelve

The Fall and Ireland

What a Manchester Band Can Tell Us about Ireland and Its Music Scene

Michael Mary Murphy

The words, music, career, and attitude of Mark E. Smith and The Fall invite debates about *music scenes* and *the music industry*. For this chapter I'm applying simple definitions of a music scene and the music industry. I'm taking a music scene to mean musicians and their supportive networks or communities. I'm positioning the music industry as a profit-driven business. That said, in practice, scenes and the industry overlap in key ways.

No music scene exists in a vacuum. Even the most do-it-yourself scene is influenced, and often inspired, by outside forces. By the same token, the globally centralized music business tries to direct the cultural and economic flows between the industry and music consumers for its own commercial advantage. But those flows are never completely one way. Local voices can emerge with enough force to be heard internationally, or to influence music-makers and fans in other places. Naturally, the centralized music industry will attempt to tame those forces commercially. Sometimes the most interesting artists escape that taming process.

The Fall are an intriguing example of a band that are often seen as belonging to the scene and avoiding the constraints of the industry. Naturally, as a Manchester band, they can tell us a lot about that city's music scene. After all, it makes sense to examine music scenes by looking at the acts from that scene. But those local acts don't explain *everything* about the music scene. While it might seem contrary to explore a music scene by looking at acts from *outside* that scene, it does allow for the voices and influence of outsiders to be included. This chapter considers the two-way flow of culture and representation between The Fall and Ireland, and it explores the experience, representation, and influence of The Fall on Ireland's music scene.

SEEING THE FALL: A SENSE OF WONDER AND SHAME

On a personal level, the first time I saw The Fall in March 1982 was a complete and utter thrill. Here in Dublin were a band whose records I had played over and over at home. I was fortunate, my older brother had been buying their singles anytime they were available in Dublin. Up our road, in suburban south county Dublin, the Cremin brothers, the Johnson brothers, and Eoin O'Sullivan were also huge Fall fans. There was a little hive of post-punk fans in Deansgrange. We'd talk at length about Mark E. Smith's *NME* (*New Musical Express*) and fanzine interviews after we'd studied them. We'd sit around listening to records in the Cremins' house. The Fall were on the turntable a lot.

So, the evening of the gig in McGonagles, off Grafton Street, was one of pure excitement. When you bring such high expectations to a gig you become part of it. You bring that hope and energy and joy to a venue that is, after all, just four walls and a bar. In my case, I felt a sense that Dublin was really lucky to have such a band in our midst. It made me feel, for a night at least, that Ireland was connected to something really vibrant: a world that could produce a band like The Fall. It is a gig that has stayed with me ever since, and I still couldn't do it justice by trying to describe it.

Mark E. Smith was unlike any other performer I had seen live. It was clear he was not desperate for our approval. He was here to do his own thing. But something happened at that gig. It made me feel embarrassed. There was often an edginess to the punk, new wave, do-it-yourself, or countercultural gigs in Dublin at that time. A distinct sense of menace. A feeling that a fight could break out at any time and for any reason. Often a fight did break out and sent fear rippling through the gathering.

My memory is that a small group of punks from the Leeson Street squat were at the front of The Fall gig, mouthing off at the band, slagging them. Smith gave as good as he got, and before the end of the show the punks shoved their way through the audience and left. There was a smattering of applause, a sense of relief that the 'troublemakers' were gone. Smith quipped brilliantly: "Where'd the boys from the museum go"? To him, in their leather jackets and spiked hair, they looked out of date.

But they hadn't left empty-handed. The reason for their swift exit was that they had stolen Mark's tape recorder from the stage. I felt embarrassed that the audience I was a member of, the Dublin audience, had done something so transgressive, so invasive, so unwelcoming to a band that had travelled to play for us.

That was an early realisation that audiences differ from place to place and from time to time. Gigs were certainly not just part of my social life but part of my self-identity. To me, the industry of live music, the ability to see the bands you like, really matters. And it seems perfectly natural to see if The Fall can help us to understand the Irish music scene as it evolved over time.

IRELAND AND THE IRISH IN SMITH'S OWN WORDS

There's one way to see the interaction between The Fall and the Irish. That's by looking at Smith's own words in his autobiography, *Renegade* (2008). The book is laced with Smith's trademark energetically jaundiced, and at times, devastatingly funny, outlook. It's interesting to note that he represents U2 as a band who are frequently imitated by career-minded bands or invoked by lazy journalists. He writes witheringly about 'a lot of British groups, obsessing about U2 or The Stone Roses' (Smith 2008, p.9). And he's equally dismissive of the music press:

> If you don't come across as readily as, say, U2, who are defined by the amount of records they sell, then journalists struggle to write anything perceptive about you. (2008, pp.79–80)

If his distrust for U2 is clear, he dislikes Bob Geldof even more: "at least Bono, for all his faults, has a career outside of all that handshaking" (2008, p.93).

But what's fascinating is the way that Smith's recollections highlight how his working-class upbringing in Manchester brought him into contact with the Irish. While scholars like Sean Campbell (2011) have illuminated the role of second-generation Irish musicians in Britain, it's interesting to see what English natives thought of the Irish. During his career with The Fall, at a time when pool tables had just been introduced to pubs in England, Smith and his manager, Kay, made money by disguising their skills and then challenging pub customers to matches. He claimed: 'It paid for the rehearsal place' (Smith 2008, p.67): 'Me and Kay would take teams of brickies on, Irish labourers.' Smith's grandfather recruited workers for his plumbing business as they were being released from Strangeways prison. He faced competition, though, from the army who were also looking to sign up the men. Smith recalled his grandfather's words to the ex-prisoners: 'He'd say, "You've got a choice, you either go to Ireland or you come with me"' (2008, p.22). It was a reminder that new recruits often didn't experience army life in exotic locations; they could find themselves on active service facing hostile locals in Northern Ireland.

But Smith didn't just see Ireland as the home of bands he didn't like, the place of 'the Troubles', or the background of the building workers whose earnings he won with his pool hall prowess. While Smith is not thought of as the most sentimental character, there's a keen sense of wistfulness about aspects of his childhood, and the place of his Irish acquaintances in it. When describing his close bonds with people on his street, he described his next-door neighbour as 'Auntie Hilda'. It wasn't until he was a teenager that he learned that she wasn't a family relative. He also wrote:

> I used to have Irish 'aunties' as well. They were people you could go and talk to and have a cup of tea with, not child molesters or anything, nice people—war widows, mostly. (2008, p.11)

Smith also had Irish friends of his own age. When he was six years old, he developed an eye condition and struggled to read. His teachers were unsympathetic and called him a 'donkey'. He wrote:

> Everybody stopped talking to me at school. It didn't bother me, because I had a lot of Irish mates who didn't give a fuck about reading or writing. I used to stay with this Irish family in Salford. They were helping my mam and dad out. They were lovely people.(2008, p.4)

Later he recalled when youngsters of his age were:

> forming gangs and things like that. I used to have a few—Psycho Mafia, the Barry Boy gang. We'd fight other gangs. It was quite interesting; there used to be Irish gangs and Orthodox Jewish gangs. But the Psycho Mafia was a real melting pot, and I was the vice president. (2008, p.16)

And if the stereotype of teenagers and alcohol persist, and are often associated with the Irish, Smith's experience suggested an alternative:

> Outside of school there were always the cider gangs and all that. But all my mates were Irish, and they didn't really drink. I like that about the Irish with their kids—they're dead strict. There was always a big lock on the drinks cabinet. (2008, p.18)

The lack of alcohol didn't mean that they were young puritans. There was plenty of fun and mischief. Smith and his young Irish friends used to sell pages torn from soft porn magazines (2008, p.16) and when they visited the cinema they didn't sit placidly:

> I remember when I used to go and watch films with my Irish mates as a kid, we'd be yelling at the screen, at Dracula with all this blood on his chin, which was obviously tomato sauce or whatever. (2008, p.23)

One of the most affectionate, and hilarious, of Smith's memories is of the musical times in the Irish family's house in Salford. They were:

always singing Elvis songs and these old Dublin ballads. But they never knew the lyrics, they'd just make them up. Their version of 'All the Young Dudes' was fantastic, better than the original—'I'm going to Woolworths, I'm going to shag a cow to death. . . .' Proper lyrics.(2008, pp.13–14)

As I'll document later, it's clear that Smith impressed and inspired many musicians in Ireland. But it's wonderful to think of him as a youngster hearing surreal, spontaneous, even ridiculous, lyrics. It's delightful to imagine him listening to his Irish friends dismantling pop songs and reassembling them to express themselves, steering the songs away from the pop charts and into a place of personal amusement.

THE FALL, ARCHIVE AND GIGOGRAPHY

It would probably annoy Mark E. Smith, but there is a useful way of examining the patterns of live music and what they reveal. On a very practical and theoretical level, Dave Laing (2011) examined how the live music industry works. He argued that you can learn about a country's live music industry by examining the who, where, and when of live music concerts. Who were the promoters, what types of bands played in which venues? Did that pattern change over time? What types of music were made available in which places and at what times?

To Laing, a gigography was not just a list of gigs played by acts. It was an opportunity to interrogate how the live music industry functioned. While he examined the tour itineraries of acts in 1960s Britain and found some dramatic regional variations, I want to adjust that methodology slightly and examine one band, the Fall, in one country, Ireland. Not every pop group has a web resource as comprehensive as the The Fall's excellent site, thefall.org, and it's thanks to the site that it's possible to study their concert history so conveniently. The Fall's first gig took place in Manchester on 23 May 1977 and, according to The Fall archives, the group performed more than twenty shows in Ireland.

The Fall made their Irish debut on 22 September 1978, when they played two shows in the notorious, yet small, venue, The Harp bar, in Belfast's Hill Street. The Harp was described in the excellent 'NI punk' site as 'a dingy, heavily fortified pub in a dimly lit, narrow, cobblestone street in a run down, dilapidated part of the city' (*N.I.Punk*, undated). The Harp was a key venue for the local scene from its first punk gig in April 1978. It hosted many of the new era of Northern Irish bands that began attracting attention and gigging between 1976 and 1978. In 2019 an application was submitted to turn the site into a boutique hotel (Scott 2019). Things change. They often don't stay the same. Live music venues which draw people to an area that is seen as unattractive can be unwittingly involved in a gentrification process. Unfortunately, for music fans, this process can lead to live music venues getting squeezed from city centres.

The Fall's first gig in Ireland, was significant for a few reasons. It was one of the earliest gigs by a visiting band to The Harp and it was a very much a local DIY production, arranged by the *Alternative Ulster* fanzine and the legendary, Good Vibrations record shop. The newspaper ad for it in the *Belfast Telegraph* (1978) newspaper was much smaller than the ad for an Elvis impersonator elsewhere in the city. It read:

INCREDIBLE PUNK: THE FALL plus Disco

The review of the gig in the self-published *Alternative Ulster* fanzine contains the warmth and unalloyed enthusiasm that were often found in the vibrant DIY fanzine scene of the punk era.

> After the gig both Mark and Kay, the band's manager, admitted that it had been some time since they'd enjoyed a gig so much. They agree that it had been a very special night there had been a marvellously warm atmosphere, a real communication between band and audience, which surprised and delighted them. (Roger 1978)

Despite how much both the band and the audience enjoyed the Belfast gigs, it was over two years before The Fall played again in Ireland. Their next Irish concert was in Cork's Arcadia ballroom in October 1980. Run by Elvera Butler, the Arcadia was a significant venue for punk, post-punk, and reggae. It typically attracted crowds of over a thousand for its weekly concerts. It was unconventional; it was alcohol-free and very community-focused (Murphy 2018a). Local Cork acts were encouraged by Butler who gave them opening slots with well-known visiting headliners. She had a policy of admitting local acts to most of the concerts free of charge, and later started a record label to promote the bands. Microdisney, led by the late Cathal Coughlan, were one of the notable beneficiaries of her DIY approach.

Butler had a reason for arranging what would be The Fall's first show in the Republic of Ireland. Frustrated by the lack of media coverage received by her venue, she wanted to host a band who were credible and well known but who weren't playing in Dublin, where most of the music journalists were based. It seems fitting that the Fall were part of an attempt to decentralise the centralised music industry, to draw attention to a vibrant 'regional' scene. Butler recalled:

I pulled a stunt sometimes where I'd bring bands in for Cork-only gigs so they had to be reviewed. I did it with the Fall for one of them. Mark E. stayed with me. Despite his reputation, he wasn't actually that curmudgeonly. (Butler interview with Butler 2017)

She confessed that although her venue was alcohol-free, she served 'hot toddies' of whiskey, coffee, and whipped cream which went down well with visiting road crews and acts. The venue's P.A. system was installed by Joe O'Herlihy who was responsible for U2's live sound on tour (Butler interview with Butler 2017). It was one of the best in the country.

Butler's gigs in Cork were very significant for local Irish acts. They gave them exposure to a wide audience interested in the better-known overseas visitors. Eoin Freeney from one of the great Irish bands of the era, the intense, challenging, and inventive Chant! Chant! Chant! recalled being excited about playing on the bill with The Fall and Microdisney. He went for a few drinks in the local Handlebars pub, knowing that Butler had provided them with some free beers in their dressing room to enjoy later:

> Their [The Fall] gig was a massive assault on the ears I seem to remember, and they played a blinder as did Micro. It was amazing experience to play the Arcadia. Elvera was really decent, she treated everyone well. We loved every crazy minute. It was an honour to share the bill with two such edgy bands. Good memories. (Freeney 2021)

But it wouldn't be a memory of a gig by The Fall without some sense of mischief or mayhem:

> We were excited to be on the bill for sure. Vinny Murphy, the brother of our bassist Larry, was part of our roadcrew and was a huge fan. Truth be told we liked the swagger of Mark E. But it was pretty strange to hear a bellowing Mark E. shouting across the ballroom at us in his wonderful broad Manc accent "wheresa alla da beera Chanta, Chanta, Chanta?

Smith was playfully taunting the band; he had 'removed' the beer from their dressing room and had decided not to share it! Freeney recalled: 'We hadn't expected them to steal our rider before we got back from having a beer or two ourselves'. Smith and The Fall may have drunk Chant! Chant! Chant!'s beer, but at least he knew their name!

Nineteen months later, in March 1982, The Fall appeared in McGonagles for their Dublin debut, at a gig arranged by Dave Clifford of the local *Vox* fanzine. It's notable that these early gigs, in Belfast, Cork, and Dublin, were all arranged by different promoters, but were all DIY events, and were not promoted by any of the traditional music industry brokers. Without wanting to romanticise DIY, in the case of The Fall, it's clear that the DIY community was helpful, and provided important opportunities to the band. The 1982 Dublin gig also provided the opportunity for local music fans to see The Golden Horde, a new band who quickly became local favourites with their punky psychedelic barnstorming performances.

That said, it should be noted that The Fall had played eleven gigs in the United States before their visit to either Cork or Dublin. They had also toured extensively in the Netherlands in both 1980 and 1981, as well as in Germany and Belgium in 1981. They had even played in Iceland before Dublin got to witness them. The Fall did return to Ireland in October 1984 and played in both Dublin and Belfast. The Golden Horde opened for them in Dublin just as they had in 1982. In the same year, another member of Ireland's underground music scene had a positive interaction with The Fall. Gavin Friday, from the theatrically provocative Virgin Prunes, appeared as a guest vocalist on *The Wonderful and Frightening World of the . . .* (1984) LP and the 'Call for Escape Route' (1984) 12-inch single. On the latter he was credited as a 'friendly visitor'. Perhaps that's a good way to think of The Fall and Ireland in the 1980s, as 'friendly visitors' to a music scene that didn't get a lot of visitors from abroad. The 1984 TV Club concert was the last gig in Dublin by The Fall in the 1980s. It seems shocking that Dublin only got two Fall shows between 1977 and 1990. But this reveals something that has been neglected in Irish popular music history. In the early 1980s Ireland felt very far away from the gig circuit across the Irish Sea.

THE DISTANCE BETWEEN IRELAND AND THE ALTERNATIVE SCENE IN THE EARLY 1980s

There is a context to the relative lack of visits from overseas bands in the 1980s. Before the emergence of punk in 1976–1977, few acts travelled to Ireland because of concerns about violence due to the 'Troubles' in Northern Ireland. But punk brought about a major change in Ireland's live music industry on both sides of the border. In 1977 the Northern Irish promoter, Paul Charles, then based in London, curated an all-Ireland gig circuit by arranging tours of Ireland by The Stranglers, The Clash, The Jam, The Adverts, and a number of other notable names in the punk scene. Bands often played in universities where the concerts were arranged by students. While they were part of student union organizations, they were not full-time members of the music industry. Despite their significance to the local music scene, they were effectively operating with do-it-yourself methods. To Charles:

It was a reliable circuit because it was the Students Unions, because it was connected with the different universities and colleges, the money was safe.... They were one hundred percent all great promoters. They were fans of music. And they all had that energy and enthusiasm, and they would go out and convert an audience to come and listen to these new bands we were booking. (Murphy 2017)

But by 1981, Charles was focused on his London booking agency and, in any event, the punk and new wave scene in Britain was no longer delivering a steady stream of new acts with high profiles, major national airplay, and chart hits to the market. The 'new romantic' movement and synthesiser bands did deliver chart stars, but they tended to bypass Ireland until they were big enough to play in major venues like the St Francis Xavier Centre, owned by the Catholic Jesuit order, the National boxing stadium, or the Royal Dublin Society's hall. The 1980s saw the ascent of MCD, who grew to become one of Europe's most powerful live music organisations. Over time they became influential on the university circuit too. But, naturally, their focus was on commercially profitable gigs, and bands without a large profile, radio airplay, and increasingly, music videos, were not a priority for them. It's hardly surprising therefore that The Fall's October 1984 visit to Ireland was their last of the decade.

In one important way, that makes The Fall's handful of gigs in Ireland very significant. At least they came. A large number of bands that were either well known, or critically acclaimed, often both, didn't play in Dublin between 1977 and the late 1980s. John Lydon didn't perform with the Sex Pistols or Public Image Ltd. Joy Division, Cabaret Voltaire, Gang of Four, Killing Joke, Spizz Energi, the Slits, Bauhaus, Sisters of Mercy, Bow Wow Wow, Soft Cell, Felt, and the Southern Death Cult didn't appear either. When U.S. hardcore emerged in the early 1980s, few of the bands, despite touring extensively in the UK, visited Dublin. There was a major gap between the local and global music scenes.

Although this has not been acknowledged in any notable accounts of the Irish music industry, it's worth considering how this impacted on the Irish music industry. The underground DIY scene was seriously underdeveloped compared to cities in Britain. Very few Irish bands made any serious inroads into the UK independent music charts, for example. Gigs in small venues were often poorly supported or were attended mostly by friends of the bands. Acts with overseas record deals and major national airplay tended to attract audiences faster. Perhaps inevitably, most new acts designed their sound to appeal to overseas record labels. Their generally very brief careers wouldn't have surprised Mark E. Smith.

The gap between the Irish music underground and the mainstream was reinforced by some of the, decidedly mixed, reviews received by The Fall. The October 1984 TV Club review by Nick Kelly in *Hot Press* magazine probably reveals more about the journalist than the band. To him, they represented the:

gap between what the music media often imagine to be of interest to the public and what members of the public actually enjoy listening to. (Kelly 1984)

Despite working for a music magazine and, presumably, listening to a lot of music, he confessed that he had 'yet to meet somebody who owned a record by the band.' It was still surprising that he didn't seem to know any songs by the band he was reviewing, and that he appeared to be proud of that. He wrote: 'There will be no songtitles or quotes in this review as not one word of Smith's rant was comprehensible.' His final conclusion was withering, although it's possible to imagine Mark E. Smith enjoying it:

> If you want to listen to something musically inventive try almost anything other than this unlistenable garargeband thrash. . . . The Fall have not sold out. Nobody would really want to buy them. (Kelly 1984)

Oh, but Mr Kelly some of us did want to buy The Fall. But that wasn't as easy as it sounds. When we were listening to records, or the John Peel show, in Dublin, we were generally listening to bands we didn't think we'd ever see playing live. And some of those records had made a complicated journey to us. In any town with a decent record shop in Britain, you could walk in and buy records, even by The Fall. In Ireland that wasn't the case. Rough Trade lacked distribution in the Republic of Ireland. A lot of independent records were not easily available. From working in my local record shop in Dun Laoghaire, I knew that even records by bands on major labels, The Cure, for example, only arrived in limited numbers. The main supplier of alternative music was Advance records located in the city centre. The dingy Dandelion market, where some of Ireland's best bands played on a makeshift do-it-yourself stage backed onto it. The whole area was soon developed into a plush modern shopping centre.

Fred, the owner of Advance Records would send his associates to Belfast with a shopping list. To avoid the expensive value added tax (VAT), they would smuggle the records across the border on the Belfast to Dublin train. One of the smugglers, Deklan, recalled the process:

> I did it on and off for 3 years, 1980–83, and I brought tons of stuff down for him in an old suitcase, hidden in the jacks [toilets] or under the seat. He used to order them by phone, from Caroline Records or Good Vibrations and give me the money to pay for them and they'd be ready to go when I got there. I used to buy my own stuff there too, much cheaper than Dublin.
>
> [As payment] He used to give me five singles and one album per trip, which was brilliant back then when money was tight and records were dear! Great times! Good Old Fred Talbot R.I.P. (Dachau 2018)

So there was a sense of contraband about our copies of 'Rowche Rumble', 'Fiery Jack', and 'How I Wrote "Elastic Man"' which had been smuggled across the heavily militarised border.

SMITH'S LEGACY IN IRELAND'S MUSIC SCENE

Smith and The Fall clearly provided opportunities for local Irish acts to open for better-known groups visiting from overseas. But they also stimulated Irish acts in another very significant way. In fact, they are a great example of how a band's influence can't be measured solely by their record sales. Some groups from Ireland openly acknowledged the influence or inspiration of The Fall. In 2006, when asked about his favourite music, Shaun Mulrooney from Humanzi wrote, 'I'm obsessed with The Fall; I now have 14 albums [by them].' His current favourite was the 1982 song, 'The Classical': 'Mark E. Smith sounds particularly nasty here and the groove is unreal.'

Musicians don't even have to mention The Fall for the influence to be inferred. Journalists writing about Dublin's Girl Band (now known as Gilla Band) often used the The Fall as a point of comparison. Here are quotes from reviews in Ireland, England, and the United States:

> These pleasantly jarring Dublin rockers blend the post-punk rhythmic patter of the Fall with manic bursts of noise-rock guitar into a wicked, electrifying performance. (Riemenschneider 2015)

> Frontman Dara Kiely delivers a spoken-word, Iggy Pop-meets-Mark E. Smith sermon about various everyday mundanities like moustaches, rashes, nylon, corn-on-the-cob and sugary drinks. (Welch 2015)

> Kiely, who sings in an addled Mark E. Smith drawl or an addled Mark E. Smith scream. (Corr 2019)

Musicians generally have a range of influences. But it's important to acknowledge that for journalists who want people to like a band they have never heard, or possibly, heard *of*, The Fall were a hook for attracting new listeners to some of Ireland's most acclaimed bands of the post-2000 era. Just like Girl Band, Fontaines D.C. were also celebrated in print with comparisons to Smith and The Fall. *Rolling Stone* magazine's David Fricke described the vocal approach of the band's vocalist Grian Chatten's approach: 'a jagged, half-shouted cocktail of Liam Gallagher in his arrogant, Oasis prime and the pub-bard confrontation of the Fall's Mark E. Smith' (Fricke, 2019). Yet, the relationship between the Fall and the new wave of what the media terms 'punk' and 'post-punk' bands is not straightforward. Fontaines D.C. have attempted to distance themselves from the tag 'punk' and 'post-punk', which is quite understandable. Few bands want to be pigeonholed. But it's notable that their interest in both poetry and music means that they are positioned by the press along with a select group of other artists. In 2019 the journalist, Ed Nash, wrote:

> I suggest that the roll-call of rock'n'roll poets typically includes the likes of Mark E. Smith, Morrissey, Leonard Cohen, Nick Cave and Shane McGowan.

In the same article he continued making references to Smith and The Fall:

> Chatten is labelled as a "post-punk Brendan Behan" and the band are compared to The Fall. None of the band are huge fans of The Fall, says Chatten, but he investigated them after their name kept cropping up in reviews.

This is really interesting. If it is true, it indicates that journalists invoking the music of Smith prompted the members of Fontaines D.C. to explore his music. In a sense, the media kept Smith and The Fall in the public's attention. His reputation is being sustained by them. That doesn't mean that Chatten and the Fontaines D.C. necessarily enjoy his work, but they have found him worthwhile and relevant:

> Whilst he isn't convinced with the comparisons, Chatten admires Smith for aligning himself with modernist poets such as Ezra Pound and T. S. Elliot and his relentless desire to blend music with creative thinking: "With Mark E. Smith, it's the intent that draws it all together. What makes him interesting is his vehemence in coming across as not a didactic person of a working-class background, but someone who was 'I'm going to make Rock and Roll as intelligent as it possibly can be. I'm going to tackle ideas.'" (Nash 2019)

To the Dublin band, Smith's artistry brought intelligence and ideas to rock music. That's high praise from a band who don't consider themselves to be fans of The Fall.

CONCLUSIONS: THE FALL AND IRELAND

Perhaps unexpectedly, The Fall reveal a lot about the music scene of Ireland. They show how far removed that scene was from the vibrant independent music situation across the Irish Sea between 1977 and the end of the 1980s. The Fall also show that a band's long-term impact can't be judged solely from the number of gigs they played in a particular country or city. In addition, and in a very meaningful way, The Fall's history demonstrates how do-it-yourself-minded individuals and small organisations can interact productively even when the centralised music industry doesn't provide obvious pathways for them. And, perhaps most importantly, Mark E. Smith showed how the Irish were present at the margins of society, in cities like Manchester, in ways that impacted meaningfully on one of the most interesting English singers of his era. Vital links between individuals often lie away from the spotlight.

All of these conclusions point to the value of analysing music scenes by referring to bands and artists from *outside* of that scene. If The Fall can teach us so much about the Irish music scene, what could other artists tell us about it? For example, what would 'the influence of Manchester on the Irish music scene' teach us? In the face of the growing concentration and centralization of the global music industry, it is important to understand how local music scenes function. Maybe if we understand small scenes, we can find ways to nurture them, support them, and help them to forge links between scenes elsewhere that have similar aims or principles. For anyone frustrated by the popular music, or even cultural landscape they are presented with, the message from Mark E. Smith and The Fall seems loud and clear: be contrary, remain an outsider, never compromise, but don't confuse that for a poor work ethic or a lack of ambition. The Fall belong in the history of Ireland's popular music. Their DNA has been invited into the gene pool of Ireland's musicians. That DNA is likely to continue to inspire creativity, daring musical escapades, and a sense of uncompromising obstinacy in the future.

NOTE

Many thanks to Garry O'Neill for his scrapbook cuttings, and to Eoin Devereux, Martin Power, and John Fleming for their guidance and support.

REFERENCES

Belfast Telegraph, ad. The Fall, 21 September 1978, p. 14.
Butler, Elvera, recorded interview with Michael Mary Murphy, 8 June 2017.
Campbell, Sean. *Irish Blood, English Heart: Second Generation Irish Musicians in England*. Cork: University Press, 2011.
Corr, Alan. "Girl Band Take It to New Extremes on The Talkies." *RTE*, 1 October 2019. https://www.rte.ie/entertainment/music-reviews/2019/0930/1079151-girl-band-take-it-to-extremes-on-the-talkies/, accessed 1 November 2019.
Dachau, Deklan, email correspondence, 22 November 2018b.
Freeney, Eoin, email correspondence with Michael Mary Murphy, 26 June 2021.

Fricke, David. "Fontaines D.C." *Rolling Stone*, 26 April 2019. https://www.rollingstone.com/music/music-features/frickes-picks-fontaines-d-c-pere-ubu-and-more-826472/, accessed 23 October 2019.

Kelly, Nick. "The Fall." *Hot Press*, 1984, no date/page number, from Garry O'Neill's scrapbook.

Laing, Dave. 'Calculating the Value of Live Music: Motives and Methods', *The Business of Live Music Conference*, University of Edinburgh, 31 March 2011.

Mulrooney, Shaun. "White Man's Funky Spirit." *Evening Herald*, 26 October 2006, p. 44.

Murphy, Michael Mary. "Punk's Secret Agent: How Paul Charles Brought Punk to Ireland, Britain and the International Market." *Punk & Post Punk*. September 2017, Vol. 6, No. 3(2017b), pp. 431–41. 11p, 2017, Vol. 6 No. 3 Intellect.

Murphy, Michael Mary. "Elvera Butler: Ireland's Ground-breaking New Wave Female Entrepreneur." *Punk & Post-Punk*. Vol. 7, No. 3, Intellect, 2018.

Nash, Ed. "Tales of the City." *The Line of Best Fit*, 9 April 2019, https://www.thelineofbestfit.com/features/longread/fontaines-dc-tales-of-the-city-interview, last accessed 24 October 2019.

N.I.Punk (undated), 'The Harp Bar—Belfast's Premier Punk Venue '78–'82', http://nipunk.weebly.com/harp-bar.html.

Riemenschneider, Chris. "SXSW's 10 breakout acts." 24 March 2015, *Star Tribune*, Minnesota, p. E3.

Roger. "The Fall, Protex: The Mystical Powers of Repetition." *Alternative Ulster*, 1978, pp. 22–23. https://thefall.org/gigography/gig78.html, last accessed 1 June 2021.

Scott, Sarah. "Original Harp Bar site. . ." *Belfast News*, 9 March 2019. https://www.belfastlive.co.uk/news/belfast-news/original-harp-bar-site-belfast-15944674, last accessed 3 October 2019.

Smith, Mark E, with Austin Collings. *Renegade: The Life and Tales of Mark E. Smith*. London: Penguin, 2008.

The Fall, *The Wonderful and Frightening World of the . . .*, Beggars Banquet, 1984.

The Fall, *Call for Escape Route*, 12-inch, Beggars Banquet, 1984.

Thefall.org.

Welch, Andy. "Girl Band Build Suspense on Unsettling and Savage New Track 'Paul.'" *NME*, 7 August 2015. https://www.nme.com/blogs/nme-blogs/girl-band-build-suspense-on-unsettling-and-savage-new-track-paul-16022, accessed 24 October 2019.

Chapter Thirteen

The Madness in My Area

Montagu Lomax and the Psychodrama of The Fall: An Examination of the Use of Psychiatric Imagery in Early Fall '77–'79

David Meagher and John McFarland

> *Good evening, we are The Fall. In UK, we spend most times wandering around institutions.*
>
> —Smith 1981, cited in Nickas et al. 2021, p.49

There can be little doubt that the punk and post-punk era fundamentally recalibrated the relationship between music and society. The first wave of punk de-coupled the perception that popular music was the preserve of the technically gifted, signalling a new era characterised by challenging sounds, sloganeering, and angular new messages. It was unapologetically homespun and individual, often delving into the mundane reality of everyday life for 'real' people. It primed a generation to receive a genuinely new meaning from music, and a post-punk extension duly followed which, although visceral in impact, maintained the capacity to challenge and inform (Meagher 2017). Over the following forty-plus years, Mark E. Smith and The Fall became a British musical institution, maintaining an insistent and unique voice, mostly from the margins, that has served to challenge and inform any comfortable convention of music and culture.

The Fall are widely acknowledged as one of the most important and enduring of the bands that emerged during the punk era. Formed in Manchester in 1976, they maintained a prolific output for forty-two years until the death of Mark E. Smith in 2018. The early output of the group consisted of a series of four singles/EPs that were released on Step Forward Records and later condensed as a compilation album titled *Early Fall '77–'79*. This early work is replete with psychiatric references but, in contrast with other bands of the punk/post-punk era, The Fall's material was aimed at specific targets such as the psychiatric system ('Psychomafia'), psychiatrists ('The Diceman'), and the pharmaceutical industry ('Rowche Rumble'). This focus is contextualised by the fact that the band emerged from the shadow of the largest psychiatric institution in Europe (Prestwich Asylum) where, in the early twentieth century, the three thousand inmates accounted for 25 percent of the total population of the town. Practices at the institution assumed international notoriety following the publication of Dr Montagu Lomax's *The Experiences of an Asylum Doctor* (1921). The book documented multiple inhumane practices in the asylum and precipitated an enquiry by the Royal Commission on Lunacy and Mental Disorder (1924–1926), which progressed to the Mental Treatment Act of 1930. This laid the foundations for the most significant reform of care for the mentally ill in British history and the replacement of the asylum system with hospitals, allowing voluntary care and outpatient treatment. By the 1970s, Prestwich hospital remained part of the fabric of everyday life in the locality (including for members of the group), as a source of employment, of treatment, and through social interactions with patients. The commonality between the observations of Lomax and the lyrical content of this early output of the group is explored in terms of its relevance in highlighting the lived experience of inadequacies of mental health care.

> Your fears, your arrears, they're all here. Some people write things about it. They have outgrew their crime. We will have revenge. (Smith 1978, cited in Nickas et al. 2021, p.17)

The death of Smith in 2018 has generated retrospective assessments of the origins of the phenomenon that was The Fall. Given their sheer longevity and persistent creativity, there are multiple angles worthy of analysis; however, the focus of the current exploration is limited to the thematic origins of the group's early work. Although *Live at the Witch Trials* was the first formal long-playing release by the group (March 1979), the later compilation, *Early Fall '77–'79* released in September 1981 (Step Forward Records), provides the most potent representation of the origins of the group, bringing together their earliest releases. The record bursts with authentic narrative and diatribes against the psych-establishment; abrasive, odd, but ultimately brimming with charisma and intrigue.

From the beginning, the group set out its identity as a spiky and unpredictable phenomenon, determined to follow a distinctive muse that was endlessly imaginative, playful, fearless, abrasive, and consistently challenging. It is ironic that, despite Smith's desire to position his group as separate from any wider movement (maintaining their base in North Manchester and away from the machinery of the mainstream music industry in London), The Fall have ultimately become the figureheads of multiple "alternative" trends in music. Their distinctive sound remains readily identifiable in contemporary krau-

```
         Burnburnburn
  DICEMAN
 Themadnessinmyarea
   Physicianhealthyself
  VARIOUSTIMES
    BINGOMASTER'SBREAKOUT
 Ourbrainsaredead
     Mentalhospitals
        Headisfulloflead    Toofasttothink
    Electrodesinyourbrain    INMYAREA
 Endedhislifewithwineandpills
  Flippedhislid   THEFALL Valium
    Nobrainsorthought
         PSYCHOMAFIA      ESP
 Becomeano-man    REPETITION
         Pushpushpush   Mentalorgasm
    Thinkthinkthink
    PSYKICKDANCEHALL
  Dopllegangar Simultaneoussuicide
      Goingonaboutdrugs
              ROWCHERUMBLE
   Thedoctorsneedprescriptions
    Prescribeddeathdance
     Pharmaceuticalcompany
           FIERYJACK
```

Figure 13.1. Word cloud of lyrics from *Early Fall '77–'79*

trock; electronica; the guitar-based musical output of bands such as Yard Act, Fontaines D.C., The Sons of Southern Ulster; and avant-pop.

Early Fall '77–'79 is an unusual official product; providing a convenient collection of their first four singles along with B-Sides but also—with typical obtuseness—containing an additional track from the album *Dragnet*. As such, for many it provides the most accessible source to engage with The Fall's early output. It is replete with psychiatric imagery as readily demonstrated in a word cloud (figure 13.1) with eight of the eleven compositions having readily discernible psychiatry-relevant content. The band's origins are steeped in an awareness of and fascination with mental illness—the album is so brimming with such depictions that it serves as a grotesque audiobook for make-shift psychopathologists. Unsurprisingly, this early output has been the subject of discussion within mainstream psychiatric literature (Woods 2021; Brown 2018).

THE PSYCHODRAMA

A particularly striking aspect of the collection is the range of mental perspectives considered; from the psychiatric system: "Oh mental hospitals / They put electrodes in your brain / And you're never the same" ('Repetition') and psychiatrists: "Physician heal thyself" ('Rowche Rumble'); to the individual experience of mental illness: "He Flipped his lid......He ended his life with wine and pills" ('Bingo Master's Breakout') and the pharmaceutical industry: "The doctors need prescriptions / The wives need their pills / So Rowche Rumble"; and even the paranormal word of the 'Psykick Dancehall' with its "ESP medium discord".

Physicians come in for further attention in 'Dice Man' where Smith likens his engagement with the "tree of showbusiness" to that of the psychiatrist protagonist in Rhinehart's novel of the same name who makes decisions based upon the roll of a dice (Rhinehart 1971). Mark E. Smith justifies this risk-friendly strategy as a means to avoid the mediocrity of the masses and not "end up emptying ashtrays", but the dialogue also extends to the listener's participation "do you take a chance, fan?" thus echoing the terms of "Rowche Rumble" where Smith challenges the triad of physician, himself, and the consumer to take responsibility ("Physician, heal thyself / Musician, heal thyself / Hey mister, heal thyself"). This resolute determination to reject the themes and musical styles of their contemporaries, aligned to a conspiratorial collaboration with the listener, is perhaps the single most important element that allowed for the peculiar longevity of The Fall. An implication of both Rhinehart's novel and the song is that breaking from the conservative machinations of mainstream psychiatric practice could challenge conventional constructs and allow sufficient chance for meaningful change—a philosophy that underpins modern-recovery-oriented care for the mentally ill.

"In My Area" sees Smith link images of psychological torment ("Your future cries of broken pain", "the traces of / The madness in my area") with the battle to resist artistic complacency within the group ("I have seen declining tracks", "the birth of bad"), sending out a warning to his groupmates of his determination to maintain forward momentum as a core philosophy. This was followed with a ruthlessness that resulted in possibly the longest list of ex-members for any group in musical history. It is estimated that over sixty different musicians played in The Fall over the years, in many cases being ejected for apparently trivial reasons. In this way, "Repetition", "Dice man", and "In My Area" lay out the manifesto for the group.

The lyrical content of the '77–'79 collection very much reflects its era, with a clear orientation toward primarily *psychiatric* perspectives rather than the current terminology around *mental health*. It addresses core themes that

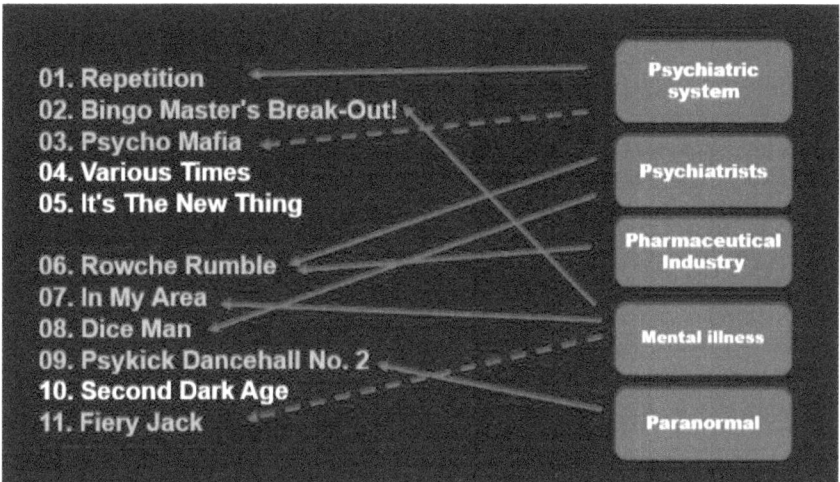

Figure 13.2. Prominent psychiatric themes linked track by track

resonate strongly with the bleak era of the mental hospital when the disconnect between those with mental illness and wider society was more socially and behaviourally apparent due to fear, stigma, and the sometimes highly visual consequences of receiving treatment with older psychotropic interventions (e.g., "Oh mental hospitals / They put electrodes in your brain / And you're never the same" ['Repetition'] or "And loads of people across the land / Who do a prescribed death dance" ['Rowche Rumble']).

Where the punk and post-punk movements took pride in their inclusion of the marginalised within society, this often manifested in inauthentic, semi-lampooned content. Although songs like "Teenage Lobotomy" and "Pretty Vacant" may have allowed for a re-appropriation of traditionally stigmatised perspectives, they are ultimately sloganistic and lack the detail and depth of the sinister narratives detailed in, for example, "Bingo Masters Breakout" which were a trademark of early Fall lyrics.

In addition to the lyrical content, the presentation of the album stands out from other releases of the time and gives due warning that there be demons inside! On the front cover the group's name sits like an old oak with its roots reaching down into the flames of various sinister goings on. Meanwhile the back sleeve includes banal shots of the group members whose appearance was clearly unaligned with punk imagery. We are served notice: this is not the cartoon insanity of The Damned or The Ramones, but something much more gritty and authentic.

From the beginning, Smith was determined to separate his 'group' from other movements. In 'Repetition', for example, he throws a dig at the early punk positionings of Richard Hell and the Voidoids' 'Blank Generation' later borrowed by the Sex Pistols as 'Pretty Vacant'. In interviews, Smith has remarked how he "loved the Pistols, but hated punk generally", nonetheless drawing a distinction between their lazy and self-regarding clichés and his work. It's no coincidence that amongst the earlier names for the group was 'The Outsiders' presumably drawn from Camus's classic novel (before settling with the title of his lesser known novel *The Fall*), reflecting the single-mindedness of the group. This ability to stand outside trends and follow their own path is a recurring and crucial aspect of The Fall's work and undoubtedly contributed to their remarkable longevity.

WRITE ABOUT WHAT YOU KNOW

All of which raises the question, how did a collection of young artists become so immersed in themes that relate to mental illness and psychiatric care?

A major clue lies in their roots in Prestwich—a suburban town perched on the edge of Manchester. Crucially, Prestwich was the site of the principal asylum for the greater Manchester area originally called the Lancashire Lunatic Asylum. The hospital was opened in 1851 to accommodate 500 patients, extended in 1863 to accommodate a further 560 patients with an annexe built in 1884 to house a further 1,100 patients that was served by bus due to its distance from the main hospital site. By 1903 it contained over 3,000 patients from Salford, Manchester, and South Lancashire, making it the largest asylum in Europe at that time. Of note, the population of Prestwich at that time was 12,800—the asylum was the largest source of employment with many employed in the hospital or in related services such that it formed a major part of the fabric of the town. In Manchester-speak the phrase "going to Prestwich" equated with becoming insane with the likely consequences of being sent to the asylum, which presumably impacted upon the reputation of the town and its inhabitants (Hopton 1999).

Members of The Fall also had significant direct links with the hospital—Kay Carroll (group manager and backing vocalist: 'Psychiatric Nurse') became involved with the Fall after meeting Una Baines (keyboards: trainee nurse) whilst working at Prestwich Hospital (Simpson 2008, pp.75–97).Smith was known to associate with inmates from the hospital, going for a drink or taking them back to his flat, commenting in his autobiography, "We lived at the back of the mental hospital. Una (Baines) worked there. Psychiatric nurses lived in every two or three houses. Biggest mental hospital in Europe; serious mental patients. I'd invite patients in for a cup of tea. Sit them down, play them some rock and roll, a bit of Telly" (Smith 2008). Tommy Mackay's

40 Odd Years of the Fall reveals how one of the earliest documented Fall performances was at the Prestwich Hospital Social club on 25 November 1978 (Mackay 2018). In effect, the group's early development occurred under and within the shadow of a monstrous asylum.

THE PRESTWICH AFFAIR

Prestwich Asylum was noteworthy not just because of its size but also as the subject of the writings of its most important employee, Dr Montagu Lomax. Dr Lomax was a retired general practitioner who took on locum work as a junior medical officer at Prestwich Asylum between 1917–1919 (Groves and Hilton 2021). He was so affected by his experiences that he felt compelled to document them in a book, *The Experiences of an Asylum Doctor* (Lomax 1921). The book is aimed principally at the layman and describes day-to-day life at the asylum, including the appalling overcrowding and squalor, mistreatment of inmates, and a poor standard of medical care and a vastly elevated mortality rate compared with the general population. He exposed a litany of inhumane practices that included malnutrition, routine use of restraint, keeping patients in 'the pen' or trapped 'behind the table', as well as the widespread use of Croton oil (a potent purgative) as a means of behavioural control. Not unreasonably, he concludes, "Probably as much perverse reasoning and defective thinking is exhibited by those responsible for the management of our public asylums as by those who are detained within them" (Lomax 1921).

However, perhaps what most makes the book so impressive is that it addresses these issues from a relatively objective perspective, focusing upon detail rather than judgmental opinion. He concludes with a series of constructive suggestions that were remarkably forward thinking for their time—movement towards voluntary care and shifting activities to community-based facilities; retiring unpleasant and pejorative terms such as 'asylum', 'lunatic', and 'pauper'; and the need to create proper career structures with training of medical and nursing staff. These may all seem like obvious developments but in 1921 would have been challengingly innovative.

Nonetheless, the book was not well received by the establishment and Lomax was vilified in a series of reports and opinion pieces in the medical press (Board of Control 1923; Lunacy Reform 1922; Occasional Notes 1922). Mainstream psychiatry circled the wagons, attacking his credibility and questioning his motives while highlighting that he lacked the experience or expertise to make such observations with any authority. It was further suggested that the descriptions were at best exaggerated and lacking in evidence and—somewhat ludicrously—that their principal effect would be to add to the anxieties of relatives of inmates.

The minister for health initially responded to the outcry about the allegations in Lomax's book by commissioning a report from a committee chaired by Sir Cyril Cobb. Neither Lomax nor the representatives of the asylum attendants participated in the process. In Lomax's case, he refused to give evidence to what he described as "official whitewash" and by this time had aligned himself with the National Society for Lunacy Reform (Lomax 1922) who wanted a Royal Commission, which had much greater weight in terms of achieving real reform. Lomax's decision appears to have been justified as the Cobb report, whilst accepting that there were grounds for some of Lomax's "allegations", rejected much of what he had reported as "gross exaggerations". The establishment were emboldened by the report and responded to it with harsh criticism of Lomax and the Lunacy Reform Society in a further piece in the *Journal of Mental Science* that concluded, "We are not surprised that the cult which has taken Dr Lomax for its high priest is decidedly not pleased with the conclusions arrived at. Its devotees continue unabatedly to inveigh that creation of their imagination, 'the system,' which is as illusory as the facts upon which they hold up the mental nurses to opprobrium" (Occasional Notes 1923).

But Lomax was a capable and determined character. As an experienced medic who had worked as a general practitioner for many years in Britain and New Zealand, he did not fit the mould for asylum doctors who typically occupied a lowly ranking in the medical hierarchy. Psychiatry was considered a less attractive branch of medicine due to the poor conditions and custodial emphasis of the work involved. Moreover, Lomax was an experienced commentator who had previously written about a variety of subjects including theosophy and female constitution (Lomax 1907; Lomax-Smith 1895).

Despite the reassurances of the Cobb report, concerns about the conditions and practices within the asylum system did not abate. Lomax's revelations caused a persisting degree of disquiet amongst the general public, perhaps also fuelled by a sense of responsibility towards the many WWI veterans who had returned from service with significant psychiatric difficulties. This was reflected in repeated coverage within the mainstream press and ultimately prompted a Royal Commission (Royal Commission on Lunacy: 1924–1926; The MacMillan Commission 1926) to which Lomax gave detailed evidence. Undoubtedly, these events contributed to the 1930 Mental Treatment Act, which remains the single most important legislative reform affecting psychiatry in England and Wales and made formal provisions for many of the suggestions raised in Lomax's 1921 publication and provided the legal basis for a new era of psychiatric care.

In the years following the Royal Commission, Lomax continued to advocate for improved standards of care in psychiatric services up until his death in 1933. Remarkably, his death passed unacknowledged by both the *BMJ* and *Journal of Mental Science*, although the *Lancet* did print an obituary recognising his passion and sincerity (Lomax 1933, p.668). As more enlightened attitudes towards the care of those with mental illness have become the mainstay of modern practices, the key contribution of Montagu Lomax to the reform of the asylum system has become better appreciated (Harding 1990). His courage as a whistle-blower in an era when challenging the establishment was likely to have a seriously damaging impact upon one's career and reputation has been acknowledged, while the complex motives around his determination have been explored, including the documented death of his eighteen-year-old son (Armine) in asylum care in 1910 (Groves and Hilton 2021).

THE MADNESS IN MY AREA?

Although Lomax's work provoked the single most important legislative change relevant to society's response to mental illness, de-institutionalizing progressed at a slow rate until the introduction of antipsychotic and antidepressant medications, which only became widespread in the 1970s, followed by the *Care in the Community* policies of the 1980s. As a consequence, the conditions that were described by Lomax were still very much evident in the 1960s and 1970s (Hopton 1999), and for Mark E. Smith (born on March 5, 1957), his developmental years occurred in the vicinity of the large asylum at Prestwich. We can only speculate about his familiarity with Lomax's work, but given his predilection for intellectual mischief, his interest in mental illness, voracious appetite for reading, and grounding in the culture of Prestwich, it is no large leap of faith to presume that he would have been aware of Lomax and Prestwich's key position in the sceptre of psychiatry.

There are also a number of striking similarities between Smith and Lomax beyond their shared connections with Prestwich (or as per the Saxon meaning, 'Priest's retreat'). Montagu Lomax had begun life as Montagu Smith but changed his surname by deed poll in 1888 (Lomax-Smith 1888, p.1), perhaps to better distinguish himself in what was a highly competitive era for young doctors seeking employment and recognition. In addition to sharing Britain's most common surname, both possessed a single-minded determination to follow the truth as they saw it with their alternative views on social politics and class system of the UK. Both were wily individuals and capable readers of the mechanics of their chosen fields who repeatedly sidestepped the trap of submitting to mainstream process. Smith enjoyed a truculent relationship with musicians and the music industry over the forty years of The Fall, a stance that may not have always been immediately financially rewarding but which afforded a degree of independence that embellished the group's output and almost certainly contributed to their longevity.

Similarly, Lomax wisely refused to be drawn into the machinations of the Cobb committee, preferring to wait for the arrival of the more substantial process of the Royal Commission. He maintained a largely independent position throughout the reform process that his work initiated.

It is also notable that both men had considerable interest in spirituality and faith healing. Lomax wrote a number of related articles in the medical literature and even published a book on spiritual healing (Lomax 1921), while Smith's interest in tarot, faith healing, and belief in his personal powers of prediction are repeatedly documented—his former wife, Brix Smith-Start, described his psychic capacity in her recent autobiography stating, "Mark is psychic and he knows it. He's a precognitive psychic, able to pick up snatches of future events before they happen" (Smith and Collings 2009; Smith-Start 2017), while Smith himself explained, "It's just precog. You write things down and you don't know what they mean but you know they're true and they come true later. It's not prophecy as such" (Bracewell and Wilde 2021).

Although tempting in light of these shared quasi-theosophical interests, it would be fantastical to draw any direct lineage between the two individuals. However, undoubtedly they shared many personal characteristics and philosophical perspectives. In all likelihood Mark E. Smith was primarily thinking of himself when he wrote 'PsyKick Dancehall', but its sentiments also readily apply to Dr Lomax, and ultimately the presence of both Mark E. Smith and Montagu Lomax resonates across time more than most who have passed through the streets of Prestwich.

> When I'm dead and gone
> My vibrations will live on
> In vibes not vinyl through the years
> People will dance to my waves.

REFERENCES

Board of Control (1923). Ministry of Health Committee on the administration of public mental hospitals (England and Wales). *Journal of Mental Science*, 69, 272–73.

Bracewell, Michael, and Jon Wilde. *Mark E. Smith. Excavate! The wonderful and frightening world of The Fall*. Edited by Tessa Norman and Bob Stanley. Faber and Faber, 2021.

Brown, M. The Man Whose Head Expanded, The Lancet, February 19, 2018 Vol 5 Issue 4, 304–305.
Groves, C., and C. Hilton (2021). Montagu Lomax: The background and motivation of a 'remarkable man' who spearheaded lunacy reform. *Journal of Medical Biography*. https://doi.org/10.1177/09677720211005268
Harding T. "Not worth powder and shot": A reappraisal of Montagu Lomax's contribution to mental health reform. *British Journal of Psychiatry*, March 1990.
Hopton J. (1999). Prestwich Hospital in the twentieth century: A case study of slow and uneven progress in the development of psychiatric care. *History of Psychiatry* (1999) 10: 349–69.
Lomax M. Agnostic theosophy. *Theosophical Review*, 1907, 39: 437.
———. The experiences of an asylum doctor: With suggestions for asylum and lunacy law reform. [S.l.]: Allen and Unwin, 1921.
———. *Spiritual healing in relation to mental diseases: An address by M. Lomax*. London: Spiritual Healing Fellowship, 1921.
———. The asylum inquiry. *Truth*, 9 August 1922: 235.
———. M.R.C.S.Eng., L.R.C.P.Edin. *Lancet*, 25 March 1933, p. 668.
Lomax-Smith M. (Announcement in Personal, etc.) *Times* (London), 11 December 1888, p. 1.
———. *Woman in relation to physiology, sex, emotion and intellect.* Russell and Willis, 1895.
Lunacy reform. *British Medical Journal*, 1(3189) (11 February 1922), p. 237.
Mackay T. *Forty odd years of the fall.* Greg Moodie, 2018.
Meagher, D. (2017). Punk rock made me a psycho-therapissed. *British Journal of Psychiatry*, 211(6), 395–95.
Nickas, B., N. Planck, and Slang King. *Mark E. Smith on stage 1977–2013.* At Last Books, 2021.
Occasional notes. The trend of psychiatry in England and Wales. *Journal of Mental Science* (1922), 67, 171–75.
———. The administration of public mental hospitals in England and Wales. *Journal of Mental Science* (1923), 69, 90–99.
Report of the Royal Commission on Lunacy and Mental Disorder. Royal Commission on Lunacy and Mental Disorder, London: H.M.S.O., 1926. https://wellcomecollection.org/works/svzt3k5g
Rhinehart, L. *The Diceman.* William Morrow, 1971.
Simpson D. *The Fallen: Life in and out of Britain's most insane group.* Canongate Books, 2008.
Smith, Mark E., and Austin Collings. *Renegade: The lives and tales of Mark E. Smith.* Penguin Books, 2009.
———. *Renegade: The lives and tales of Mark E. Smith.* Viking Books, 2008.
Smith-Start, Brix. *The Rise, The Fall, and The Rise.* Faber and Faber, 2017.
Woods, G. (2021). The Fall: 'Rowche Rumble'—psychiatry in music. *British Journal of Psychiatry*, 218(3), 150–50.

Index

A Tribe called Quest 183n1
Adorno, Theodor 172, 173–4, 178, 183n2
The Adverts 238
afterlife 62
alcohol 149, 236–7
alienation 159
Alighieri, Dante 95, 114, 204, 205, 214, 215, 216, 225n19
Alternative Ulster (fanzine) 236
Ancient Egypt 56
Anderson, Jenny 39n7
Appointment with Fear 32, 39n8
Archer, Simon 'Ding' 198, 199
Arctic Monkeys 152
Aristotle 45, 191
art 9–25, 35, 49, 126, 181; outsider art 26; working–class art 12, 106
The Atrix 106
Australia 72, 103, 104; Brisbane 103, 107
authenticity 45, 173, 177–8
avant–garde 1, 10–11, 175, 179, 196
avant–pop 247

Bacon, Francis 65, 66
Badly Drawn Boy 95
Baines, Una 76, 104, 250

Ballard, JG 71, 101
Bangladesh 62
Barbican 18
Barthes, Roland 206
Bassey, Shirley 16
Bauhaus 239
BBC vii, 10, 15, 18, 19, 20, 39n12, 44, 61, 65, 68, 83, 84, 85, 88, 91, 94, 111, 143, 187, 213, 261
Beatles 113, 129, 151, 191, 200
Beckett, Samuel 191, 192, 194
Behan, Brendan 242
Belfast Telegraph 236
Belgium 238
Benjamin, Walter 97
Bessy, Claude 70
Big Star 113
Big Youth 178
The Birthday Party 224n10
Birtwistle, Spencer 65
Blackpool 28
Blake, William 6, 11, 20–21, 76–8, 88–9, 125, 167n2, 197, 203, 205, 218, 223n1, 223n5, 226n38
Blast manifestos 14, 21
body 138–43
Bono 77
Borges 224n8

Bosch, Hieronymous 215, 220
Bourdieu, Pierre 86–7
Bow Wow Wow 239
Bowery, Leigh 18, 71, 98n2, 181
Bowie, David vii, x, 13, 95, 102, 203, 221, 227n49, 259
Bradbury, Malcolm 190–91
Bradley, Michael 93
brain function 9
Bramah, Martin 11, 66, 69, 104, 106
Branson, Richard 125
Brecht, Berthold 45, 54
British TV 104–5
Britpop 76, 93
Brown, James 176
Burchill, Julie 75
Burgess, Tony 55
Burns, Karl 177
Burroughs, William S. ix, 6, 13, 110, 125, 166, 205, 221
Bush, Kate 77, 151
Butler, Elvera 236–7
Buzzcocks 92
The Byrds 113

CIA 62, 71
Cabaret Voltaire 239
Cambridge 12
Camus, Albert 1, 11, 12, 13, 110, 204–5, 224n9, 250; *The Fall* (novel) 11, 204
CAN 1, 6, 172, 173, 175–8, 182, 183n1
Caillois, Roger 192
Captain Beefheart 113, 137, 201n4
The Carpenters x
Carroll, Kay ix, 17, 66, 75, 76, 216, 233, 236, 250
Castenskiold, Claus 217
Cave, Nick 242
celebrity death 90–91, 101–3
Chant! Chant! Chant! 106, 237
The Charlatans 143
Charles, Paul 238
Clark, Michael x, 10, 16, 17, 18, 98n2, 172, 180, 181. *See also* dance
Clarke, Arthur C 74

The Clash 113, 238
classical music 171, 175
classism 12
The Clint Boon Experience 199
Cocteau Twins 206
Cohen, Leonard 102, 171, 203, 242
Coldcut 1, 180–81
Cole, Jack 14
collage 53
Collins, Edwyn 1–2, 107
Cologne 177, 183n1
colonialism 12
comics 10, 14, 26, 66–7, 111, 140
conspiracy theory 71–2
Cook, Peter 15, 113
Corman, Roger 124, 190
corpus–based text analysis 119–67; corpus pragmatics 154–5
Costello, Elvis 106
Coughlan, Cathal 236
cover art 49–52, 105, 107, 187, 197, 203, 217
COVID–19 pandemic 77
Crosby, Stills, Nash and Young 220
Crowley, Aleister 205
cubism 224n13
Curtis, Ian 91, 102. *See also* Joy Division, New Order
Czukay, Holger 175

D.O.S.E. (band) 181
Dadaism 2, 13, 39n1, 195, 217, 222
Dad's Army 35, 39n12
Dali, Salvador 26
The Damned 249
dance 180–82; ballet 17, 18, 19, 85, 87, 98n2, 172, 180, 181
Das Boot 20
DC Nien 106
death of Diana Spencer (1997) 65
defamiliarisation 44–5, 48
Deleuze, Gilles 76, 203
depression 74–5
design 45–6
Dick, Philip K. 42, 67, 69–71, 113, 125

Dickens, charles viii, 205, 217
Diddley, Bo 13
Disneyland 42, 68
DIY ethic 1, 182, 231, 232, 236, 237, 238, 240, 242–3, 245
Dolan's Warehouse 3
Domino Records 182
Donne, John 205
Dostoevsky, Fyodor 205
Dragnet 12
drugs 149, 205
Duff, Graham 10, 15–16, 19, 42
Duncan, Helen 66
Dylan, Bob 113, 187, 203

Echo and the Bunnymen 224n10
electronic music/EDM 176, 181, 247
Eliot, T. S. 13, 205, 207, 211, 242
estrangement 45
Eton 12
Eurovision Song Contest 122, 152
evolutionary biology 72
existentialism 11, 204
expressionism 26

Facebook 103
Factmag 120
Factory Records 92, 93, 207, 208
The Fall: *Annotated Fall* (website) 15, 153, 166–7n1, 177, 189–90, 214. *See also* fandom; anti–nostalgia 185, 186, 197; Brownies performance (Manhattan) 66; career 2, 91–2, 110, 185–201, 213; 'creative deformation' 48–50; final gig (QMU Glasgow 2017) 85–7, 89, 98n3; 'folklore' 83–4, 92–3, 96; language viii, 6, 15, 41–3, 47, 54, 55–6, 57, 58, 72, 120, 125, 135, 151–66, 176, 179, 186, 187, 203, 204, 207, 208, 209, 210–11, 214–6, 217, 218, 221–3, 260, 263; lineup 4, 5, 91, 171, 195–6; *Live at the Witch Trials* vii, 104, 105, 106, 153, 246; lyrical themes and features 124–45; name:
See Camus, Albert; obfuscation 190, 191, 196, 204, 218; PR and image 75, 86; scholarship 5; sound 123–4, 188–201, 212; *The Wonderful and Frightening World of the Fall* x, 4, 209, 213, 238; thefall.org 235
fandom 2, 6, 10, 21n2, 91, 101–3, 124, 126, 153, 166–7n1
Faust 57, 74
Felt 239
film 19–20, 35
fine art 20–21
Flickering Lexicon 126–8, 146n4, 146n7
Fontaines DC 2, 241, 242, 247
Forster, Robert 101–18, 191; drug use 109
France 71
Frazer, Elizabeth 224n10
Freeney, Eoin 237
Freud, Sigmund 72, 84, 85, 87, 92, 94–5, 97
Friday, Gavin vii–xi, 4, 238, 259
Friel, Tony 11, 69, 205
Frost, Anthony 30, 31, 35
funk 176, 180
Fust, John 57
futurism 205

Gallagher, Liam 241
Gang of Four 106, 239
garage music 182
Garland, Judy 17
Geldof, Bob 233
gender 2, 132–5, 137, 158–9, 164, 252
Gentry, Bobby 15
Germany ix, 15, 26, 42, 66, 74, 122, 159, 172, 180, 183n1, 220, 225n17, 238
Ghostdigital 181
gigography 235–43
Gilla Band (formerly Girl Band) 241
Ginsberg, Allen 205
Glastonbury Festival 65
Glorious Revolution (1688) 18

Go–Betweens 101–18
The Golden Horde (band) 238
Gorillaz 1, 181
gothic rock 152
GQ Magazine 120
Green Man Festival 74
Greenway, Pete 4, 196
Grosz, Georg 26, 39n1, 217
The Guardian 120
Guattari, Felix 76
Gurdjieff, G. I. 69. *See also* occult/paranormal
Gutenberg, Johannes 56–7
Gysin, Brion 221

habitualisation 43, 44, 46, 48
habitus 86, 89
Hanley, Paul ix, x, 10, 14, 21, 21n1, 213, 218
Hanley, Steven ix, x, 65, 110
Hardy, Thomas 205
Harris, Rolf 104
Harvey, Alex 26, 39n3
heavy metal 152
Hebden Bridge Festival 17
Hecht, Ben 220
Hex Enduction Hour 52
Hey! Luciani 17–18, 28, 31, 71, 98n2, 181
Holland Festival 18
Holland, Jools 71
homelessness 31, 39n7
Homer 215
Hook, Peter 92
horror 12, 13, 32, 42, 54–5, 124, 205, 208, 219. *See also* science fiction; gothic literature 12
Hot Press 239–40
Hucknall, Mick 92
Humanzi 241
hybridity 179

I Am Curious, Orange 18, 98n2, 223n1. *See also* Clark, Michael
Iceland 238

Ideal (TV series) 19
Iggy Pop 241
Imperial Wax (band) 4
In Camera (Sartre) 20
In God's Name 71
Inch (band) 181
indie vii, 93, 152
Inspiral Carpets 2
intertextuality 186, 204
Iran 62
Ireland and Northern Ireland vii, viii, ix, 3, 6, 7, 106, 231–44; Belfast 235–6, 237, 238, 240; Black–and–Tans viii; Cork 236, 238; distance from alternative scene 238–43; Dublin 238; Irish in England 233–5; music smuggling 240–41; NUI Galway 187; Troubles 233, 238; University of Limerick Symposium on The Fall 2–5, 150
Iser, Wolfgang 191–2, 195
Islamic Jihad/Hezbollah 62
Italian Futurism 224n13

Jackson, Michael 90
Jagger, Mick 104
The Jam 106, 238
Jamaica 172, 178
James, M. R. 12, 42, 71, 189, 205
Jameson, Fredric 174, 175
Jarry, Alfred 13, 205
jazz 175, 180
Jesus and Mary Chain 183n1, 224n10
Joy Division viii, 92, 106, 114, 239, 259, 260
Joyce, James viii, 13, 120, 198, 199, 207, 217

Kafka, Franz 205
Karoli, Michael 176, 177
Kelly, Nick 239–40
Kershaw, Liz 18
Kiely, Dara 241
Killing Joke 224n10, 239
King Tubby 172, 175, 179, 182, 183n6

The Kinks 113, 128
Kirby, Jack 14. *See also* comics
Kirchner, Ernst 26, 39n4
Kitt, Eartha 16
krautrock 172, 176, 246–7

Laing, RD 76
language 6, 54–6, 149–70, 203–230; dialect 125, 137, 152; semantic categories 119. *See also* corpus-based text analysis
Larkin, Philip 205
LCD Soundsystem 2
Lebanon 62
Leckie, John x, 62,
Lee, Stewart 16, 226n36
Leftfield 180
Lewis, Wyndham 11, 14, 21, 113, 120, 190, 205, 207, 208, 214, 216
Liebezeit, Jaki 175–6, 177
Ligeti, Gyorgi 175
literariness 11–16, 119, 120, 143, 149, 188, 204
literature 101
Liverpool vii, ix, 220, 227n45
Lomax, Montagu 246, 251–4
The London Underground (band) 17
Lord Byron 125, 137
Louder Than Words Festival 145n1
Lovecraft Country (TV series) 12
Lovecraft, H. P. 6, 12, 54, 124, 189, 201, 205
Lowry, Malcolm 13, 205
Ludd, Ned 137; Luddite 207
LUX gallery 12, 20
Lydon, John (Johnny Rotten) x, 180, 183n1, 239. *See also* Sex Pistols, Public Image Ltd
lyrical interpretation 12, 123–4, 126, 149–67, 173, 190, 218–9. S*ee also* corpus based text analysis, fandom

Machen, Arthur 10, 12, 69, 205
Madchester 76, 93

Magazine (band) 106
magical realism 110, 149
Mailer, Norman 205
Manchester viii , ix, 3, 10, 11, 12, 16, 17, 19, 21, 25, 31, 34, 35, 39nn9–10, 66, 68, 69, 91, 92, 93, 97, 103, 105, 110, 137, 145n1, 182, 213, 217, 231, 233, 235, 243, 245, 246, 250, 260, 263. *See also* Northern England, place, Prestwich, Salford; city centre bombing (1996) 68; Cornerhouse Centre 182; Hacienda ix, 213, 214; Manchester Art Gallery 12; Manchester City (football team) 10; Strangeways Prison 31, 233
Mann, Thomas 205
Marcus, Ben 55
marginalisation 159
Marlowe, Christopher 203, 205
McCulloch, Ian 220
MCD 239
McFarlane, James 190–91
McGowan, Shane 242
McGurk effect 189, 201n2
McLennan, Grant 101, 102, 107, 111–2
media 75
Melling, Kieron 4, 196
Melody Maker 20, 105
Michael, George 95
Microdisney 236
middle class 44
Middles, Mick 67, 68, 145n1
Milland, Ray 124, 190
mimesis 191–2
MIT 9
Mitchell, Joni 203, 220
modernism 13, 43, 47, 50, 52, 69, 120, 204–5, 206–8; working–class modernism 5, 6, 185–8
Moldavia 74
Moldova 74
Montgomery, Don 76
Mooney, Malcolm 176

Morning of the Magicians (Pauwels and Bergier) 71
Morrison, Jim 203
Morrison, Lindy 107
Morrissey 92, 151, 203, 224n14, 242
Mouse on Mars 2, 19, 172, 180, 181
The Move 128
MTV 105
Mulrooney, Shaun 241
Mumford and Sons 77
Munch, Edvard 36, 39n13
The Murder Capital 2
music production 174, 178–9, 182–3, 183n3; reification of music 173–4, 183n2; 'scene' vs 'industry' 231–43
musique concrete 176

Nabokov, Vladimir 13, 205
narrative 72
Nasser, Abdel 71
National Front 75
neologisms 135–6, 197, 198
Netherlands 215, 238
Neu! 1
New Order 92, 224n10
new romantics 239
new wave 93, 104, 106, 232, 239, 241
New Zealand 252
Newsnight 143
Nietzsche, Friedrich 74, 143
nihilism 203
NME (*New Musical Express* magazine) 6, 31, 105, 107, 180, 195, 232
Nobel Prize 187
Northern England 9, 10, 87, 102, 106, 149, 216–7, 233, 238, 240. *See also* Liverpool, Manchester, place, Prestwich, Salford
Nostradamus 77
NY–MOMA 12

Oasis 241
Oates, Joyce Carol 13

O'Brien, Flann (Brian O'Nolan) 203
occult/paranormal 54–7, 61–78, 144, 205, 208. *See also* horror; Devil 32. *See also* religion; popular belief in 63–4; psychic abilities 58; psychokinesis 62
The Old Grey Whistle Test 17, 105
Olympic Studios x
Ono, Yoko 9
Orton, Joe 113
Osborne 113
The Otherwise (film script) 15–16, 19, 20, 42, 96. *See also* Duff, Graham
Oulipo 220
Ouspensky, P. D. 69
Oxford English Dictionary 15

P[illay], Lanah 16–17, 71
Pander, Panda! Panzer! 19, 67
Paris Opera Ballet 181
Parker, Steve 213
Parsons, Tony 75
Parton, Dolly 125. 137
Pasolini, Pier Paolo 221
Pavement 2
Peel, John vii, 9, 65, 91, 93–4, 105, 123, 128, 129, 132, 140, 181, 187, 199, 200, 240, 260
performance 87–9, 98n3, 149, 150, 173, 185, 188, 191, 232
Perry, Lee 'Scratch' 172
Perverted by Language 16, 210–14, 217–22
Picasso, Pablo 12, 30
Pinter, Harold 113, 205
place 137–8. *See also* Liverpool, Manchester, Northern England, Salford; local vs geographical 92, 97, 105, 246; urban vs rural 103
Plato 56, 130
Plutarch 15
Pluto Studios 213
poetry 48
pop art 26
pop music 171, 172, 174, 180, 186

Pope John Paul I 10, 18, 28, 30, 39n5, 71, 98n2, 125, 183n7
popular culture 9, 12
postmodernism 186
The Post Nearly Man 19
Poulou, Eleni 14, 15, 20, 88, 196
Pound, Ezra 6, 203–30
precognition 10, 42, 61–78, 124, 149, 254
Presley, Elvis 102, 235, 236
Prestwich vii, viii, 6, 21, 34, 39nn9–10, 54, 66, 76, 77, 85, 95, 96, 97, 114, 138, 216–7, 226n33, 246, 250, 251–2, 253, 254; Prestwich Asylum 6, 76, 246, 250, 251–3. *See also* Lomax, Montagu
Price, Vincent 124
Prince 102
The Prisoner (TV series) 18
psychiatry 6, 73, 245–56; anti-psychiatry 76; antipsychotic medication 253; parapsychology 62; stigmatisation of mental illness 249, 251
Public Image, Ltd (PIL) 239. *See also* John Lydon, Sex Pistols
punk vii, 1, 2, 11, 70, 75, 76, 93, 96, 105, 106, 108, 176, 178, 183, 183n1, 191, 206, 207, 223n7, 232, 235, 236, 238, 239, 242, 245, 249–50, 260, 262; proto–punk 191; post–punk vii, xi, 1, 2, 6, 11, 19, 93, 105, 149, 178, 183n1, 194, 204, 206–9, 222, 223n7, 232, 236, 241, 242, 245, 249, 261
Pythagoras 15

Queen Victoria 125

The Radiators 106
Radiohead 183n1
The Ramones 249
Reed, Lou 113
reggae 6, 180; dub reggae 172, 178–80
religion 18, 31, 57, 144, 193, 218–21
repetition 43, 87, 95, 129, 172, 175, 176, 178, 182, 188, 191, 194, 201, 218, 220
Reynolds, Joshua 77
Rhine, JB 62
Rhinehart, Luke (George Powers Cockcroft) 13–14, 205, 248
Richard Hell and the Voidoids 250
Riley, Marc 51, 52, 92
ritual 86, 87
Robinson, Sandy 48–9
rock 48, 166, 171, 172, 180
Roeg, Nicolas 104, 109
Rolling Stone magazine 241
Romania 74
Rough Trade viii–ix, 212–3, 240
Roxy Music vii
RSPCA 84

Salford 61, 67, 69, 98n1, 110, 123, 137, 234, 250. *See also* Northern England, place
Sartre, Jean–Paul 13, 20
Scanlon, Craig x, 65, 71, 212
Schmidt, Irwin 175
science fiction 42, 44, 74
Serling, Rod 19
Sex Pistols 92, 106, 239, 249, 250
Shakespeare, William 18, 125
Sheeran, Ed 77
Sherwood, Adrian 178
Shipman, Harold 125
Shklovsky, Viktor 43, 44, 45, 46, 48
The Singing Detective 19
Silverman, Burton 39n7
Simmel, Georg 84, 85, 87, 92
Simon and Garfunkel 104
Simpson, Dave 9, 68
Sister Sledge 128, 172
Sisters of Mercy 239
skinheads 28
Skinner, Frank 61, 67
Slash (magazine) 70
The Slits 239

Smith, Irene 68
Smith, Mark E: autobiography 110–11, 112; creative process ix, x–xi, 1, 2, 14–16, 17, 19, 30–31, 48, 53, 57, 77, 112, 149, 150, 213; death 3, 5, 20, 78, 83–118, 120, 185, 188, 245; film and TV appearances 10, 20; gangs 234; health 32, 86, 102, 165; influences 1, 5–6, 13, 113, 125, 149, 158–9, 166, 176, 190, 199, 201, 201n5, 208, 223; media portrayal 91, 96, 97, 195, 237; paranoia 62, 70, 110; precognition 6, 61–82, 84, 98n1. *See also* occult/paranormal; surrealism vii, viii, 2, 15, 120, 221, 226n36, 235; tarot 69, 70; voice viii, 150, 173, 188, 189, 198, 212
Smith, Patti 203
Smith, Suzanne 3
Smith–Start, Brix ix, x, 18, 63, 68, 70, 116, 120, 128, 212–3, 224n14, 226n22, 226n24, 254
Soft Cell 239
song structure 149
Sonic Youth 2, 77
Sons of Southern Ulster 247
soul 180
Southern Death Cult 239
"Spectre vs Rector" 12, 69, 123, 135, 144, 161, 179, 189. *See also* horror
spelling and grammar 151–2, 153, 196, 223. *See also* typography
Spencer, Simon 65
Spizz Energi 239
Spurr, Dave 4, 196
St Werner, Jan 182
Stansfield, Lisa 180
Stein, Gertrude 196
Stockhausen, Karlheinz 175
Stoker, Bram 205
The Stooges 199, 201n5
The Stranglers 106, 238
streaming music 175
Strummer, Joe 102
Stuart, Becky 30

Sudan 62
Sumner, Bernard 92
Suzanne Smith 51–2. *See also* cover art
Suzuki, Damo 125, 171, 176, 177
SW1 Gallery London 126
taboo 125

Tate Modern 12
theatre 16–19, 45, 181
theosophy 69, 252, 254
Thompson, Hunter S. 125, 195
Tintoretto 35, 39n11
Tolstoy, Leo viii
Top of the Pops 105
Total Recall (1990) 71
translation 54
transliminality 73–4
Trump, Donald 77, 90
Tschichold, Jan 46, 207
Tull, Jethro 31
The Twilight Zone 19, 74, 125
Twitter 83
Tyler, the creator 183n1
typography 6, 41–60, 16, 203. *See also* cover art; and capitalism 47; International Typographical Style 46–8; unobtrusiveness 43–4, 47

U2 viii, 233, 237
UK Decay 224n10
UK secret services 71
Ukraine 74
uncanny 50–51, 84, 94–5, 97
The Undertones 93
university gigs 238–9
University of Regensburg 152
USA 238, 241

Van Greenaway, Peter 124
Vander, Pamela 86
Vandermeer, Jeff 16
Varney, Reg 194
Velvet Underground 176
Village Voice 188
Vincent, Gene 128, 199

Virgin Prunes viii, ix–x, 4, 238
visual language 50, 54. *See also* cover art, typography
Von Sudenfeld 182
Vorticism 11, 14, 21, 204, 207, 208–10, 222, 224n13
Vox (fanzine) 237

Waite, Terry 62–3, 64, 68
Wallis, Alfred 26, 39n2
Warde, Beatrice 43, 46
weird literature 12
West, Kanye 90
Wheatley, Dennis 205
White, Nancy 95
White Rastas 28
Wilde, Oscar 11
Wilding, Neville 65
Wilkinson, Dave 10
William of Orange 125
Wilson, Colin 44, 71, 125, 205
Wilson, Harold 71
witch trials 57, 66
Wither, George 197–8
Withnail and I 108
Wolstencroft, Simon 3–4, 65
Woolf, Virginia 122
working class modernism 187
working–class culture 85, 87
Wright, Peter 71–2
writing 42
World War I 252
World War II 66, 71, 74
Wyndham, Lewis 190

XTC 106

Yard Act 247
Yeats, W. B. 58
YouTube 105
Yugoslavia 42, 68

Zagreb 68, 74
Zappa, Frank 113
Zimbabwe Rhodesia (June–December 1979) 137

About the Editors and Contributors

EDITORS

Eoin Devereux
Professor Eoin Devereux is co-director of the Centre for the Study of Popular Music and Popular Culture at the University of Limerick Ireland. He is also an adjunct professor in Contemporary Culture at the University of Jyvaskyla, Finland. He has previously co-edited (with M. Power and A. Dillane) books on Morrissey (Intellect, 2011), David Bowie (Routledge, 2015), Songs of Social Protest (Rowman and Littlefield, 2018), and Joy Division (Rowman and Littlefield, 2018). A creative writer, his work has been published and broadcast in numerous settings including *The Irish Times* and RTE Radio 1. He has written sleeve-notes for the re-issued versions of The Cranberries' *Everybody Else Is Doing It, So Why Can't We?* and *No Need to Argue*. Eoin co-scripts and co-performs *The Cedarwood Chronicles*, a monthly radio programme on U2X radio with Gavin Friday.

Martin J. Power
Dr Martin J. Power is a senior lecturer in Sociology and co-director of the Centre for the Study of Popular Music and Popular Culture at the University of Limerick, Ireland. Among his recent publications are the co-edited books *Football and Popular Culture: Singing Out from the Stands* and *Football, Politics and Identity* (Routledge, 2021). Martin has previously co-edited (with E. Devereux and A. Dillane) books on Morrissey (Intellect, 2011), David Bowie (Routledge, 2015), Songs of Social Protest (Rowman and Littlefield, 2018), and Joy Division (Rowman and Littlefield, 2018).

CONTRIBUTORS

Kieran Cashell lectures in Critical & Contextual Studies, Limerick School of Art and Design (TUS). He is author of *Photographic Realism: The Art of Richard Billingham* (Bloomsbury, 2020) and *Aftershock: The Ethics of Contemporary Transgressive Art* (I. B. Tauris, 2009). He has contributed to edited collections on popular music culture including *Working for the Clampdown: The Clash, the Dawn of Neoliberalism and the Political Promise of Punk*, Colin Coulter (ed.) (MUP 2019); *Heart and Soul: Critical Essays on Joy Division*, M. Power, E. Devereux, A. Dillane (eds.) (Rowman and Littlefield, 2018); and *Popular Music and Human Rights*, I. Peddie (Ashgate, 2011); he has also published articles in the journal *Punk & Post Punk*.

Brian Clancy is a lecturer in applied linguistics at Mary Immaculate College, Limerick, Ireland. His research work focuses on the blend of corpus linguistic methodology with the discourse analytic approaches of pragmatics and sociolinguistics. His primary methodological interests relate to the use of corpora in the study of language varieties and the construction and analysis of small corpora. His published work explores language use in intimate settings, such as between family and close friends, and the language variety Irish English. He is author of *Investigating Intimate Discourse: Exploring the Spoken Interaction of Families, Couples and Close Friends* (Routledge, 2016) and co-author, with Anne O'Keeffe and Svenja Adolphs, of *Introducing Pragmatics in Use* (Routledge, 2011 and 2020).

Matt Davies is senior lecturer in English Language at the University of Chester. His research interests include the relationships between language and power, news discourse, and the ideological power of artificially constructed textual oppositions. His monograph, *Oppositions and Ideology in the News*, and several book chapters, explore syntactic techniques used to demonise and delegitimise individuals and groups through the power of 'us'/'them' oppositions. He also teaches about conflicts and controversies in English language and linguistics. He has been an avid follower of The Fall since he first heard 'Rowche Rumble' on John Peel's 1979 Festive 50, soon after which he drove himself to distraction trying to unpick the lyrics of 'Spectre vs. Rector'. He has given several public and academic presentations on using computer-assisted techniques to explore the lyrics of Mark E. Smith. He also plays (Steve Hanley–influenced) bass guitar in the Salford/Manchester-based band Factory Acts.

Samuel Flannagan is a freelance writer who writes mostly about literature and music. His first Fall records were *Reformation Post TLC* and *Shiftwork*, but they still became his favourite band. This may be the reason that he has an unconventional take on The Fall's oeuvre. He is sincere in his belief that *The Remainderer* is a more important Fall record than *Slates*. He lives in Berlin.

John Fleming's award-winning writing spans five broadcast radio plays (including *The Invisible Hand Report* and *Downheaval*, the latter given separate productions by RTÉ and BBC), five short stories for RTÉ and BBC World Service (including *The Young Charles Laughton* and *Whaling Slang*), and a dozen essays on music and literature for *Dublin Review of Books*. He co-directed a film about London in the 1980s (*Guests of Another Nation*), and curated Eamon Carr and Eamonn Dowd's *Fever Ship* album. He works as a subeditor/journalist for *The Irish Times* and contributes Irishman's Diaries, pieces on post-punk subculture and, for foreign pages, bag-handle-blistered semiological takes on the many cities he has visited. Educated at Terenure College, he did a BA in communication studies in NIHE/DCU and an MA in film and TV studies at Polytechnic of Central London/University of Westminster. A Dubliner and fictionalist, he has lived in London, New York, and Paris.

Mike Glennon is a Dublin-based composer, audio artist, and creative arts researcher. He is a lifelong fan of The Fall. Mike was awarded his PhD by TU Dublin in 2021 for his research on Mixtapes and Mix-Based Modes of Making Music. He has presented his research and composition work at locations including the Research Pavilion of the Venice Biennalle. His writing has been published by platforms including Organised Sound, RTE Brainstorm, and Sounding Out. He frequently collaborates with artists across various disciplines creating sound and music for installation, video, performance, and more. Mike was part of the creative team behind the *Hy Brasil II* installation which was awarded a Gold Kinsale Shark Award in 2019. He has also released two albums as a member of the band The 202s. Mike currently lectures in BIMM Institute Dublin where he teaches a range of creative and cultural courses.

K. A. Laity is an award-winning author, scholar, filmmaker, critic, editor, and arcane artist. She currently holds the position of associate professor of English at the College of Saint Rose (New York). Her scholarship at present covers medieval Scots, crime fiction and films, and the fiction of Leonora Carrington. Her short film *A Fire Ritual for the Heart* was featured in the Silent Fire exhibition co-curated by the Yale Institute of Sacred Music and Nasty Women Connecticut. Her fiction includes crime, thrillers, gothic, fantasy, and humour. She has edited many anthologies in addition to writing short stories, scholarly essays, songs, and plays. Laity served as History Witch for Witches & Pagans. Her 2011–2012 Fulbright Fellowship at the National University of Ireland, Galway, focused on Digital Humanities. Follow her on Twitter,

Instagram, or Facebook. She creates the podcast *Is It Funny?* and her radio programme *Surreal Noir* can be found on NoBounds Radio.

Ben Lawley is a researcher and writer with a focus on music, culture, and thought. He has published papers on diverse subjects with research strands encompassing urbanism, health, medicine, and music. His current research concerns music history and literary theory. He lives and works in England.

Michael Mary Murphy was part of Dublin's small DIY/punk music scene during the 1980s. He wrote for fanzines, helped to organize gigs, and worked in his local indie record shop. In 1989 he was hired by the Virgin record label in London before being employed by the Imago record label in New York owned by Terry Ellis, who had previously founded Chrysalis Records. There he worked with acts including Henry Rollins. He subsequently founded his own music management company and was personal manager for artists on each of the major labels. He writes about the music industry, punk, youth subculture, and Dungeons and Dragons. He lectures at IADT Dun Laoghaire. A co-authored book with Jim Rogers, *Sounds Irish, Acts Global: Explaining the Success of Ireland's Popular Music Industry* (Equinox) is forthcoming.

David Meagher is the chair of Psychiatry at the School of Medicine, University of Limerick, and consultant psychiatrist at University Hospital Limerick. He is the guitarist in the Sons of Southern Ulster. He has published on punk and psychiatry and is the co-author of a book chapter with Eoin Devereux and Walter Cullen on Ian Curtis in *Heart and Soul: Critical Perspectives on Joy Division*, edited by Martin Power, Eoin Devereux, and Aileen Dillane (Rowman and Littlefield, 2018).

Martin Myers is a sociologist of education at the University of Nottingham. His work is primarily interested in the intersections of class and race/racism as a means of reproducing inequalities through educational practice. In particular, it has focused on Gypsy, Roma, and Traveller experiences of schooling and education, including the long-standing impact of eugenics and segregation within European policymaking. His current research (with Kalwant Bhopal) explores the role of elite universities within global educational economies. This work forms the basis for a forthcoming book, *Elite Universities and the Making of Privilege: Exploring Race and Class in Global Educational Economies*. He has also written about The Fall, and often talked at too great a length about them. He (probably) first saw The Fall perform live in 1979.

John McFarland, after graduating from Trinity College Dublin in 1998, Dr McFarland completed basic specialist training in Medicine and began training in Psychiatry in 2002. He became a member of the Royal College of Psychiatrists in 2005 and is also a member of the College of Psychiatry of Ireland. John spent three years in research, focused on the area of brain morphological changes in psychotic individuals and holds the additional degrees of Medical Doctorate (MD), a higher diploma in Health Care Management, and a higher diploma in Cognitive Behavioural Therapy. He is currently consultant psychiatrist for the North Care Mental Health Services, senior lecturer in Psychiatry in the University of Limerick, and dean for Post Graduate Education in the University of Limerick Deanery.

Suzanne Smith designed artwork for singles, EPs, and LPs by The Fall. She currently lives in Manchester, UK. She has exhibited her work in London, Berlin, and Copenhagen. Her works include the paintings *Remit 2*, *Joan Praying*, *Andrew 2*, and *Douglas* as well as a series called *Nothing to Fear*. She has just completed illustrations for two books on poetry: *Ordinary Others* (2020) and *Vulgar Variants* (2021), in collaboration with the poet Jonathan Wonham. Suzanne designed the artwork for The Fall's *Wise Ol'Man* album.

Elaine Vaughan lectures in Applied Linguistics and TESOL at the University of Limerick, Ireland. Her research interests include corpus pragmatics, Irish English pragmatics, and using/building corpora to explore language varieties and different domains of discourse. Her published work focuses on the pragmatics of Irish English; media representations of language, humour, and laughter; and community and identity in language. Of particular interest to her are the ways in which different disciplinary perspectives and methods can be blended through the use of corpora and corpus-based approaches for intra-varietal, pragmatic, and sociolinguistic research, as well as corpus-based critical discourse analysis.

Paul Wilson is a researcher, designer, and writer whose work explores the intersections of language, landscape, community, and communication. His current research involves the production of designed narratives of community and place and, in particular, investigates the potential for critically engaged typographies and language-acts, focusing on sites of class experience and situated knowledge at moments or points of change or transition. Much of his work orbits ideas and ideals of utopianism found in manifestations of the utopian action and has resulted in a broad range of activities: surveying the noticeboards found in the interior landscapes of Working Men's Clubs; mapping the route of the march which marked the closure of Britain's last deep coal mine; and exploring the post-Brexit significance of the Esperanto-English dictionary held in Keighley Library, West Yorkshire. He is a lecturer in the School of Design at the University of Leeds.

www.ingramcontent.com/pod-product-compliance
Lightning Source LLC
Chambersburg PA
CBHW021847300426
44115CB00005B/50